The Financialisation of Social Reproduction in the Age of Neoliberalism: From Theory to Case Studies

Studies in Critical Social Sciences

Series Editor
David Fasenfest (*York University, Canada*)

VOLUME 290

The titles published in this series are listed at *brill.com/scss*

The Financialisation of Social Reproduction in the Age of Neoliberalism: From Theory to Case Studies

Critical Reconstructions of Political Economy

VOLUME 4

By

Ben Fine

With

Kate Bayliss, Mary Robertson and Alfredo Saad-Filho

BRILL

LEIDEN | BOSTON

Library of Congress Cataloging-in-Publication Data

Names: Fine, Ben, author. | Bayliss, Kate, 1965- author. | Robertson, Mary (Economist) author. | Saad-Filho, Alfredo, 1964- author.
Title: The financialisation of social reproduction in the age of neoliberalism : from theory to case studies / Ben Fine ; with Kate Bayliss, Mary Robertson and Alfredo Saad-Filho.
Description: Leiden ; Boston : Brill, [2024] | Series: Studies in critical social sciences, 1573-4234 ; volume 290 | Includes bibliographical references and index. | Summary: "Drawing upon comprehensive research across five countries, including case studies of housing, water, and health, comprehensive theoretical and empirical accounts are offered of the impact of financialisation on economic and social reproduction, alongside the corresponding material cultures of neoliberalism. Economic is understood as embedded within social reproduction, with neoliberalism, as the current stage of capitalism, fundamentally underpinned by, but not reducible to, the financialisation of everyday life. Considerable emphasis is placed upon the variegated outcomes attached to the neoliberalisation of social reproduction, as highlighted by the comparative study of economic and social provisioning across different countries and sectors"– Provided by publisher.
Identifiers: LCCN 2024033598 | ISBN 9789004706286 (hardback) | ISBN 9789004706293 (ebook)
Subjects: LCSH: Neoliberalism. | Financialization. | Social class.
Classification: LCC HB95 .F56 2024 | DDC 320.51–dc23/eng/20240923
LC record available at https://lccn.loc.gov/2024033598

Typeface for the Latin, Greek, and Cyrillic scripts: "Brill". See and download: brill.com/brill-typeface.

ISSN 1573-4234
ISBN 978-90-04-70628-6 (hardback)
ISBN 978-90-04-70629-3 (e-book)
DOI 10.1163/9789004706293

This book is printed on acid-free paper and produced in a sustainable manner.

Contents

Figures

Preface

This is the fourth in a series of volumes looking back upon my journal contributions to select topics and locating them in terms of their own time and subsequent developments (Fine, 2024a–c for the first three volumes). This one is different from the others. First and foremost, most of the material included has not been previously published other than as Working Papers. Second, the source of the previous work, and the theme/topic is derived from the EU-funded Fessud project on the impact of financialisation (see Appendix 1 to Chapter 1). Third, although other volumes occasionally relied upon co-authors for a contribution, those here draw heavily upon co-authors, and especially Kate Bayliss, Mary Robertson and Alfredo Saad-Filho. In addition, many other researchers contributed through their research and Fessud Background and Working Papers even though these are not reproduced here (see Appendices 2 and 3 to Chapter 1 – these are given their own set of references and give a sense of the weight and momentum of the contribution made by the Fessud research). Last and least, I was in the middle of preparing a fourth volume when switching to this one. It was targeting development economics/studies. It is liable to be next up, most likely to be split in two to form both Volumes five and six.

As always, thanks are due to my co-authors and all those who have contributed, directly or indirectly, wittingly or unwittingly, to making this volume possible. Fuller acknowledgements along these lines and the rationale for this series is to be found in the Prefaces to the previous volumes.

CHAPTER 1

The Fessud Years and Beyond

1 How We Got Here

Towards the end of the noughties, I was informed of the opportunity to bid for a major EU research project on financialisation, with the rare indication that a heterodox bid would be welcome. Initially, the idea was that the project would be located at the School of Oriental and African Studies, SOAS. I undertook some preliminary substantive research on the proposal, whilst also sounding out colleagues at SOAS – arguably the UK's if not the EU's leading site for heterodox economics – about taking the lead in completing the proposal and administering the research should it be successful. In the event, I was bitterly disappointed that I could not muster up sufficient support to run the application and the project from SOAS. Fortunately, the lead was taken up by the University of Leeds, with Malcolm Sawyer at the helm.[1]

After much endeavour (and, reportedly, some attempts to undermine the success of the proposal, by those making the choice opposed to it through making unreasonable or spoiling demands on which we were advised always to accept), the bid proved successful and Financialisation, Economy, Society and Sustainable Development (FESSUD) was born.[2] It ran for five years, ending on November 30th, 2016. I led a major programme of work from SOAS.[3] It is some of the results of that research, often written up as previously unpublished working papers, that make up the bulk of what is reproduced in this volume. This is, however, only a small part of the overall research in which I was involved, and, by the same token, this fails to acknowledge through authorships, a dozen or more other researchers who participated more or less directly in the Fessud research that I led or in which I was involved.[4]

---

1 For the continuing Fessud website, see https://fessud.org This is much less informative and less populated than the website that ran during the project, forcibly closed shortly after the project ended.

2 See Appendix 1 for the briefest of overviews of the Fessud project (a sort of official notice to accompany publications). Note that fifteen universities were involved with numbers of researchers involved from each.

3 As did Jan Toporowski.

4 For a list of working papers completed in Fessud as a whole, running to over two hundred, see https://fessud.org/working-papers/ On the Fessud site, some other publications are listed also.

 | DOI:10.1163/9789004706293_002

There has, though, been some delay in bringing the research covered here to publication although other parts of the research have been published.[5] There was an intention, towards the end of the project and afterwards, involving the authors of the contributions included here, to publish an overview of the research synthesising its main results and bringing out its broader implications. This began during the research itself with the drafting of one of the chapters included here, the first after this, on the nature of neoliberalism and its relationship with financialisation. Alfredo Saad-Filho, not previously a Fessud researcher, was added as a co-author to Kate Bayliss, Mary Robertson and myself, both to add his expertise on neoliberalism (and its vast literature) and some freshness and oversight in drafting, given how the three of us old hands were Fessud-weary. The result proved to be much too long for journal publication, and a shorter version (Fine and Saad-Filho, 2016b), shedding the case study material on housing and water (and co-authors Kate and Mary, upon their insistence and against ours) was published instead.

This left high and dry the unpublished case study material and much else besides. So we determined to put it together in a book. Over a six-year period, to put it bluntly, we failed even though we had a ready and willing publisher, choice from a number of schemes by which to organise the material, and the vast majority of Chapters were redrafted and, at one time or another, ready to go. However, the enterprise continually stalled. The main reason appeared to revolve around bouts of ping pong across authors, each revising and updating in light of others' revisions in sequence, as individual time, availability and energy and real-world developments impinged. No sooner would one round of revisions be completed than another had already been initiated.

However, now having gone over the selection of the material for publication in this volume, I realised that there was another, more challenging reason for the delays in, and ultimate abandonment of, publishing the book, for which we had brought in Alfredo to facilitate the end result. This is the nature of the raw material from which we were trying to put the book together, deriving from the practices of the Fessud project itself. First, the project was comprised of a number of 'Work Packages', with our own efforts occupying major parts of two Packages, as well as spilling over to others, especially where cross-Package syntheses were involved. Second, within each Package, there was a programme of work, research and corresponding reports (not least five country case studies for each of housing and water, as well as overall framings and literatures

5 In Appendix 2 are listed the Fessud Working Papers arising out of the research with which I was involved. Appendix 3 lists further publications by authors of this volume that arose directly or more or less indirectly out of the Fessud research.

reviews). Third, attached to each Package was a set of 'Deliverables'. These were texts reporting to the EU as funder on the results of the research in set format. Fourth, coming out of these various drafts were more or less polished working papers. Last, there were more formal publications arising out of the research. Details of these are listed in Appendices 2 and 3.

As a result of these compendia of written materials, with cross-cutting and repetitive drafts across the multifarious purposes for which they were written, at different times and of different qualities, it was more or less impossible to compile a book out of cut, paste and amend, over and above the challenge (which we did meet through considerable dialogue) of providing an overall analytical framework for the material. Rather, quite apart from discontinuities of timings over our own availabilities, updatings and revisions, what was needed was someone to start afresh and write the book without drawing upon existing texts other than as raw materials. Easier to see this in retrospect but, in the event, too late.

Nonetheless, what has remained as an option is to publish a selection of the pieces as standalone chapters, as in this volume. It comes at the expense of some repetition around some of the basic concepts, especially for the pinpointing of the nature of financialisation for example. These pieces do stand the test of time as they are relatively recent, are grounded in comparative case study material, and cover basic conceptualisations that remain relevant and benefit from being discussed as they are being deployed, rather than being taken for granted. The writers were struggling to come to terms with conceptual framings in light of, and informing, case study research. This meant some patient attention to how this should be done, how to express it (in part for other researchers as well as potential readers), and how to justify it against possible objections and alternatives.[6] Exposition of such ex ante material may be of more value to readers than ex post contributions that take too much for granted.

2 From Globalisation to Variegated, Volatile Vulnerabilities

Subsequently, though, I have found a way of developing and summarising the results of our research, or at least their framing, through a sequence of acronyms, although these elements are not linear but need to be in continual

6 Kate Bayliss, in particular, has been exemplary in insisting upon making the frameworks adopted to be as simple and accessible as possible, and to be accompanied on how to do corresponding research in chosen case studies.

dialogue with one another as well as between the theoretical, the historical, the contemporary (empirical and discursive) and case studies – Glob, NL, finn, CCFCC, (PS)SoPs, Norms, MC as 10Cs, ER&SR, and V^3. I cover these in turn.

Globalisation is a buzzword and fuzzword (Cornwall and Eade, eds, 2010), with a huge literature across every (social science) discipline, and with a huge range of coverage by topic.[7] My own approach to globalisation, at least in the first instance, is by reference to economic reproduction (and restructuring and transformation) of the world economy, with an attention to production (and the accumulation of capital) and the relations, agencies, structures and processes (trade and finance for example) through which it occurs with corresponding consequences for economic and social reproduction (uneven development, inequalities, global cultures and conflicts, environmental degradation, etc). More specifically, such globalisation has been dominated by multinational corporations throughout the post-war boom (the so-called Keynesian/welfarism period, see below), and has continued to do so to the present day. The vast majority of provisioning draws directly or indirectly on a relatively small number of multinational corporations, with those in or around social media most to the fore in the contemporary scene,without overlooking the continuing role for vast numbers of smaller companies and local and nation-state provisioning and policymaking (with a lesser role for 'civil society' in provisioning as such). Whilst there is a healthy literature on such globalisation, with global production networks to the fore,[8] economic and social analyses tend to overlook this vital, determining aspect of contemporary capitalism.

This is especially so when it comes to neoliberalism (NL) which has also attracted a huge and varied literature. I have myself been a latecomer onto the scene. I do recall being invited to contribute on neoliberalism and labour markets to Saad-Filho and Johnston (eds) (2004),[9] and feeling bad at refusing given my personal and general feelings of obligation to contribute wherever I can (often, possibly, to a fault). But I was convinced I had nothing to say on the topic and was not particularly impressed by the voluminous literature that had already been attracted by it. It tended to fall into the category of attaching whatever was being analysed as being neoliberalism, by which it could then serve as both descriptor and explanandum. But, extreme pro-market ideology apart, which I have never accepted as being part of neoliberalism in practice,

7 For some discussion of my position, and differences with others, see Fine (2004a and 2006a).

8 Previously known as Global Commodity Chains before using Global Value Chains as a stepping stone to GPNs. For some critical commentary on this continuing journey, see Bayliss and Fine (2021, Chapter 2).

9 Having relatively recently completed a book (Fine, 1998).

most of what was being said about a distinctive neoliberalism was part and parcel of what had often if not systemically always been characteristic of capitalism from time to time, from attacks on wages and trade unions through to cuts in welfare and austerity.

Two factors subsequently changed my position. The first and more important was to have become increasingly in contact with the financialisation literature, and so its empirical importance in practice, from the mid-noughties, with Epstein (ed.) (2005) proving an important starting point as with most everybody else. This dovetailed with the second factor as I began work at more or less the same time on social policy. This itself had been prompted by two triggers. On the one hand, I was asked to look at social policy for a conference in India in 2009 even though I had no track record on the topic. I suspect they were just matching speakers to sessions. Significantly, the conference was entitled "The Crisis of *Neo-Liberalism* in India: Challenges and Alternatives", emphasis added.[10] As a result, by reviewing the literature, I connected three dots – social policy, neoliberalism and financialisation.

In a nutshell, it became apparent to me that neoliberalism should be considered a stage of capitalism which was defined by the pervasive presence of financialisation in economic and social reproduction. This offers a sharp contrast with the previously, to some degree, misnamed Keynesian period for which state intervention and multinational corporation restructuring in production had played the major roles in such reproduction (albeit with a major, if lesser role than under neoliberalism for finance) both internationally and nationally. This carried a number of implications. First is that neoliberal ideology of non-interventionism and withdrawal of the state is simply false. Rather neoliberal interventionism has targeted the financialisation of economic and hence social reproduction. Second is to have delineated two different stages of neoliberalism in the first instance, the first in which privatisation, deregulation and other such policies promoted financialisation through what has aptly been termed shock therapy. It was followed by the Third Wayism stage in which the dysfunctions and protests against the consequences of the first phase are addressed as a means to continue to sustain financialisation.

During the course of the Fessud research, I began to argue that a third phase of neoliberalism was then in place. I came to this conclusion as a result of coming across the work of econophysicists, who had examined the networks

10 It was jointly organised by the Tata Institute of Social Sciences (TISS), Mumbai and International Development Economics Associates (IDEAS), 13–15 March. My paper was entitled, "Social Policy and the Crisis of Neo-Liberalism", and is available at https://www.networkideas.org/ideasact/jan09/PDF/Fine.pdf.

of relations between globally-organised financial corporations, their production counterparts, and the state (Vitali et al. 2011). The analysis pointed to overt interventionism by the state in promoting private finance to be involved in industrial restructuring. In a sense, this was to revisit the 'Keynesian' period, with the major difference being the more prominent role of private finance (with two-thirds of the major global corporations being involved being engaged in finance). The shifts towards the third stage of neoliberalism both preceded the GFC and were accelerated by it (as is the case with the pandemic).

In short, neoliberalism as a stage of capitalism is defined by its being underpinned by, but not reducible to, financialisation. Unsurprisingly, from the beginnings of the new millennium, increasing evidence and (scholarly) discussion of the role of finance in economic and social reproduction gathered considerable momentum. But this created a problem of its own, as financialisation itself became a buzzword and fuzzword, now commanding a huge literature. It is not a parody to suggest that anything that was at all loosely associated with finance, money or monetary ethos became incorporated into the definition of financialisation. This had two effects, one extremely important and positive, and the other more questionable. For, on the one hand, there has been a huge empirical literature on financialisation from varieties of positions, across most disciplines, and covering an equally wide range of subject matter. Most of this is critical and associates financialisation with dysfunction of one sort or another – hardly surprising given the poor performance in general, if not uniformly, of the neoliberal economy, and the GFC and its impacts. On the other hand, theory around financialisation has been underdeveloped, and, in the extreme, it has been reduced to looking for the 'bad' and its associated presence with something called 'financialisation'.

To escape this conundrum, in my own work, a narrow definition of financialisation was adopted in which it was confined to the creation of financial assets that could be traded on the basis of anticipated rewards either through speculation or the funding of productive activity whether directly or indirectly. On this basis, the effects of financialisation through economic reproduction more generally and social reproduction as a whole need to and can be traced (rather than being rounded up as financialisation itself). Thus, for example, a mortgage as such is not financialisation, but its bundling up into an asset (on the expectation of trading it for gain) is. And it is a moot point whether such financialisation generates productive activity (housebuilding) or simply leads to speculation in mortgage markets and property purchases.

Appeal to financialisation as such cannot answer what balance occurs between these two stylised extremes, although there might be some presumption in favour of the deadweight of increased speculative activity. But, before the effects of financialisation can be assessed, it is necessary to frame and categorise what can be its effects across economic and social reproduction. To do this, our approach focused on unpicking the notion of commodification. For much of the literature, this has also been seen as an important aspect of neoliberalism, and understood as lying across full scale, private production for profit (as with privatisation) and the introduction of commercial motives and criteria irrespective of the extent to which commercial exchange is involved (as with the introduction of user charges for state services or cost-benefit analysis to determine whether a project should be financed). For 'full' commodification, we deployed the term itself exclusively, abbreviating it as C. For the exchange of money for provision but not full commodification, we referred to Commodity Form (CF). And for the presence of monetary motives but not the use of money as such, we talk of Commodity Calculation (CC). Putting the three together yields CCFCC.

Now CCFCC allows for both financialisation and its effects to be addressed. For financialisation itself can depend upon at least a stream of revenue to be securitised for which C and CF can qualify, but not CC although it can be ideologically induced by neoliberalism. For the latter, there is a tendency to press for the introduction of CC, for CC to be strengthened to CF, and for CF to be strengthened to C. But this is not necessarily a uniform, linear set of trends across neoliberalism both across and within sectors. For example, the promotion of mortgage finance and owner-occupation has led to those who are hard to house, especially with the decline of social housing. This had led to an expansion of housing benefit to support those dependent upon, but unable to afford, private renting, increasingly placing them outside purely commodified provision. More generally, under neoliberalism, interventionism to promote commodification gives rise to those who are hard not only to house, but to feed, clothe, educate, and so on, through market provision, meaning non-commodity forms of provision that can, admittedly but not necessarily, involve CF or CC.

This points to a key challenge for neoliberalism, and those who study it, namely how does it organise and deliver social policy especially in light of its ideological predilection for individual (family) self-reliance and market provision? An answer is to be found in application of the system of provision (SoP) approach, first posited over thirty years ago in the context of consumption studies (Fine and Leopold, 1993), with Bayliss and Fine (2021a) offering a comprehensive overview, some extension and a retrospective. The SoP approach suggests that consumption depends upon integrally organised and vertical chains of relations, processes, structures and agencies, differentiated from one another as is acknowledged in popular discourse by reference to the fashion system, the food system, the transport and education systems and so on. Attached to each SoP will be particular (social) Norms of consumption. These are not simply average levels of consumption but who gets what (the distribution of consumption by quantity and quality) and how, all to be studied as part and parcel of understanding why SoPs are reproduced and/or transformed in the broader contexts of economic and social reproduction. In addition, each SoP will be attached to a material culture (MC) – how consumption, and its provisioning, is understood by those engaged with it, what it means to them, with an evolving tension between experiencing and reflecting upon that provisioning and the roles to be played within and in light of it – from passive individual consumer to engaged collective activist. Such material cultures have been framed in terms of what has been dubbed the 10Cs – that they are Constructed, Construed, Conforming, Commodified, Contextual, Contradictory, Closed, Contested, Collective and Chaotic (Fine, 2013a for a first account of, and justification for, these 10Cs).

Unsurprisingly, given the themes of Fessud, and the Work Packages with which I was engaged, the SoP approach was deployed as a major analytical entry point, with financialisation to be examined for its impact upon SoPs in general and on housing and water in particular across the five country studies and beyond.[11] Indeed, the SoP approach had figured in a major way in the formulation of the Fessud application for funding. However, the SoP approach had been initially focused on consumption generated by private, commodified provision – in deference to this (postmodernist) focus of the literature at its origins. What had been notably absent was consumption by other means – collective, public or even consumption through the welfare state and social policy.

This is something over which I had felt a lingering guilt of omission but the previously mentioned venture into social policy allowed for it to be alleviated, and to be done so by extending the SoP to the PSSoP approach, prefixing SoP with Public Sector (PS).[12] The qualification was much more than nominal. For it involved a major, critical breach with the prevailing literature on (neoliberal)

---

11 The countries were UK, Portugal, Poland, Turkey and South Africa, with some attention also to pensions and, to a lesser extent, health.

12 Note that PSSoP has fallen out of favour to a large degree in subsequent work. This is for two closely related reasons. On the one hand, all SoPs incorporate a heavy role for the state under neoliberalism (in promoting financialisation and its effects), so it is hard drawing the line between them (other than on form of ownership of provision alone). On the other hand, drawing a distinction between SoP and PSSoPs tends wrongly to suggest analytically that there are (non-PS)SoPs that are without state intervention.

social policy. I found it to be extremely informative in its extensive, often comparative, empirical studies by country and sector. But it was also unduly complacent in its understanding of neoliberal social policy for a number of reasons.[13]

First, it tended to see neoliberalism as being well understood, with new rounds of policy readily framed as involving more privatisation, commodification, harshness or austerity, or some reaction against these. In other words, what need for renewal of understanding of the crises of social policy – we have seen this all before over the last thirty years or so.[14]

Second, by the same token, it tended to see neoliberal social policy as the antithesis of the Keynesian or Keynesian models of social provision. Indeed, this is a consequence of using the models of social policy that had been put forward during the Keynesian period (or even as it was coming to a close), with the neoliberal successors being seen as merely policy shifts. But this all begins to wear a bit thin once it is recognised that neoliberalism has lasted longer than the post-war boom, and so however it is characterised, and however correctly, should not be taken as the model for neoliberalism by way of deviation from it. Neoliberalism and its social policy has to be examined on its own terms, not those of (departure from) the Keynesian period.

Third, in short, the major omission from the social policy literature was the defining characteristic of neoliberalism, financialisation. The task in examining social provisioning under neoliberalism involved engaging the analytical sequence previously laid out and tying it to public sector SoPs, albeit in the processes of being subject to CCFCC. In particular, this also required distinguishing such provisioning by sector, location and over time.

But to engage with PSSoPs in the context of neoliberalism as laid out is to locate them in relation to economic and social reproduction (ER&SR). Corresponding literature has had some increasing prominence since the end of the Fessud project but with some aspects with which I would disagree (whilst welcoming the incorporation of gender, race and environmental aspects). First, there is a tendency to see ER&SR as a structured dualism, with tensions

13 Especially the Welfare Regime Approach (WRA) (Fine 2012, 2014 and 2016a). Such over-reliance on neoliberalism as not the Keynesian period is characteristic of the developmental state paradigm (DSP), the Social Compacting Paradigm (SCP) and the Varieties of Capitalism (VoC) approach. See Ashman and Fine (2013) and Fine (2016b). See further discussion below.

14 A major exception has been the global social policy school but this has arguably exaggerated global at the expense of national determinants with corresponding implications for tending unduly to homogenise social policy across country and sector.

between them. This is simply wrong as there is so much overlap between them (SR depends heavily upon all aspects of economic delivery as well as the state straddling both ER and SR). Instead, ER should be seen as embedded within SR (as should gender, race and the environment and their mutual interactions and those with ER) rather than as one amongst a number of structures that sit alongside SR.

Second, partly as a result of the origins of the distinction between ER and SR arising out of interrogating how labour is reproduced, and debates over the productivity and role of domestic labour, SR has tended to be confined, within its dualism with ER, to this focus alone. What is the role of caring and other such labour in the processes of SR. But, SR, as already implied, ranges far beyond what happens in the household with domestic labour, and it has become increasingly so. This is precisely because of the presence of the welfare state, social policy and PSSoPs across so many sectors.[15]

Third, precisely because of the conceptual 'domestication' of SR, there is a neglect of the social reproduction of class relations. This is not just an omission of an influence on SR – it is heavily contingent on what role is played by dominant classes – it is an omission over the very nature of SR. For it involves the reproduction of class relations as a whole (as well as those of gender, race and the environment – and, it should be added, the global order) rather than just the reproduction of the workforce. And, again, class relations are not another structure to be added. Rather SR is about the reproduction, and restructuring and transformation, of class relations as a whole, and their corresponding politics and ideologies. Thus, and most obviously, it is impossible to understand neoliberalism without due attention both to financialisation and how corresponding capitalist class relations have been transformed in and of themselves and in relation to the forms taken by ER. After all, neoliberalism has witnessed the growing hegemony of finance as the mode of SR.

Last, and by no means least, in our formulaic framing is V^3. Drawing on what has gone before, this acronym points to the Variegated nature of social provisioning across time, place and sector (as is explicitly suggested by the SoP approach). But this is complemented by Volatility in such provisioning as a consequence of the speculation and crises within and across sectors at national and global levels. These are themselves a consequence of both neoliberalisation and financialisation, not least with priority to the financial sector

15 See Bobek et al. (2023) for a useful "state of the art and beyond" look at "the financialization of households". From our perspective, although implicitly pointing to variegation, it scarcely looks at specific sectors beyond mortgages, welfare and credit, nor the relationship between financialisation and neoliberalism as a stage of capitalism.

in policymaking, especially during crises, and the herded speculation in shifting from one to another (global) market in search of financialised rewards across energy sources, foods, and so on, if especially foreign currencies. This all gives rise to Vulnerabilities within and across social provisioning, not least with growing inequalities and the increasing uncertainties around who gets the means to sustain livelihoods given the variegated volatilities involved and the lack of commitment or capacity for states to respond appropriately and sustainably.

This retrospective account of the key elements of the Fessud research is at most original in how it is put together. The different aspects involved can be found across the pieces included in this volume, albeit with different emphases upon them from chapter to chapter. The first chapter, other than the last, though, is different from the others in having been drafted initially after all of the others, thereby being able to incorporate both analytical and empirical material from them. It does so with the specific aim of specifying the nature of neoliberalism as a stage of capitalism, and both these chapters draw upon, and critically depart from, the neoliberalism literature by emphasising the defining role of financialisation. It also seeks to dispel certain misunderstandings of neoliberalism, specifically around those that define it by features that are far from confined to the current period, and those that unduly accept neoliberalism's presentation of itself ideologically as being non-interventionist – as opposed to being heavily interventionist on behalf of capital as a whole and finance in particular. Further, other misunderstandings of neoliberalism, even leading to its dismissal as an apt moniker for contemporary capitalism, can be readily set aside – especially that neoliberalism is homogenising and eroding of social policy, as opposed to variegated and challenged by how to sustain both financialised accumulation and handle its V^3 consequences for social reproduction.

The theme of neoliberalism as interventionist is also taken up in the final chapter, itself set apart from the others in having been written most recently. Following the pandemic, and extensive and even unprecedented levels of state intervention in response to the crises it prompted, there was a strong current suggesting that neoliberalism was dead or, at least, in its death throes, something also suggested in response to other developments, such as those associated with the environment, reregulation of finance and the so-called new industrial policy. From our longstanding position, not only was state intervention not dead but it had never gone away. And the developments suggesting its demise are entirely consistent with neoliberalism's third phase as we have characterised it.

Otherwise, the chapters sandwiched between the first and last, follow a logic of developing and applying the concepts previously laid out. Chapter 2 begins with an account of financialisation but is more concerned to specify the SoP approach. Chapter 3 focuses upon extending the SoP approach to public provisioning, PSSoPs. Chapter 4 revisits financialisation in greater depth both in terms of what it is and what are its consequences, and how to frame them in practice, with corresponding application to case studies for housing and water. Chapter 5 assesses the deficiencies of mainstream economics in light of its inabilities, not even able to incorporate financialisation into its world vision.

3 Where We Differ

On rereading and preparing these chapters for publication, they remain relevant and timely despite a short passage of time. But it is worth highlighting both where we have major differences with other contributors over and above those already indicated, as well as how our contributions relate to subsequent work and issues. First and foremost is at most the token acknowledgement of the environment in our Fessud research. As if by way of compensation, if not excuse, the SoP approach has subsequently been adopted in major research projects, and for reasons that make sense in terms of the diversity and variegated nature of environmental issues. Looking at (greening) consumption alone is sorely inadequate from a systemic point of view, its origins need to be traced back through differentiated systems of provision in terms of the attached environmental relations, structures, processes and agencies through which they impact upon environmental outcomes, all as part of economic and social reproduction.

Second, contributions on, and debates over, financialisation extend from before and after the Fessud research. Of particular prominence has been the critique of one wide definition of financialisation which sees it as an extra layer of exploitation, more or less of finance against everybody else. Quite apart from corresponding differences over what is financialisation, ours being narrowly confined to what is termed interest-bearing capital in Marx's terms – with a close correspondence to fictitious capital, the formation of assets that make a claim on surplus and can be exchanged as such – we depart from two other ways in which financialisation has often been conceived.

The first, associated with finance as an extra layer of exploitation, is more or less explicitly tied to the idea that finance, as financialisation, is a general appropriation of surplus at the expense of all but those who are attached (beneficially) to the financial system.[16] Here, though, there is considerable slippage involved, with an image, cliché even, created of an economy in which exploitation through and as a result of financialisation involves higher unemployment, lowered wages and social provisioning alongside privatisation and user charges, and excessive reliance upon credit (cards) and unduly exploitative interest payments in order to seek to sustain stressed and reduced standards of living.

There is no doubt that such a picture is accurate, but only for certain sections of the population which vary in size from one place to another, and better seen in terms of the growing inequalities and V^3 associated with neoliberalism. Fessud research, for example, shows that the wealthier you are the more likely you are to be more (proportionately) indebted, and positively benefit from being so through access to credit, capital gains in, and occupation of, homes, and ownership of financial assets themselves including subsidised pensions. There is also a healthy literature showing how non-financial corporations are heavily embroiled in financial operations, not least through buy-back options. Nor is this uniformly at the expense of investment, as is apparent in the energy and food sectors, which underpin global warming and the global pandemic of obesity (Bayliss and Fine, 2021b) and what they call the political economy of excess more generally. Financialisation can lead to excessive investments as long as revenues are assured and can be securitised.

This is acknowledged in what might be seen as a parallel literature to the financialisation as exploitation of us all, that attached to finance as parasitic, especially associated with Mazzucato (2018). This is part and parcel of a broader literature and set of concerns around what finance is productive, whether it produces value because it appropriates so much, and whether this leads to a more general understanding of contemporary capitalism oriented around appropriating rents from diverse sources ranging from finance to monopolistic corporations especially in IT sectors.[17]

Yet a second take on financialisation is to attach it to uneven development and, in a sense, an approach that parallels finance exploits us all to one in which some countries (financially) exploit others, with explicit resonances with dependency by reference to subordinate or peripheral financialisation. I have always been wary of such framings, in part because of their focus on exploitation between countries, or regions, as opposed to classes. In addition,

16 The leading proponent has been my colleague, and former PhD student, Costas Lapavitsas (especially Lapavitsas, 2013). See Fine (2010a) for (unanswered) critique.

17 See debate between Christophers and Fine (2020) and, most recently, Christophers (2020).

my own work on South Africa, even if dubbed a middle-income country, has focused upon its becoming at the fore of globalisation, neoliberalisation and financialisation in the post-apartheid period.[18] Significantly, much of the more recent literature on the uneven incidence and impact of financialisation, especially if taken as a whole and through empirical case studies, can be interpreted as emphasising its variegated nature at a global level, with uneven structures and processes of dominance through what are many different monetary/financial structures, relations, agencies and processes.[19]

In brief, there is no analytical short cut from globalised, neoliberalised, financialisation tendencies to their incidence and outcomes. There is a common and understandable tendency to seek empirical regularities – financial exploitation of us all, subordinate or peripheral financialisation, either productive or parasitic financialisation, financialisation as a form of rent appropriation – and to read these off, inevitably selectively to favour hypotheses, as both financialisation, etc, and its explained effects. Counter-tendencies, counter-evidence and corresponding variegation are overlooked or seen as marginal exceptions to what may be appropriately identified, but not uniform, empirical developments. In many respects, this is tantamount to adopting what we have termed a horizontal perspective – common properties across varieties of aspects of economic and social reproduction – as opposed to the vertical perspective attached to the SoP approach in which the chain of provisioning is followed from production through to consumption whilst being contextualised for contemporary capitalism within economic and social reproduction as a whole.

Similar critical conclusions apply to a greater or lesser degree to what have been prominent approaches to economic and social reproduction, with a tendency to place emphasis on the economic and stasis in institutionalised forms of provision. Attention has already been drawn to the Welfare Regime Approach, deriving from the work of Esping-Andersen, and its having been forged in the Keynesian era. In addition, at least initially, it depends upon three ideal types or templates for social policy regimes but these have been expanded in response to burgeoning case studies in response to ill-fitting evidence between or within countries by location and policy sector. As suggested, the neoliberal period tends to be seen as departing from these (Keynesian period) regimes rather than its being specified on its own terms (if history were reversed, would we define Keynesian as not neoliberal?).

18 See Fine (2019) and Ashman et al. (2021), for example.

19 For some commentary, see Fine (2020a and b and 2022).

Three other broad approaches share in common some of these characteristics. One is the Varieties of Capitalism (VoC) approach which had the remarkable feature of neglecting the role of finance in the first instance even though it was first put forward as finance was experiencing its meteoric rise. The Social Compacting Paradigm (SCP), suggesting that the Keynesian period was characterised by positive-sum collaboration between capital and labour, has lost prominence as collective bargaining and the presence of trade unions, and progressive organisations more generally, in policymaking has been eroded. This does capture a significant aspect of the neoliberal era but how, why and with what effects needs to be addressed through the restructuring of policymaking in the presence of financialisation, and implications from this in terms of formation and representation of interests. And the Developmental State Paradigm (DSP) has also gone into decline, from a position of prominence around the successful catch-up industrialisation of the East Asian NICs. Instead, it has been diluted to signal any intervention of the neoliberal state that can be deemed to be successful, why and how, as opposed to significant economic and social development as a whole.[20] Thus, for those seeking to resuscitate the DSP, there has to be a clear recognition of the changed global conditions in which development is being sought, and especially how to delimit the dysfunctions attached to financialisation.[21]

4 Alternatives: Posing and Achieving

This brings to the fore the question of alternatives, what they are and how to achieve them. First, consider the narrower question of struggles around consumer issues which have become most prominent recently around the environment but have a longer tradition across child labour, other labour conditions, and boycotts of various sorts for various reasons. What became apparent, however, in recognising the neglect of public or collective consumption in formulating the SoP approach, is that there were good reasons why consumer struggles, or consumerism, are liable to be of limited impact (Fine, 2005). This derives from the need to trace back their origins and determinants in SoPs as a whole with two major overlapping implications. One is to transform the struggle into a broader or different struggle, over child labour and conditions more generally for example, rather than over its products. The other is to begin to

20 See Fine et al. (eds) (2013), Fine (2016b) and Fine and Pollen (2018).

21 But for a more positive take on the development *welfare* state (DWSP), see Fine (2014).

create a distance from the eponymous consumer (i.e. everybody) and to target a different focus for struggle, between workers and capitalists for example. On the other hand, the recognition of the need for, and ethics underpinning, collective consumption (for the public not for profit), transforms what is provided into something else, social policy or the welfare state, displacing the policy, delivery and activism into something other than consumption as such. Either way, for consumer struggles to become prominent and effective, they are transformed into, and are expressed as, something else and so no longer are, or recognised as, consumerist struggles as such. Indeed, putting it the other way around, confining struggles to those of consumerism, has the effect and even the intention of limiting their scope and effectivity, something that is well-illustrated by the confined role played by consumer councils and the like in the wake of privatisation of public services.

At the other extreme to detailed consumerist policies, and their prospects to become something more and different, is to consider the general scope for policymaking and alternatives within the neoliberal stage of capitalism. Our starting point is not to put forward a whole series of policies, something that is important but neither particularly challenging nor particularly necessary. Evidence for such bald claims can be made in general terms by reference to climate change and to welfare provision. Everyone in the world knows, for example, that associated policies need to be more and different (and the same applies, if to a lesser extent, to finance where there is too much and of the wrong sort). The issue is not what policies but how to get traction for them. Thus, for example, despite what are the many deficiencies of policymaking during the Keynesian/welfarism period, and extensive continuing state intervention under neoliberalism, a step forward in progress would be made in targeting such social reformism and the conditions that make it possible.

But it is precisely the nature of economic and social reproduction under neoliberalism that has undermined the conditions that render more progressive policymaking possible. Most important has been the erosion of the strength and organisation of progressive forces, not least trade unions and the prominence and presence of collective bargaining extending from wages and conditions of work to areas of policymaking in economic and social reproduction. In its place, neoliberalism has tended to be associated with the displacement of policymaking from popular participation, its removal and authoritarian centralisation to central government albeit with the devolution of responsibilities to lower levels without the resources to deliver, and increasing presence and influence of financial interests and considerations at all levels, not least through a concentration of ownership and control of all forms of media, and revolving doors across these and business, politics and consultancy.

Of necessity, the presence and influence of these factors is both uneven in presence and (pathways to conflicts over) impact. However, decline in the presence of progressive institutions in policymaking, and more generally, has had another effect in the context of continuing electoral democracy. This is to create limited opportunities for (collective) expression of dissent to the dysfunctions of neoliberalism. As a result, these are open to capture by waves of populism in which the media, charisma and simplified, if appealing, postures can play a major role, not least through various forms of nationalism, racism and the like. In short, electoral outcomes are both variegated and volatile, with vulnerabilities in the rise and fall of governments and political parties. In this context, the left (as opposed to the 'centre' or the 'neoliberal') can gain unanticipated successes against the establishment (as with Corbyn in the UK) but, equally, and more often and secure are those from the right even if open to populism and challenges to the establishment (as with Johnson and Brexit). In addition, so extensive and increasingly overt is interventionism under neoliberalism that it offers unlimited opportunities for those from the right to appropriate support under the banner of restoring small government and the freedom of the individual, not least from the corruptions and dysfunctions of big government.

All of this paints an extremely bleak picture in terms of the potential and scope for progressive alternatives – it is worth recalling that the Keynesian period was marked by debates over whether reformism or revolution (or one as the path to the other) needed to be on the agenda but now it is whether we can get reformism at all of the sort that featured in the post-war boom. In this light, there are two sorts of entry points for alternatives to emerge. There are those that are wide-ranging and command the potential in principle to engage large numbers. Most obvious, in this respect, are climate change, the environment, and the predations and dysfunctions of financialisation, ranging over the effects experienced directly or indirectly through austerity and inequality. Increasingly, there are concerns over global instabilities and wars, and what were previously denominated as new movements around gender and race.

None of these can be discounted as the potential for the organisational umbrella under which deeper understandings and pressure for successful change can flourish. But it is precisely their generic natures that render them elusive as the foundations for mobilising for more fundamental change. By contrast, an entry point for change at the opposite extreme is to mobilise around specific provisioning – for employment, health, transport, water, housing and so on. Demands for basic income fall across these two entry points although I am more inclined to press for provisioning of basic needs in detail than for the income to access them (which does nothing to guarantee supply under what conditions).

One shift that favours specific entry points is the discursive tensions within neoliberal policymaking, especially in its third phase. Specifically, there are profound contradictions in terms of the idea that the state should use its resources and policymaking capabilities to support private finance to fund private providers because the outcome will be superior than the state managing delivery itself – and this has been found again and again in water, health, transport and, most obviously, renewable energy provision, motivating campaigns for renationalisations and for the application of social as opposed to commercial criteria. Precisely because the state plays a vital role so it carries the potential for conflict over what that role should be – provision for whom, under what criteria, raising the spectre of people before profit.

How such considerations play out in practice is highly variegated, not least because that is the nature of provisioning under neoliberalism. What must be sought is collective endeavour around individual struggles for progressive change and unity across such struggles and their connections to the grander challenges we face.

Appendix 1: Short Fessud Blurb

Financialisation, Economy, Society and Sustainable Development (FESSUD) is a 10 million euro project largely funded by a near 8 million euro grant from the European Commission under Framework Programme 7 (contract number: 266800). The University of Leeds is the lead co-ordinator for the research project with a budget of over 2 million euros.

The Abstract of the Project

The research programme will integrate diverse levels, methods and disciplinary traditions with the aim of developing a comprehensive policy agenda for changing the role of the financial system to help achieve a future which is sustainable in environmental, social and economic terms. The programme involves an integrated and balanced consortium involving partners from 14 countries that has unsurpassed experience of deploying diverse perspectives both within economics and across disciplines inclusive of economics. The programme is distinctively pluralistic, and aims to forge alliances across the social sciences, so as to understand how finance can better serve economic, social and environmental needs. The central issues addressed are the ways in which the growth and performance of economies in the last 30 years have been dependent on the characteristics of the processes of financialisation; how has financialisation impacted on the achievement of specific economic, social, and environmental objectives?; the nature of the relationship between financialisation and the sustainability of the financial system, economic development and the environment?; the lessons to be drawn from the crisis about the nature and impacts of financialisation?; what are the requisites of a financial system able to support a process of sustainable development, broadly conceived?

The views expressed during the execution of the FESSUD project, in whatever form and/or by whatever medium, are the sole responsibility of the authors. The European Union is not liable for any use that may be made of the information contained therein.

The partners in the consortium are

Participant number	Participant organisation name	Country
1 (Coordinator)	University of Leeds	UK
2	University of Siena	Italy
3	School of Oriental and African Studies	UK
4	Fondation Nationale des Sciences Politiques	France
5	Pour la Solidarite, Brussels	Belgium
6	Poznan University of Economics	Poland
7	Tallin University of Technology	Estonia
8	Berlin School of Economics and Law	Germany
9	Centre for Social Studies, University of Coimbra	Portugal
10	University of Pannonia, Veszprem	Hungary
11	National and Kapodistrian University of Athens	Greece
12	Middle East Technical University, Ankara	Turkey
13	Lund University	Sweden
14	University of Witwatersrand	South Africa
15	University of the Basque Country, Bilbao	Spain

Appendix 2: Working Papers from Our Fessud Research

Not all Working Papers listed here are cited in the text but those listed in the references are also included here (with same date designation as in the main list) for completeness. Note also that some Working Papers came out at time of preparation, but others were turned rapidly from Project 'Deliverables' (requirements of the funding as opposed to manuscripts for public consumption as such) into Working Papers at the close of the official Project website, with or without minor or major revision. The Deliverables no longer seem to be available. All of the Working Papers for the Project as a whole are available at https://fessud.org/working-papers/ The Working Papers listed here are drawn from four of the twelve Fessud Work Packages – Work Packages 5 (Finance and Well-Being), 8 (Finance, Real Economy and the State), 11 (Foresight) and 12 (Synthesis and Conclusions).

Those Involving the Co-authors of This Volume

Bayliss, K. (2014) "The Financialisation of Water in England and Wales", FESSUD Working Paper Series no 52, https://fessud.org/wp-content/uploads/2015/03/Case-study-the-financialisation-of-Water-in-England-and-Wales-Bayliss-working-paper-REVISED_annexes-working-paper-52.pdf

Bayliss, K. (2016) "The Financialisation of Health in England: Lessons from the Water Sector", FESSUD, Working Paper Series, no 131, https://fessud.org/wp-content/uploads/2015/03/Financilisation_Health_England_WorkingPaper131.pdf

Bayliss, K. (2016a) "The System of Provision for Water in Selected Case Study Countries", FESSUD, Working Paper Series, no 194, https://fessud.org/wp-content/uploads/2015/03/FESSUD_WP194_The-System-of-Provision-for-Water-in-Selected-Case-Study-Countries.pdf

Bayliss, K. (2016b) "Neoliberalised Water in South Africa", FESSUD, Working Paper Series, no 204, https://fessud.org/wp-content/uploads/2015/03/FESSUD_WP204_Neoliberalised-Water-in-South-Africa.pdf

Bayliss, K., J. Churchill, B. Fine and M. Robertson (2016) "Summary Report on the Impacts of Financialisation and of the Financial Crisis on Household Well-Being", FESSUD, Working Paper Series, no 199, https://fessud.org/wp-content/uploads/2015/03/FESSUD_WP199_Summary-report-on-the-impacts-of-financialisationfinancial-crisis-on-household-well-being.pdf.

Bayliss, K. and B. Fine (2016) "Finance and Economic and Social Reproduction: Origins of the Present and Implications for the Future", FESSUD, Working Paper Series, no 189, https://fessud.org/wp-content/uploads

/2015/03/FESSUD_WP189_FinanceEconomicSocial-Reproduction-Origins-of-the-PresentImplications-for-the-Future.pdf.

Bayliss, K., B. Fine and M. Robertson (2013) "From Financialisation to Consumption: The Systems of Provision Approach Applied to Housing and Water", FESSUD, Working Paper Series, no 02, https://fessud.org/wp-content/uploads/2013/04/FESSUD-Working-Paper-021.pdf.

Bayliss, K., B. Fine and M. Robertson (2016) "The Role of the State in Financialised Systems of Provision: Social Compacting, Social Policy, and Privatisation", FESSUD, Working Paper Series, no 154, https://fessud.org/wp-content/uploads/2015/03/Role-of-the-state-working-paper-154.pdf.

Fine, B. (2013a) "Towards a Material Culture of Financialisation", FESSUD Working Paper Series, no 15, https://fessud.org/wp-content/uploads/2013/04/Towards-a-Material-Culture-of-Financialisation-FESSUD-Working-Paper-15.pdf, see Fine (2017a).

Fine, B. (2016c) "The Endemic and Systemic Malaise of Mainstream Economics", FESSUD, Working Paper Series, no 190, https://fessud.org/wp-content/uploads/2015/03/FESSUD_WP190_The-EndemicSystemic-Malaise-of-Mainstream-Economics.pdf, see Chapter 6.

Fine, B. and K. Bayliss (2016d) "Paper on Theoretical Framework for Assessing the Impact of Finance on Public Provision", FESSUD, Working Paper Series, no 92, https://fessud.org/wp-content/uploads/2015/03/FESSUD_WP192_Theoretical-Framework-for-Assessing-the-Impact-of-Finance-on-Public-Provision.pdf, see Chapter 4.

Fine, B., K. Bayliss and M. Robertson (2016b) "Housing and Water in Light of Financialisation and 'Financialisation'", FESSUD, Working Paper Series, no 156, https://fessud.org/wp-content/uploads/2015/03/Housing-and-Water-in-Light-of-Financialisation-and-"Financialisation"-working-paper-156.pdf, see Chapter 5.

Fine, B., K. Bayliss and M. Robertson (2016c) "From Financialisation to Systems of Provision", FESSUD, Working Paper Series, no 191, https://fessud.org/wp-content/uploads/2015/03/FESSUD_WP191_From-Financialisation-to-Systems-of-Provision.pdf, see Chapter 3.

Fine, B., A. Saad-Filho, K. Bayliss and M. Robertson (2016a) "Thirteen Things You Need to Know about Neoliberalism", FESSUD, Working Paper Series, no 155, https://fessud.org/wp-content/uploads/2015/03/13-Things-you-need-to-know-about-Neoliberalism-working-paper155.pdf, see Chapter 2.

Robertson, M. (2014) "Case Study: Finance and Housing Provision in Britain", FESSUD Working Paper no. 51, https://fessud.org/wp-content/uploads/2013/04/Case-Study_-Finance-and-Housing-Provision-in-Britain-working-paper-51.pdf

Robertson, M. (2014) "Housing Provision, Finance, and Well-Being in Europe", FESSUD Working Paper no 14, https://fessud.org/wp-content/uploads/2013/04/Housing-provision-Finance-and-Well-Being-in-Europe-Working-paper-14.pdf

Robertson, M. (2016) "The System of Provision for Housing in Selected Case Study Countries", FESSUD Working Paper, no 193, https://fessud.org/wp-content/uploads/2015/03/FESSUD_WP193_The-System-of-Provision-for-Housing-in-Selected-Case-Study-Countries.pdf

Santos, A. and M. Robertson "Definancialising Well-Being: The Case of Housing", FESSUD Working Paper, no 178, https://fessud.org/wp-content/uploads/2015/03/FESSUD_WP178_Definancialising-well-being-the-case-of-housing.pdf

***Those Commissioned by, or Working in Collaboration with, Us*[22]**

We worked particularly closely with the Portuguese team (and especially Ana Santos and Nuno Teles) and also some of the Leeds team (especially Marco Boffo, Andy Brown and Dave Spencer), with considerable joint and overlapping work. Fuzzy boundaries prevail over where to draw the line between our Working Papers, theirs, and those that are joint. But some more or less arbitrary choices have been made in what follows. Mary Robertson was initially part of the Leeds team as well as joining ours, and teams would exchange responsibilities for work with one another according to expertise and inclination. But see previous footnote over the conversion of Deliverables into Working Papers.

22 The one exception is for the following group which has apparent inconsistencies across them in terms of authorships as well as problems of mix and match of the materials covered. In the volume, I have replaced all references to these by reference to Santos and Teles (2014) and/or Santos et al. (2016). Santos, A. and B. Fine (2014) "Empirical Report on Cross-National Comparative Analysis of Household Financial Behaviour: Recent Trends", Leeds, UK: FESSUD project, (Deliverable D5.03). Santos, A. and N. Teles (2013) "Empirical Report on Cross-National Comparative Analysis of Household Financial Behaviour – Recent Trends", FESSUD WP5 empirical work, mimeo.

Santos, A. and N. Teles (2014) "Recent Trends in Household Financial Behaviour", in Santos and Fine (2014).

Santos, A. and N. Teles (2014) "Recent Trends in Household Financial Behaviour", FESSUD Working Paper Series, no 171, https://fessud.org/wp-content/uploads/2015/03/FESSUD_WP171_Recent-Trends-Household-Financial-Behaviour.pdf.

Santos, A., N. Teles, R. Matias, A. Brown and D. Spencer (2013) "Empirical Report on Cross-National Comparative Analysis of Household Well-Being: Micro Analysis", Leeds, UK: FESSUD project, (Deliverable D5.04).

Santos, A., N. Teles, R. Matias, A. Brown and D. Spencer (2016) "Cross-National Comparative Analysis of Household Well-Being", FESSUD Working Paper Series, no 172, https://fessud.org/wp-content/uploads/2015/03/FESSUD_WP172_Cross-national-comparative-analysis-household-well-being.pdf.

I managed to 'convert' Deliverables (often referenced in the Working Papers) into corresponding Working Papers, with a little imagination, as referenced here and throughout the volume.

Çelik, Ö., A. Topal and G. Yalman (2015) "Finance and System of Provision of Housing: The Case of Istanbul, Turkey", FESSUD Working Paper Series, no 152, https://fessud.org/wp-content/uploads/2015/03/Housing_Istanbul_WP152-FESSUD.pdf

Churchill, J. (2014) "Towards a Framework for Understanding the Recent Evolution of Pension Systems in the European Union", FESSUD Working Paper, no 12, https://fessud.org/wp-content/uploads/2013/04/Towards-a-framework-for-understanding-the-recent-evolution-of-pension-systems-in-the-European-Union-FESSUD-working-paper-12.pdf

Happer, C. (2013) "Financialisation, Media and Social Change", FESSUD Working Paper Series, no 10, https://fessud.org/wp-content/uploads/2013/04/Financialisation-Media-and-Social-Change-FESSUD-Working-Paper-10-.pdf, see Happer (2017).

Isaacs, G. (2016) "The Commodification, Commercialisation and Financialisation of Low-Cost Housing in South Africa", FESSUD Working Paper, no 200, https://fessud.org/wp-content/uploads/2015/03/FESSUD_WP200_Commodification-Commercialisation-Financialisation-Low-Cost-Housing-in-South-Africa.pdf

Karacimen, E. (2014) "Dynamics behind the Rise in Household Debt in Advanced Capitalist Countries: An Overview", FESSUD Working Paper Series, no 9, https://fessud.org/wp-content/uploads/2013/04/Dynamics-behind-the-Rise-in-Household-Debt-FESSUD-Working-Paper-09-1.pdf

Lis, P. (2015) "Relationships between the Finance System and Housing Markets", FESSUD Working Paper, no 99, https://fessud.org/wp-content/uploads/2015/03/1-LisP_FESSUD_WP3_finance_housing-working-paper-99_CorrectedVersion.pdf

Lis, P. (2015a) "Financialisation of the Water Sector in Poland", FESSUD Working Paper, no 101, https://fessud.org/wp-content/uploads/2015/03/FESSUD_WP8_Financialisation_of_the_water_sectorInPoland_working-paper101.pdf

Lis, P. (2015b) "Financialisation of the System of Provision Applied to Housing in Poland", FESSUD Working Paper Series, no 100, https://fessud.org/wp-content/uploads/2015/01/2-LisP_FESSUD_WP8_housingPoland-working-paper-100.pdf

Rodrigues, J., A. Santos and N. Teles (2016) "Financialisation of Pensions in Europe: Systemic and Variegated Effects in Semi-Peripheral Portugal",

FESSUD Working Paper, no 175, https://fessud.org/wp-content/uploads/2015/03/FESSUD_WP175_Financialisation-Pensions-in-EUVariegated-Effects-in-Portugal.pdf
Santos, A. (2014) "Financial Literacy, Financialisation and Neo-liberalism", FESSUD Working Paper Series, no 11, https://fessud.org/wp-content/uploads/2013/04/Financial-Literacy-Financialisation-and-Neo-liberalism-FESSUD-Working-Paper-11.pdf, see Santos (2017).
Santos, A. (2016) "Financialisation, Social Provisioning and Well-Being in Five EU Countries", FESSUD Working Paper, no 176, https://fessud.org/wp-content/uploads/2015/03/FESSUD_WP176_Financialisation-social-provisioningwell-being-in-5EUcountries.pdf
Santos, A., N. Serra and N. Teles (2015) "Finance and Housing Provision in Portugal", FESSUD Working Paper Series no 79, https://fessud.org/wp-content/uploads/2015/01/FESSUD_Working-Paper-Series_Santos-Serra-Teles-2015-79.pdf.
Santos, A., N. Teles, R. Matias, A. Brown and D. Spencer (2016) "Cross-National Comparative Analysis of Household Well-Being", FESSUD Working Paper Series, no 172, https://fessud.org/wp-content/uploads/2015/03/FESSUD_WP172_Cross-national-comparative-analysis-household-well-being.pdf.
Saritas, S. (2014), "Review of Pension Provision across the European Union Countries", FESSUD Working Paper Series, no 13, https://fessud.org/wp-content/uploads/2013/04/REVIEW-OF-THE-PENSION-PROVISION-ACROSS-THE-EUROPEAN-UNION-COUNTRIES_13.pdf
Teles, N. (2015) "Financialisation and Neoliberalism: The Case of Water Provision in Portugal", FESSUD Working Paper, no 102, https://fessud.org/wp-content/uploads/2015/03/Financialisation-and-neoliberalism-the-case-of-water-provision-in-Portugal-working-paper-102.pdf
Yilmaz, G. and Ö. Çelik (2016) "Finance and System of Provision of Water: The Case of Istanbul", FESSUD Working Paper Series, no 153, https://fessud.org/wp-content/uploads/2015/03/Water_METU_WP_FESSUD-153.pdf

Appendix 3: Subsequent Publications (on) from Fessud

Unsurprisingly, Fessud proved to be a major staging point in applying and developing a range of research, drawing upon what had gone before and feeding into subsequent contributions after the research programme had been completed. What follows is a wide-ranging and extensive, if still select, list of publications deriving in one way or another from the Fessud programme in which the co-authors of this volume have been involved,[23] ranging from those directly derived from the research itself (or in preparing the proposal that necessarily preceded the start of the research itself by some time) through to those drawing upon Fessud research subsequently.[24]

A major aspect of the research was to develop and apply the system of provision (SoP) approach, if especially in the contexts of both financialisation and public/social provisioning. The Fessud research has ultimately fed into a major retrospective covering the history of the approach in terms of its evolution, how to do it, and what are its most recent applications (Bayliss and Fine, 2021a). It is complemented by the chapters on the SoP approach within this volume, with corresponding case studies. There were also many other SoP studies, not included in this volume, across the five country case studies for water and housing, as well as other studies for pensions and health alongside those for more general topics such as well-being and culture. All of this has been recorded in Appendix 2. Our own work on the SoP approach has gathered momentum across Bayliss et al. (2018), Bayliss and Fine (2022) and Robertson (2020).

Kate Bayliss has been particularly active in deploying and promoting the SoP approach through blogs, policy activism and scholarly contributions. Water has been in the lead (Bayliss and Hall, 2017; Bayliss, 2020, 2021, 2022a-c; Bowles et al. 2021; Bayliss and Buse, 2022; and Bayliss et al. 2020, 2021 and 2023). Other sectors across infrastructure (and energy, health and transport)

23 By way of partial exception, it is worth mentioning the PhD theses under my supervision by students who contributed to the Fessud research, and/or drew upon it, listed below. There were also other PhD students who contributed to our research, notably Elif Karacimen and Jennifer Churchill, who completed PhDs at SOAS with other supervisors, and yet other research students who contributed to Fessud research other than our own.

Robertson, Mary. The Financialisation of British Housing – A Systems of Provision Approach, 2014.

Saritas, Serap. Financialisation and Turkish Pension Reform, 2016.

Isaacs, Gilad. The Financialisation and Internationalisation of Post-Apartheid South Africa, 2017.

Unsal, Ezgi. A Political Economy of Electricity and Housing Provision in Turkey since 1980: Change, Financialisation and Market-Based Social Provision, 2017.

Baloyi, Basani. The Financialisation of Mozambique's Roads, 2018.

Haines-Doran, Tom. Understanding the Changing Role of Central Government in Britain's Railways since Privatisation: A Systems of Provision Approach, 2019.

Moore, Glennie. From Francoism to Financialisation: The Financialisation of Mortgages in Spain, a Case Study Analysis and a Framework for Future Studies, 2020.

24 As in Appendix 2, there will be works here which are not cited in the main list of references, but those that are there are reproduced here as they appear in the main list, for consistency.

are covered in Bayliss and Pollen (2021), Bayliss et al. (2020 and 2021), Bayliss and Gideon (2020) and Bayliss (2022). The SoP approach has also been deployed across major research programmes, iBuild (on UK infrastructure), https://research.ncl.ac.uk/ibuild/; Lili (on Living Well within Limits), https://lili.leeds.ac.uk; and urban infrastructure in the global south, https://www.inclusiveinfrastructure.org Across these, and other research, the SoP approach has been increasingly applied to environmental issues. Mary Robertson (2017a and b and 2024) has continued to examine housing SoPs empirically and for their analytical implications.

Unsurprisingly, given the Fessud theme of finance, financialisation figures extremely strongly in our Fessud contributions and ongoing work. Neatly combining aspects of the SoP approach to financialisation and culture, drawing upon our own and commissioned work, was the special issue on the Material Culture of Financialisation (MCF), published in 2017 in *New Political Economy*, vol 22, no 4, reproduced in Bayliss et al. (eds) (2018), including our own contributions Bayliss et al. (2017), Bayliss (2017), Fine (2017a) and Robertson (2017a). Continuing contributions to, and debate over, how to understand financialisation and trace its effects, are to be found, in the context of rent, in Robertson (2024) and more generally in Fine (2013–14 and 2022) and Christophers and Fine (2022), the latter serving as the opening contribution to Mader et al. (eds) (2020).

Unavoidable within the Fessud research was its situation within a neoliberal context. As a result, neoliberalism figures as a major target of research in its own right. During the Fessud research, neoliberalism as a stage of capitalism was directly addressed in general in Fine et al. (2016a), published without case studies as Fine and Saad-Filho (2016a). It was considered in the context of development and politics in Fine and Saad-Filho (2014), and Fine et al. (eds) (2012), with Fine (2012a), Fine et al. (2012) and Chang and Fine (2012) as contributing chapters. Paraphrasing Bill Clinton's "It's the economy, stupid", I was soon to coin the phrase, "Neoliberalism, it's financialisation, stupid", but it has yet to catch on. Each of these previously, and other, cited contributions explicitly identifies financialisation as the underlying aspect of neoliberalism, as does Fine (2019 and 2020a and b). Neoliberalism and the variegated, volatile vulnerability (V^3) of political outcomes is studied in the context of the rise of authoritarianism in Boffo et al. (2019), and Corbyn's election as leader of the Labour Party in the UK in Fine and Saad-Filho (2019) which considers the content of, and contents of, the Party's economic programme under Corbyn (and John McDonnell). An assessment of her own is made by Mary from an insider's perspective, as she served as Corbyn's Chief Economic Advisor (Robertson, 2023).

But the major continuing contributor to the study of neoliberalism has been Alfredo, with a sheaf or publications, over and above those already mentioned, that both preceded and succeeded Fessud (Saad-Filho, 2017, 2018, 2021a and b, with 2022a on climate and 2020 and 2022b on the pandemic; and Saad-Filho et al. 2021, see also Bayliss and Fine, 2021b). His expertise in the area was specifically brought on board towards the end of Fessud. No doubt, there would have been a continuing momentum if taking the counterfactual of the non-existence of Fessud. However, Fessud may have contributed to the weight of contributions as well as enhancing substantive content.

Last, and by no means least, the themes of neoliberalism, financialisation and SoPs were taken up across a range of other work. South Africa has figured strongly, in part because it was one of the country case studies, but also because of my own research, policy and activist interest over decades, Ashman et al. (2021) and Reynolds et al. (eds) (2019), including Reynolds et al. (2019), Fine (2019) and Fine and Van Niekerk (2019). Social policy has also been prominent during the Fessud programme and in continuing work, Fine (2012, 2014 and 2016a). Here the major theme has been the critique of the Welfare Regime Approach and the need to take account of financialisation in understanding evolving neoliberal social policy and its differentiated impact across sector, (country) location and time. The same applies to privatisation and the search for public sector alternatives (Fine and Hall, 2012; Bayliss and Mattioli, 2018; and Bayliss and Fine, 2020). Increasingly, such work has been located in the context of neoliberalised economic and social reproduction, as well as particular forms that it takes, such as Public-Private Partnerships, Fine (2020a and 2020b). And the practices and discourses of the neoliberal and financialised 'developmental state' have been covered in Fine and Pollen (2018) as well as Fine (2016b) which also engages with the social compacting paradigm (SCP) and WRA again. A more positive stance on the Developmental Welfare State is taken in Fine (2014). And the nature of mainstream economics, and how to offer alternatives in teaching and research in the neoliberal context, see Chapter 6, has remained an abiding focus, not least with the earlier volumes in this series, (Fine, 2024a–c, and, otherwise, most recently, Fine, 2016d, 2017b, 2018 and 2022, Fine and Dimakou, 2016; and Robertson, 2020).

Ashman, S., B. Fine and E. Karwowski (2021) "The Relevance of Financialization for African Economies: Lessons from South Africa", SOAS Department of Economics Working Paper, no 245, https://www.soas.ac.uk/economics/research/workingpapers/file156232.pdf

Bayliss, K. (2020) "Moving the Goalposts: Reconfiguring the Role of the Private Sector in the Provision of Water", in Gideon and Unterhalter (eds) (2020), pp. 79–97.

Bayliss, K. (2021) "Water Companies Are Safe Investments – and Too Important to Be Driven by Profit", *The Conversation*, August 13.

Bayliss, K. (2022) "Can England's National Health System Reforms Overcome the Neoliberal Legacy?", *International Journal of Health Services*, vol 52, no 4, pp. 480–91.

Bayliss, K. (2022a) "England's Water: Is the Privatised Model a Fair System?" *Guardian*, November 30.

Bayliss, K. (2022b) "Why Clean, Affordable Water Should not Be in the Hands of Private Companies Targeting Profit – New Research", *The Conversation*, August 26.

Bayliss, K. (2022c) "Water Privatisation: A Costly Policy Distraction", *Smart Water Magazine*, January 21.

Bayliss, K. and K. Buse (2022) "England's Privatised Water: Profits over People and Planet", British Medical Journal, 378:02076, doi.org/10.1136/bmj.02076

Bayliss, K. and B. Fine (2020) "Financialisation and the Future for SOEs", in Bernier et al. (eds) (2020), pp. 354–71.

Bayliss, K. and B. Fine (2021a) *A Guide to the Systems of Provision Approach: Who Gets What, How and Why*, Basingstoke: Palgrave MacMillan.

Bayliss, K. and B. Fine (2021b) "Food, Diet and the Pandemic", *Theory and Struggle*, vol 122, no 1, pp. 46–57.

Bayliss, K., B. Fine and M. Robertson (2017) "Introduction to Special Issue on the Material Cultures of Financialisation", *New Political Economy*, vol 22, no 4, pp. 355–70, reproduced in Bayliss et al. (eds) (2018), pp. 1–16.

Bayliss, K., B. Fine and M. Robertson (2018) "The Systems of Provision Approach to Understanding Consumption", in Kravets et al. (eds) (2018), pp. 27–42.

Bayliss, K., B. Fine and M. Robertson (eds) (2017) "Material Cultures of Financialisation", special issue of *New Political Economy*, vol 22, no 4, reproduced as Bayliss et al. (eds) (2018).

Bayliss, K., B. Fine and M. Robertson (eds) (2018) *Material Cultures of Financialisation*, London: Routledge, reproduced from, Bayliss et al. (eds) (2017).

Bayliss, K. and J. Gideon (2020) "The Privatisation and Financialisation of Social Care in the UK", Working Paper for the Women's Budget Group, and SOAS Working Paper, no 238, https://www.soas.ac.uk/sites/default/files/2022-10/economics-wp238.pdf

Bayliss, K. and D. Hall (2017) "Bringing Water into Public Ownership: Costs and Benefits", Technical Report, Public Services International Research Unit (PSIRU), University of Greenwich, London, https://gala.gre.ac.uk/id/eprint/17277/10/17277%20HALL_Bringing_Water_into_Public_Ownership_(Rev'd)_2017.pdf

Bayliss, K. and G. Mattioli (2018) "Privatisation, Inequality and Poverty in the UK: Briefing prepared for UN Rapporteur on Extreme Poverty and Human Rights", Working Paper, no 116, Sustainability Research Unit, University of Leeds, https://www.see.leeds.ac.uk/fileadmin/Documents/research/sri/workingpapers/SRIPs-116.pdf.

Bayliss, K., G. Mattioli and J. Steinberger (2020) "Inequality, Poverty and the Privatization of Essential Services: A 'Systems of Provision' Study of Water, Energy and Local Buses in the UK", *Competition and Change*, vol 25, no 3/4, pp. 478–500.

Bayliss, K. and G. Pollen (2021) "The Power Paradigm in Practice: A Critical Review of Developments in the Zambian Electricity Sector", *World Development*, vol 140, pp. 1–12, doi.org/10.1016/j.worlddev.2020.105358

Bayliss, K., M.-J. Romero and E. Van Waeyenberge (2021) "Uneven Outcomes from Private Infrastructure Finance: Evidence from Two Case Studies", *Development in Practice*, vol 31, no 7, pp. 934–45.

Bayliss, K., E. Van Waeyenberge and B. Bowles (2023) "Private Equity and the Regulation of Financialised Infrastructure: The Case of Macquarie in Britain's Water and Energy Networks", *New Political Economy*, vol 28, no 2, pp. 155–72.

Bernier, L., M. Florio and P. Bance (eds) (2020) *Handbook on State-Owned Enterprises*, London: Routledge.

Boffo, M., B. Fine and A. Saad-Filho (2018) "Neoliberal Capitalism: The Authoritarian Turn", in Panitch and Albo (eds) (2018), pp. 247–70.

Bowles, B., K. Bayliss and E. Van Waeyenberge (2021) "London's 'Super Sewer': A Case Study for the Interdisciplinary Possibilities of Anthropologists and Economists Investigating Infrastructure Together", in Wood (ed.) (2021), pp. 5–30.

Brennan, D., D. Kristjanson-Gural, C. Mulder, E. Olsen (eds) (2017) *The Routledge Handbook of Marxian Economics*, London: Routledge.

Cahill, D., M. Cooper and M. Konings (eds) (2018) SAGE *Handbook of Neoliberalism*, London: Sage.

Chang, K.-S. and B. Fine (2012) "Conclusion", in Chang et al. (eds) (2012), pp. 299–318.

Chang, K.-S., B. Fine and L. Weiss (2012) "Introduction: Neo-Liberalism and Developmental Politics in Perspective", in Chang et al. (eds) (2012), pp. 1–26.

Chang, K.-S., B. Fine and L. Weiss (eds) (2012) *Developmental Politics in Transition: The Neoliberal Era and Beyond*, Basingstoke: Palgrave MacMillan.

Chang, K-S., B. Fine and L. Weiss (eds) (2012) *Developmental Politics in Transition: The Neoliberal Era and Beyond*, Basingstoke: Palgrave Macmillan.

Chester, L. and T.-H. Jo (eds) *Heterodox Economics: Legacy and Prospects*, Bristol: World Economics Association Books.

Christophers, B. and B. Fine (2020) "The Value of Financialization and the Financialization of Value", in Mader et al. (eds) (2020), pp. 19–30.

Deane, K. and E. Van Waeyenberge (2020) *Recharting the History of Economic Thought,* London: Bloomsbury Publishing.

Decker, S., W. Elsner and S. Flechtner (eds) (2018) *Advancing Pluralism in Teaching Economics*, London: Routledge.

Fasenfest, D. (ed.) (2022) *Marx Matters*, Leiden: Brill.

Fine, B. (2012) "Financialisation and Social Policy", in Utting et al. (eds) (2012), pp. 103–22.

Fine, B. (2012a) "Neo-Liberalism in Retrospect? – It's Financialisation, Stupid", in Chang et al. (eds) (2012), pp. 51–69.

Fine, B. (2013–14) "Financialisation from a Marxist Perspective", *International Journal of Political Economy*, vol 42, no 4, pp. 47–66.

Fine, B. (2014) "The Continuing Enigmas of Social Policy", prepared for the UNRISD project on Towards Universal Social Security in Emerging Economies, UNRISD Working Paper, no 2014–10, June, http://www.unrisd.org/80256B3C005BCCF9/%28httpAuxPages%29/30B153EE73F52ABFC1257D0200420A61/$file/Fine.pdf, shortened and revised in Ye (ed.) (2017), pp. 29–60.

Fine, B. (2016a) "The Systemic Failings in Framing Neo-Liberal Social Policy", in Subaset (ed.) (2016), pp. 159–77.

Fine, B. (2016b) "Across Developmental State and Social Compacting: The Peculiar Case of South Africa", ISER Working Paper no. 2016/1, Grahamstown: Institute of Social and Economic Research, Rhodes University. https://eprints.soas.ac.uk/34148/1/iserwp.pdf

Fine, B. (2016d) *Microeconomics: A Critical Companion*, London: Pluto.

Fine, B. (2017a) "The Material and Culture of Financialisation", *New Political Economy*, vol 22, no 4, pp. 371–82, reproduced in Bayliss et al. (eds) (2018), pp. 17–28.

Fine, B. (2017b) "From One-Dimensional Man to One-Dimensions Economy and Economics", *Radical Philosophy Review*, vol 20, no 1, pp. 49–74.

Fine, B. (2018) "In and Against Orthodoxy: Teaching Economics in the Neoliberal Era", in Decker et al. (eds) (2018), pp. 78–94.

Fine, B. (2019) "Post-Apartheid South Africa: It's Neoliberalism, Stupid!", in Reynolds et al. (eds) (2019), 75–95.

Fine, B. (2020a) "Framing Social Reproduction in the Age of Financialisation", in Santos and Teles (eds) (2020), pp. 257–72.

Fine, B. (2020b) "Situating PPPs", in Gideon and Unterhalter (eds) (2020), pp. 26–38.

Fine, B. (2022) "From Marxist Political Economy to Financialisation or Is It the Other Way about?", in Fasenfest (ed.) (2022), pp. 43–66.

Fine, B. (2022a) "Towards Interdisciplinarity as Instinctive", in Chester and Jo (eds) (2022), pp. 290–325.

Fine, B. (2024a) *Economics Imperialism and Interdisciplinarity: Before the Watershed; Critical Reconstructions of Political Economy*, Volume 1, Leiden: Brill, and Chicago: Haymarket.

Fine, B. (2024b) *Economics Imperialism and Interdisciplinarity: The Watershed and After; Critical Reconstructions of Political Economy*, Volume 2, Leiden: Brill, and Chicago: Haymarket.

Fine, B. (2024c) *Cliometrics as Economics Imperialism: Across the Watershed: Critical Reconstructions of Political Economy*, Volume 3, Leiden: Brill, and Chicago: Haymarket.

Fine, B. and K. Bayliss (2022) "From Addressing to Redressing Consumption: How the System of Provision Approach Helps", *Consumption and Society*, vol 1, no 1, pp. 197–206.

Fine, B. and O. Dimakou (2016) *Macroeconomics: A Critical Companion*, London: Pluto.

Fine, B. and D. Hall (2012) "Terrains of Neoliberalism: Constraints and Opportunities for Alternative Models of Service Delivery", in McDonald and Ruiters (eds) (2012), pp. 45–70.

Fine, B. and G. Pollen (2018) "The Developmental State Paradigm in the Age of Financialisation", in Hyland and Munck (eds) (2018), pp. 211–27.

Fine, B. and A. Saad-Filho (2014) "Politics of Neoliberal Development: Washington Consensus and post-Washington Consensus", in Weber (ed.) (2014), pp. 154–76.

Fine, B. and A. Saad-Filho (2016a) "Thirteen Things You Need to Know about Neoliberalism", *Critical Sociology*, vol 43, no 4–5, pp. 685–706.

Fine, B. and A. Saad-Filho (2019) "Economic Policies for the Many Not the Few: Assessing the Economic Strategy of the Labour Party", *Theory and Struggle*, vol 120, pp. 76–88.

Fine, B., A. Saad-Filho, K. Bayliss and M. Robertson (2016b) "Thirteen Things You Need to Know about Neoliberalism", FESSUD, Working Paper Series, no 155, https://fessud.org/wp-content/uploads/2015/03/13-Things-you-need-to-know-about-Neoliberalism-working-paper155.pdf, see Fine and Saad-Filho (2016a) and Chapter 2.

Fine, B. and R. Van Niekerk (2019) "Conclusion: Harold Wolpe: Towards the Politics of Liberation in a Democratic South Africa", in Reynolds et al. (2019), pp. 338–68.

Gideon, J. and E. Unterhalter (eds) (2020) *Critical Reflections on Public Private Partnerships*, London: Routledge.

Hyland, M. and R. Munck (eds) (2018) *Handbook on Development and Social Change*, Cheltenham: Edward Elgar.

Kravets, O., P. Maclaran, S. Miles and A. Venkatesh (eds) (2018) *The SAGE Handbook of Consumer Culture*, London: Sage.

Mader, P., D. Mertens and N. van der Zwan (eds) (2020) *The Routledge International Handbook of Financialization*, London: Routledge.

McDonald, D. and G. Ruiters (eds) (2012) *Alternatives to Privatisation: Exploring Non-Commercial Service Delivery Options in the Global South*, London: Routledge.

Panitch, L. and G. Albo (eds) (2018) *A World Turned Upside Down?, Socialist Register*, 2019, vol 55, London: Merlin Press.

Reynolds, J., B. Fine and R. Van Niekerk (2019) "Introduction: Revisiting Harold Wolpe in Post-apartheid South Africa", in Reynolds et al. (2019), pp. 1–28.

Reynolds, J., B. Fine and R. Van Niekerk (eds) (2019) *Race Class and the Post-Apartheid Democratic State*, Pietermaritzburg: University of KwaZulu-Natal Press.

Robertson, M. (2017a) "The Great British Housing Crisis", *Capital and Class*, vol 41, no 2, pp. 1–21.

Robertson, M. (2017b) "(De)constructing the Financialised Culture of Owner-Occupation in the UK, with the Aid of the 10Cs", *New Political Economy*, vol 22, no 4, 398–409, reproduced in Bayliss et al. (eds) (2018), pp. 398–409.

Robertson, M. (2020) "How and Why Are Things Consumed?", in Deane and Van Waeyenberge (eds) (2020), pp. 69–88.

Robertson, M. (2023) "Reform versus Transformation: Reflections on the Legacy of Corbynism's Economic Programme", *Historical Materialism*, vol 31, no 3, pp. 3–32.

Robertson, M. (2024) "Rent and Financialisation as Concrete Totality: The Case for Provisioning Approaches as Method of Abstraction", *Progress in Human Geography*, vol 48, no 1, pp. 18–34.

Saad-Filho, A. (2017) "Neoliberalism", in Brennan et al. (eds) (2017), pp. 245–54.

Saad-Filho, A. (2018) "Monetary Policy and Neoliberalism", in Cahill et al. (eds) (2018), pp. 335–46.

Saad-Filho, A. (2020) "From COVID-19 to the End of Neoliberalism", *Critical Sociology*, vol 46, no 4–5, pp. 477–85.

Saad-Filho, A. (2021a) *Growth and Change in Neoliberal Capitalism: Essays in the Political Economy of Late Development*, Leiden: Brill.

Saad-Filho, A. (2021b) "Endgame: From Crisis in Neoliberalism to Crises of Neoliberalism", *Human Geography*, vol 14, no 1, pp. 133–37.

Saad-Filho, A. (2022a) *Progressive Policies for Economic Development: Economic Diversification and Social Inclusion after Climate Change*, London: Routledge.

Saad-Filho, A. (2022b) *The Age of Crisis: Neoliberalism, the Collapse of Democracy, and the Pandemic*, London: Palgrave.

Saad-Filho, A., M. Arsel and F. Adaman (2021) "Authoritarian Developmentalism: The Latest Stage of Neoliberalism?", *Geoforum*, vol 124, pp. 261–66.

Santos, A. and N. Teles (eds) (2020) *Financialisation in the European Periphery: Work and Social Reproduction in Portugal*, London: Routledge.

Subaset, T. (ed.) (2016) *The Great Financial Meltdown: Systemic, Conjunctural or Policy Created?*, Cheltenham: Edward Elgar.

Utting P., S. Razavi and R. Buchholz (eds) (2012) *Global Crisis and Transformative Social Change*, London: Palgrave MacMillan.

Weber, H. (ed.) (2014) *Politics of Neoliberalism: A Survey*, London: Routledge.

Wood, D. (ed.) (2021) *Infrastructure, Morality, Food and Clothing, and New Developments in Latin America*, Research in Economic Anthropology, vol 41, Bingley: Emerald Publishing Limited.

Ye, I. (ed.) (2017) *Towards Universal Health Care in Emerging Economies: Opportunities and Challenges*, London: Palgrave MacMillan.

CHAPTER 2

Thirteen Things You Need to Know about Neoliberalism

Postscript as Personal Preamble

Although this piece appears in this volume as the first contribution from the FESSUD project, it was written last and, almost certainly, after funding had already been exhausted and employed research completed apart from the limited time allowed for continuing the writing up of results from the project, see Preface and Chapter 1. My leading co-researchers, Kate Bayliss and Mary Robertson, and myself were joined by Alfredo Saad-Filho to add his expertise on neoliberalism and to revitalise our energies.

As a result, the chapter is marked by a number of features. In general, it reflects at the time of writing the most mature account of our endeavours across a number of dimensions. First is theoretical, ranging however skimpily at times in relative and/or absolute terms across the nature of neoliberalism as a stage of capitalism, the role of the state, how to understand financialisation, and the application of the system of provision (SoP) approach in and of itself, to social reproduction and social norms, and to material culture (and everyday life) through the 10Cs. These issues to a greater or lesser extent are covered in greater detail and depth in later chapters to which reference can be made although the intention is that this Chapter should be able to be followed as a standalone contribution. Second is empirical with integral, if selective, reference for illustrative purposes to the case studies undertaken in the comparative research, especially but not exclusively for the provisioning of housing and water. Third, as a consequence, is reference to the variegated nature of provisioning under neoliberalism and the increased volatilities and vulnerabilities surrounding economic and social provisioning. Fourth, heavily emphasised in our latest contribution on the post-pandemic period in response to the idea that its associated interventionism witnessed the death of neoliberalism (Bayliss et al. 2024 and the longer version, Chapter 7), is the stance taken here against the idea that neoliberalism, despite its ideology (or should that be ideologies), is laissez-faire. Rather, it has always favoured and is heavily characterised by interventionism in practice. Indeed, we demonstrate that neoliberalism transforms state interventionism in variegated and shifting ways but is no less interventionist as a result.

 | DOI:10.1163/9789004706293_003

Despite these briefly summarised achievements, there are also some notable absences. Most significant is the failure to have identified the third phase of neoliberalism (as opposed to the two that are highlighted – shock therapy and Third Wayism). The latest phase is one in which financialised accumulation (and corresponding influences upon economic and social reproduction) rests on much more explicit state interventionism, not least in state support in financing and provisioning for private involvement in public services, economic and social infrastructure and (the 'new') industrial policy. This has been accelerated by the pandemic but preceded it. In principle, this ought to raise the question of whether the purpose of the state is to underwrite profitability or to put people before profit. Whether it does so in practice, and in policy and political conflicts, remains to be seen.

Introduction[1]

Oh no, not another piece on neoliberalism, synthesising what has gone before, adding its own particular angle and, thereby, compounding the confusion as much as clarifying what has gone before.[2] And, what's more, written with a popular title along the lines of Ha-Joon Chang's (2011) *23 Things They Don't Tell You About Capitalism* (neoliberalism can be handled with a parsimonious, ten fewer things, especially if the 23 are already on board). But appearances can be deceptive. For, whilst what follows is a stocktaking exercise, delivered to some degree in popular and stark form, it gains depth from three sources. One

1 Originally drafted as Fine et al. (2016a). Unlike the other chapters, no number is given for the introduction section in deference to the one-to-thirteen things as sections that follow, so that each can have its corresponding number. Stripped of its case study illustrations, this chapter first appeared in print as Fine and Saad-Filho (2016a), without co-authors Bayliss and Robertson upon their insistence and against our own.

2 Much of the neoliberal conundrum is neatly illustrated by Wacquant (2009, p. 306), "Neoliberalism is an elusive and contested notion, a hybrid term awkwardly suspended between the lay idiom of political debate and the technical terminology of social science, which moreover is often invoked without clear referent. For some, it designates a hard-wired reality ... while others view it as a doctrine ... It is alternately depicted as a tight, fixed, and monolithic set of principles and programs that tend to homogenize societies, or as a loose, mobile, and plastic constellation of concepts and institutions adaptable to variegated strands of capitalism." See also Prügl (2015, p. 616) who, in the context of 'Neoliberalising Feminism', suggests that, "Neoliberalism has become somewhat of a master variable, an explanatory hammer that fits all nails, used to account for a multiplicity of contemporary phenomena, and largely replacing other master concepts such as capitalism, modernity, and globalisation."

is longstanding scholarship on neoliberalism itself.[3] Another is being able to view, and to present, neoliberalism in light of the global crisis. The third is to have illustrated the nature of neoliberalism through comparative five country case studies around housing and water, themselves situated in the broader context of study of the impact of financialisation on economic and social functioning.

This intellectual exercise is both significant and timely because the current 'age of neoliberalism' has already lasted beyond one generation – exceeding the lifetime of the preceding Keynesian 'golden age' – and there are no signs that it is about to give way. The solidity of neoliberalism, its continuing ability to renew itself and intensify its hold on governments and societies, despite economic volatility and the depth of the current crisis, warrants recognition and detailed investigation.[4]

1 The First Thing …

… you need to know about neoliberalism is that it represents a new stage in the development of capitalism emerging in the wake of the post-war boom.

In the social sciences literature, neoliberalism has generally been understood in four closely-related and not always easily separable ways: (a) as a set of economic and political ideas inspired, unevenly and often inconsistently, by the (neo-)Austrian School and monetarism;[5] (b) as a set of policies, institutions and practices inspired and/or validated by those ideas;[6] (c) as a class offensive against the workers and the poor led by the state on behalf of capital in general and finance in particular (this attack is normally justified by recourse to neoliberal ideas and carried out through so-called economic 'adjustment', especially in developing but increasingly in developed countries in crisis),[7] and (d) as a

3 See, for example, Ayers and Saad-Filho (2008 and 2015), Bayliss et al. (eds) (2011), Chang et al. (eds) (2012),[[I_12283n]]] Fine (2010a and b), Fine and Hall (2012), Fine and Saad-Filho (2014), Saad-Filho (2007, 2008 and 2010), Saad-Filho (ed.) (2003), Saad-Filho and Johnston (eds) (2005) and Saad-Filho and Yalman (eds) (2010).

4 For the persistence of neoliberalism, despite the crisis, see the aptly named "The Strange Non-Death of Neo-liberalism" (Crouch, 2011), and especially Chapter 7.

5 See Dardot and Laval (2013), Mirowski (2009) and Mirowski and Plehwe (eds) (2009) and Stedman Jones (2012).

6 Thus, for Dardot and Laval (2013, p.7), "Since the late 1970s and early 1980s, neo-liberalism has generally been interpreted both as an ideology and as an economic policy directly informed by that ideology."

7 See, for example, Duménil and Lévy (2004) and the works reviewed in Cahill (2014).

material structure of social, economic and political reproduction underpinned by financialisation, in which case neoliberalism is the current phase, stage, or mode of existence of capitalism. Each conceptualisation of neoliberalism necessarily involves a further issue: does this understanding of neoliberalism offer anything of substance in capturing the contemporary world beyond poorly specified notions of 'free market' capitalism, post-fordism (underpinning postmodernism), the 'knowledge economy', the ever-popular consumer society (neoliberally underpinned by excessive credit), or whatever?[8]

Our own starting point is to characterise neoliberalism in light of approach (d). This immediately raises three further questions. First is how do we define a stage of capitalism. This is done through the distinctive ways in which economic reproduction (the accumulation, distribution and exchange of value) is organised and reorganised and its implications for social reproduction (the structures, relations, processes and agents that are not necessarily directly or predominantly economic, including the political and the ideological). As Dardot and Laval (2013, p.14) rightly puts it, "the originality of neoliberalism is precisely its creation of a new set of rules defining not only a different 'regime of accumulation', but, more broadly, a different society".

Second is how do we characterise previous stages of capitalism. This is to some degree academic as there tends to be uniformity over the periodisation of capitalism into separate stages even if slightly different criteria from ours are used to do so.[9] Some sort of laissez-faire period in the nineteenth century is presumed to give way to a more monopolistic stage in the first half of the twentieth century which then passes to a stage in which state intervention is significant, conventionally termed the Keynesian or Fordist period.[10] More significantly, stages of capitalism are distinguished by global and not merely (a collection of) national conditions, so it would be inappropriate to start inductively from the classification of countries into those that are more or less (neo) liberal, Keynesian or whatever. Rather, different countries exist within, and influence, the dominant stages of global capitalism in different ways, and this has implications for what might be termed the variegated outcomes for the

8 Similar, if not identical, questions might be asked of 'globalisation' which is the most prominent way of characterising the contemporary world, not necessarily as a stage of development, but with multiple, competing, contested and not always consistent interpretations (Kiely, 2005; Kozul-Wright, 2006; Labica, 2007; and Rosenberg, 2000 and 2005).

9 Of course, there may be exceptions if periodising by relatively disconnected criteria such as political systems, wars and technologies.

10 This leaves open how to characterise the stage after Keynesianism if not neoliberalism, with post-fordism also having proven incapable of delivering anything other than at most a temporary and unsatisfactory answer (Mavroudeas, 1999 and 2006).

economic, the political and the ideological more generally at different levels and in different arenas.

The third issue is why, then, should neoliberalism be considered a new and separate stage of capitalism. Our answer is to be found throughout what follows but is fundamentally based upon the insight that the most salient feature of neoliberalism is financialisation. As is shown in the fifth thing, the rise of financialisation over the past thirty years, defined as the intensive and extensive accumulation of interest-bearing capital, has transformed profoundly the organisation of economic and social reproduction. These transformations include not only outcomes but the structures, processes, agencies and relations through which those outcomes are determined across production, employment, international integration, the state and ideology. Correspondingly, the term financialisation encapsulates the increasing role of globalised finance in ever more areas of economic and social life. In turn, financialisation underpins a neoliberal system of accumulation that is articulated through the power of the state to impose, drive, underwrite and manage the financialisation and internationalisation of production and finance in each territory, even if often under the ideological veil of preference for, and goal of, non-intervention.

Our favoured approach, then, not only claims that neoliberalism is the current stage, phase or mode of existence of capitalism but also explains how and why it should be understood as such. It also implies that the starting point in specifying neoliberalism must have both logical and historical content. The former concerns the nature of economic reproduction under neoliberalism, while the latter focuses on the (uneven) ways in which neoliberalism exists across different countries including both economic and social reproduction. For, as will be seen under the tenth thing, neoliberalism is distinctive but not homogenising. Instead, it fosters diversity and differentiation underpinned by common aspects, or driving forces and conditions. It is the latter that have to be identified in the first instance, together with their internal contradictions, tensions and sources of dynamics and, consequently, potential to realise uneven outcomes and the mechanisms and determinants through which they do so in specific instances. In contrast, the commonly held presumption that neoliberalism is homogenising is grounded at an excessively concrete level and in a selective manner, either missing out on the diverse consequences of the common drivers of neoliberalism, or inevitably concluding that it is an incoherent specification of contemporary capitalism in light of this empirically unavoidable diversity.[11]

11 See Castree (2006) and Ferguson (2007). For Venugopal (2015, p. 165), "neoliberalism has become a deeply problematic and incoherent term that has multiple and contradictory

Within this understanding of neoliberalism as a stage of capitalism, housing and water feature as two aspects of economic and social reproduction that have been transformed over the last thirty years. The case studies offered below corroborate the view that the defining feature of this transformation is the intensive and extensive accumulation of interest-bearing capital – in short, financialisation – supported by the state under the veil of non-intervention. For example, a key trend across all of the housing case studies for five countries was the extension of homeownership which, with varying degrees of success, has served as a means to incorporate more households into mortgage markets, and as a basis for developing secondary mortgage markets. States have played an active role in this shift, with interventions ranging from creating the legal and regulatory frameworks for primary and secondary mortgage markets to exist, to subsidising mortgages and even the building of houses to which it is hoped mortgages will be attached. Yet such interventions tend to be couched in pro-market rhetoric, with lesser commodified forms of provision constrained if not prohibited. Within these patterns, there is wide variation in the content and degree of state intervention across the case studies which, along with variation in the extent to which intensive and extensive financial accumulation has taken hold in the housing sector, serves to emphasise the unevenness of neoliberalism, and the associated importance of attending to its historical as well as its logical content.

Evidence from the water case studies also supports the notion of neoliberalism as a stage of capitalism, see below. However, water also offers salutary lessons concerning the history as opposed to the logic of capitalist development through, and within, stages. For, early private providers were taken into the public domain in the post-war period in large part due to the failings of private providers to reach rural and low-income areas. Even so, the compartmentalising of stages is not clear-cut and gives rise to contradictions where they overlap as the case studies in Poland, Portugal and South Africa demonstrate. In these countries state resources were invested in the 1990s to expand access to unconnected rural and low-income areas. At the same time, neoliberal policies were gaining ground so that households were facing tariff increases to ensure that charges would cover costs. The result in some cases has been that the water provided by the state-led infrastructure investment is too expensive for households to afford. Some have been disconnected as a result. State-led expansion is increasing access while neoliberal financial management is limiting it! This

meanings, and thus has diminished analytical value". But also, for the contrary, see Hart (2002 and 2008) for neoliberalism's contingent diversities as opposed to incoherencies, and also Peck (2010).

is indicative that development through stages of capitalism is not unilinear, and they can overlap or even be reversed; this is a further source of variegation in outcomes (with the corresponding inclination, in case of neoliberalism, for it be dismissed on empirical grounds of not homogenising to a template of features and trajectories).

In contrast, the approach to neoliberalism in what follows is informed by a specific understanding of two key features of the contemporary political economy. The first is that financialisation has transformed global patterns of growth. The rates of investment and GDP growth in the advanced economies have tended to decline since the crisis of the so-called Keynesian, Fordist or social-democratic 'golden age', regardless of the unprecedentedly favourable conditions for capital accumulation in the recent past, in part imposed through neoliberalism itself. These conditions include the West's victory in the Cold War and the collapse of most nationalist movements in the Global South, and the closely related liberalisation of trade, finance and capital movements, the provision of unparalleled support to accumulation by competing states, the containing of taxation, transfers and welfare provision in most countries, the secular decline in the power of trade unions, peasant movements, left parties and social movements (the traditional sources of resistance within previous forms of capitalism), and the unprecedented ideological hegemony of a bogus but vociferous 'free market' capitalism. Finally, the unprecedented availability of new technologies serves as a potential source of productivity increase and driver of the restructuring of accumulation, alongside significant increases in the global labour force, not least with China's integration into the capitalist world economy. Instead of thriving on the basis of these conditions, global accumulation in the core countries has been hampered by continuing instability and, since 2007, by the deepest and longest economic crisis since the Great Depression.

The second key feature is that neoliberal patterns of production, employment, finance and consumption have simultaneously sustained impressive rates of investment and GDP growth in particular regions, with Northeast and Southeast Asia to the fore and, more recently, the transformation of China into the assembly hub of the world.[12] This is far from suggesting that neoliberalism fosters an unproblematic 'global convergence'. Rather, it creates new patterns of uneven and combined development, in which unparalleled prosperity within and across countries and regions, and for specific social strata (possibly identified as financial or other elites or oligarchs, the top 1%, the top 0.01% or

12 Bellamy Foster and McChesney (2012).

whatever), both coexist with new patterns of poverty as well as its reproduction in areas where it already prevailed.

2 The Second Thing …

… you need to know about neoliberalism is that it is not reducible to a cogent ideology, but it is attached to a wide spectrum of ideas. These ideas display a changing relevance in rationalising current conditions and selected policies, quite apart from their leverage over state policy and their role in confining and steering political and other contestations.

Ideologically, neoliberalism draws heavily, if at times indirectly, upon the Austrian tradition of Ludwig von Mises, Friedrich von Hayek and their neo-Austrian successors, and the US monetarist school associated with the Department of Economics, University of Chicago in general and with Milton Friedman in particular. They argue, albeit in sharply dissimilar and logically incompatible ways, that differently endowed property-owning individuals exchanging goods, services and information in minimally regulated markets constitute the most desirable form for allocating resources and should prevail over an interventionist role of the state and, even if less apparent in popular discourse, democratic processes: the neoliberal ideology of free markets can never entirely part company with its antithesis in some respects, the authoritarian state.[13]

Despite their shared purposes and conclusions, even casual examination reveals considerable tensions between these scholarly underpinnings of neoliberalism. For example, while the (neo-) Austrians emphasise the inventive and transformative subjectivity of the individual and the spontaneous emergence of an increasingly efficient order through market processes, neoclassical economics focuses on the efficiency properties of a static equilibrium achieved entirely in the logical domain on the basis of unchanging individuals, resources and technologies and, possibly, mediated by the semi-divine intervention of the Walrasian 'auctioneer'. Nor does either capture the political economy and moral philosophy associated with Adam Smith, despite

13 See Ayers and Saad-Filho (2015) and note the putative 'de-politicisation through economisation' (Madra and Adaman, 2014). The neoliberal dilemma across freedom of, and yet control over, individual choice is neatly addressed in scholarship, ideology and, increasingly, policy in practice, by the notion of 'nudging' behaviour (Fine et al. 2016b).

their obsessive rhetorical recourse to the 'invisible hand', with its meaning and rationale subject to varieties of (mis)interpretations.[14]

The analytical inconsistencies and policy failures of monetarism have been exposed in merciless detail by Keynesian and heterodox economists, but these shortcomings have been largely ignored by many mainstream economists, policymakers and the media.[15] They promoted, instead, a populist understanding of 'competitiveness', 'individual freedom' and 'democracy' that has validated neoliberal policy reforms and repression of opposition in country after country, while also providing reassurance that the neoliberal reforms spawn the best of all possible worlds.

Despite its impressive strengths, neoliberal ideology remains too fragmented to provide a coherent representation of society. It offers, instead, a fuzzy conception of self and society based on universalism, individualism, formal egalitarianism and meliorism. This worldview justifies a set of loosely articulated finance-friendly state policies and practices giving neoliberalism a semblance of coherence in the realm of ideas, and considerable resilience in practice; these policies cannot be contested easily, for the neoliberal restructuring of the economy and society not only narrows drastically the scope for, and directions of, debate, but also hollows out the institutional channels from which alternatives could emerge (see thirteenth thing). These limitations are notable, for example, in stridently defended privatisations that are habitually awarded to, or create, monopolies, and in decentralisation of state provision, in which a leading thrust is to 'devolve' responsibility for delivery to lower levels of administration (claiming also to democratise), whilst not providing sufficient resources to allow for provision to meet requirements whether formal or otherwise, and imposing the requirement to rely on private suppliers (see ninth thing).

The fraught relationship between neoliberal policy and ideology, and the often incoherent nature of the latter, is evident in the way that homeownership has been promoted and pursued, as revealed across the case studies. It

14 See Hands (2010) and Witztum (2013) for the poverty of the attempted socialisation of the individual in mainstream economics relative to Adam Smith. Medema (2009) demonstrates the tension between appealing to pursuit of self-interest as a rationale both favouring and opposing state intervention.

15 Following the decline of Friedman's monetarism in the 1980s, the emerging neoliberal ideas were strapped more or less awkwardly to different versions of 'supply-side' and New Classical Economics, new Keynesianism and new institutionalism, depending on how imperfectly working markets were conceptualised and incorporated into macroeconomic analysis (see Fine, Lapavitsas and Pincus, 2001; Fine and Milonakis, 2009; and Milonakis and Fine, 2009).

was said above that homeownership and the opportunities it presents, via primary and secondary mortgage markets, for financial accumulation, is a defining feature of housing provision under neoliberalism. Yet homeownership has been justified in a range of often incompatible ways. For example, privately-owned homes are portrayed as both an investment good or lucrative asset, and as more homely and better at providing places of stability, comfort and security than other tenures. Similarly, homeownership is celebrated for cultivating calculating rationalities in agents making decisions about housing, at the same time as it is seen as fulfilling a natural and innate desire to own one's own home (Payne, 2012). Despite the tension between these implied uses of, and attitudes towards, housing – which depict privately-owned homes as both economic and emotional assets – each conception occupies an uneasy coexistence within neoliberal rhetoric (as opposed to realities of homeownership exclusion), and in relation to one another.

To the extent that there is a common element across the different portrayals of homeownership, it takes the form of a preference for self-reliance through the market, and a presumption against collective forms of provision, particularly via the state. Here housing dovetails with the pro-market, anti-state interventionist stance that pervades neoliberal ideology more generally. In practice, however, housing policy has been much more pragmatic than this individualistic and anti-state ideology would suggest. States have been proactive and heavily interventionist in creating and extending markets for both mortgages and owner-occupied properties. For example, all of the case studies have at some point utilised mortgage subsidies to expand the section of the population covered by mortgage markets. Furthermore, in the UK and Poland, homeownership received a big push from the privatisation of previously state-built housing, while in Turkey and South Africa the state is heavily involved in building housing for low-income homeownership. The rhetoric of non-intervention has, thus, served as a smokescreen behind which states have intervened, often heavy-handedly, to abet the transformation of housing into private assets.

The decentralisation of responsibilities to local government units, without the resources necessary to meet these responsibilities, or freedoms to choose how to meet them, has been another feature of neoliberal housing policy. In both the UK and Poland, the dynamics of decentralisation were tied up with privatisation. Ownership of the state-produced housing stock formally resided with municipalities but, in both cases, these municipalities were forced by central government to offer tenants a discounted right to buy, leading to the privatisation of the bulk of the public housing stock. The heavy discounts attached to this right, along with strictures on new building – again imposed by central government – have made local governments increasingly unable to meet their devolved responsibilities with regards to housing the otherwise deprived.

The centrepiece of Turkey's neoliberal housing strategy has been the Mass Housing Administration (TOKI), which has used its comprehensive land-use powers to facilitate a process of state-led gentrification (Çelik et al. 2015). However, the transfer of land-use powers to TOKI has hollowed out local level democratic processes and limited the role of municipalities to convincing, or enforcing, dwellers to relocate in order to make way for new developments. In South Africa, the content given to the post-apartheid constitutional right to decent housing was developed at the national level, but the onus for fulfilling this right has been progressively transferred to municipal governments (Isaacs, 2016). The delivery model settled on by central government, which involved a one-off capital subsidy for the provision of a basic housing unit or 'top structure' to low-income groups, has tended to favour sprawling and peripheral developments. Such developments have high infrastructure costs and low tax intakes which, in turn, increase the burden and reduce the proceeds of delivery. Consequently, municipalities have not only been denied a say over the shaping of housing policy, but their ability to meet their housing responsibilities has been actively undermined by the content given to housing policy at a national level. The national government eventually realised these limitations and sought to rectify them by shifting policy away from mass unit production and towards the creation of so-called 'sustainable human settlements'. But this served to increase drastically the demands placed on municipal authorities which had neither the resources, the capacities nor, on occasion, the political will, to deliver them.

Across the case studies we can, therefore, see how the interplay of ideology and institutional reform has hollowed out the space for alternatives to neoliberal housing policy. First, responsibility for meeting the housing needs of marginalised populations and addressing market fall-out have been devolved to local authorities without the requisite capacities to fulfil them. This has served to erode the quality and availability of such provision, and denigrate those reliant on it. Second, while decentralisation is often presented under the guise of democratisation, the limited options and resources available to local governments have meant that decentralisation has not tended to facilitate the emergence of alternative forms of provision, and may even stifle it, reinforcing the notion that (local) state provision of housing is inferior both in principle and in practice.

The case studies indicate that neoliberal ideology has taken root in all of the water case studies with each adopting remarkably similar policies in the early 1990s including, to varying degrees, commercialisation, corporatisation, decentralisation and privatisation. These are underpinned by a neoliberal logic purporting to turn policymaking into a technocratic process removed from political influence. Hence, rather than a public decommodified service, water is increasingly reduced to the status of an 'economic good',[16] with the increasing presumption that prices need to reflect costs, and billing should relate to individualised consumption. In practice this has led to the widespread adoption of pricing methodologies based on 'cost recovery' and 'user pays', intended to lead to more efficient price signals. More specifically, water consumption has increasingly been metered so that individuals are responsible for managing their own consumption. The neoliberal package has become the only available option with policy debates increasingly narrowing around details such as 'willingness to pay' and 'value for money'.

Commodification of water faces particular challenges in and of themselves and in relation to a neoliberal ideology of leaving things to an ideally conceived and functioning market, against which compromises have to be made in practice. As is occasionally acknowledged by those more carefully undertaking such exercises, there are unavoidable ambiguities, if not inconsistencies in seeking to calculate a 'cost recovery' price for a natural resource with network effects and extensive externalities in provision. What costs should be recovered and how should they be calculated and distributed? How to account for leakages? What about historical costs, financing costs, and the impact on the ecosystem? In practice, the case studies show that there is inevitably considerable discretion when it comes to water pricing. For example, the case studies in England and Wales[17] (E&W) and Portugal (Bayliss, 2014; and Teles, 2015, respectively) show that the way in which capital investment is reflected in charges is flexible depending on assumptions about the cost of capital, the timeframe over which costs should be recovered and the allowable returns for investors. Where prices are set in advance for a five-year period (as is the case in E&W), prices are not based on actual costs but estimates of future costs and these have often been in favour of private investors.

In practice, then, water prices are contested and subject to bias and not reducible to simply applied neoliberal principles as they cannot be deployed as such. Furthermore, outcomes are contextually specific and equally incapable

16 As reflected in the adoption of the Dublin Principles at the United Nations World Summit in Rio in 1992. According to the fourth of these principles, "Water has an economic value in all its competing uses and should be recognized as an economic good".

17 The case study focused on water in England and Wales only, rather than the UK as a whole, because the SoPs for water in Scotland and Northern Ireland are run on different lines as water has not been privatised there.

of being interpreted as simply relying upon, or departing from, the market. In Portugal and Poland, contestation takes the form of local authorities trying to keep costs down to garner political support, while in E&W private water companies are trying to increase the prices they can charge to end users.[18]

Decentralisation has been one of the more problematic neoliberal water policies. Water providers vary greatly in their size and technical and financial capacities which derive in large part from the areas which they serve. In practice, decentralisation leads to reduced scope for pooling of financing and capacity. This is particularly significant in South Africa where there are entrenched regional inequalities. The provinces with the higher levels of poverty are the ones with the lowest rates of water access. More generally, decentralisation has created fragmented structures in the provision of water. This was most significant in Poland where 2,479 local authorities are responsible for water provision. Elsewhere in South Africa and Portugal, there has been some consolidation in the sector with, for example, amalgamation of some of the bulk water companies in South Africa and the merging of some bulk and retail water providers in Portugal.

Contrary to the suggestions of neoliberal postures concerning the individual freedoms that derive from the withdrawal of the state, the case studies suggest that neoliberalism in practice can work against democratic processes in the provision of water. In E&W, democratic accountability has been compromised by privatisation, with companies owned by foreign conglomerates or in some cases by unknown investors. Where the utility is owned by a financial special purpose vehicle based offshore, it is sometimes impossible for an outsider to determine the identity of the ultimate shareholders. Complex ownership structures and opaque financial transactions via tax havens make it difficult to trace financial flows. Global transactions in which ownership stakes of water providers are bought and sold to owners around the world (see third thing) create a geographical, financial and administrative distance between water users and corporate decision-makers which is incapable of being supportive of genuine democratic accountability.

In short, as illustrated by the case studies, if not reducible to their own specificities as much the same will be found in other areas of economic and social provision, neoliberalism is heterogeneous in the ideologies that it deploys and equally diverse in how these are applied in practice. For the promotion of the private sector in general, and of finance in particular, is at most

18 For Polish water, see Lis (2015a) and Yilmaz and Çelik (2016) for Istanbul, and for overview of case studies Bayliss (2016a).

opportunistically attached to broader goals of democracy, decentralisation and accountability, let alone efficacy and equity in the provision of basic goods such as water and housing.

3 The Third Thing …

… you need to know about neoliberalism is that it is not fully nor appropriately understood as the mirror image of, or a reaction against, Keynesianism, itself often inadequately seen as the explanation for the post-war boom.

Whilst, in practice, almost every area of economic and social reproduction has been reconfigured under neoliberalism (see first and second things), neoliberal ideology (especially when it comes to the economy and the unidimensional promotion of, and reliance upon, the market) tends to induce a shallow opposition between neoliberalism and Keynesianism, as if the former could be reduced to the rollback of the latter in parallel with the market/state dualism. In turn, (a broader notion of) Keynesianism is often specified in terms of 'state intervention' and collectivised forms of provision, including the short-run macroeconomic manipulation of effective demand, the welfare state, nationalised industries, some measure of planning and social contracting, which might progress to socialism through incremental reform.

It may be appealing to see neoliberalism as the counterpart to this conception of Keynesianism, offering a swing in the balance between market and state provision (see fourth thing). Even acknowledging that Keynesianism is associated with more or less progressive forms of state expenditure and intervention, the post-war boom was not driven by a bland and presumably incremental socialism but by economic and social restructuring with internationalisation of all forms of capital to the fore, especially that of productive capital, supported by (mainly US-dominated) finance, with a heavy role for the state in promoting such restructuring through both national and international corporate champions.[19] In turn, Keynesianism was driven to collapse because of the economic and social transformations that it engendered and supported, and the contradictions embodied in its own policies.[20] The simplistic dualism between Keynesianism and neoliberalism fails to acknowledge the broadly spread and deeply-rooted transformations in the processes of economic and social reproduction that have been wrought by neoliberalism, and

19 See Duménil and Lévy (2004), Fine and Harris (1985) and, especially, Panitch and Gindin (2012).

20 See Gowan (1999) and Saad-Filho (2007).

their reflection in the profound changes across each of scholarship, ideology and policy in practice.[21]

This failure to recognise the complex relationship between neoliberalism and Keynesianism has fed two additional illusions. One strand of thought, especially within Marxism, sees the emergence of neoliberalism in general and financialisation in particular as either the epiphenomenal consequence of, or the functionalist response to, the still unresolved crisis of the Keynesian period.[22] Such reductionism is insufficient because it simply sets aside three decades of global restructuring of production, employment, trade, finance, ideology, state and society, and overlooks the role of financialisation (see fifth thing) in promoting and supporting the contemporary (neoliberal) forms of accumulation and the social reproduction that accompanies it.[23]

The antithetical illusion, associated with social democracy, is that a return to Keynesianism can restore more favourable economic and social conditions today. Even though higher taxes, controls on trade, domestic finance and capital flows, expanded social provision and the fine-tuning of aggregate demand can help to address competing short-term macroeconomic objectives and promote short-term improvements in economic performance and social welfare, these policies would have only limited bearing on the long-term performance and underlying dynamics of the global economy and, even if achievable and achieved today, would remain hostages to neoliberal imperatives. Highlighting the contradictions of neoliberalism by contrast with (the strengths and virtues of) what existed before is an important analytical task in its own right, but it will neither reveal alternatives to neoliberalism nor make the limitations of Keynesianism disappear in practice.

It follows that neoliberalism and the potential for overcoming it cannot be encapsulated in conventional debates in macroeconomics, which express the rivalry between more or less sophisticated versions of monetarism and Keynesianism over whether and how to manipulate effective demand and other macroeconomic variables in order to deliver rapid and stable accumulation.[24]

21 See Fine and Milonakis (2009 and 2011).

22 Most recently, see Kliman and Williams (2015).

23 The most prominent example of this sort of reasoning is the Brenner hypothesis of investment overhang involving competitiveness between nations and large national capitals discouraging new investment. See, however, Fine et al. (2005) for a critique focusing on the extraordinary restructuring in the steel industry. Hypotheses of lack of movement since the 1970s can rarely provide evidence from particular sectors of the economy for which, of course, little has remained the same.

24 It is part and parcel of the inheritance from Keynesianism and its debate with monetarism that health, education, welfare, industrial policy, finance for investment, and so

This bypasses almost entirely the problems of economic and social restructuring and reproduction. Even if alternative policies are appropriately identified, the means to secure them against neoliberal imperatives remains unaddressed as neoliberals themselves would suggest in terms of the imperatives of the market, globalisation and so on.

In the provision of water, neoliberal policies have brought about profound changes in social structures. In the UK the privatisation programme of the 1980s Thatcher Government specifically set out to restructure social relations by dismantling the power of trade unions, and the water case study demonstrates that this has been effective (see seventh thing). In the case studies, water institutions have been restructured in ways that are underpinned by a neoliberal ethos that is difficult to reverse. Financial practices have become more sophisticated and deeply embedded so that even public companies engage in hedging and use derivatives while issuing international bonds. Public utilities are now ranked by global credit ratings agencies.

Furthermore, water privatisation in the context of globalisation has led to a fundamental shift in the locus of sector control. Since the early privatisations of the 1990s, new investors have entered the sector and the 2000s saw a shift in ownership structures with a process of global consolidation with new Asian investors as well as financial companies buying up water companies. For example, French firm, Veolia has sold its water investments in Portugal to an investor from Beijing. Japanese conglomerate Marubeni has bought out water companies from Portuguese construction company AGS. Marubeni also has power generation assets in Portugal. Both of the remaining water privatisations in South Africa have now been bought by Singapore-based company, Sembcorp, that also owns an English water company!

Accordingly, ownership stakes are now bought and sold around the world, and national boundaries may have little significance in the ownership of water utilities. Water is just one of a portfolio of investments for these companies, some of which own power plants, airports, hotels, supermarket chains and many other investments worldwide. The case studies show that the privatised utilities are immersed in global corporate structures that are far more

on, as opposed to effective demand, are sidelined alongside the focus on the short run as if it were independent from the long run. In this respect, monetarism only completed what Keynesianism started, finishing with the failure to acknowledge financialisation, itself merely the tip of the iceberg in the neglect of the other determinants of economic policy and performance. Hence the insights from, and limitations of, Crouch's (2009a and b and 2011) notion of privatised Keynesianism, that neoliberalism is based upon demand management through private credit rather than state expenditure.

complex than was imagined, possibly even desired, at the time of privatisation. Governance, that was once conceptualised on a local, certainly within a national, physical geographical basis, is now global with investments connected by finance. The neoliberal model of large numbers of small companies, competitively engaged with one another, at a local level and subject to some combination of market and decentralised, democratic accountability is a myth of massive proportions in every respect, with reality better represented by the mirror image of the myth!

In short, the idea of Keynesianism failed to get to grips with the dominating role of the internationalisation of production, as represented by multi-affiliate multinational corporations. By the same token, understanding neoliberalism as a reaction against Keynesianism means overlooking the increasing subordination of national infrastructure to global provision in the context of financialisation. Such developments have profound effects. The water companies involved are usually expected to provide further investment in infrastructure, especially in light of currently imposed fiscal constraints on governments. Governments need to maintain an attractive climate for investors, not just for water but for infrastructure in general, and this affects the regulatory process (disproportionately favouring corporates).

Housing has similarly undergone major restructuring under neoliberalism, in ways that cannot be understood as the mirror image of Keynesianism. First, most of the case study countries never experienced a welfare state, and so had no Keynesian-style social housing provision against which to react. This serves to emphasise the point that, although stages of capitalism define the global economy, countries are differentially integrated into it. Second, and relatedly, to the extent that a distinctly neoliberal form of housing provision can be discerned, it cannot be reduced to a swing of the pendulum from state to market. On the one hand, all of the case study countries barring socialist Poland had extensive market structures prior to neoliberalism and, on the other, states have continued to be heavily involved in housing provision under neoliberalism. What changed is rather that there was a shift towards treating housing as an asset, which was associated with expanding homeownership and mortgage lending, and that state support for housing provision was residualised. This shift has, of course, been accompanied by a transformation of the supply and demand structures that underpin housing provision, in different ways in different countries, though never in ways that can be reduced to a simple opposition with the Keynesian era. For example, in the UK and Poland, state capacity for building has been lost and supplanted, in the former, with an increasingly concentrated private housebuilding industry and, in the latter, with emergent private firms and a widespread practice of self-build. In all of the case studies there is a section of the population whose wealth is tied up in their housing. Third, as a result of the shift towards treating housing as an asset, housing has been subject to heightened international investment in both mortgages and their derivatives, and in real estate directly, embroiling housing and housing-related debt in global financial networks.

Neoliberalism in the context of globalisation, then, has created intertwined multinational structures of corporate control over water – and other utilities – which are not easily reversed, and these social structures around water continue to evolve. Such complexities in global, national, and other levels of economic and social restructuring, whether in water or otherwise (with housing itself different in the restructuring of ownership, with the global decisive in consumer credit or mortgages and their derivatives) can hardly be captured through the notion of neoliberalism as Keynesianism's alter ego.

4 The Fourth Thing ...

... you need to know about neoliberalism is that it is not primarily about a (possibly pendular) shift in the relationship between the state (or the Polanyian social or collective) and the market. Analytically, the market-state dualism is insufficient because neoliberalism is not defined by the withdrawal of the state from social and economic reproduction.[25] As Wacquant (2009, p. 307) suggests:

> A central ideological tenet of neoliberalism is that it entails the coming of 'small government': the shrinking of the allegedly flaccid and overgrown Keynesian welfare state and its makeover into a lean and nimble workfare state ... stressing self-reliance, commitment to paid work, and managerialism ... [But] the neoliberal state turns out to be quite different *in actuality*.

Under neoliberalism state institutions intervene upon and through markets and other institutions in specific ways that tend to extend and/or reproduce neoliberalism itself.[26] Exactly the same is true of other systems of accumulation, not least those attached to the Keynesian, developmental or Soviet-type

25 As Wade (2013, p. 7) rightly puts it, "[t]he 'market' is the polite way of referring to 'the owners of capital', especially financial capital".

26 See, for example, Lemke (2001).

states that are presumed to have been more interventionist.[27] In all these cases, the roles of 'the state' and 'the market' (unduly undifferentiated) cannot be usefully identified through their simplistic opposition. Instead, the relevant patterns of accumulation, restructuring and social and economic reproduction can be understood only through relatively concrete and historically-specific analyses. These must include the interaction, contestation and cooperation among specific institutions within, across and beyond that putative divide. Those processes are themselves heavily influenced by, but not reducible to, the underlying economic, political and ideological interests that act upon and through such institutions.

In practice, then, first, much has been achieved through state provision in the past, and this has itself become the basis for privatisation, for example, in terms of availability of productive facilities. In both the UK and Poland, a substantial share of the total housing stock is state-built, albeit now privatised, and in the UK this includes some of the better quality stock. The scope for such achievements can only have been enhanced over time through improved technological capabilities and new management techniques. Yet, these successes are rarely if ever recognised, while public provision is invariably and arbitrarily deemed to be inferior to private provision often on the basis of casual or flawed studies, that rarely even consider firm and market structure, finance, degree of monopoly and so on.[28]

Second, state intervention has been transformed rather than simply 'reduced' under neoliberalism (see sixth thing). Currently, while the overall logic of state policies and interventions remains to promote economic and social reproduction and the restructuring of capital, the interests and role of finance have increasingly come to the fore either directly or indirectly. Such is evident, for example, from the policy responses to the global crisis of 2007/8 and the continuing recession; but it is equally characteristic of the policies implemented over the entire neoliberal period, as the interests of private capital in general and of finance in particular have been favoured by the state (see eighth thing). This is well illustrated by both housing and water, reflecting both the diversity of developments under the post-war boom, across sectors and countries, and how they have been transformed under neoliberalism.

The deficiencies of the notion of market-state dualism are exposed by the SoP approach, which draws attention to the multiple ways in which the state intervenes in provisioning. In housing, for example, the role of the state

27 See Fine et al. (eds) (2013) in the context of the developmental state paradigm that accepts the analytical agenda of state versus market.

28 See Bayliss and Fine (eds) (2008).

cannot be reduced to the question of whether the state provides some housing directly or not, but also concerns how the state shapes land use, both development and house purchase finance, private production and other alternatives, and the tax, subsidy and benefit regimes that underpin consumption decisions (Robertson, 2014). Attending to these areas reveals that the character of state intervention has changed, but seldom in ways that can be readily characterised as a withdrawal let alone a retreat from intervention. For example, a distinctive feature of housing policy in the neoliberal era has been a uniform reluctance to allow land to be diverted from its highest value commercial use for other purposes, but this has commonly led, not to a laissez-faire approach to land markets, but to state intervention to facilitate proactively the allocation of land according to a commercial rationality. Turkey provides a stark illustration of this. There, comprehensive land use powers have been concentrated in the hands of TOKI, which has used authoritarian, and at times violent, measures to make potentially high-value urban land available to private developers. Even in the UK and Poland, where the idea of the retreat of the state might be thought to have gone furthest, due to both the ending of direct state provision and the privatisation of the public housing stock, the state has continued to intervene on the demand side in the form of mortgage subsidies. Admittedly, these were phased out in the UK by the end of the 1990s, except in the major, if readily overlooked, tax relief on mortgage costs of the burgeoning buy-to-let market. But demand subsidies have resurfaced following the disruption caused by the financial crisis, for example, through Help to Buy, whereby the government guarantees part of the mortgage taken out by users of the scheme.

By rejecting the idea of the state retreating from intervention, neoliberal housing policy is best characterised in terms of the restructuring of housing provision in the interests of private capital. Notwithstanding important national and regional diversities in how this has been achieved, it has tended to mean: promoting owner-occupation (the benefits of which to capital include expanding primary and secondary mortgage markets, remoulding individuals as asset-owning entrepreneurial saver-investors, and helping to ensure political passivity); the application of a commercial rationality to land use, aiding the accumulation and appropriation of rent, and making real estate a site for capital investment; a general reliance on the private sector for provision of new build and repair and maintenance; and an allowance made for a minimal though often dysfunctional safety net, in which the private sector again plays a central role in delivery (Robertson, 2016). States have intervened to support all aspects of this neoliberal housing agenda, though in widely different ways depending on context. Mortgage subsidies and land use policies have already been mentioned, and there is also even evidence on supply-side measures where these are deemed necessary. For example, in Portugal a private building boom received crucial state support in the form of infrastructure investment, while in South Africa the spread of homeownership among the poor, black population has been pursued through supply-side subsidies (Santos et al. 2015; and Isaacs, 2016). That the latter were provided with the explicit aim of equipping that population with a financial and economic asset that would allow them to enter secondary housing markets and move up the property ladder, is made no less true by having proved largely unsuccessful.

Despite the best efforts of neoliberal policy makers, the state continues to play a significant role in the provision of water. In the case studies, water is mostly provided by state institutions. Privatisation is not widespread and has even declined, for example in South Africa where just two concession contracts remain. Even with the commitment to neoliberal policies, it is the state (with financial support from the EU) that has been responsible for extension of the water supply network to increase access in Poland, Portugal and South Africa in the 1990s.

Only in E&W has water been completely taken over by private enterprise. Here, the publicly-funded infrastructure was transferred to the private sector upon privatisation, at a fraction of the asset value, but the state maintains a crucial – and demanding – role. There are a number of state agencies that are involved in different aspects of regulation including the Environment Agency and the Competition Commission. The economic regulator, Ofwat, plays a central role in setting prices as well as performance targets and monitoring firms' activities. In Portugal, the regulator ERSAR has a central role in the construction of 'market' forms in the provision of water, while municipalities have been responsible for negotiating and monitoring contracts (albeit with limited capacity). While the introduction of neoliberal policies is supposedly associated with a reduction in the role of the state and greater reliance on 'market' outcomes, in water the parameters of the so-called market are entirely created by the state, and subject to lobbying from private water companies.

5 The Fifth Thing …

… you need to know about neoliberalism is that it is underpinned by, although not reducible to, financialisation.[29] Whilst seeing neoliberalism as tied to financialisation is pushing against an open door, especially in the wake of the

29 See first thing and Fine (2013–14).

current global crisis, financialisation itself has often been imprecisely defined and variously understood across a burgeoning literature. In much of this literature, financialisation is merely a buzzword reflecting the greater significance of finance, money and commercial ethos in economic and social reproduction in recent decades, and the (closely related) growth and proliferation of financial assets. However, if financialisation is defined as the increasing presence and influence of finance, then, given its remarkable rise over the last thirty years, it is tautological to define neoliberalism as attached to financialisation. This leaves open the question of the drivers and contradictions of financialisation and neoliberalism, and how they should be addressed in terms of analytical content and their effects.

Our more specific view of financialisation focuses, instead, on the role of finance as (interest-bearing) capital and not just as financial or credit relations in general. It is precisely in this respect that financialisation marks a departure from the past both in the scale and in scope of financial activity in pursuit of financial returns at the expense of production. In this sense, a mortgage, for example, remains a simple (transhistorical) credit relation between borrower and lender. However, it becomes embroiled in financialisation once that mortgage obligation is sold on as part of some other asset, which becomes routinised only under neoliberalism. With such financialisation spread more generally, so grows the influence of finance over the control of resource allocation – including the flows of money, credit and foreign exchange and, correspondingly, the level and composition of output, employment, investment and trade, and the financing of the state – by money-capital embodied in an array of (more or less esoteric) financial assets.[30] Those assets are created, held,

30 Quoting at length from Ashman and Fine (2013, pp. 156–57), "[F]inancialisation has involved: the phenomenal expansion of financial assets relative to real activity; … the proliferation of types of assets, from derivatives through to futures markets with a corresponding explosion of acronyms; the absolute and relative expansion of speculative as opposed to or at the expense of real investment; a shift in the balance of productive to financial imperatives within the private sector whether financial or not; increasing inequality in income arising out of weight of financial rewards; consumer-led booms based on credit; the penetration of finance into ever more areas of economic and social life such as pensions, education, health, and provision of economic and social infrastructure; the emergence of a neoliberal culture of reliance upon markets and private capital and corresponding anti-statism despite the extent to which the rewards to private finance have … derived from state finance itself. Financialisation is also associated with the continued role of the US dollar as world money despite … its deficits in trade, capital account, the fiscus, and consumer spending, and minimal rates of interest … [H]owever financialisation is defined, its consequences have been perceived to be: reductions in overall levels and efficacy of real investment as financial instruments and activities expand at its expense

traded and regulated by specialist institutions that, under neoliberalism, are integrated in a distinctly US-led global financial system (Panitch and Konings, 2008; Panitch and Gindin, 2012; and Rude, 2005).

The creation and circulation of these financial assets are intrinsically speculative activities that tend to become unmoored from the constraints of production, even though this autonomy can never be complete (Fine, 2013–14; and Fine and Saad-Filho, 2016b). The ensuing tensions and limitations lead to a number of outcomes that characterise financialised accumulation. These include the diffusion of a peculiar form of short-termism in economic decisions (e.g., not only through purely speculative activities but also through securitisable long-term investment, with pursuit of immediate profitability at the expense of productivity growth);[31] the imperative for generating and appropriating surplus out of finance; and the explosive growth of rewards to high-ranking capitalists and managers in every sector, especially finance itself, fuelling the concentration of income under neoliberalism. These financialised forms of accumulation are mutually reinforcing, but they can also dysfunctionally diverge (see twelfth thing).

The relations of mutual determination between finance and economic and social reproduction, identified above, establish the material basis of neoliberalism as a system of accumulation, described in the first thing (Albo, 2008; and Saad-Filho and Johnston, eds, 2005). In turn, financialisation has supported the global restructuring of production, that has become known as 'globalisation', and the reconstitution of US imperialism in the wake of the collapse of the Bretton Woods System, the US defeat in the Vietnam War and the Iranian revolution.[32]

This understanding of financialisation has four significant implications. First, financialisation underpins neoliberalism analytically, economically, politically and ideologically, and it has been one of the main drivers of the

even if excessive investment does take place in particular sectors at particular times; … prioritising shareholder value, or financial worth, over other economic and social values; pushing of policies towards conservatism and commercialisation in all respects; extending influence of finance more broadly, both directly and indirectly, over economic and social policy; placing more aspects of economic and social life at the risk of volatility from financial instability and, conversely, placing the economy and social life at risk of crisis from triggers within particular markets … Whilst, then, financialisation is a single word, it is attached to a wide variety of different forms and effects of finance."

31 Note that reducing wages in pursuit of profit is by no means unique to neoliberalism. But, for the latter, the pressure is that much greater in view of financial imperatives (also explaining why rewards within or linked to that sector have become so disproportionate).

32 See, for example, Duménil and Lévy (2004), Gowan (1999) and Kotz (2015).

restructuring of the global economy since the 1970s; financialisation is, then, the defining feature of accumulation today. Second, financialisation has been buttressed by institutional transformations expanding and intensifying the influence of finance over the economy, ideology, politics and the state. Third, contemporary financialisation derives both from the post-war boom and from its collapse into the stagflation of the 1970s.[33] Fourth, financialisation has been closely associated with the increasing role of speculative finance in economic and social reproduction, with water and housing offering clear examples.

One of the most striking examples of financialisation in relation to housing is the subprime market in the USA. On this market, mortgage lending to borrowers with low credit ratings – that is, subprime borrowers – was sustained, at least for a while, by lenders selling on subprime debts in order for them to be packaged up with 'normal' mortgage debts and traded as residential mortgage-backed securities (RMBSs). These RMBSs served in addition to transform illiquid housing debts that were attached to particular, spatially fixed housing units, into liquid assets that could be purchased by investors all over the world. Uncertainty about the credit rating and (falling) value of these securities would eventually lead the system to unravel, triggering the series of events that culminated in the 2007–9 global crisis. However, while the crisis instigated a retreat to safety among mortgage lenders, securitisation has not been abandoned as a technique for rendering illiquid assets liquid. The case study countries exhibited much lower rates of mortgage securitisation than that seen in the USA, though some was evident in most countries, and a substantial amount in the UK. More generally, the role of finance in this aspect of social reproduction is seen to have been extended across the case studies by a push towards owner-occupation, which, in most cases, is contingent upon taking out a mortgage.

Another way in which housing is implicated in financialisation concerns the realisation of Harvey's augury that land would come to behave like a financial asset (Christophers, 2010). True to Harvey, a distinctive feature of the era of neoliberalism is that urban real estate has become an important site for the circulation of fictitious capital. Development companies, Real Estate Investment Trusts and wealthy individuals increasingly invest in property in pursuit of augmented ground rents, not least in the form of self-fulfilling capital gains. Even where such investment is not limited to residential property, the latter is affected by the reshaping of urban landscapes in response to the

33 For a historical overview see Panitch and Gindin (2012), Rude (2005) and Saad-Filho (2007).

needs of capital, of which gentrification and the displacement of working class housing are key aspects.[34] In the area of housing, financialisation has therefore progressed through the creation of financial assets out of both mortgage repayments and rental streams, and through the trading of such assets on international financial markets.

For water, in the case of E&W, ownership of utilities has become heavily embroiled in global financial dealing, which is patently a diversion from the provision of domestic supplies. All water providers have some involvement with the financial sector. Investment in water – and infrastructure more generally – is largely funded by bond issues. Both public and private water companies engage in financial practices such as hedging and derivatives to mitigate the effects of changes in exchange and interest rates. However, the case studies show that privatisation lays the foundations for more financialised structures. Outside E&W, water privatisation has taken the form of a long-term concession, which has a specified duration. The two largest companies that operate in this area, French companies, Veolia Environment and Suez, have taken part in privatisations in all of the case studies. These two companies are the main private operators in the sector and were awarded the highest number of private water contracts globally between 2001 and 2010.[35] Stakes in these companies form part of investment portfolios, for example in water-related Exchange Traded Funds (ETFs) listed on the New York Stock Exchange. In this way, water has become a tradeable asset class (Bayliss, 2013).

This is a relatively mild form of financialisation when compared with the experience in England. Here privatisation took a different form. Instead of long-term concession contracts, English water and sewerage companies were floated on the London Stock Exchange (LSE). Despite an initial putative intention of creating a popular class of share-owning voters, most firms were privately bought out and taken off the LSE. Four out of the ten water and sewerage companies were taken over in the 2000s by consortia of financial firms. These companies have used extensive financial engineering to increase distributions to shareholders in ways which are far removed from the abstraction and distribution of water. By creating complex structures involving the securitisation of future water bill payments and routing funds through offshore jurisdictions, these companies have provided substantial distributions to shareholders. Within the limits of price controls, firms have managed to increase greatly

34 See Aalbers and Christophers (2014) for the central role played by housing in economic and social reproduction, in terms of both its material weight and as a marker of more general determinants and issues across the political economy of financialisation.

35 PPI Database 2012, https://ppi.worldbank.org/en/ppi.

both debts and dividend payments while remaining just within the required limits for their credit ratings. This process has led to an enormous increase in financing costs which have been incorporated into consumers' water bills (note that high levels of financing costs is not judged as a source of inefficiency – see seventh thing).

With its attachment to finance in this way, problems of regulating water have been compounded. The financial complexity of some of the water companies places some of their activities to a large extent beyond the control of the regulator, Ofwat. Regulation is based on a system of price controls established at privatisation, designed to mimic a competitive market (for both water and finance). Other elements of financial activity, notably dividend payments and debt, are regarded as 'market outcomes' falling outside the remit of the regulator. The only constraint on these financial aspects of corporate activity is that firms have to maintain a credit rating that is 'investment grade'. It is now clear that some companies have increased debt through complex financial engineering in order to finance distributions to shareholders.[36] In part this is achieved by loans from shareholders at high rates of interest. Furthermore, additional financial rewards are generated in the sale of ownership stakes for undisclosed amounts. Financial returns, then, result from investors' use of financial operations to work around the regulatory price controls, rather than the production of water.

Significantly, then, housing and water have been subject to financialisation in the neoliberal era even though they are in their own respects far in some sense from standardised objects for capitalist production, circulation and speculation. The parallel, and readily recognised, role of financialisation in globalisation and corporate restructuring of what might be deemed to be more standardised sectors of the economy (pursuit of stakeholder value, etc) is indicative of the defining significance of financialisation for neoliberalism. However, financialisation, like neoliberalism, is uneven in incidence and outcomes, contingent upon whether and how its imperatives are realised, or not.

6 The Sixth Thing …

… you need to know about neoliberalism is that it does not merely involve a change in policies that, in principle, could be readily reversed.

36 See PWC (2013) and Bayliss (2014) for more details.

The neoliberal 'policy reforms', implemented through Reaganism, Thatcherism and the (post) Washington Consensus, are supported by five ontological planks.[37] First is the dichotomy between markets and the state, implying that these are rival and mutually exclusive institutions. Second is the assumption that markets are effective if not always perfectly efficient while state intervention is wasteful because it distorts prices and misallocates resources in comparison with what an ideal market would have done, induces rent-seeking behaviour and fosters technological backwardness. Third, the belief that technological progress, the liberalisation of finance and capital movements, the systematic pursuit of 'shareholder value' and successive transitions to neoliberalism around the world have created a global economy characterised by rapid capital mobility within and between countries and (an ill-defined process of) 'globalisation'. Where they are embraced, rapid growth ensues through the prosperity of local enterprise and the attraction of foreign capital; in contrast, reluctance or 'excessive' state intervention (however it may be determined) drives capital, employment and economic growth elsewhere. Fourth, the presumption that allocative efficiency, macroeconomic stability and output growth are conditional upon low inflation, which is best secured by monetary policy at the expense of fiscal, exchange rate and industrial policy tools. Fifth, the realisation that the operation of key neoliberal macroeconomic policies, including 'liberalised' trade, financial and labour markets, inflation targeting, central bank independence, floating exchange rates and tight fiscal rules is conditional upon the provision of potentially unlimited state guarantees to the financial system, since the latter remains structurally unable to support itself despite its escalating control of social resources under neoliberalism.

But crucially, and more fundamentally, neoliberalism has not only changed the policies adopted by governments, and their accompanying ideologies, but also the conditions within which policy is conceived, formulated, implemented, monitored and responded to – and which, in turn, renders the reverse of policy and ideology heavily constrained as well as the emergence of alternatives in principle and practice. This has been recognised clearly, if partially, in the literatures that seek to distinguish different types of capitalism.[38] For example, the Varieties of Capitalism (VoC) approach perceives differences in the institutional construction of policy and, in the case of social policy, the

37 Saad-Filho and Johnston (2005).

38 Thus, for example, the social structures of accumulation approach has been modified to suggest that neoliberalism is a particularly dysfunctional articulation of social structures (Kotz et al. eds, 2010).

Welfare Regime Approach (WRA) focuses on the balance of power and resources between capital and labour and how they are mediated through (influence upon) the state. Presumably, each of these approaches would emphasise the encroaching gains of neoliberal capitalism, although neither was originally grounded upon the changing role of finance in specifying the varieties and regimes, respectively, and their evolving fortunes.[39] Instead, these approaches are caught on the intellectual cusp between the post-war boom and neoliberalism, seeking to defend or promote what is perceived to be the best of the past (boom) against the worst of what was yet to come, itself extrapolated from the past as a less successful liberal form of post-war capitalism.

That neoliberalism is not reducible to changes in macroeconomic policy is not a novel insight, as neoliberalism has, often, been defined instead by microeconomic shifts, not least through privatisation and commercialisation as symptomatic of the presumed withdrawal of state intervention. However, such distinctions between the microeconomic and the macroeconomic cannot generally be sustained not least as, for example, the provision of economic and social infrastructure, including water and housing, straddle both, as do trade, industrial, commercial and, not least, financial policy itself. Our interpretation of neoliberalism as grounded upon finance-driven economic and social restructuring can encompass both (admittedly parodied) extremes of the micro and the macro, integrate them and develop their insights further.

As was seen under the third thing, changes to housing provision under neoliberalism go beyond a mere policy shift, amounting to a restructuring of the structures, agents, processes and relations underpinning supply and demand. The state has not retreated, but its role has been transformed, leading to changes in state functioning that cannot be easily reversed. For example, where the state has been a direct provider of housing, as in the UK and Poland, its development capabilities have been hollowed out, and the state's role in housing provision in the era of neoliberalism characterised in terms of being an enabler rather than a provider of housing. This is true even in countries, such as Turkey and South Africa, where the state continues to play an active role in financing and overseeing development, because in these cases actual delivery is carried out by the private sector.

An additional feature of the emergence of the enabling state is that planning processes have been reconstituted around commercialised land use,

---

39 See, in this light, Ashman and Fine (2013) and Fine (2014) for critiques of VoC and WRA, respectively. Note that each approach to different types of (parts of) capitalism is grounded in methodological nationalism in which the global as such is just one factor amongst many.

growth partnerships with business interests, and inter-regional competition (Rydin, 1998). These changes to the institutional context in which housing policy is developed and implemented make reversing that policy difficult, though not impossible. The difficulty is compounded by the emergence of new groups with vested interests in current forms of provision. These include mortgage lenders, who benefit from an expanding pool of borrowers through the spread of homeownership, and large sections of homeowners themselves, who have acquired wealth through credit-inflated capital gains to housing. The scope for reversibility is further narrowed by the marginalisation of some groups in policymaking processes. Most notable for housing is an increasingly casualised labour force, and the relegation of social housing safety nets serving those excluded from the market to a residual role within a narrative of self-responsibility.

The neoliberalisation of water has led to profound yet subtle changes in attitudes which have gained traction through a discourse of 'scarcity', justified by a shift in narrative from one of abundance to one where resources are in short supply. Neoliberal water pricing is also known as 'demand management' based on the idea that consumption decisions will be based on more appropriate information if the price of water reflects its true cost. If water bills are higher, people will consume less. The financial crisis has also been used to promote neoliberal policies in water in the context of financial scarcity. This has been particularly significant in Portugal where municipalities have tried to block the imposition of cost recovery prices but resistance has been more difficult with the financial crisis and calls for austerity. A new law introduced in 2014 granted the Portuguese water regulator powers to impose cost recovery tariffs on municipalities. Neoliberalism has become associated with more than just the provision of water but is now attached more deeply to environmentalism and fiscal restraint such that a reversal could be construed as leading to environmental and financial profligacy. The micro level policies of pricing and commercialisation are enmeshed in macro and global concerns.

But the harnessing of the market to non-market objectives, such as environmental sustainability, most evident in the creation of carbon trading for example, is not merely a shift in, and deployment of, ideology. It also reflects profound shifts in the neoliberal institutionalisation of policymaking in which private provision takes priority, and against which other objectives are not so much absented as residualised, and in ways that are themselves marked by diversely formed neoliberal imperatives and conditions, see tenth and eleventh things.

7 The Seventh Thing …

… you need to know about neoliberalism is that it represents more than a shift in the balance of power, primarily against labour and in favour of capital in general and of finance in particular, undoubtedly true though this is. Neoliberalism invariably has a significant impact on class relations and the distributional balance between them, for example, through financialisation, globalisation and neoliberal reforms. This includes the 'flexibilisation' and intensification of labour, the limitation of wage growth, the rollback of collective bargaining and the adverse changes in welfare provision, and how each of these has affected workers, women, minorities, immigrants, and so on. Neoliberalism has also affected social relations through privatisation and the appropriation of the 'commons' (i.e., areas where property rights were either absent or vested upon the state),[40] and through the financialisation of social reproduction (see eleventh thing). Finally, neoliberalism has triggered macroeconomic crises that penalise the poor disproportionately (see twelfth thing).[41] In these ways, neoliberalism has both expanded the power of capital and created an income-concentrating dynamics of accumulation that can be limited, but not reversed, by marginal (Keynesian) interventions.

These shifts in the balance of power are both symbolic of the establishment of neoliberalism and fundamental to its reproduction, with the anti-labour policies and assaults of Reaganism and Thatcherism initially to the fore. These are so significant that, especially in US political economy literature, they are often taken to be the defining characteristic of neoliberalism, with financialisation as its consequence.[42] This argument follows from an analysis of neoliberalism primarily in distributional terms, suggesting that lower economic and social wages cause high inequality as well as deficient demand, to which speculative finance is a corollary through both investment by the wealthy and the

40 Harvey (2005) calls this process "accumulation by dispossession", an umbrella term for an extremely diverse range of phenomena that at most and only occasionally has a limited connection to primitive accumulation in the classical Marxist sense and, more often than not, are underpinned by financialisation (as, for example, in futures carbon trading, which is probably the most fetishised form of dispossession).

41 See, for example, Duménil and Lévy (2011) and McNally (2014).

42 Thus, for the monopoly capital school, US capitalism has been chronically beset, even during the post-war boom, by deficient demand, in this case deriving from the underconsumption attached to high monopoly prices, and correspondingly low real wages and output. For Polanyi Levitt (2013, p. 164), "The objective of the neoliberal counter-revolution was to restore the discipline of capital over labour, and the principal means of achieving it were deregulation, liberalization, privatization and explicit attacks on trade unions."

expansion of credit to the poor (for consumption, mortgages, and other short-term responses to wage compression). This is, however, to reduce economic and social restructuring in general, and neoliberalism specifically, to the spheres of circulation (effective demand) and distribution (between wages and profits, and degree of social wage). Yet the neoliberal restructuring of housing provision, for example, has not only – nor even necessarily – involved the erosion of wages in the construction industry. It has also seen changes in the forms taken by employment relationships, with a shift towards, or consolidation of, sub-contracting and piece work, not to mention the stratifying effects of changes in the terms under which people can access housing – the hoarding of housing wealth and diminished availability of alternatives to owner-occupation being most notable here (Robertson, 2014). In the context of specifying both the balance and the nature of power under neoliberalism, focusing on circulation and distribution is too limited, and it extrapolates unduly and too narrowly in scope (mortgaging and pricing alone) from US (and, to some extent, UK) conditions without reference to levels and means of supply (which vary considerably across countries with corresponding implications for forms taken by housing crises in the wake of the global crisis).

This point can be made by reference to what might be termed the social compacting paradigm (SCP), which has been deployed to characterise economic and social 'settlements' over the post-war boom, typically in order to explain comparative national performance; for example, why did West Germany and Japan grow faster than the USA or the UK.[43] SCP suggests that formal and institutionalised negotiation between capital and labour offered fuller and stronger labour representation in policymaking, and that the social partnership agreement around wage restraint in return for expanding social wages induced higher investment and faster productivity growth than the Anglo-Saxon paradigm.

Irrespective of the extent to which differential performance across countries can be explained primarily by industrial relations,[44] however broadly conceived, the contrast with the neoliberal period is striking. The weakening power of labour has led to, and been reflected by, its systematic exclusion from policymaking. Consequently, social compacting has itself been widely

43 For a critical review, see Fine (2016b).

44 Significantly for what was to come, germane to comparative performance during the post-war boom were debates about different financial systems (typically, bank-based vs market-based) and how conducive they were for economic and social restructuring, in both generating finance for investment and interacting with the policymaking processes (Ashman and Fine, 2013; Fine and Harris, 1985; and Zysman, 1983).

dismantled and, where it has survived, it has shrivelled into a tokenistic ritual or illusory role of legitimation of neoliberal policies addressing the implications of faltering growth, rather than negotiating the distribution of gains due to productivity, output and income growth. Most importantly, financial policy and the functioning of the financial system invariably remain outside the scope of any social compacting.[45]

Such considerations are well-illustrated by examples in Eastern Europe and South Africa where, with the collapse of the Soviet regime and apartheid, respectively, in the early nineties, neoliberalism both arrived late and sought to make up for lost time. Necessarily, the forms taken by policymaking and the powers underpinning and exercised through the transition to neoliberalism were subject to considerable variation across countries and over time, and were hardly reducible to a shift from the state to the market (see fourth thing). For example, whilst forms of tripartism flourished in post-Soviet Eastern Europe, their content was eviscerated as they were used to ease the emergence of new elites and consolidate the old in new circumstances. Consequently, in these neoliberal experiences, reliance upon, or marginalisation of, tripartism has been a matter of convenience, leading to an 'illusory corporatism' that bears little relationship either to the post-war boom social corporatism in the West or to the influence of, and support for, labour characteristic of the Soviet period.[46]

A similar account can be told of South Africa, where the form taken by social corporatism is the Triple Alliance of the ANC, the South African Communist Party and COSATU, the confederation of trade unions. Yet, the ANC Government is generally recognised as having taken a neoliberal turn in the mid-1990s, not least with the adoption of the Growth, Employment and Redistribution (GEAR) policy framework. As the economy was thoroughly restructured through financialisation during the post-apartheid period, the

45 The leading example is provided by the Irish Republic, not least in the wake of the global crisis; see Doherty (2011) and Regan (2009).

46 For example, in Hungary, "[c]ommitted to introducing new fiscal discipline and to cutting real wages, the Socialist government unilaterally imposed it austerity budged and reinstituted wage controls, bypassing the IRC [Industrial Relations Code] while continuing to claim commitment to the tripartite process" (Ost, 2000, p. 510). In Poland, "the main task of ... [the] tripartite commission has been to secure labor's consent to its own marginalization", p. 515. In sum, "The best that can be said is that tripartism means formal negotiations over very broad issues, with no guarantees that the agreements will become law or be respected by employers ... equally likely are tripartite sessions where the government simply informs "social partners" of its intentions and seeks labor assent to fait accompli" (Ost, 2000, p. 515). See also Ost (2011).

main forum for tripartite policymaking, the National Economic Development and Labour Council (NEDLAC), became increasingly ineffective because of the non-participation of the most powerful businesses and lack of influence over major policies and issues, especially thoseinvolving finance (Webster et al. 2013).In short, social compacting under neoliberalism, if and when it occurs, actually undermines the labour movement, and much the same is liable to be so of new social movements, in and of themselves, in the absence of strong and supportive left movements and organisations.

In the provision of water, the case studies show that neoliberalism has been associated with a weakening in the power of labour. In E&W, trade unions have become fragmented with the break-up of the national water framework upon privatisation, and this was part of the government's intention (third thing). National bargaining processes have been replaced by separate labour negotiations for each water company even though these are represented by national trade unions (GMB and UNISON). Terms and conditions vary considerably across the country.[47] Furthermore, labour is not regarded as a stakeholder in the price-setting process in the same way as investors or consumers. Remuneration of labour has lost out since privatisation. The case study shows that there has been a substantial increase in the proportion of turnover allocated to interest payments and to directors' remuneration over the past twenty years while the proportion going to salaries and wages has declined in the E&W water and sewerage companies. The regulatory structure supports such a shift in allocation of income away from wage labour to directors, shareholders and financiers. Firms are required to meet efficiency targets and this typically impacts on labour with employment numbers lowered in order to increase productivity. However, since privatisation, interest payments have rocketed with some loans at interest rates as high as 18%. Such high interest payments could be regarded as a gross inefficiency but rentier payments are not judged in the same way as labour costs. Company performance is partly assessed by the operating profit or the EBITDA (earnings before interest, taxes, depreciation and amortisation), so a company with low wage costs and high interest payments is considered to be efficient. Neoliberalism results in downward pressure on wage costs while allocations to the financial sector are primarily unchecked in every sense.

In E&W there has also been a growing gap between payments to directors and employee wages. Directors' remuneration is designed so that their interests are aligned with those of shareholders, with their receiving rewards

47 Interview with GMB union.

of shares in the company and bonuses based on financial targets and shareholder returns. Labour unions are not considered as stakeholders in the sector; for example, trade unions were not consulted in the price-setting process in 2014, unlike investors and consumers. Also in Portugal, union power has been weakened by restructuring of the water sector. Corporatisation processes have involved the proliferation of 'individual labour contracts' that are not covered by collective agreements. Meanwhile the current restructuring of the bulk sector is expected to involve lay-offs, according to the trade unions.

This is, then, much more than the erstwhile public sector becoming (more like) the private sector to a greater or lesser extent in its ethos and practices (commercial criteria to the fore, widening relative remuneration, etc). It also reflects a shift in the balance of forces in the making of policy and, equally, how policy is formulated, implemented and monitored as most obviously reflected in what has come to be known as the new public management, with doubts about positive results (Hood and Dixon, 2015a and b).

8 The Eighth Thing …

… you need to know about neoliberalism is that it involves varied and shifting combinations of scholarship, ideology, policy and practice, with connections to one another but not necessarily with coherence across and within these elements.[48] The tensions across the domains of scholarship, ideology, policy and practice can be illustrated at three levels. First, the meaning and significance of neoliberal scholarship, the ensuing ideology, and their policy implications have shifted across time, place and issue, and there can be inconsistencies across their component parts. These are, often, due to tensions between the rhetorical and policy worlds built by the advocates of neoliberalism, and the realities of social and economic reproduction. For example, support for homeownership has been couched in pro-market, anti-state rhetoric but, as discussed under the fifth thing, states have been proactive in creating mortgage markets and facilitating owner-occupation, including maintaining both through subsidies where necessary. They have also put safety nets in place to deal with the fall-out where the market fails to ensure stable social reproduction, all the while expounding the merits of market-based provision and disparaging the public sector. Another striking example is provided by the shift from privatisation to

48 See, especially in the context of 'development', Bayliss et al. (eds) (2011), Fine (2010b) and Fine and Saad-Filho (2014).

public-private partnerships, especially where large-scale state support for private provision of economic and social infrastructure is concerned.[49]

Second, even the most ardent supporter of freedom of the individual in general, and market freedom in particular, concedes that those freedoms can only be guaranteed through state provision of, and coercion for, a core set of functions and institutions, ranging over fiscal and monetary policy to law and order and property rights, through to military intervention to secure the 'market economy' when this becomes necessary. The coercive use of state power to support the market can go beyond simply maintaining the rules of the game. In Turkey, for example, the allocation of land to its commercially most valuable uses has relied on the deployment of state power to relocate existing communities forcibly. In practice, then, neoliberalism can be closely associated with authoritarianism, while its attachment to classical liberalism and political democracy is hedged and heavily conditional in practice (see second thing).[50]

Third, the tensions and inconsistencies across scholarship, ideology, policy and practice were sharply revealed by the policy responses to the current global crisis, with the ideology of free markets, especially those of finance, smoothly giving way to heavy intervention on its behalf, what has been dubbed socialism for the bankers and capitalism for the rest of us, followed by a bewildered response from the discipline of economics to events that were not so much unpredicted as deemed to be either impossible or subject to policy control. Paradoxically, while unlimited resources have been made available to salvage finance, no concession has been offered at the level of ideology or scholarship, where the intolerant hegemony of mainstream economics remains virtually unscathed.

Some of the inconsistencies and contradictions between neoliberal rhetoric and policy are highlighted in the provision of water, as the case studies demonstrate. For example, the adoption of cost recovery pricing has attracted numerous – and contradictory – objectives. The pricing policy is supposed to be equitable (in the sense that payment is related to consumption costs) and to ensure that services are financially and environmentally sustainable (see sixth thing). But, aside from the questionable methodological approach (see second thing), this pricing structure creates prices that are regressive and are not affordable[51] for a significant proportion of the population.

---

49 See Bayliss and Fine (eds) (2008), and Alexander (2014) for a critique of recent developments.

50 See, for example, Barber (1995) and Bresnahan (2003).

51 There is no fixed definition of affordability for domestic water supply but the UN has recommended that water costs should not exceed 3% of household income.

While presented as neutral and scientific, cost recovery techniques are potentially inequitable in two main respects. First, low-income consumers are likely to be the most costly to serve. It is far cheaper per unit to provide water to large industry than low volume consumers located far from the network in rural areas or high-density slums. Second, when it comes to water – which is consumed by the whole population – poorer households pay a larger proportion of their incomes towards infrastructure costs where these are financed from user fees. Three of the case studies, for Portugal, South Africa and E&W, looked in detail at the system of cost recovery pricing, and it is found that a cost recovery tariff is not affordable for a significant proportion of the population. The case studies in E&W and South Africa show that a lack of affordability has led to high household debts accruing. In Portugal, municipalities have kept tariffs below cost recovery levels, and households are paying an affordable amount for their water bills but municipalities are not collecting sufficient revenue to pay their bulk water providers, so debts are amassing at this level in the water system of provision. In all three cases the resulting debt levels look set to threaten the very financial sustainability that cost recovery is supposed to engender.

The neoliberal response to water affordability concerns in South Africa, Portugal and E&W is to provide means-tested financial support for low-income households. This creates significant administrative challenges and often fails to reach the most marginalised. If universal access is a genuine priority, a more effective approach would be to start with affordability as the core objective and to organise price structures around this. Instead, social policy requires households to prove that they cannot afford the cost recovery price in order to qualify for a discounted price. The contradictions arising in the push for both cost recovery and affordability are particularly prominent in the case of South Africa where the state has financed the rolling out of infrastructure to increase access to water while, at the same time, pressure to achieve cost recovery risks disconnecting those that the government extension programme has connected. The forced installation of prepayment meters for low-income households means that some that cannot live within the free basic water amount then effectively self-disconnect.

Water privatisation also highlights neoliberal contradictions. Private water companies face the dual imperatives of meeting the demands of both shareholders and local consumers. According to the regulator in E&W, these interests are compatible – what is good for investors is good for customers. Clearly, however, there are conflicting priorities. Investors want profits and consumers want lower prices. Prices have gone up by 40% since privatisation in E&W and are subject to intense negotiations in the regulatory process. Cost recovery pricing has been promoted as a tool of 'demand management' to reduce water consumption (see sixth thing). This raises problems when combined with privatisation if the private operator is remunerated on the basis of units sold (as was the case in E&W, Poland and Portugal). The case studies show that where private water providers suffer a loss due to reductions in consumption (i.e. successful 'demand management'), this is recovered by increasing consumer prices. Thus, if users consume less water, they pay a higher price in the future.

Privatisation in the case studies has sometimes been introduced in practice to get round fiscal constraints. Private finance is presented as an alternative to public funding. Yet these are not substitutes. Private finance has to be repaid either by end users or from the public purse and is considerably more expensive than government funding. Privatisation then relies on greater efficiency to justify itself but the empirical support for this is far from compelling (Bayliss, 2011). There is an irony in that fiscal targets, established to encourage careful management of public finances, lead governments to sign up to public-private partnerships that are considerably more costly than government borrowing. But private finance is politically attractive because the associated debts are 'off balance-sheet'. In the wake of the financial crisis, governments are facing increased pressure to cut back on spending which can increase reliance on the private sector even though this potentially exposes governments to higher liabilities.

Scholarship can be overridden when it comes to practical policy implementation as utility privatisation demonstrates further. According to neoliberal theory, privatisation increases efficiency because private shareholders, with recourse to the residual (profit) of the enterprise, have a greater incentive to ensure the monitoring of management of the organisation. In practice, however, the case study of E&W water showed that some companies are partly owned by foreign governments. If privatisation theory is to be believed this would create inefficiency but there were no such concerns raised when stakes in water companies were sold to sovereign wealth funds from China, Singapore and Abu Dhabi. Similarly, the state-owned South African water utility, Rand Water, has taken part in privatisations in other African countries. The ease with which the fundamentals of theory are ignored when they contradict practical policy implementation highlights the lack of coherence across neoliberal ideology, scholarship and policy in practice.[52]

---

52 In this respect, the greatest irony for Thatcherism (and its nationalism) is the extent to which British electricity has become owned by the monopolistic state-owned, French EDF.

9 The Ninth Thing ...

... you need to know about neoliberalism is that it has been subject to two phases, loosely divided by the early 1990s. The first of two phases of neoliberalism is aptly characterised as the transition or shock phase, in which the promotion of private capital proceeded in country after country without regard to the consequences. This phase requires forceful state intervention to contain labour, disorganise the left, promote the transnational integration of domestic capital and finance and put in place new institutional frameworks (see first and third things).

The second (mature) phase has been, if only in part, a reaction to the dysfunctions and adverse social consequences of the first phase, not least in social welfare provision. This ('Third Way') phase focuses on the stabilisation of the social relations imposed in the earlier period, the consolidation and continued expansion of the financial sector's interventions in economic and social reproduction, state management of the new modalities of international economic integration, and the introduction of specifically neoliberal social policies both to manage the deprivations and dysfunctions created by neoliberalism and to consolidate and reconstitute social and individual agents along neoliberal lines (see tenth thing).

Both phases require extensive (re)regulation, despite the rhetorical insistence of all manner of neoliberals on the need to 'roll back' the state, interpreted, in the first phase of neoliberalism, as 'hollowing out', followed by the 'rolling out' of new and, occasionally, more explicit forms of intervention on that foundation in the second phase (see fourth thing). Inevitably, these phases are more logical than chronological, as they can be sequenced, delayed, accelerated, or even overlain in specific ways depending on country, region and economic and political circumstances, such as transition in Eastern Europe and from apartheid in South Africa.

The two phases are clearly demarcated in the case of UK housing. 'Roll back' commenced in the 1980s with a comprehensive assault on local authority housing that saw swathes of the existing stock sold off and local government (councils) prevented from replacing them. The 1990s then saw efforts to manage the costs of this policy – principally a lack of affordable housing – in what can be seen as the 'roll out' phase. This involved use of the planning system to increase affordable housing supply in the form of conditionalities attached to planning permissions, attempts to introduce private finance into the management and refurbishment of the remaining social housing through PFIs (private financial initiatives), and the promotion of housing associations through stock transfer and as providers of new housing. Housing associations, in particular, are archetypal of 'Third Wayism', combining an acknowledgement of the need for social housing, with an ongoing aversion to direct state provision and new avenues for private finance to become embedded in social reproduction. Indeed, scope for private finance's involvement in housing associations has been extended as state subsidies have been progressively reduced, with some housing associations now issuing their own bonds as well as borrowing from banks (Robertson, 2014).

In Poland, as elsewhere in Eastern Europe, 'roll out' took the form of 'shock therapy' following the collapse of socialism. A series of reforms, intended to achieve a sudden transition from state-planned socialism to market-based capitalism were introduced, including price liberalisation, the removal of currency controls, the curtailing of subsidies, and the privatisation of public assets, housing among them. Though relatively modest in comparison with other countries in the region, these reforms plunged Poland into a deep recession and twenty percent unemployment. The programme was consequently tempered a few years in, including the establishment of the Associations of Social Housing to address growing housing need (Lis, 2015b). However, this change in direction should be viewed as consolidation rather than retreat as the quest to conform to neoliberal reforms continued, not least under Poland's pursuit of accession to the EU.

Water sector reforms were implemented around the early 1990s in each of the case studies. In E&W the initial water privatisation led to dramatic price increases. The incoming Labour Government in 1997 introduced a windfall tax, and prices came down in the 1999 price review. However, they have since crept up to the levels of the late 1990s.

Shock therapy was less pronounced elsewhere. In South Africa, neoliberalism was moderated by a policy focus aiming to reverse the inequalities of the apartheid era and so there was a roll out of public investment to increase access. Poland and Portugal have also seen increases in public investment to increase access. Prices in both of these countries have been kept low by municipal providers, so the impact of shock therapy had less of an impact on water consumers. In Portugal the effects of the shock therapy were muted by the availability of cheap funding from the EU in the 1990s. The regressive effects of the shock therapy reforms have more recently, however, been exposed with the external shock on the Portuguese economy resulting from the international crisis. The full impact of the cost recovery pricing has not yet reached consumers in Portugal as municipalities have kept their water charges low but the debts that municipal water providers owe to bulk water companies have escalated as their tariffs have become cost reflective. The Portuguese water regulator, ERSAR, was in 2014 given the power to intervene in municipal tariff setting so that these incorporate the cost recovery pricing approach. Retail water tariffs are expected to increase substantially so the full impact of shock therapy will reach end users in due course.

Inevitably, the logical sequencing of neoliberalism into two phases is not always followed chronologically by sector and place for various contingent reasons. This leads to confusion over the nature of neoliberalism, and even to the denial that it is a useful category of analysis, and only prevails as a pejorative ideological device by its putative opponents, see first thing. Together with the uneven incidence and impact of financialisation, this means neoliberalism is highly variegated across economic and social reproduction as part of its nature and for a complex of other reasons.

10 The Tenth Thing ...

... you need to know about neoliberalism is that it is highly variegated in its features, impact and outcomes. Although neoliberalism has an identifiable material and ideational core (see first, second and fifth things), and neoliberal policies share readily recognisable features, neoliberal experiences take a wide variety of forms in different countries and over time (see ninth thing).

There are three reasons for this. First, despite its common core, neoliberalism can be associated with significant differences in the forms, degrees and impact of financialisation, the depth and modalities of internationalisation of production and dependence on external trade, societal changes, ideology, structures of political representation, and so on.

Second, these variegated relationships interact among themselves and with specific aspects of economic and social reproduction in historically contingent ways. Thus, for example, the more or less universal expansion of mortgage markets has interacted with the pre-existing housing systems in different ways across countries.

Third, whilst financialisation is a core aspect of neoliberalism, it remains not only uneven but also confined in its direct grasp over economic and social reproduction – not everything is financialised even where finance or even just the market is present. Thus, many public services are not commercialised, let alone financialised. As a result, even though financial institutions may not directly dictate how these services are provided, this does not mean that financialisation exerts no influence. The result is to create space for diversity in deviating not only from exclusive reliance upon financial imperatives where they do apply (such as the extent and level of user charges, for example) but also, and inevitably, where they do not.[53]

In sum, while the secular rise of financialisation and its extended reach across both economic and social reproduction is what motivates our understanding of neoliberalism as the current stage of capitalism (see first and fifth things), the impact of financialisation is variegated across industrial production and other types of enterprise, and so on.[54] Concretely, whilst financialisation feeds in part by transforming economic and social activity in ways in which the associated revenues can be packaged into corresponding assets, the extent and influence of financialisation across the various elements of economic and social reproduction is highly contingent, reinforcing the variegated nature of outcomes. In short, economic and social reproduction cannot be reduced to financialisation, but nor is the latter entirely absent of influence where it is not immediately present as such.[55]

With the increasing role of financialisation, whether directly or indirectly, there will remain dysfunctions and dissonances where the logic of the market does not prevail, most obviously with the hard to employ, house, educate, provide for in old age, raise out of poverty, provide for health, and so on. This is to raise the issue for scholars (and practitioners) of neoliberalism of how it intervenes where market provision fails or is absented and which, in practice, is necessarily contingent upon how markets and the non-market are formed and contested. Such issues are obvious in case of social policy but by no means confined to it where for example, neoliberal ideology of (un)deserving poor dovetails with interventionist support for those in or into work. Precisely because dysfunctions in the hard to serve through the market are multi-dimensional and uneven in their incidence, individual anomalies are liable to be created across them either in the form of 'undue' benefits (to be cut) or 'undue' harshness (to be alleviated). In the context of chronic increases in inequality and the acute impact of crisis and recession,[56] there are inevitable pressures both

53 See Gingrich (2015) for variability in institutional forms of social provision in light of what is provided and how and corresponding implications for 'cost' of neoliberal change.

54 Note that beyond the pursuit of the eponymous stakeholder value, analysis of the relationship between financialisation and the restructuring of productive capital remains seriously underdeveloped, partly because it is limited to macroeconomic generalisations in terms of lower levels of investment in deference to financial dealing. For a telling illustration in the context of financialisation of global production networks, see Coe et al. (2014).

55 See, for example, Graeber (2014) on the neoliberalisation of the university.

56 For the capacity of the top 10% of the income distribution to grow at the expense of the bottom 40%, see Palma (2009) on the 'neoliberal art of democracy'.

to reduce individual and overall benefits and to protect the most vulnerable, even if this contest can be highly uneven. How these and other tensions within neoliberalism are resolved is not pre-determined.

Somewhat different considerations apply where the forms taken by neoliberal economic and social reproduction are of more direct interest to the various fractions of capital than moderating social conflict and dysfunction in general. The state has long intervened to represent the interests of particular capitals, against the interests of others and, in some respects, for capital as a whole against the potentially destructive impact of competition between capitals. This remains the case under neoliberalism and implies that the state does not privatise everything, does not rely exclusively on private finance, and can even exclude such in order to pursue other interests and dynamics not least those of productive capital (on which financialisation in other spheres may heavily depend). Nonetheless, such interventions tend to be marked by the neoliberal condition, especially where private and/or international finance is involved, whether directly or indirectly, or even where it is absent because, for example, of continuing state provision (itself to be contingently explained and related to the broader role of finance, not least in funding the state and influencing its policies). As will be seen below, such an abstract discussion is readily brought down to earth by reference to South African water, not least in how it relates to internationally, financialised productive capital, the dynamics of economic and social reproduction and the evolving policies of the state.

Whilst the current grip of neoliberalism raises doubts about what might have previously been taken for granted of the strength and viability of social resistance against the commodification of 'sacred' types of provision (including public goods and the environment), our perspective is distinctive in two respects. On the one hand, there is a social content to all objects of provision, including commodities, and each is open to particular types of reaction against market forms as is evident, for example, in the differences between housing, water, transport and health, and the wide variety of the targets of charity, from food banks through woodlands to opera. On the other hand, the dualism between neoliberal (re-)commodification and decommodification under, despite or against neoliberalism, is too crude. In other words, simply focusing on market forms is insufficient because these are far from homogeneous (Fine, 2013b), as they can reflect everything from production for profit to user charges with (more or less targeted) subsidies. It also obliterates the ways in which commodities serve provision along the chains of activities that attach production to the market. For these reasons, we have found the SoP approach to be particularly useful in delineating the variegated nature of neoliberalism in general, and for housing and water in particular.

The capacity of the SoP approach to depict accurately the variegation of neoliberalism derives from two of its key features. First, by taking as its units of analysis the entire chain of activities underpinning the provision of a good, the approach is able to illuminate the way in which neoliberalism manifests differently across these activities, whilst they are also integrated with one another. The construction industry will be affected differently by financialisation than will housing consumption, for example. Yet this is missed by focusing on the commodity or market forms alone. Second, while emphatically not eschewing theory, the chain of activities that constitute a SoP are investigated at a concrete level with a high level of empirical content. The boundaries of a SoP are in turn determined inductively, based on the reach of the relations that form it, and usually falling at a national or even regional level (with the exception of fully globalised production networks). These levels of analysis ensure that SoPs are highly situated and specific, capturing the historically-developed social, economic, and political context within which each SoP operates (Bayliss et al. 2013). Such traits enable the approach to capture the role of context and historical contingency in generating variegated forms of neoliberalism.

To take the example of housing and financialisation, the growth of mortgage markets has been a defining feature of neoliberal housing provision. But mortgage markets differ markedly in what caused their growth and the extent to which they have been subject to processes of financialisation, not to mention in structure, size, and the levels and forms of state support. While mortgage market growth in general has been underpinned by increased international capital flows, it has also reflected different circumstances in different countries. Two crucial factors in the growth of the mortgage market in the UK were the ending of segmentation in lending markets and the decimation of social housing. The former allowed banks to enter mortgage markets that had previously been the preserve of mutuals known as building societies, increasing competition there (Robertson, 2014), and boosting the supply of, and demand for, mortgages. In Portugal, accession to the euro played a key role in expanding mortgage markets, by improving lending rates, while in Poland foreign currency loans provided a significant boost to lending (Santos et al. 2015; and Lis, 2015b). In Turkey the state is a large mortgage lender, but in South Africa a major section of the population continues to be excluded from mortgage markets (Çelik et al. 2015; and Isaacs, 2016). In terms of financialisation, the US subprime market, which relied heavily on securitisation, is the consummate example of a financialised mortgage market. But it is the exception rather than the rule, as securitisation rates were much lower in the rest of the world, reflecting smaller market size and the later development of the legal and institutional frameworks necessary for securitisation to occur. The general trend of mortgage market growth across the case studies, therefore, conceals significant variegation in both its form and extent.

Different countries also differ markedly in the impact the growth of mortgage credit had on the rest of their housing SoPs (Robertson, 2016). One crucial aspect concerns the way in which mortgage credit fed through into housing production. In both Portugal and Turkey, a boom in mortgage lending was accompanied by a construction boom, whereas in the UK credit has tended to feed far more into house prices. Again, the difference arises from the different institutional contexts that have developed historically in each country. One example is the arrangements for governing land use planning. Whereas both Portugal and Turkey had planning systems that encouraged large-scale development, the planning system in the UK is more restrictive. Or, to put it more starkly, while in Turkey state power was mobilised to clear low-income groups from central urban land in order to make way for large-scale luxury developments, in the UK state power has been enthralled to a NIMBYism (Not in My Back Yard) that has stifled development. This led, in combination with the speculative character of housebuilders in the UK, to a secular under-supply of housing and above-inflation house price increases. Another example concerns development finance. In Portugal and Turkey, increased international capital flows and favourable interest rates boosted lending both on mortgage markets and to housebuilders, whereas in the UK the availability of credit for mortgages and for housebuilders were asymmetrical, skewed to the former.

It was said above that attempts to manage the dysfunctionalities created by neoliberalism are a significant source of variegation, reflecting differences in how those dysfunctionalities manifest and in how they are contested. In both Turkey and South Africa, managing the hard-to-house has been incorporated into the promotion of owner-occupation. The Turkish state both lends and builds for low-income house purchase, while in South Africa the state has subsidised an extensive building programme for low-income homeownership. In the UK, Portugal and Poland, by contrast, support for the market-excluded has taken the form of the direct or indirect provision of social housing for rent, contributing to the maintenance of a parallel housing subsector. These social housing systems are governed by a logic that is distinct from both the owner-occupied and private rented sectors, but this is not to say it is 'decommodified', as private capital is implicated in both the financing and building of such housing.

There are also some aspects of the neoliberalisation of water that are shared across the case study countries (and many parts of the world). For example, water has been commodified (to differing degrees, Bayliss, 2016a), and governments (sometimes at the behest of the World Bank and IMF) have stated a commitment to charging cost recovery pricing and implementing the 'user pays' approach to pricing (see second thing). But, as stated above, there is scope for arbitrary, that is contested, decisionmaking in the application of this in practice.

While neoliberal policies project a homogenising force, they are implemented in diverse historical, institutional, political, geographical and socio-economic contexts, and this affects outcomes. The water case studies demonstrate the variegation of neoliberal approaches and impacts both within and between countries. Taking privatisation, E&W is an outlier with water privatised by listing companies on the stock exchange. Meanwhile, in South Africa, Poland, Portugal and Turkey, privatisation is less widespread and has taken the form of long-term concession contracts. Privatisation is strongly associated with cream-skimming and has tended to be implemented in locations that offer the most lucrative opportunities for investors.[57] Neoliberalism, then, creates an uneven structure where some water providers have been hived off into global corporate investment portfolios (see third thing), while others remain part of local economic and municipal structures. Within the same country, depending on where a consumer pays their water bill, the corresponding funds might be uplifted to pay dividends to shareholders in another country or they could remain within the local municipality. Privatisation is diverse in the forms and outcomes taken attached to the system of provision.

The way in which privatisation was conducted in E&W has created a more deeply financialised structure than elsewhere (Bayliss, 2014). The case study demonstrates that financial investors have been significant beneficiaries of neoliberal policies (see fifth thing). In South Africa, by contrast, while the sector is run on strongly neoliberal lines, there has been relatively little privatisation and financialisation (Bayliss, 2016b). Water production is horizontally segregated along three tiers across the country. Water in its initial stage of abstraction is known as 'raw water'. This can be bought directly by big industry and mining companies or by one of the country's twelve bulk water providers. The latter then sell water to municipalities who sell it to end users. At each stage there is a mark-up on price. The resulting structure then means that households pay a higher price than large industry that can use water at an earlier stage of the distribution system. Furthermore, the country is water-stressed and large industry and mining firms are able to pay a premium to

57 In Portugal, for example, although only 29 utilities have been privatised out of 380 managing entities, they are located in the coastal regions and account for over 13% of the population, mostly serving densely populated areas which are easier and cheaper to provide for than rural areas. In South Africa, only two long-term privatisation concessions remain.

assure their water supplies. The water sector is, then, best understood in terms of separate consumer groups. The result is that economically and politically powerful users potentially have a cheaper and more secure water supply than (poorer) households.

Infrastructure investment in South Africa is either financed through the government or via 'off-budget' financing, arranged through the state-owned enterprise, TCTA. Off-budget infrastructure finance is only available for consumers of 'raw water', including industrial consumers as well as the bulk Water Boards that are considered to be 'economically viable'. This will include the Water Boards serving wealthy areas such as Rand Water which provides for the main economic region of the country, Gauteng Province. Other Water Boards providing water to less prosperous regions, for example in the north west of the country, rely on government funding. Infrastructure is financed this way, rather than through taxation, to apply the neoliberal logic as far as possible of 'user pays'. This leads to the hiving off of provision for the most wealthy industries and regions, which finance and use their own infrastructure separately from the less economically viable users, who rely on the state for service provision. Effectively, then, the logic of 'user pays' means that the wealthy do not have to engage with government financing but are encouraged to contribute to separate private financial structures. The state is left with the hardest to serve, and the scope for pooling and cross subsidy across regions and user types is diminished.

These examples indicate that the logic of neoliberalism is not neutral but is open to manipulation to serve the politically and economically powerful segments of the economy. This occurs in different ways depending on the context. In E&W, it takes the form of financialisation which has been far more significant than elsewhere, and shareholders have made substantial returns. In South Africa, more significant has been a kind of cream-skimming where the 'economically viable', including mining and industry, are prioritised when it comes to the provision of water.

11 The Eleventh Thing …

… you need to know about neoliberalism is that its economic and social reproduction is attached to particular material cultures that give rise to what might be termed the (variegated) neoliberalisation of everyday life. It was consistently shown by the previous things that neoliberalism has redefined the relationship between the economy, the state, society and individuals. It has constrained the latter to give their lives an entrepreneurial form, subordinated social intercourse to economic criteria, and neutered the previous structures and institutions of political representation. The ideology of self-responsibility has been especially significant since it deprives the citizens of their collective capacities, agencies and cultures, values consumption above all else, places the merit of success and the burden of failure on isolated individuals, and suggests that the resolution of every social problem requires the further individualisation and marketisation of social provision and intercourse.[58]

The scholarly literature has pinpointed these features of neoliberalism in different ways, for example, through the idea that finance 'exploits us all'.[59] This notion draws upon, first, the intuition that low and stagnant wages, high unemployment, privatisation of basic services and the introduction of user charges have undermined the ability of many to sustain customary or desired living standards in the absence of credit, so that exploitative indebtedness results by way of (strictly temporary) remedy. Second, it is seemingly validated by the proliferation of financial relationships and institutions into daily life under neoliberalism. Such a perspective contains an element of truth in that financialisation has been associated with increasing inequalities of access and with volatility and insecurity in the provision of many aspects of economic and social life, with the potential for deprivation to be mutually compounding and multi-dimensional. But the nature and incidence of such deprivations are far from uniform across different social strata, age groups and areas of provision, and it is doubtful that the financialisation of everyday life is primarily, let alone generally, characterised by exploitative indebtedness.

A broader approach suggests that the financialisation of daily life is better understood in terms of the subjection (which may or may not include relations of exploitation) of households to financial markets and processes. For example, for Bryan and Rafferty (2014, p. 404):

> [H]ouseholds have become a frontier of capital accumulation, not just as producers and consumers, but also as financial traders … The requirements of this emergent financial citizenship for the house and households extend beyond just honouring payments on a home purchase, it is requiring a culture of financial calculation that becomes absorbed as part of the daily norms and dispositions of social being.

---

58 Although, ever inconsistent, neo-liberalism is equally associated with non-market and collective forms and ethos where it is in some sense 'traditional', ordered and authoritarian, etc.

59 See especially Lapavitsas (2013) and Fine (2010a and 2013–14) for wide-ranging critique with alternatives.

However, this framing immediately begs the question of which activities attached to the household are subject to a culture of (financial) calculation, why and how, and whether (in the absence of profit as the bottom line) they cohere into an integral system including both calculation and stable trade-offs. In turn, the corresponding social norms of financial behaviour are highly contingent upon the extent to which financialised forms of provision are prevalent, and what are the norms for provision of what is not financialised.[60] Inevitably, then, across commodity consumption, housing, education, health, transport and so on, the impact of financialisation will be highly uneven and differentiated and far from reducible to, or even primarily influenced by, an increasing presence of financial calculation.

A more promising approach can be rooted in the work of Foucault in seeing the neoliberalisation of everyday life – including the financialisation of social intercourse – as the subjective, if resisted and reflexive, internalisation of specifically neoliberal norms and dispositions.[61] For Dardot and Laval (2013, p. 8):

> Neoliberalism is not merely destructive of rules, institutions and rights. It is also *productive* of certain kinds of social relations, certain ways of living, certain subjectivities ... This norm enjoins everyone to live in a world of generalized competition; it calls upon wage-earning classes and populations to engage in economic struggle against one another; it aligns social relations with the model of the market; it promotes the justification of ever greater inequalities; it even transforms the individual, now called on to conceive and conduct him- or herself as an enterprise. For more than a third of a century, this existential norm has presided over public policy, governed global economic relations, transformed society, and reshaped subjectivity. The circumstances of its triumph have often been described – in its political aspect (the conquest of power by neoliberal forces), its economic aspect (the expansion of globalized financial capitalism), its social aspect (the individualization of social relations to the detriment of collective solidarities, the extreme polarization between rich and poor), and its subjective aspect.

Even though this is more than an agenda of what needs to be discovered than discovery itself it suggests, once again, that the content of, and pathways

60 Such financialisation of everyday life directly leads to the notion that the over-indebted are in need of financial literacy programmes as a result of being irrational (see Santos, 2014 for a critique).

61 See, for example, Langley (2008) and Kear (2013).

to, neoliberalisation and the responses to it are highly diverse. For this reason, we address the variegated material cultures of neoliberalism through the SoP approach and the 10Cs associated with it: these material cultures are Constructed, Construed, Conforming, Commodified, Contextual, Contradictory, Closed, Contested, Collective, and Chaotic.[62]

Housing is heavily implicated in neoliberalism's reshaping of individual subjectivities (Gurney, 1999; Payne, 2012; and Van Gent, 2010). This is because homeownership – neoliberalism's favoured form of housing tenure – by providing individuals with an asset, is perceived to play a crucial role in reconstituting individuals as entrepreneurial, self-reliant saver-investors. Payne (2012) elaborates this in relation to the UK, situating the promotion of homeownership within a broader project of welfare restructuring which has sought to shift welfare provision from a social-collective to a market-individualist model and ethos. The problem with Payne's analysis, as with the association between homeownership and individualistic and entrepreneurial behaviour, is that both focus on the goals and rationale of neoliberal housing and welfare policy rather than the extent to which it has been successful (and internalised). In practice, the extent to which neoliberalism has reconstituted social norms in relation to housing is constrained by a number of factors. First, while owner-occupation has grown in recent decades, in most countries there remains a substantial proportion of the population that has no housing assets and is relatively insulated from this kind of neoliberal socialisation. Second, among those who do own a home, treating that home as an asset implies a mentality of rational, financial calculation, which exists in tension with the value people attach to their housing as home. As Fine (2013b, p. 17) puts it:[63]

> the role of mortgage finance is telling, not least with an appreciating asset serving both as a form of saving and as access to credit for consumption (or even other purposes) whilst also, of course, being a home not a house except for those who suspend the distinction.

This clash of meanings is evident even in countries such as the UK and Portugal, where an asset-based approach to housing has to some extent taken root, as reflected in increases in the hoarding of housing wealth. It is even more pronounced in countries in which mortgage markets and owner-occupation are less functional and established. In South Africa, for example, the majority

62 See Fine (2013b), and Fine (2013a) for the 10Cs approach applied to financialisation itself.

63 See also Christophers (2010).

of poor black homeowners report that, far from using their house as a basis from which to move up the housing ladder and accumulate wealth, they would never sell their house because they have an emotional attachment to it as a home (Isaacs, 2016). Despite attempts to encourage households to treat housing as an economic and financial asset, then, the poor black population continues to regard housing more as physical shelter and emotional asset than it does a financial one.

The example of housing serves to illustrate that social norms under neoliberalism emerge not simply from the imperatives of financial calculation, but from the interaction of those imperatives with the pre-existing and continuing social meanings and norms attached to particular items of consumption. As noted above, this interaction can be characterised in terms of the 10Cs, or some of them. Thus, the cultures that shape the consumption of housing under neoliberalism are contradictory and chaotic, reflecting the multiple meanings attached to housing. These meanings are in turn constructed by political and economic agents in particular contexts and construed by reflexive consumers in ways that often involves contestation over both meanings and outcomes.

Attitudes to water vary across location and over time. To some degree this will relate to availability. In water-stressed regions, attitudes will be different from those in an area which is prone to flooding. But it is not just geological issues that shape attitudes. Water cultures are affected by the ways in which water is provided. Neoliberal policies have specifically aimed to effect a change in cultures with the portrayal of water as an 'economic good' rather than as a public service. With water perceived as scarce, consumption is rationed by price. Universal metering is associated with self-responsibility to manage consumption and payments. To some extent, the conception of water as an economic good appears to run counter to the recent adoption of water as a human right,[64] where it was acknowledged that clean drinking water and sanitation are essential to the realisation of all human rights. The details of the UN resolution are explicit that everyone has the right to a 'sufficient' level of water for basic consumption. This has been set at 50–100 l/c/d (enough to meet basic needs according to the World Health Organisation) and it needs to be 'affordable' (not exceeding three per cent of household income), http://www.un.org/waterforlifedecade/human_right_to_water.shtml. Water, therefore, as a human right, is clearly not like other economic goods. Yet the rights-based approach is not, in principle, incompatible with neoliberal policies. Indeed,

64 In 2010 the United Nations General Assembly explicitly recognised the human right to water and sanitation (UN Resolution 64/292).

it might even be seen to promote them insofar as rights are designated to be delivered through private, financialised provision, underpinned by subsidy.[65]

While the right-to-water rules out a pricing structure that makes water unaffordable, the approach comes down to meeting basic needs and does not prevent unequal structures of provision that are exacerbated under neoliberalism. In recent decades, the water case studies show that there has been a shift in the understanding of equity. Neoliberalism in provision is associated with a notion of fairness by which everyone should pay for what they consume. But everyone needs to have water, and cutting consumption is not an option for many low-income households. In neoliberal terms, equity relates not to fairness in the distribution of resources but merely to ensuring that the most disadvantaged have access to the bare minimum for survival. In the case studies where social policy was assessed (E&W, Portugal and South Africa), efforts to support low-income households were far from adequate, based on complex means testing and providing a very small (often insufficient) amount of social funding (or a modicum of free water in South Africa) for deprived households. In neoliberal terms, this is how equity is addressed. Yet, nowhere is there any mention of the impact of policies on the wealthiest consumers (and this can include the industrial). Equitable provision needs to be mindful of the impact across the realm of consumer types. The neoliberal understanding of equity is limited to easing the more severe aspects of policy on the social reproduction of the residualised and impoverished.

12 The Twelfth Thing …

… you need to know about neoliberalism is that it is associated with specific modalities of economic growth, volatility and crisis.[66] The neoliberal restructuring of economic reproduction introduces mutually reinforcing policies that: dismantle the systems of provision established previously (which are defined, often ex post, as being 'inefficient'); reduce the degree of coordination of economic activity; create socially undesirable employment patterns; feed the concentration of income and wealth; preclude the use of industrial policy instruments for the implementation of socially determined priorities; and make the balance of payments structurally dependent on international flows

65 Here, there is a parallel with the principle of universal access to health care, with a major issue being not whether but what and how!

66 As Fiorentini (2015, p.128) puts it, "The dominance of neoliberal policies in the last three decades has produced worldwide greater inequalities, financial instability and crisis."

of capital. In doing this, and despite ideological claims to the contrary, neoliberalism fuels unsustainable patterns of production, employment, distribution, consumption, state finance and global integration, and it increases economic uncertainty, volatility and vulnerability to (financial) crises.

In particular, financial sector control of economic resources, and the main sources of capital, allows for the draining of capital from production; at the same time, neoliberalism systematically, if unevenly, favours large capital at the expense of small capital and the workers, belying its claims to foster competition and 'level the playing field'. As a result, accumulation in neoliberal economies tends to take the form of bubbles which eventually collapse with destructive implications and requiring expensive state-sponsored bailouts. These cycles include the international debt crisis of the early 1980s, the US savings and loan crisis of the 1980s, the stock market crashes of the 1980s and 1990s, the Japanese crisis dragging on since the late 1980s, the crises in several middle-income countries at the end of the twentieth century, and the dotcom, financial and housing bubbles of the 2000s, culminating with the global meltdown starting in 2007.

In turn, neoliberal policies are justified ideologically through the imperatives of 'business confidence' and 'competitiveness'. This is misleading, because confidence is elusive, materially ungrounded, self-referential and volatile, and it systematically leads to the over-estimation of the levels and effectiveness of investments that will ensue from the pursuit of finance-friendly policies. Moreover, those policies are not self-correcting. Instead of leading to a change of course, failure to achieve their stated aims normally leads to the deepening and extension of the 'reforms' with the excuse of ensuring implementation and the promise of imminent success the next time around.[67]

We can see how neoliberalism's dynamics of bubble, crisis and retrenchment have played out in relation to housing and its role in the 2007–9 financial crisis. The crisis was preceded by a widespread, mutually reinforcing cycle between mortgage lending and house prices, in which mortgage lending fed speculative rents (and capital gains on house prices), and these were in turn used to justify further mortgage lending. It was the subprime market that was to burst the resulting house price bubble. As subprime borrowers began to default on their mortgage loans in early 2007, panic spread through the financial system as the opaque character of the risks and returns carried by RMBSs became evident. While it was only the USA and, to a lesser extent, the UK that

67 This is evident in the 'evaluatory trap' associated with privatisation (Bayliss and Fine, eds, 2008) and in the hype surrounding private sector funding of the public sector.

had subprime sectors, banks had purchased subprime securities on a global scale. Doubts about the credit rating of those securities, therefore, had knock-on effects on mortgage lending all over the world, leading to a global house price crash. However, despite the catastrophic consequences of the resulting economic crisis, the widespread policy response has been to promise new regulation to tame the most controversial financial excesses – themselves treated as an aberration – while seeking to return the financial sector to normal functioning as quickly as possible. In the UK, the state has even attempted to override a retreat to safety by mortgage lenders, by guaranteeing a portion of mortgage loans and thus returning loan-to-value ratios to pre-crisis levels – levels now seen as too risky by mortgage lenders themselves.

Unsurprisingly, then, however we interpret the differences between the post-war boom (including Keynesianism, developmentalism, Soviet regimes and their variants) and the neoliberal period, economic performance for the latter in terms of growth and volatility has been generally worse and, ultimately, led to a global crisis driven by finance and financialisation, despite unambiguously and unprecedentedly favourable conditions for capitalism worldwide (see first thing).

13 The Thirteenth Thing …

… you need to know about neoliberalism is that there are alternatives, both within and beyond neoliberalism itself. To conclude, it was shown in the sixth thing that neoliberalism cannot be reduced to a collection of policies, which would suggest that alternative policy initiatives could reverse the neoliberal reforms and even transcend neoliberalism. Policy changes are certainly essential, but the scope for such changes can be questioned in the light of the political means and forms available to the opposition, the strength of the coalitions potentially committed to them, and the scope to drive the required distributional, regulatory and policy reforms given the neoliberal transformation of production, international integration, the state, ideology and society itself. None of these can be adequately assessed without a prior understanding of the systemic features of neoliberalism and the transformations that it has wrought on class relations and institutions and the processes of economic and social reproduction.

It was also shown in the seventh thing that neoliberalism is not a 'capitalist conspiracy' against the workers, in which case there would be nothing systemic or historically-specific about it, since capitalists and the state have always readily conspired against the workers.[68] Conversely, in this case, neoliberalism could be dislocated through a counter conspiracy, or even by changes in the law. Alternatively, this approach can also be read as implying that 'things were much better' under previous systems of accumulation (Keynesian, developmentalist, and so on), which, in principle, should be restored.

The latter goals are laudable but implausible. For, while neoliberalism is incompatible with economic democracy, it simultaneously hollows out political democracy.[69] On the one hand, the discourse and practice of TINA (There Is No Alternative), often now muted and implicit, under neoliberalism blocks the political expression of dissent even in moderate forms and feeds apathy, populism and the far right, courting destabilising implications for neoliberalism itself. On the other hand, the institutional shifts, the changes in the structures of political representation, and the social and economic transformations wrought by neoliberalism systematically reduce the scope for the expression of collective interests, the emergence of transformative programmes, and even the aspiration to change society beyond neoliberalism. The options for water policy have severely narrowed in the past three decades with the World Bank, the IMF and other international institutions promoting neoliberalism. For example, EU member states were given until 2010 to establish water-pricing policies according to the terms of the EU 2000 Water Framework Directive (WFD) including adopting the principles of cost recovery. Governments are prevented from using any other approach to pricing. Similarly for housing, responsibility for delivery tends to lie with local government units, whose hands are tied by central governments both directly, through restrictions on the policy options available, and indirectly, through the imposition of excessive burdens of delivery without the requisite resources.

In short, the post-war consensus inspired a political contest over whether collectivism in the forms of (Keynesian) reformism or socialist revolution would be capable of continuing to deliver progressive outcomes. Neither now is on the agenda, not least as the dominant form taken by collective economic and social reproduction has been appropriated by finance. Nevertheless, the economic contradictions of neoliberalism, the incremental sclerosis of the political institutions regulating its metabolism and the cumulative corrosion of its ideological foundations make this system of accumulation resistant to economic change, but also vulnerable to a multiplicity of political challenges.

---

68 In Adam Smith's (2009) famous words, "People of the same trade seldom meet together, even for merriment and diversion, but the conversation ends in a conspiracy against the public, or in some contrivance to raise prices."

69 Ayers and Saad-Filho (2015).

The costs of neoliberal housing provision, for example, are in some places giving rise to political mobilisations against neoliberal policy strictures. Hence, community resistance to gentrification and relocation was observed in Turkey, South Africa and the UK and, in some instances, local struggles have been linked to broader demands for more inclusive and collective forms of housing provision. However, these movements have yet to develop beyond defensive struggles into a more comprehensive challenge to neoliberalism, from particular interests within a sector to social transformation beyond it.

This does not imply that electoral strategies are sufficient, nor that changes in social, industrial, financial or monetary policies can fulfil radical expectations. Quite the contrary; neoliberalism has repeatedly demonstrated its resilience both in practice and in the realm of ideas. But the demand for the expansion and radicalisation of political and economic democracy can integrate widely different struggles, delegitimise neoliberalism and support the emergence of alternatives. These are now urgently needed.

CHAPTER 3

From Financialisation to Systems of Provision

Postscript as Personal Preamble

As is implicit in the newly-drafted introduction that follows, allowing this Preamble to be brief, this Chapter was written towards the end of the Fessud project. As a result, and as a theoretical contribution, it both brings together many of the elements that had been developed during the research and is especially marked in closing by what we had been working on at that late stage. Whilst our research had been primarily focused on the impact of financialisation on state provisioning, and especially housing and water if partially extending to health and pensions, our attention turned to how those at the rough (or smooth) end of such provisioning understood their experiences. In particular, we focused upon what we termed the material culture of financialisation, MCF. To this end, I used project funds to commission some specific contributions from outside the erstwhile Fessud team of researchers. I was particularly pleased to solicit a piece from the Glasgow Media Group, whose work I had long admired especially from its coverage of the 1984/85 UK Miners Strike, and on which I had drawn – as had others – to argue that to be a striking miner was to be criminalised by both the courts and complicit media (Fine, 1990). Ultimately, our work on the MCF was published as a special issue of *New Political Economy*, subsequently appearing as a standalone book (Bayliss et al. eds, 2017).

1 Introduction[1]

The purpose of this Chapter is to give a wide-ranging overview of the nature and implications of financialisation and 'financialisation', a distinction between what financialisation is and how it is understood, respectively, see also Chapter 4. Section 2 suggests, as is now commonly accepted and represented in a burgeoning literature, that financialisation has experienced a meteoric rise. This has, however, not been uncontested, and the rejection of

1 Originally appearing as Fine et al. (2016c), with this introduction newly drafted for this Chapter in lieu of a previous Fessud preface.

 | DOI:10.1163/9789004706293_004

its use is also addressed. In section 3, the groundwork is provided both for a rationale for the deployment of financialisation, and how this should be done, through interrogation of what questions should be placed upon financialisation in order to be able to put it on sound foundations. Section 4 answers these questions by placing a narrow definition upon financialisation as the intensive and extensive expansion of interest-bearing capital (money-making through money-lending as capital for the purposes of generating a surplus). By narrowing the definition of financialisation in this way, a distinction can be drawn between financialisation as such and its effects, something which is deficient within much of the literature given its tendency to dub as financialisation anything associated with the use of monetary relations and their practices and ethos.

Nonetheless, the relationship between financialisation and its effects are not immediate but need to traced. One way of doing this is to unpick the notion of commodification (often associated with financialisation) into three different aspects, commodification as such, commodity form and commodity calculation. At a grand level, this allows for financialisation to be seen as systemic and underpinning neoliberalism as a stage of capitalism, in terms of its presence across economic and social reproduction. As a result, the incidence and impacts of financialisation are both variegated and associated with what we have termed the material culture of financialisation (MCF) as laid out in the following sections. They range over MCF by drawing upon the system of provision approach (and its associated 10Cs – see other Chapters as appropriate), and how to engage in the cultural through interdisciplinarity and a foothold in political economy.

For, how financialisation is experienced in everyday life, and more generally, is heavily conditioned by its taking place behind the backs of those who suffer its consequences, as it impacts upon them from afar (in financial markets and the institutions of, and influences upon, policymaking), establishing new social norms and forms of provisioning. The final section, if briefly, suggests that existing, well-established frameworks for unravelling these developments – especially those associated with the social compacting paradigm and the welfare regime approach – are sorely inadequate and outdated. Instead, detailed attentions needs to be placed upon differentiated systems of provision, the material cultures with which they are attached, the 10Cs framing for example, and corresponding MCFs as the basis on which to build targeted, collective and, hopefully, joined up activism for alternatives. Each of these different elements, and how to bring them together, is examined in greater detail throughout the book.

2 What Is Financialisation, or Should That Be Whether?

Sporadic previous forays apart,[2] over its relatively short life, the notion of 'financialisation' has experienced a meteoric rise, accelerating in prominence in the wake of the global crisis. In this respect, it has shared some of the common features of other 'buzzwords' that have been deployed across the social sciences, and may have even emulated them more rapidly even if with some way still to go.[3] Here, in particular, comparisons might be drawn with the more longstanding, but still relatively recent, concepts such as globalisation, neoliberalism, and social capital. Indeed, financialisation has already been associated with the first two of these. As Epstein (2005, p. 3) puts it, "In short, this changing landscape has been characterised by the rise of *neoliberalism, globalization* and *financialization*". But financialisation has also been studiously ignored by the third, social capital, in view of the latter's lack of attention to the global, national and international elites and the exercise of systemic power.[4]

This is itself indicative of what is often a key characteristic of a buzzword, especially as it evolves to maturity. On the one hand, whilst it is extremely wide-ranging in its use, there tend to be no go areas that may or may not be filled out at later stages. In case of financialisation, its rise has been extensive across the social sciences but with the notable exception of its total exclusion from mainstream economics, an absence that is not liable to change. This is despite heterodox economics taking a lead in the development and use of financialisation. The reason for this is not then that financialisation is in some sense non-economic and, in any case, mainstream economics has increasingly encroached on the non-economic as subject matter.[5]

Rather, by its origins and nature, financialisation does not fit into the mainstream, see also Chapter 6. Its momentum, if not its origins, is derived from the Global Financial Crisis which, self-confessedly, left the mainstream floundering for an explanatory response on its own terms and without the option of

2 The term, at least as it is used now, can be traced back at least to Magdoff and Sweezy (1987), with an early intervention for the more recent literature deriving from Arrighi (1994). As Goldstein (2009) observes, the idea only has a significant presence over the past decade or so. To begin with at least, we place it in inverted commas to distinguish it as understood as opposed to how it is in contemporary capitalism (although there are necessary connections between the two).

3 See Cornwall and Eade (eds) (2010).

4 See Fine (2010b) for such critical reflection on social capital, and Vitali et al. (2011) for evidence of the social capital of finance.

5 As with economics imperialism, see Fine and Milonakis (2009).

drawing upon financialisation even as a stopgap.[6] For financialisation is heavily attached to the notion that the economy is subject to systemic forces and processes that are far from equilibrating, notions that do not fit comfortably within mainstream methodology and methods with its preoccupations with aggregating from the individual (optimiser), (narrowly conceived, static, allocative) efficiency and (at most deviations from a given) equilibrium.

On the other hand, across social sciences otherwise, 'financialisation' has very rapidly been deployed with different meanings and with different methods and theories.[7] As a result, three fundamental features mark the rise of 'financialisation' across the social sciences. One is the frequent observation of neglect of finance in the past. Second is the wide variety of approaches taken to financialisation, essentially ranging from construction of the neo-liberal subject whether as worker, consumer, entrepreneur, investor or policymaker through to grand narratives concerning the nature of contemporary capitalism. Third, closely related but distinct, is the equally wide variety of subject matter covered by financialisation, dealing in everything from the nature of the relationship between financialisation and neoliberalism in characterising contemporary capitalism to the pervasive influence of financialisation on everyday life, let alone as a generic term for finance itself and, correspondingly, wherever it intervenes (Sawyer, 2014).

In short, whether as inspiration or reflection (or both), it has been commonplace for the starting point for many contributions to the financialisation literature to reference Epstein's (2005, p. 3) definition of financialisation as "the increasing role of financial motives, markets, actors and institutions in the operation of the domestic and international economies". This is extraordinarily open and wide-ranging and highly descriptive as opposed to analytical in substance. As already implied, it is an invitation to see financialisation more or less everywhere, and it is an invitation that has been readily accepted!

Not surprisingly, itself typical in the evolution of a buzzword, the idea of financialisation has already attracted controversy, and rejection, as a minority sport. Debate has ranged over the extent, historical uniqueness, likely longevity and homogeneity of the incidence and effects of the rise of finance that 'financialisation' is putatively designed to capture. Michell and Toporowski

6 Interestingly, this seems to have led the mainstream to deny that the continuing global, if especially US, recession is a consequence of finance as the recession should have been over by now if so. Instead, explanations are sought in the traditional terms of real factors on either the supply or demand sides. See especially Summers (2015) and the *American Economic Review* collection of which it is a part.

7 See Mader et al. (eds) (2020) for a more recent and extensive retrospective.

(2014, p. 80), for example, see financialisation as a neologism, reflecting over-reaction to the greater contemporary presence of finance but its neglect in the past. They conclude, "For this reason, the understanding of finance requires the abandonment of financialization as a project of intellectual inquiry".

Similarly, Christophers (2015a and b) rejects the use of financialisation as overblown, highlighting five fundamental features.[8] These concern what he sees as limits in the success that is liable to accompany attempts at promotion of the notion of financialisation. First is Analytic – that the term has spread too much in meaning and application to be useful. Second is Theoretic – that nothing new has been added. Third is Strategic – that, whilst financialisation may have placed finance more fully on the agenda of scholarship, it has paradoxically done so in a way that has also led to neglect of close consideration of the details of money and finance itself, as financialisation serves as an all-embracing point of reference.[9] Fourth is Optics – that the novelty of the rise of finance is exaggerated and not new, especially if allowance is made for the exceptionalism of the Keynesian period. And fifth is Empiric – that finance can only prevail to a degree constrained by other economic activity upon which it depends.

In this light, Christophers anticipates that there are two prospective ways forward for financialisation. One is to seek to overcome the amorphous creation it has become with renewed attempts, especially theoretical, at forging different and better definitions of what it is. And the other is to continue along the road of more of the same, with the literature feeding and expanding upon itself, especially empirically, as earlier studies of financialisation provide a template for successors of the same type with or without a novel wrinkle or two. It should be observed that these two ways of moving forward are precisely ones that have been followed by the social capital literature (Fine, 2010b) although, possibly not realised by Christophers, these two directions are not necessarily alternatives but can be mutually reinforcing and overlapping.[10] This is because the acknowledgement of the ambiguities in the definitions and use of financialisation induces new and improved versions that simply add to the chaos,

8 Subsequently, Christophers (2020 and 2022) has been captured by the notion that finance must produce value as it appropriates so much of it, and to see it as part and parcel of a portfolio of rents that characterise contemporary capitalism. But see debate between Christophers and Fine (2020) that opens the Mader et al. (eds) (2020) volume.

9 There is, then, much referencing to the black boxing of finance, see also Poovey (2015) and below.

10 And possibly a similar story can be told for globalisation and neoliberalism!

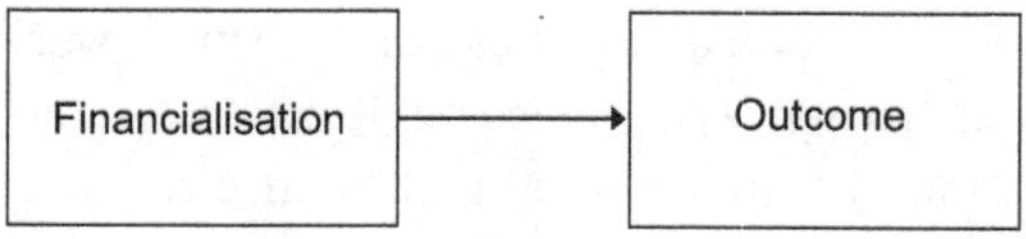

FIGURE 1 From financialisation to outcome

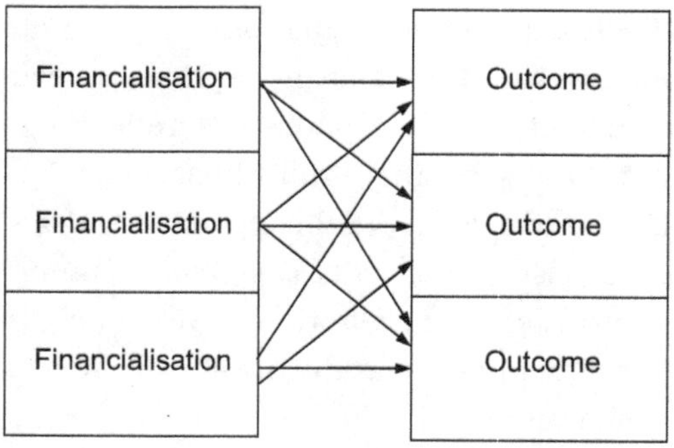

FIGURE 2 From financialisations to outcomes

rather than clean it up as definitions proliferate alongside the case studies they illustrate.

Indeed, the representation of the process for social capital by Fine (2010b) readily carries over to financialisation. The initial starting point is that financialisation is seen as causing something else, see Figure 1. Subsequently, as indicated in Figure 2, both financialisation as cause and its effects can become extremely wide-ranging, with just three of each illustrated.[11] Nor is the expanding scope of financialisation's causes and effects confined to this analytical mechanism, as illustrated in Figure 3.[12] On the one hand, it can be located relative to other parallel, and not single, factors, B, (such as levels of inequality, for example), that mutually determine effects, and by underlying determinants of both financialisation and B, as represented by A (which might, for example, include neoliberalism or globalisation, themselves multi-dimensional and complex).

11 Note, even at a relatively early stage, in locating financialisation geographically, Lee et al. (2009, p. 727–8) observe, "What is perhaps relatively new is the extent to which finance has found its way into most, if not all, of the nooks and crannies of social life. To illustrate, it is easily possible to identify at least 17 notions of financialization."

12 Figure 3 is indicative of how financialisation is a middle-range concept, with all its attendant strengths and weaknesses (Merton, 1957).

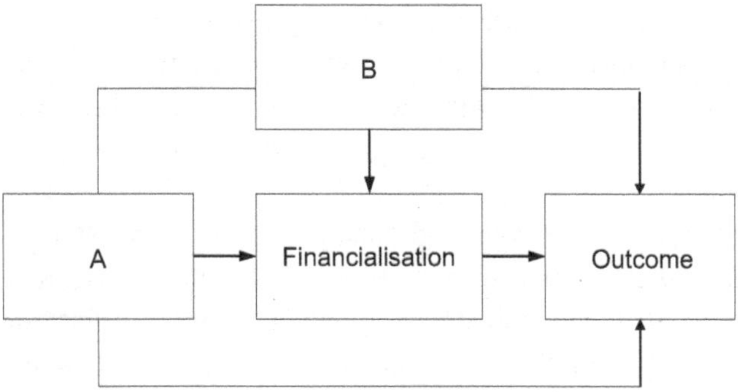

FIGURE 3 Locating financialisation

In short, the simplicity of Figure 3 is misleading in deference to ease of presentation since each of the boxes should be fragmented with a corresponding plethora of arrows across the boxes. Moreover, whilst already indicative of the expanding scope of causes and effects associated with financialisation, there is a further impetus to this outcome. It is the tendency for the notion of financialisation to incorporate substance from the other boxes, thereby conflating the nature, causes and consequences of financialisation with one another. Recall, for Epstein, that it refers to "the increasing role of financial motives, markets, actors and institutions in the operation of the domestic and international economies", if not societies, households, policymaking and so on!

3 Taking Financialisation Forward: What Are the Questions?

For those wedded to intellectual purity, this is a disastrous state of affairs. But it does not follow that buzzwords, as they become fuzzwords (Cornwall and Eade, eds, 2010), are thereby rendered analytically degenerative. This may or may not be the case and may change over time.[13] We have, for example, learnt an enormous amount through the scholarship attached to globalisation and neoliberalism, although Fine (2010b) argues the opposite for social capital in viewing it as degrading the scholarly traditions on which it draws and misinterpreting the empirical evidence that it provides. In response to Christophers (2015a), then, Aalbers (2015, p. 215) in particular, welcomes the role that financialisation has played in unravelling complexity, for "The literature on financialization thus is part of a larger attempt to understand the nonlinear,

13 Think, for example, of the rise and fall of 'modernisation'.

multidimensional, multi-scalar complexity of contemporary societies/economies". In addition, it serves to promote interest in intra-disciplinary and interdisciplinary endeavour, and in attaching the micro to the macro levels, p. 216, given the:

> potential for financialization as a concept facilitating the conversations between different (sub)disciplines that otherwise do not necessarily talk much to each other … The power of the financialization literature is not only that it connects different disciplines but also different levels of analysis, from the very micro to the very macro – and demonstrating how these are related.

Such is also the thrust of other responses to Christophers, with a heavy bias in these idiosyncratically towards the role played around (agricultural) land. For example, Fairbairn (2015) welcomes how the rise of financialisation helps to explain why and how new forms and levels of speculative purchase of farmland (for capital gains) have now become readily accepted as legitimate, whereas Murphy (2015), in the context of housing markets and urban development, sees financialisation as able to address the details in developments in drawing upon, but going beyond, Harvey's grand theorising around secondary circuits of capital (associated with infrastructural provision and the like).[14]

Christophers' (2015b) response to these positive postures has a number of dimensions. One is to accuse the literature of continuing to fail to address financialisation as opposed to its effects, "The financialization literature represents the study of the effects of finance rather than the study of finance per se", p. 230. This black boxing is surely true of much of the literature, but certainly not all, and it is far from a logically necessary nor dominant feature. And, to the extent that it does apply, it may reflect the empirically driven character of the literature in its relatively early stages. On the other hand, Christophers shifts ground, almost coming to the position of accusing scholars of financialisation of intellectual and political opportunism by suggesting that they confine their (limited) understanding of finance to a critique of its application beyond its 'normal' spheres of operation, something, it should be closely observed, that has been brought to prominence by the financialisation literature itself, p. 232:

---

14 See also Lawrence (2015) and Ouma (2015) for comment on Christophers and, for the remarkably rapid rise of financialisation in agrarian studies, Isakson and Ryan (2014), Dixon (2014), Fairbairn et al. (2014), Fairbairn (2014) and McMichael (2012). This has been particularly and understandably driven to a large extent, if with different focuses, by attention to global food chains and land grabs.

> I would therefore put it like this: financialization is a politically limited critique insofar as it is essentially a critique of what finance does, especially elsewhere – of where its tentacles extend to, of the constituencies thus enrolled and ensnared, of the 'nonfinancial' logics thus adulterated – and not of what finance is. The object of critique is the extension of finance's rules and logics to domains where they are not welcome, not natural, and not historically normalised. The object of critique is thus not capitalist finance per se. The latter's rules and logics are left curiously intact, even if their illegitimate imperialism is castigated. The implication, needless to say, is that finance – its relations, practices, and ideas – is somehow unproblematic and irreproachable just so long as it sticks to its 'legitimate' sphere of operation and influence (however that might be demarcated).

There must, however, be serious doubts about whether this is accurately representative of the political and/or intellectual positions of many of those who have engaged in the financialisation literature as many of these are heterodox within their disciplines and remain, rather than have become, critical of the role of finance in contemporary capitalism in light of finance's 'imperialism' of application.

Whilst such criticism, then, is misplaced, the Christophers debate does raise crucial issues around what is to be understood as financialisation and what are its essential features, although these are not necessarily best captured in terms of what he somewhat obscurely terms its five limits around the Analytic, Theoretic, Strategic, Optics and the Empiric. Rather, the first issue is how to narrow the definition of financialisation so that it can be used to distinguish its causes from its effect.

The second issue is closely related and contingent on the first, and concerns specifying the mechanisms which attach causes to effects (in order to avoid the sort of reasoning in which the presence of finance or even just the idea of money, often labelled financialisation, is deemed to be sufficient to explain whatever happens to whatever are its associates, not least as housing, energy, food and all sorts of other associated crises, are putatively explained by financialisation).

The third issue is to unpick the nature and impact of financialisation both within and between the economic and the non-economic (or the social), these themselves giving rise to the challenge of interdisciplinarity. This is not simply a matter of opening its own black box but also the black box of how finance is economically and socially embedded. In this respect, the literature on financialisation does have considerable strengths precisely because of the depth and breadth of its case studies and empirical analyses. In this light, the issue is more a matter of how to order such studies, and the variables they bring to bear, in an appropriate analytical framework, the demands upon which, as will be seen below, are considerable.

The fourth issue is to locate financialisation historically, not least in light of criticisms that it represents nothing new or distinctive. Here, again, the literature displays some strengths, not only in charting the quantitative dimensions of the growing scale and scope of financialisation but also through the qualitative nature of contemporary capitalism in a variety of ways, especially through attachment to neoliberalism, but also through growing inequalities and the power of finance.

A final issue covered here concerns how to relate grander theory to more detailed analysis or, if in slightly inappropriate terms, the shift from macro to micro levels. Here the literature has been collectively strong in identifying the scale and scope of the problem given its own wide range of empirical subject matter and topics. This has revealed how diverse are the incidence and effects of financialisation. The literature has been less successful in bridging the micro detail with macro posturing, other than in deploying the notion of financialisation as an all-embracing analytical fix – although this can be given some substance, however appropriately, as in Lapavitsas' (2013) idea that we are all financially exploited, or, for others for example, that financialisation represents the rise of the rentier. In this light, the issue is how a theory of financialisation allows for heterogeneity in practice.

4 Defining Financialisation: One Step Back, Two Steps Forward

In addressing these conundrums around conceptualising financialisation, we will draw selectively upon the work delivered under two of the "Work Packages", WP5 and WP8, or research themes of the Fessud project. These themes are particularly suitable for meeting the challenges raised above for the following reasons. First, with one relating financialisation to well-being, and the other to provision of water and housing, the location of financialisation within the research has extended from economic to social (and even cultural) reproduction. Second, WP5 has understood well-being from an interdisciplinary perspective and has been particularly concerned with the material culture of financialisation through which both the construction and delivery of well-being can be assessed. Third, WP8 has both drawn upon such research from WP5 and has undertaken cross-country comparative work, thereby allowing for the diversity of the incidence and impact of financialisation in different contexts (by sectors as well as countries). And, fourth, all of the research has been mindful not only of debates around financialisation but also of those across the social sciences more generally.

Central to addressing the issues identified is to make progress in defining financialisation, and in a way that distinguishes it both from its effects and the mechanisms that bring about those effects (without descending into fuzziness as suggested in Figure 3). Inevitably, this means the adoption of a lean and mean alternative to the literature's empirically rich but conceptually chaotic collective posture and, in this respect, much of the research in WP5 and WP8 has been inspired by defining financialisation by reference to Marx's theory of interest-bearing capital, that is money capital that is advanced in the anticipation of a return based on the accumulation of productive capital. Here, the important point is not the appeal to Marxist theory as such but to seek both to avoid associating financialisation with, on the economic terrain, the simple presence of (more) credit and to associate it more positively with the role of finance in its driving of the economy, including broader financial activity itself.

By contrast, post-Keynesian approaches, for example, tend to see financialisation in terms of the impact of finance on levels (and forms and rewards)[15] of effective demand. This can come through distribution at the expense of wages, speculative at the expense of real investment or financial-interest induced austerity. As previously mentioned, other approaches, in a sense narrowing down to some degree from Epstein's all-encompassing definition, tend to adopt a similar procedure if with different content – exploitation of us all by finance (as with Lapavitsas, 2013), the transformation of the household to financial agent (Bryan and Rafferty 2014), the increased power of the financial rentier (Duménil and Lévy, 2004), or the broadly-based notion of financialisation as bricolage (Erturk et al. eds, 2008; and Johal et al. 2014). At most, these offer a definition of financialisation based on how longstanding features of capitalism have wrought qualitative through quantitative change.

To some degree, the same applies to our own alternative definition of financialisation in terms of interest-bearing capital, with more detail to follow. For, the reason why this is salient for understanding contemporary capitalism is because of the intensive and extensive accumulation of such capital, intensive within what are longstanding if inventively proliferating financial markets, and extensive by the incorporation of new domains, especially those related

15 In desperately abbreviated summary, the literature is heavily concerned with different regimes of (more or less successful) growth, depending upon whether they are driven by consumption or (productive) investment, distribution between both profits and wages, and the share in surplus of speculative finance. See Hein (2022) for a recent overview.

to social reproduction such as housing most prominently but also in privatisation, commercialisation and the varieties of financial intrusions into everyday life.[16]

By adopting such a narrow, and abstract, definition of financialisation, however, the space is opened for tracing the complex and diverse avenues through which it exerts its effects. The approach brings out two useful strategies in this regard. On the one hand, financialisation is dependent upon, but not coterminous with monetary relations. On the other hand, financialisation also exerts its influence through non-economic relations, most obviously in the power of finance in political, ideological and cultural arenas.

Indeed, financialisation, thus understood, does not necessarily extend its scope to include the advance of all capital, let alone credit, whether for industrial or commercial purposes, because capital might be funded from retained earnings or whatever rather than borrowing from which a return is anticipated. Only the latter case involves financialisation in that a claim on earnings is created that can be bought and sold separately in what Marx termed fictitious capital. Of course, the current period has witnessed the massive expansion of such interest-bearing (and fictitious) capital in intensive forms, as has been recognised in the stakeholder value literature on financialisation, although it extends much further than this in the proliferation of types and growth of financial derivatives.

With a narrow definition of financialisation, it is possible to examine how it has effects (or, indeed, is itself affected) rather than taking it as coterminous with its own effects as in broader definitions. But this also requires unpicking, or disaggregating, monetary and non-monetary relations that interact with, but are distinct from, financialisation. A starting point in doing so is to recognise that financialisation is dependent upon commodity relations since its monetary rewards ultimately derive from commodity production (as finance never made any return by itself other than appropriating it from elsewhere as a result of the putative trading in risk or providing financial services).[17] But commodity relations are much broader than financialisation as buying and selling can take place in the absence of credit, let alone credit relations that have themselves been financialised. Accordingly, the most prominent form in which everyday life says hello to financialisation is in the indirect form of commodity relations, buying and selling. As mentioned, this may not involve finance as such in case of cash purchases (although financialisation may well

16 See Fine (2013–14) most recently, and Fine (2022) for an update.

17 For an outstanding account of how finance as productive has been rationalised, see Christophers (2013).

have occurred intensively further up the chain of provision). But, equally, commodity relations for consumption have increasingly become embroiled in credit relations, most notably with mortgages, credit cards, and so on.[18]

This is not financialisation as such by its tight definition as interest-bearing capital. Mortgages have long existed, for example. What makes them financialisation is the securitisation of the potential interest payments (or the debts as such) and their bundling into derivatives for speculative purposes. One implication is that (re-)commodification, even if not financialisation itself, offers fertile opportunities for financialisation, both in the productive sphere itself (as with privatisation and corresponding creation of financial assets representing ownership) and with its 'weaker' counterparts of commercialisation with user charges, public-private partnerships, and contracting out.[19] The associated revenues of such commodified operations offer the scope for securitisation and, so financialisation, that may or may not (be allowed to) take place.[20]

But, quite apart from commodification, in addition, economic and social life can depend upon what can appropriately be termed the 'commodity form', payments of money, in the absence of commodity relations as such, as with pensions, social security and so on.[21] Significantly, such payments are also capable of being securitised to form the basis of extensive financialisation even if not directly financialisation themselves. The leading example is pensions,[22] for which this increasingly prominent element of social reproduction (of the aged) has been subject to individual responsibilisation, driven by, and as a consequence of, financialisation. This has given rise to a set of rich and contradictory cultures as a result of the clash of financialisation of pensions with a traditional ethos of collective provision for the retired, not least in the wake of the variously understood crises of pension systems (putatively assigned to a demographic time bomb). Apart from the narrowly interpreted

18 With the corresponding notion that everyone is financially exploited, Lapavitsas (2013) and Fine (2010b and 2013–14) for critique, or that the household is necessarily forced into being the equivalent of a financial operative, Bryan and Rafferty (2014).

19 Weaker only in the sense of less than full reliance upon the private sector but, equally, stronger for continuing to rely upon the backing of the state!

20 See Leyshon and Thrift (2007) for a relatively early, if implicit, suggestion that financialisation be reduced to capitalisation/securitisation.

21 And, quite apart from pocket money, this might even include wages as commodity form, given the special nature of labour power as a commodity, not least with the securitisation of wage revenues as an asset against which debts can then be bought and sold, and underpins the increasingly formal short loan business set against, and first call upon, pay packets as has occurred in South Africa, and elsewhere, through garnishee orders.

22 But see Saritas (2014) and Churchill (2014)

parameters of pension systems themselves (levels of payments by whom, with what rewards), how these have been constructed on a broader perspective depends upon differential access to, participation within, and rewards from labour markets, the taxation systems and the levels of provision of social or familial welfare provision outside of the pension system, quite apart from the vagaries of financial returns when these are a proximate determinant of individual or collective pensions.[23]

The relationship between pensions and finance offers a salient example of why it is necessary to distinguish between commodification and commodity form in engaging with the effects of financialisation. Pensions have been financialised but not, in general, in the direct experience and knowledge of pensioners themselves! Yet, whilst commodification and commodity forms both form the basis for financialisation, the same cannot be said, or at least to the same degree, of what might be termed commodity calculation, in which some sort of monetary calculations are made in the absence of monetary exchange itself (in traditional academic terms, cost-benefit analysis for example). As with commodities and commodity form, the presence of commodity calculation is not itself financialisation, although often conceived as such when, notions, such as the neoliberalisation of this or that, are interpreted as its financialisation, not least in the university for example.[24] But, unlike the other two, commodity calculation is not capable of providing the basis for financialisation, as we have defined it at least, as there is no monetary exchange, nor flows of income, as such.

The benefits of approaching financialisation through a tight, i.e. narrow and precise, but abstract definition is that it allows for diversity of outcomes through the troika of commodity, commodity form and commodity calculation, distinguishing financialisation from its effects rather than reducing or, more exactly, expanding the former to the latter if financialisation is simply conceived of as the general, if multiple and diverse, presences and influences of monetary exchange and calculation.[25] In addition, apart from approaching financialisation through such a troika, the intensive and extensive expansion

23 Significantly, the SoP/10Cs approach adopted here, see below, is capable of addressing how such wide-ranging systemic factors feed into the shifting cultures of what pensions are and what they mean.

24 See Engelen et al. (2014), Martin (2011) and Morrish and Sauntson (2013), and also Graeber (2014).

25 There is a sense in which this approach to financialisation parallels that to money, and the dispute – between Zelizer (1994, 1996, 1998 and 2000), on the one hand, and Fine and Lapavitsas (2000), Fine (2002a) and Lapavitsas (2003), on the other – over whether a general theory of money as opposed to a theory of multiple monies is appropriate. Inevitably,

of interest-bearing capital points to the increasing role of financialisation in economic and social reproduction and restructuring. This is, of course, a prominent theme in the political economy literature on financialisation, especially for the economic, with financialisation from a variety of perspectives generally and understandably seen as having deleterious effects on performance whether it be growth, employment, distribution or stability.[26] As a result, a tight definition of financialisation, wedded to the broader troika of commodification, commodity form and commodity calculation in the context of economic and social reproduction allows for considerable scope for interdisciplinarity as both the economic and social are straddled by such an approach.

This, however, also points to a further major issue that needs to be confronted by financialisation, once it is defined. If financialisation is to move beyond the acknowledgement of the greater presence and power of finance, it requires systemic understanding of the contemporary period. What are the dynamics of capitalism in the presence of financialisation and how do they differ from those that came before? In this respect, we have argued at great length that financialisation can be understood as underpinning neoliberalism understood as the current stage of capitalism, Fine et al. (2016a), and correspondingly influential over the neoliberalisation of everyday life. This is not to reduce neoliberalism to financialisation but to perceive the last thirty years as having witnessed considerable intervention on the part of the state to promote (the processes, interests, etc, associated with) financialisation. To some extent, it is precisely this systemic and dynamic significance of financialisation for contemporary capitalism that renders it, like globalisation and neoliberalism, so suitable for adoption by the social sciences in which it can sit comfortably across a variety of methods and disciplines despite, or even because of, a collective lack of coherences. The major, perverse, exception is mainstream economics, in contrast to heterodox political economy, for it is incapable of addressing the systemic and the historically dynamic. And, other than for mainstream economics, the nature of financial developments also legitimately allows contributions to the financialisation literature in general to be seen as positive and constructive even if they are confined to the descriptive since they will pinpoint some aspect of the influence of financialisation even if not grounded in a rigorous definition, lines of causation and configuration of mechanisms.

---

multiple monies means multiple financialisations and the tendency to see nothing common in diverse empirical outcomes.

26 The impact of financialisation on study of social reproduction, especially social policy, has been much more limited if not negligent, see Fine (2014).

Further, though, in locating financialisation in a systemic context, as observed, there is an equal need to address the issue of its diversity, not only in its content, forms and incidence but also in its impacts. Reference to the troika of commodification, commodity form and commodity calculation, and attachment of these to neoliberal economic and social reproduction, is to open not to close analyses. In this respect, for example, the renewal of interest in Polanyian double movement is welcome (Polanyi Levitt, 2001; and Dale, 2012) but limited, as the movements are not confined to finance, land and labour, nor is it a double movement between commodity and non-commodity forms but a multi-dimensional and differentiated set of movements across all economic and social reproduction, with corresponding resistances and contingent outcomes in circumstances, to coin another phrase, of everyday lives that those that live them do not make themselves and of which they may be only distantly conscious.

5 From Political Economy …

Interestingly, the presumption behind the Polanyian double movement is that there is a social reaction against economic (or commodification) consequences. This involves both economic effects (presumably unequal access to employment, finance or land, or the conditions attached to access) and ideological effects (that these 'commodities' are more than economic in terms of non-market criteria and ethos). Within the financialisation literature, there is much by way of bringing out these economic effects, especially where political economy is concerned (and its location across the social sciences). As summarised by Ashman and Fine (2013, pp. 156/7), quoting at length:[27]

> In brief, financialisation has involved: the phenomenal expansion of financial assets relative to real activity (by three times over the last thirty years); the proliferation of types of assets, from derivatives through to futures markets with a corresponding explosion of acronyms; the absolute and relative expansion of speculative as opposed to or at the expense of real investment; a shift in the balance of productive to financial imperatives within the private sector whether financial or not; increasing inequality in income arising out of weight of financial rewards; consumer-led booms based on credit; the penetration of finance into ever more

27 Unfortunately, more than repeating what is already to be found in Chapter 2.

> areas of economic and social life such as pensions, education, health, and provision of economic and social infrastructure; the emergence of a neoliberal culture of reliance upon markets and private capital and corresponding anti-statism despite the extent to which the rewards to private finance have in part derived from state finance itself. Financialisation is also associated with the continued role of the US dollar as world money despite, at least in the global crisis of the noughties, its deficits in trade, capital account, the fiscus, and consumer spending, and minimal rates of interest.
>
> And, however financialisation is defined, its consequences have been perceived to be: reductions in overall levels and efficacy of real investment as financial instruments and activities expand at its expense even if excessive investment does take place in particular sectors at particular times (as with the dotcom bubble of a decade ago); prioritising shareholder value, or financial worth, over other economic and social values; pushing of policies towards conservatism and commercialisation in all respects; extending influence of finance more broadly, both directly and indirectly, over economic *and* social policy; placing more aspects of economic and social life at the risk of volatility from financial instability and, conversely, places the economy and social life at risk of crisis from triggers within particular markets (as with the food and energy crises that preceded the financial crisis). Whilst, then, financialisation is a single word, it is attached to a wide variety of different forms and effects of finance with the USA and the UK to the fore. And, even if exposed in acute form by the crisis, its expansion over the last few decades has been at the expense of the real economy despite otherwise extraordinarily favourable "fundamentals" for capitalism in terms of availability of new technologies, expansion and weakening of global and national labour forces, and the triumph of neoliberalism in political and policy arenas.

Such multi-faceted postures are part and parcel of the way in which the amorphous nature of financialisation has been addressed. But, whether directly or indirectly, it leads to two important conclusions. The first is that financialisation is differentiated across these various aspects by its degree and form of incidence, and by location, sector and socio-economic status. Just as not all productive capitals are financialised in the same way, to the same extent and with the same results, so not every household is mortgaged to the hilt and at the cusp of, or beyond, credit card abuse. In short, as already suggested, financialisation involves something much more complex than a single movement of commodification.

Second, by the same token, the Polanyian dual movement against commodification even, or especially, when it is underpinned by financialisation, is not a single movement either. Financialisation is only experienced primarily indirectly, or at a distance, through commodification, commodity form and commodity calculation. This does, however, tend to give rise to at least one uniform effect, and that is to locate the sources of power and knowledge over them away from those who experience their effects, as is most apparent in crises, austerity programmes and so on.

Such is hardly to suggest that crises have been absent previously irrespective of the presence and role of financial considerations which, nonetheless, tend to weigh heavy as with the Great Depression of the 1930s. Rather, it is to observe that, especially in the context of neoliberal authoritarianism (which is based to a large degree on centralisation of authority in control of resources and policy but decentralisation of responsibility whether through the market or otherwise), financialisation is associated with limitations on democratic participation in decision making either by shifting or constraining the policy process (with privatisation of public services a prime example).

6 ... through Material Culture and the SoP/10Cs Approach ...

Once again, though, the degree to which and the form in which such developments have occurred is uneven (or differentiated, or variegated, take your pick) although there are general factors of considerable importance such as the decline in strength, organisation and representation of labour movements, the role of 'independent' central banks in making 'monetary' policy, and the increasing significance of public and private supranational organisations such as the World Bank and the World Economic Forum. As laid out in Fine (2016b), this has meant the decline and transformation in the presence of (the potential for) social compacting or social consensus[28] but the shifting balance and nature of the exercise of power in policymaking is multi-faceted and extensive in the wake of neoliberalised financialisation, that goes far beyond the demise of Keynesian-type post-war settlement-making.[29] Thus, for example, Binderkrantz et al. (2015) point to the increasing coincidence of corporate power across government, other institutions and the media.

28 A similar transformation in the developmental state paradigm is also observed.

29 Indeed, Fine et al. (2016a) argue that it is inappropriate to see neoliberalism as departure from Keynesianism as opposed to a period of capitalism with its own features.

As already repeatedly emphasised, these considerations are highly differentiated in incidence and impact, raising the issue for scholarship of how to operationalise corresponding general insights at the level of more detailed research. In the Fessud work on housing and water, but also more generally, the method adopted to allow for such diversity has been the systems of provision, SoP, approach, which sees the economy as constituted by overlapping, (commodity-specific) systems of provision. These SoPs are defined in terms of the structures, agents, processes and relations that characterise the entire chain of provision underpinning particular commodities. The operation of a SoP is shaped by multiple factors – social, political, economic, geographic and historical – and in turn gives rise to distinct, commodity-specific cultures of consumption, the pattern of practices, ideas and meanings that shape patterns of consumption. For the SoP approach, then, Bayliss et al. (2013, p. 1) suggest:[30]

> The material properties of a good or service fundamentally affect consumption patterns (for example water has different material attributes from housing) and goods and services are imbued (often subtly) with cultural significance. ... For the narrowly-defined physical characteristics attached to provision, and consumption, are necessarily culturally endowed in the widest sense. Such cultural content is also subject to wider considerations that range far beyond the immediate provision of the good itself (such as gender, class and nationality). Each SoP needs to be addressed by reference to the material and cultural specificities that take account of the whole chain of activity, bringing together production, distribution, access, and the nature and influence of the conditions under which these occur.

Use of the SoP approach allowed for investigation of the role and impact of finance and financialisation on housing and water (Bayliss et al. 2013; Bayliss, 2014; and Robertson, 2014). By locating finance within the integrated chains of provision of these two commodities, it was possible to reveal how both have been restructured along the chain of provision by the expanded and transformed presence of finance.

The SoP approach has also been extended to examine corresponding material cultures of consumption – by which we intend the desires, meanings and

30 The SoP approach first appeared in print in Fine and Leopold (1990) in debating the putative UK Consumer Revolution of the eighteenth century. It was fully laid out in Fine and Leopold (1993) but, for a retrospective account, see Fine (2013a), as well as other references cited here. More recently, see Bayliss and Fine (2021a).

practices to which the SoP is attached – through what is known as the 10Cs that have become part and parcel of the SoP approach to the material culture of consumption. The significance of such material culture is that it frames how forms and levels of provision are received and, as a consequence, accepted or challenged with potential for influencing policy and the directions of change. The 10Cs are made up of the following components: Constructed, Construed, Conforming, Commodified, Contextual, Contradictory, Closed, Contested, Collective, and Chaotic. This complex characterisation of consumption cultures, across at least these ten dimensions, mitigates against any tendency to exaggerate the extent of financialisation's cultural hegemony by drawing attention to agents' capacities for reflection and resistance, as well as the multi-faceted influences on their subjectivities that derive from factors more distant than acts of financing, purchasing and consuming. The 10Cs also facilitate a deconstruction of these influences, in discursive terms and in terms of economic and political power. In short, they present a holistic understanding of the multiple channels through which the Foucauldian governance of the financialisation of everyday life is maintained, in conjunction with any dissonances in how financialisation and its effects are practised and perceived.

Now, the SoP/10Cs approach can come together with the insights gained from distinguishing between financialisation as such and its consequences through commodification, commodity form and commodity calculation. For the material culture of financialisation is associated with pressing for commodity calculation to be more pervasive, for it to lead to commodity form, and for commodity form to lead to commodification. None of this is, however, linear or guaranteed, and it is contradictory in that commodification at one point, housing for example, may condition or even lead to decommodification elsewhere (the hard to house, addressed through burgeoning housing benefit). Nonetheless, commodity calculation is necessarily (as logically) the most pervasive form through which financialisation is materially, and hence culturally, experienced since it is a pre-condition for both commodity form and commodification, and, in turn, for financialisation, although one or other or all of these can be far removed from the direct experience of everyday life and even more so in how it is interpreted/experienced.

Nor is the presence of commodity calculation unique to the era of financialisation and its material culture, as was recognised by Oscar Wilde's quip concerning the cynic knowing the price of everything and the value of nothing and, in more scholarly fashion, by Simmel's view not that every relation had become monetised in practice so much as in thought.[31] This is why, if we are to specify financialisation distinctively, it needs to be in terms such as the current period of capitalism, see above for its attachment to neoliberalism, and the tendency for economic and social reproduction to become incorporated into extensive and intensive forms of financialisation (and not just as the greater presence of an unstructured understanding of finance).

7 ... to Interdisciplinarity in Practice

In the previous sections, then, we have sought to define financialisation in a particular way and to prepare the ground for examining its incidence and its effects by carefully distinguishing financialisation as such from commodification, commodity form and commodity calculation. The latter have themselves been approached in the Fessud work through the SoP/10Cs framing, with a focus on the transformative impact of financialisation on households and everyday life. And, indeed, the expanded presence of finance in social reproduction, and the ways in which households have become increasingly embroiled in financial markets, have been extensively documented elsewhere (Langley, 2008; Montgomerie, 2009; Seabrooke, 2010; Brassett et al. 2010; Froud et al. 2002; and Pike and Pollard, 2010). Building on this work, our interest is in how the dominance of finance has taken root and manifested at a subjective level, and how it has in turn transformed agents' subjectivities, both reflecting the broad material transformations previously delineated and how they constrain and influence how they are perceived and acted upon. For Marron (2013, p. 787):

> With the growth of what is termed 'financialisation', the widening breadth and scope of financial markets has [sic] been inherently bound up in transformations in terms of how individuals live their lives: their habits and reflexive choices, their modalities of self-discipline and their subjectivities.

As should be apparent, the SoP/10Cs approach, whilst rooted in political economy and its use and application across the social sciences, also engages with interdisciplinarity more broadly through its interrogation of the

31 See Simmel's *The Philosophy of Money* (1978), published in 1900, and commentary by Dodd (1994), and also in Gronow (1997) and Fine (2002a).

financialisation of everyday life. For the multiple forms taken by households' engagement with financial markets are explored alongside the often contradictory formation of the subjectivities that underpin these material practices (Froud et al. 2007). This means attending to how the needs, ideas and meanings attached to finance have facilitated finance's encroachment into everyday life, and the transformative implications for people's lives and self-understandings. The goal is to begin to grasp, on the one hand, "the way in which financial risk, metrics and practices have become bound up with and normalised through everyday activities such as buying or improving a home; learning and obtaining skills; having children and providing for old age" (Christopherson et al. 2013, p. 354) and, on the other, the structures and configurations of economic, political, and cultural power that underpin this normalisation.

As Christopherson et al. rightly note, p. 354:

> An acceptance of the relationship of financial processes to changing subjectivities and understanding of the self and society contravenes conventional beliefs about the economy as a separate sphere and personhood as fixed over time in relation to changing economic roles, practices and expectations (see Pollard, 2013). Instead, it emphasises a broader anthropological conception of economic activity as encompassing a 'way of life' that is mutable and socially structured.

Accordingly, the Fessud work more generally is situated within, and contributes to, the 'cultural turn' in political economy, which rejects old binaries, Polanyian or otherwise, in favour of the hybridisation of culture and economy and of use value and exchange value (Barnes, 2004). This reorientation is motivated by the recognition that culture is rooted in the material world, "[c]ulture exists neither in our minds, nor does it exist independently in the world around us, but rather is an emergent property of the relationship between persons and things" (Graves-Brown, 2000, p. 4). Further, it is imperative to acknowledge in turn that economies are "formatted by discourses" (Montgomerie, 2009, p. 2), and hence that we need "cultural terms such as symbol, imaginary, and rationality ... to understand crucial economic processes" (Peet, 2000, p. 1213). Addressing culture's material foundation opens the door to comprehending the role of economic and political power in shaping financialised cultural forms, including, without being limited to, "the extent to which elite actors can sway public opinion and assist in the framing of incentive structures" (Seabrooke, 2010, p. 57). However, such considerations exist in conjunction with agents' capacities for reflection and resistance. These in turn focus attention on how dominant norms attain legitimacy and compliance in terms of

Foucauldian ideas of governmentality: in principle a legitimate social system can only function through "cumulative, individual acts of compliance or confidence" by non-elites towards those who seek to govern (Bendix, 1977, quoted in Seabrooke, 2010, p. 57; and see also Stanley, 2014).

The challenge for such a cultural political economy is how to pay due recognition to cultural specificity, the efficacy of cultural properties, agent reflexivity, and the co-constitution of subject and object, while "continu[ing] to emphasise the materiality of social relations and the constraints involved in processes that also operate behind the backs' of the relevant agents" (Jessop and Sum, 2001, p. 94). As is apparent from the Fessud case studies, the impact of financialisation is to strengthen and broaden the ethos of commodity calculation, through financial literacy, the media, the promotion of the homeowner and, perversely, through dichotomising it with an alter ego of financial exclusion or well-being independent of financial affairs. It is highly conducive to perceiving the economy, and ideologically promoted as such, as if a household, weighing economic and non-economic imperatives against one another but with Micawberite financial balance as the priority of both national and everyday life as opposed to provision independent of market logics (Stanley, 2014). Commodity calculation does its work by occupying the space of material culture and excluding other tenants, especially those associated with the ethos of collective and non-market forms of provision, lest it be for those who are not in and cannot be in the market. In short, as with capitalist commodity production more generally, territories are laid out by financialisation on which it does or does not prevail in economic and social reproduction. What goes on outside of its borders is complex and varied but far from independent of what goes on inside.

This is where the SoP/10Cs approach is intended to do its work. But a serious and obvious challenge, not explicitly addressed here,[32] in applying the SoP approach to the material culture of financialisation is how SoPs are to be defined and distinguished from one another. As Fine (2013b) notes financial services themselves are not a commodity in any straightforward sense.[33] While they include an array of (speculative) assets and (credit-related) services

32 But see Bayliss et al. (2013), and earlier SoP work, where this is taken to be an empirical, inductive issue in part subject to the research questions being addressed.

33 But note that the 10Cs approach can be adopted as a general approach to material culture, without necessarily being rooted in commodity production (from which it originated) or consumption as such as is apparent from its application to public provision and social policy (Fine, 2002a and 2014) and to topics such as identity (Fine, 2009b and c), and the ethics of economics (Fine, 2013c).

that are not readily categorised in terms of either consumption or production other than by inappropriately stretching the meanings of these terms, they are, nonetheless, subject to material practices in how they are constructed and accessed, and in how they have effects. There is, after all, a financial system that can itself be interpreted as a system of provision. This is the procedure adopted by Fine in dealing with the nature of the financial system as a whole, and how it impinges on everyday lives.[34]

Significantly, though, none of the Fessud case studies, focusing upon the material culture of the financialisation of everyday life, bears directly upon financialisation as the expansion of interest-bearing capital. This is because, as observed through the prism of commodification, commodity form and commodity calculation, such activities take place, to recoin a phrase, behind the backs, not only of 'consumers' but also even of many of the producers and commercial operatives as well, even though it is well-observed in the financialisation literature how extensive and important are the profits that derive from the financial arms of non-financial companies.

By virtue, then, of both the 'distance' of such financial operations from the nitty-gritty of everyday life and their intrinsic complexity,[35] the material culture of financialisation is far removed from direct 'knowledge' or experience of such activity and so, accordingly, is only engaged as such indirectly. But, as Fine closely argues, in light of the 10Cs and in parallel with the so-called diet paradox, such (lack of) knowledge is not primarily, and certainly not purely, a consequence of such distance. Indeed, our everyday knowledge of food, and its effects given obesity at epidemic proportions, is extensive and often, if ignored, knowable and known within everyday life, however much observed in the breach. The major difference with finance, intensified by financialisation, is that we not only are ignorant of its dynamic chaos but that, as such, it is systemically unknowable in its own way, with corresponding results filtering down to everyday lives, occasionally acutely in case of crisis just as chronically in the case of the diets of affluence.

The point, then, is not that the food, in contrast to the financial system is knowable – after all it has been subject to (unknowable) crises of its own from mad cow to horsegate – but that the nature of knowledge, and corresponding cultures, are specific to how food and finance are differentially organised

34 Fine draws the parallel for finance with food, For the latter, there are imperatives to eat (from the food industry) and to diet (from its industry) that correspond to those both to spend (on credit) and to save for finance.

35 Even testing the limits of academics, whose knowledge of the 'markets' often remains a black box (Poovey, 2015; and Christophers, 2015b).

and provided (which the SoP/10Cs approach seeks to address). In general, and hardly unsurprisingly, the way in which the unfillable gap in the financial knowledge of everyday life is accommodated is one that essentially turns a blind eye to its fundamental feature of systemic uncertainty,[36] either through individual reliance upon the practices and experiences of managing individual financial affairs or through addressing these more collectively as a form of Foucauldian governance.

This syndrome is beautifully illustrated by other Fessud studies (Bayliss et al. eds, 2017). Santos (2014), through a study of financial literacy programmes and their promotion through national and international bodies, argues that, despite their many contradictions, such programmes perform an ideological function of inculcating calculating and individualistic attitudes among individuals. Financial literacy programmes are specifically designed to insert the financial subject into a world in which the external environment is admittedly uncertain but in which the subject can get by if only gaining and applying the appropriate knowledge.[37]

Gabor and Brooks (2017)[38] trace the depoliticisation of the concept of financial exclusion through scholarly and policy discourses, and its post-crisis resurgence as a critical concept through an explicit tying of financial exclusion discourses to the Foucaldian production and maintenance of financialised subjectivities. Financial exclusion does acknowledge that systemically

36 And, of course, such blindness is food and drink to the treatment of finance in mainstream economics, not least with its efficient market hypothesis, and even if it is taken as critical point of departure with the notion, in what might be called the inefficient market hypothesis, that financial markets can be tamed, or their deleterious effects mitigated, by appropriate regulation or other state intervention.

37 Recent research has shown just how limited is financial literacy, even within the USA, the country leading the drive of financialisation. For Lusardi and Streeter (2023, p. 173) in the newly-established *Journal of Financial Literacy and Wellbeing*, reporting on three elementary questions about inflation and interest rates, "Less than 50% of the respondents know about interest rates and inflation, and fewer than 30% of the respondents got all three questions correct. Nearly 20% answered none of the questions right. More than half of the respondents indicated they did not know the answer to one or more questions, and nearly 10% did not know how to answer all three questions. These are alarming findings given the complex financial decisions that individuals must make." But they are even more alarming over economic and political decisions to be made on the role of the financial sector. See next but one footnote also.

38 Note, in the original, this was referenced as Gabor, D. (2015) "Financial Exclusion", Fessud Mimeo.

financial literacy might not be enough to get by but that the system can be rendered less dysfunctional with sufficient compensating and targeted support.[39]

As a further example, Boffo et al. (2013) offer a critique of the turn towards happiness economics as a metric of well-being for its failure to take into account cultural interferences in reported happiness. Well-being, they argue, and the myriad ways in which it has been affected by financialisation, can only be comprehended through the integrated study of how perceptions of needs and wants are constituted, and of how their satisfaction is facilitated or constrained. Measures of well-being proceed oblivious to the views that its subjects might have over the workings of the financial system, how it reduces their aspirations, and can allow for limited shifts in reports of happiness despite devastating reductions in standards of living.

Across each of these case studies from Work Package 5, if each for a different topic with correspondingly different aspects, there are common elements. One is how the individual is taken as starting point – for lessons in financial literacy, for support out of financial hardship, or for assessment of well-being, respectively. Another is how these starting points are not tied at all, or at most in the most superficial and erroneous fashion, to the systemic functioning of finance. All can be financially literate, all can be financially included, and happiness begins and ends at home irrespective of how it has been delivered there as long as it has been. In contrast, the SoP/10Cs approach directs attention to the material culture of financialisation in denying knowledge of the financial system (from the extent of government support to its iniquitous rewards through to its inability to be governed), in promoting financial exclusion as a condition of financial inclusion, and in reducing aspirations in reporting well-being.

The material cultures of financialisation do not, of course, pertain only to the financial system itself. The financialisation of everyday life has led finance to intersect more extensively with the other SoPs embroiled in social reproduction, reshaping the material practices and consumption cultures associated with those SoPs. The material cultures of financialisation must, therefore, be approached from the perspective of both the material culture of the financial system itself, and that of the material cultures created through the financialisation of other SoPs and other activities. Happer (2013) helps to bridge

39 I recall at a meeting to discuss food poverty, and how to negotiate credit card debt, a mainstream economist suggested as plenary speaker that it was simply a matter of present value discounting on compounded interest, to which a representative of the Citizen's Advice Bureau responded that those who come to it for help have no idea what compound interest is, such is their level of financial literacy, and they are just trying to get by from day to day.

these two perspectives by looking at the role of the media in shaping perceptions and understandings of the financial system, and explaining this role in terms of the structures underpinning the production and dispersion of information. She deploys the circuit of communication model to complement the SoP approach. She finds that reduced democratic accountability, a revolving door between the political, financial, and media sectors, and journalistic reliance on expert financial knowledge have all played their part in marginalising media narratives that are critical of financialisation and its effects. Moreover, precisely in the representation of finance and of the crisis in the media, in the absence of direct experience of its workings, the knowledge gap is filled by those experts and commentators who are generally heavily implicated in securing its interests, representing its views and precluding alternative forms of financial let alone economic and social organisation.

Similarly, Robertson (2014) in part offers an illustration of the role of the media in promoting, and condoning, financialisation through close attention to the way it has, in conjunction with government discourses and material advantages, promoted owner-occupation as the most favoured form of housing tenure. Robertson draws attention away from the financial system per se to look at the financialisation of the housing sector. Taking mortgage-facilitated owner-occupation as the defining feature of financialised housing provision, Robertson investigates how a desire for owner-occupation has been inculcated and normalised in the UK. The discursive reshaping of the meanings and perceptions attached to owner-occupation emerges as a key part of the story. The paper also exposes the roots of these normalising discourses in the economic and political power imbalances that are part and product of a financialised economy such as Britain's.

Thus, the financialisation of the housing SoP is located at a distance from those taking out mortgages. On the face of it, subject to terms and conditions, buying a house through a mortgage in the UK today is no different than in the previous 100 years or more even though what was primarily a system of not-for-profit building society provision has been displaced by for-profit banking provision. But, as Robertson shows, such shift in the forms of financial provision, even if located away from the borrower as such, has contributed to a profound shift in the UK in the material culture of housing towards one unambiguously favouring individual private homeownership (as well as this being underpinned by genuine advantages to those who achieve it against the marginalised forms or quality of alternative tenures). Moreover, although common to a greater or lesser extent across many countries, this shift is not reducible simply to the greater availability of mortgage finance but this in conjunction with the conditions of housing supply, including access to land, the role of the state and planning system, and the nature of the construction industry – reinforcing the virtues of approaching the material culture of (housing) finance through the prism of the SoP/10Cs approach.

Much the same is true in its own way of the Fessud pension work. The SoP/10Cs approach rejects the tradition of defining pension 'systems' in terms of the various forms taken by, and levels of, costs and benefits, important and shifting though these are. Instead, pension systems are understood in terms of economic and social reproduction (of the aged) in the broader contexts of both other forms of support (labour markets, the welfare state and social policy) and the ideological transformation of pension provision from an ethos of collective care to individualised financial responsibility (see Churchill, 2014; Saritas, 2014; and also above).

Similarly, the financialisation of water is located at some distance from the day-to-day engagement with consumers. As in housing (even if with shifts in the balance of tenure types), the way in which consumers access water has on the surface changed little in the past thirty years in England and Wales. Even the names of the water providers are largely the same. Yet this apparent continuity conceals a transformation in the underlying social relations. The provision of water, it transpires, has proven particularly well-suited to financialisation (through securitisation) with its stable and predictable revenue streams. Some private water companies have securitised future payments of water bills for decades into the future to raise funds (and corresponding debts) to boost shareholder returns. Notably, however, this outcome has only emerged in the case study of England and Wales where transformations in the troika of commodity form, commodity calculation and commodification are at their most advanced. In addition, a sympathetic regulatory environment has protected investor interests. In contrast, the other case studies have seen more muted financial transformations in the provision of water with the promotion of commodity form (payment of water bills), commodity calculation (for example, 'cost recovery' pricing) but stopping short of commodification (production for profit). In these locations, there has been little private sector involvement, and where privatisation has occurred, it takes the form of concession and lease contracts as opposed to the full divestiture carried out in England and Wales. And, unsurprisingly, each case exhibits its own specific features as SoPs which are neither directly financialised as such nor unaffected by financialisation.

The upshot of this attention to how other SoPs are affected by financialisation is three-fold. First, that there are multiple, competing, and contradictory pressures on material practices and cultures across commodities. Second, that, reflecting distributional and other inequalities, different agents and groups are differentially affected by financialisation. And, finally, that each of these features gives rise to limitations and, potentially, resistance to the financialisation of everyday life. All of this serves as a reminder that, "financialisation does not impose one new logic, but makes and remakes the world in complex ways" (Froud et al. 2007, p. 343).[40] This is precisely why the SoP and 10Cs approach offers some insight into material cultures attached to financialisation, why resistances have been so muted, and how this might become otherwise.

8 The Qualitative and Quantitative by Way of Conclusion

Within the study of consumption, the SoP/10Cs approach has a long history and record of mixing quantitative and qualitative methods. The organising frame for doing so is to focus upon 'norms of consumption'. But these are interpreted in a specific way in terms of standards of living that differ for each item of consumption by socio-economic and socio-cultural variables. In this light, the SoP/10Cs approach seeks: (a) to identify such norms, that is differentiated patterns of consumption for which quantitative analysis is clearly needed but informed by qualitative analysis in investigating what sorts of differentiation, why and how; (b) to explore how they are constructed and construed; and (c) to analyse how and why they change and, in the Fessud research, through the impact of financialisation (with each of (b) and (c) also integrating qualitative and quantitative analyses). In case of housing, for example, financialisation is associated with the promotion of mortgage-funded owner-occupation, with corresponding implications for unequal access to housing and the marginalisation of social housing. Once again, though, the extent and forms of provision are uneven (as well as role of private renting) as is the (policy) response to those who are excluded from owner-occupation as the preferred tenure form.

Not surprisingly, at least in part, one way of examining norms conceived as differentiated is through focusing on inequality. Another way is through those who are marginalised or excluded. In addition, the Fessud research has put forward the notion of 'variegated vulnerabilities'. For the forms and levels taken

40 And, in addition, it is crucial to avoid the two, increasingly clichéd, logics associated with financialisation: on the one hand, especially in the context of everyday life, the unemployed or low waged household, public service deprived and over-indebted on mortgage and credit cards desperately seeking to sustain norms of consumption, see Karacimen (2014) and Santos and Teles (2014); and, on the other hand, the fat cat financier responsible for low investment and growth, rising inequality and speculative crises. No doubt, these exist but they are in part misleading in understanding the nature, incidence, driving forces and consequences of financialisation, see Fine et al. (2016a).

by norms of provision have, with financialisation, been increasingly subject to commodification, commodity form, and commodity calculation. Whether through market or non-market forms of provision, especially with financial instabilities, crisis, recession and policies of austerity, provision has become increasingly volatile on top of structured disadvantages and inequalities. In the context of income inequality, Palma (2009) has shown dramatic increases in income of the share of the top 10% in most countries at the expense of the bottom 40%. On the basis of these data, he identifies neoliberal ideology as "the *art of* getting away with ... a remarkably asymmetric distributional outcome within a *democracy*", emphasis added. More generally, the neoliberal art of democracy might be conceived of as how to manage greater inequalities and variegated vulnerabilities across systems of provision in the wake of financialisation.

CHAPTER 4

Towards a Theoretical Framework for Assessing the Impact of Finance on Public Provision

Postscript as Personal Preamble

Although it appeared as a Working Paper relatively late in the Fessud programme, the chapter in the version reproduced here is marked by its having been primarily drafted at an early stage in the research, with at most minimal account taken of what had been done in the passage of time from the original to the final version – reference is made to case studies having been undertaken but results from them are notable for their absence.[1] Its purpose at the time of writing was manifold. To some degree, it offers an overview of the system of provision (SoP) approach, steered towards dealing with the impact of financialisation in the neoliberal context (especially of privatisation of public provision and its more general commercialisation). For this reason, it puts forward the notion of a *Public Sector* System of Provision (PSSoP) to highlight the extent to which the role of the public sector in provisioning is to be distinguished from what had previously been the main target of consumption studies, commodified provision for private consumption. Necessarily, even if it covers many if not all of the elements involved in the SoP approach, and seeks to integrate them into a framework for analysis, subsequent developments cannot be present, whether analytical or empirical, especially around the nature of neoliberalism and the consolidation of its third phase – see Chapter 1 for the details of the latest developments in the SoP approach and its place within Fessud research, and other chapters for more exposition and justification of its core elements.

Even more significant, for its character and content, is the purpose for which the chapter was written, alongside its timing. On the one hand, it is an exercise in persuasion, in general but especially for the researchers on the Fessud project who were not necessarily chosen for their commitment to the SoP approach, and may even have been antagonistic towards it in deference to

1 Inconsistently, the original is dated December, 2016 but refers to case studies that are to be completed in June, 2015. Results from the latter are spread across and unevenly incorporated into other chapters but, in the event, this chapter was acceptable as it was in its lack of reliance upon case studies.

 | DOI:10.1163/9789004706293_005

their own expertise in the case studies for which they were being engaged (for housing and water by country). On the other hand, it was not simply a matter of persuasion but of offering guidance to our researchers on how to do SoP studies given willingness to be guided (something that could not always be taken for granted).

In both of these regards, persuasion to come on board the SoP approach and how to row the boat, we had mixed success. More important, though, for the substance of this chapter, is that the case studies for England for housing and water had already made considerable progress. As a result, they could be referenced to illustrate the arguments being made in favour of the SoP approach and as a guidance on how to do SoP research (including emphasis on the fallacy of seeking a case study template in light of the contextual significance of SoPs by country and sector). All of these considerations are covered in its own way in the, slightly modified, abstract and preface to the piece as it ultimately appeared and which now follows.[2]

This chapter offers a framework for analysing public provisioning based on the system of provision approach that addresses the material and cultural specificities to take account of the whole chain of activity, bringing together production, distribution, access, and the nature and influence of the conditions under which these occur. Consumption is fundamentally affected by the material properties of a good or service, and the factors that shape cultural systems are grouped under 10 headings (known as the 10Cs). These interact with the elements of the chain of provision which are understood in terms of relations between agents, embedded in historically-evolved structures and processes. All of these elements combine to derive a SoP which is unique for a specific good or service in a particular location at a given time. Drawing on case studies from the UK, the chapter shows how finance is understood in the SoP framework in terms of relations between agents in the chain of delivery. The SoP approach embraces the messy, conflicting and contested arena of the real world and, thereby, opens the way for a more grounded interpretation of policy impact and outcomes.

Any paper on the theoretical framework for assessing the impact of finance on public provision is of potentially enormous scope, from grand theory (of the nature of contemporary capitalism and the state within it), through the macroeconomics of state expenditure, to the microeconomics of sectoral provision in terms of state versus market. It possibly ranges over public and

2 Ironically, the preface ends by suggesting the contribution is not ready for publication until the other case studies had been undertaken and incorporated. Judgement in retrospect differs.

private finance, as well as ethical and cultural considerations (politics and ideology), as determinants in public provision. And across economics, let alone other disciplines, there is a huge range of theoretical frameworks that can be brought to bear. Clearly, such a wide coverage is beyond this chapter, and we have needed to be selective.

In being so, we have been mindful of the overall programme of work attached to examining public provisioning (especially of housing and water) in light of financialisation. We have been guided by work already undertaken, and that yet to be delivered. In particular, as comparative studies of housing and water for five EU countries are to be undertaken, we have drawn upon the pilot studies that have already been undertaken for the UK and which were completed earlier than the others in order to act as a guide if not rigid framework for them. In addition, we have been able to benefit from other work on the material culture of financialisation and case studies of housing and pensions (as leading elements in personal finance underpinning well-being).

Through this and earlier work, it was already determined that a (public sector) system of provision, (PS)SOP approach would be adopted and developed in framing the relationship between finance (and financialisation) and public provision. In addition, this approach is highly inductive in content in the sense of not being atheoretical nor purely descriptive but in insisting that appropriate theory can only be fully developed in the context of attention to the specific public provision (and its relationship to finance) under consideration – in other words, our framing suggests no general theory should be applied to public provision (and finance). Possibly, this general, negative theoretical conclusion is the most important to be drawn as it leans against most other approaches which seek to take theory off the shelf and apply it to case studies.

To a large extent this negative conclusion on a general theory is reflected in the paper that follows, drawing on empirical illustration of the diversity of the content, form and factors in public provision. It is also, by the same token, a paper at an intermediate stage in the research programme since it denies that there is a linear process of developing the theory, which is then complete, and read to be applied. In contrast, we expect to refine the theory and framing in light of the fuller set of case studies once they are completed. And, whilst we have drawn upon the earlier work that has already been done on SoPs, we have not considered it appropriate to reproduce what has been done before as opposed to illustrate its significance through select topics and illustrations (privatisation and material culture for example).

As a result of all of these considerations, this chapter is not and cannot be either tightly structured or sequenced. It is 'bitty', developing and applying some aspects of the SoP approach without doing so fully in and of themselves nor comprehensively across all aspects. It is both work in progress and a guide and raw material for future work. It should be assessed as such and not seen as intended for publication prior to integration with work that has already been completed and the case studies that have yet to be carried out.

1 Introduction – Why Do We Need a New Theory?[3]

Private finance is making increasing inroads into the delivery of public services as privatisation, at one stage a radical policy, introduced tentatively into limited sectors, has now been repackaged to some degree as public-private partnerships (PPPs) and, across the world, has become core policy, adopted to varying degrees, implemented by governments, and promoted by international agencies. In the UK, the government spends about £187bn each year on goods and services and about half of this is allocated to contracting out services (NAO, 2013b). In Europe, countries are increasing the role of the private sector in essential services with the European Commission insisting on water privatisation in the indebted countries of Greece and Portugal. Elsewhere the World Bank's International Finance Corporation (IFC) is promoting greater private sector involvement in health and education as well as water and energy. Moreover, privatisation is increasingly a vessel for financialisation as elements of a previously public service become tradable assets and are, thereby, (potentially) incorporated into circuits of global (financialised) capital. Economic theory is as yet ill-equipped to deal with the multiple effects and interactions of such transitions which need to address privatisation, social policy and global trends.

Traditionally, welfare economics presents social policy as a response to market imperfections generating the need for social intervention and/or targeted, if possibly universal, support. Privatisation is supposed to increase efficiency because ownership brings profit from operations (and lower costs), ownership can be bought and sold, and the public sector tends to be staffed by self-interested bureaucrats.[4] In the parallel literature outside of welfare economics, Esping-Andersen and his followers have approached matters differently, seeking to organise the diverse approaches of different (nation) states to social policy into groupings of ideal types in the welfare regime approach (WRA).

3 Based on Fine and Bayliss (2016).

4 For critique of privatisation theory for its grounding in rational individuals operating in a world devoid of context and history, see Bayliss and Fine (eds) (2008) and Bayliss (2011) for example.

However, this has resulted in a burgeoning number of regimes and limited classificatory coherence as a result, especially across the different elements of social provision. In addition, the approach is static with limited explanatory scope or implications for how policy might be changed in light of the determination of welfare regime at a country level with underlying causal factors (Fine, 2014).

There are then considerable limitations in the theoretical literature when it comes to the growing permeation of public services by private finance, especially in light of a global context of considerable diversity of substance and forms of continuing public and relatively recent privatised provision. Significant issues are ignored or glossed over, especially those related to diversity of outcomes although these are often highlighted in specific case studies as conditioning factors. Health care, education and social care are hugely different fields and different again from water, housing and roads. Differences also emerge in the financing of welfare and public services and with the coverage (universal, means-tested or based on qualification criteria). What applies to one service or commodity may not apply to another or to the same one in a different country or at a different time.

Diversity also stems from the structures within which goods and services are embedded. Such structures may include neoliberalism, globalisation and financialisation which may impact differently across sectors as well as locations. Other factors, for example, the level of development, may have an impact on the level and effectiveness of public services – especially as the teleology of development as modernisation towards some form of welfare state has been rudely disturbed over the three decades of neoliberalism.

A further limitation of existing theoretical frameworks is that relations between agents are only superficially understood. For example, according to privatisation theory, the private firm is considered to be a single entity with managers, financiers and workers all potentially working harmoniously in the pursuit of greater efficiency in order to maximise profits, albeit subject to conflicting interests more or less efficiently resolved through market or non-market forms. But such theory tends to say relatively little about the contestation within the firm, whether over production itself or for the achievement of broader goals. Yet greater profits are achieved by lowering wages and increasing effort from, or deteriorating conditions of, the workforce. Such efficiency gains accrue to the owners and the impact is regressive (Shaoul, 2008). Originally, in the WRA, reference was made to the access to power, and the resources to deploy it, but these considerations have tended to fade in deference to identifying, rather than explaining, ideal types. This is despite a transformation in the way in which power and resources have been configured within neoliberalism in general and through financialisation in particular.

Finally, then, as just indicated but on a more general scale, the theoretical literature with regard to both privatisation and social policy is patchy in the way in which it deals with the rising impact of finance and emerging financialisation. The expansion of the neoliberal paradigm has been associated with a substantial increase in the scale and scope of the financial sector over the past thirty years, particularly in the UK and USA but with global reach. The impact has been varied but there are profound implications for the relationship between the state and the private sector, discussed below, and not least for public provision.

A theoretical framework, then, needs to be able to incorporate the diversity of social policy and public services which differ across sectors and locations and over time rendering each case unique. The risk is that little can be said beyond the fact that 'it's complicated'. However, it is essential both to address the nature and significance of underlying and general influences. These include the nature and influence of neoliberalism and globalisation and the role of financialisation in determining social policies both directly and indirectly. Further, as demonstrated in Fine (2014), these grand variables are not at all forces for homogenising social policies but are fundamental in bringing about their heterogeneity.

This chapter proposes an alternative theoretical approach from those already discussed, and others. It derives not from typologies or idealised states but takes the system of provision (SoP) as the frame of analysis. The SoP approach aims to provide an analytical theoretical framework that can be applied to different research questions to plug some of the gaps outlined above. The SoP approach was developed in the 1990s and was originally devised as an alternative perspective to orthodox understandings of consumption, applied to food and clothing industries for example (Fine and Leopold, 1993). In contrast to neoclassical economic theory, where consumption patterns are assumed to derive from the aggregated decisions of rational, self-serving individuals, the SoP approach sees consumption as inherently linked to integral and distinct chains of provisioning (from production through to consumption) which, in turn, are shaped by many parameters including social, political, economic, geographical and historical factors (Bayliss et al. 2013) for a recent overview.

This chapter seeks to expand on the earlier SoP work to apply the framework to public consumption or public sector SoPs (PSSoPs). States vary in their functions and activities and a wide literature exists on what should be the role of the state, see below. Some states have privatised elements of services such as health and education and some aspects of infrastructure. Private sector pensions are increasingly widespread. This chapter focuses on the provision of basic goods and services for which the state has some or all responsibility (even though these may be provided by the private sector). This includes services such as: health, education and social care; utilities and infrastructure; and welfare as well as other areas that are traditionally the realm of the state but where the private sector is increasingly present such as security and defence.

The SoP approach is built on the premise that different services, goods and commodities are derived from different and diverse integral systems or chains of provision. The aim is to devise a framework for examining the provisioning and consumption of a service or commodity with reference to the mechanics of the system that provides it. The SoP approach offers considerable advantages over traditional approaches to consumer theory largely because it is firmly anchored in real world practices. To achieve this, requires recognition of the complexity and diversity of goods and of the societies in which they are consumed. By locating consumption in the context of a chain of processes and structures brought about by relations between agents, the SoP approach opens the way for a more grounded interpretation of policy impact/outcomes.

This chapter sets out something of the history of the SoP approach and its original applications. This provides a generic framework and raises key issues that need to be covered in SoP analyses. The chapter then turns to the specific research issue of the impact of finance on public provision. Two sections set the scene for the SoP approach in doing this. The first provides a brief discussion on the role of the state, drawing on different theoretical schools, and the second considers the role and nature of finance and the rise of financialisation. These themes are brought together in the following section on public sector systems of provision which highlights the distinctive contribution and innovative framing provided by the SoP approach. Moving more towards practical application, this is followed by an overview of material culture as applied to public services in general and privatisation in particular. This serves the dual purpose of both framing privatisation in terms of the SoP discourse instead of more traditional, orthodox approaches, as well as providing a practical example of the way that SoP analysis can be applied. Then comes an overview of some of the issues and questions to be addressed in framing a SoP analysis of the impact of private finance after which the final section concludes.

The SoP approach provides an innovative approach to a long-running research question which stems from the impact of privatisation on public services. While the focus is on the analytical framework, SoP is about real-world practical application. The chapter draws on examples, often from the UK and in particular from two case studies that have been undertaken using the SoP approach in the UK, one on housing (Robertson, 2014), and one on water (Bayliss, 2014). The chapter moves on from stale debates organised around state versus market that have been too crude and misplaced to address both diversity of outcome in practice and how that diversity is underpinned by the structures, agents, processes and relations involved. The SoP approach presented here aims to provide an alternative framework for understanding and interpreting the way in which states interact with private enterprise and finance. Possibly, one of the paper's most important conclusions is to acknowledge how analyses must be inductively engaged in order to address the diversities involved. This explains why the chapter engages both theoretically and empirically with its object rather than remaining at a theoretical level alone.

2 An Overview of the Systems of Provision Approach

As mentioned above, the SoP approach was originally devised in response to the limitations of consumption theory, rejecting the notion that different disciplinary perspectives on consumption (for example, from economics, sociology, psychology) can be collated to derive a general theory universally applicable to all goods as is often found, for example, in various forms across marketing studies. The SoP approach, in contrast, is built on a vertical analytical framework in which the study of consumption (and the consumer) is attached to distinct, and distinctly structured, systems that are commodity-specific. The premise of the application of the SoP framework to public consumption is the same. The way in which different public services are consumed is shaped by the way in which they are produced and distributed as well as by paying attention to their specific material cultures and how these interact with provisioning.

A system of provision (SoP) for a good[5] is understood as the integral unity of the economic and social factors that go into its creation and use. Each SoP is seen as distinct from, if interacting with, others and to vary significantly from one commodity (or commodity group) to another. The SoP approach, then, examines consumption in terms of commodity-specific chains of provision, appropriately acknowledged in popular discourse and understood as food, clothing, energy, housing systems, etc.

5 The SoP approach was initially applied specifically to commodities for private, commodity-provisioned consumption but it can equally, if mindfully, be carried over to non-commodity provision. In part, this can be justified by the 'mimetic' forms taken by non-commodity SoPs, especially in view of their location within capitalism and the greater or lesser pressures towards commodity forms and calculation.

The SoP approach was originally developed in detail by Fine and Leopold (1993) in a comprehensive response to the perceived failings of consumer theory across the social sciences. At one extreme, the orthodox approach to consumer studies has been built on neoclassical economics where the processes of production are assumed to be more or less "harmoniously and efficiently linked through the free play of the market mechanism" (Fine and Leopold, 1993, p. 20). Individual utility is both a determining explanatory factor and a desirable outcome giving rise to the idea of consumer sovereignty. Production systems are assumed to respond to the whims of consumers. For Fine and Leopold (1993, p. 20), according to orthodox theory:

> The system of production responds as a servant to the needs and wishes of consumers subject to the availability of resources. In this sense, consumption can be traced back from the individual, through exchange, to act as a determining moment upon production – even if allowance can also be made for distortions in efficiency and competitiveness along the way.

Neoclassical economics, then, conceives of reality as a departure from an idealised equilibrium (with deviations accounted for by monopoly, externalities, merit goods, etc). Essentially the starting point is a pro-market position, and specific goods are examined in terms of market imperfections. This approach is built on a raft of unrealistic assumptions, taking as its model the perfectly competitive industry, with well-informed consumers, and rigidly formed or inherited preferences and meanings of goods in and of themselves and to the consumer.

Within neoclassical economics, but at the other end of the spectrum from consumer sovereignty, are approaches where monopolistic producers predominate over consumers, not only through pricing but also through heavy reliance on manipulative advertising. Theories of consumption within mainstream economics have also been attached to Keynesian considerations of aggregate effective demand. In a way, though, this reflects a failing of more micro-oriented studies in which the understanding of consumption is generalised and universalised across different goods.

The other extreme in consumer theory, taken as critical point of departure by Fine and Leopold, was the exploding presence of postmodernism across the social sciences in general, other than economics in particular, and its overwhelming presence in an expanding field of consumer studies. Whilst for neoclassical economics, the subjectivity of the consumer has been tied to a mechanically-applied optimisation of a given utility function (across objects of consumption with given meanings), the postmodern consumer is subjectively capable of endless and unlimited reinvention of the objects of consumption and own identity. In this parallel universe to orthodox economics, reference to the material properties (and provisioning) of commodities tends to evaporate by giving way to deconstruction of the meaning of consumption to the consumer and the latter's own inventiveness.

Between, these two extremes, Fine and Leopold also found a common set of deficiencies across consumer theory more generally. First, the study of consumption had been heavily organised around a disciplinary division of labour to the extent that one or more 'horizontal' theories were applied within each discipline – utility theory for economics, semiotics for postmodernist study, emulation and distinction for sociology, and so on, usually with commodity-specific consumption taken as a universal and generalisable norm. It is no accident, for example, that the postmodernist invention of the deconstructing consumer should focus on the more fantastic as opposed to the more mundane items of consumption and those subject to heavy advertising or cultural prominence, the better to be able to appropriate exotic material to deconstruct. In formulating the SoP approach, the idea was rejected that these separate, generally mutually inconsistent (by method and concept), horizontal theories could be stacked to give a general theory universally applicable to all goods (although that is how consumer or marketing studies might be conceived with their appetite for combining different approaches for the practical purposes of selling goods or working out, however successfully, which marketing strategies might or do work and why). The SoP approach, in contrast, is built on a vertical analytical framework in which, as already indicated, the study of consumption (and the consumer) is attached to distinct, and distinctly structured, systems that are commodity-specific.

Second, then, it was recognised that the varieties of factors that make up the study of consumption across the social sciences could be integrated, if only inductively according to their weight of presence, mode of combination and specific (historical and social) context as well as incidence across society. There are, for example, different issues for consumption by reference to gender, not least in clothing, and the factor of fashion correspondingly has a different presence for men and for women. Further, the water system is different from the housing system by virtue of what is provided as well as by national and other contextual considerations. In this way, it follows, for example, that gendered consumption is itself SoP-specific in terms of how commodities are provided and perceived, with different and shifting gender content of consumption across commodities (from fashion to motor cars at opposite extreme of content and more mundane objects such as TVs being more gender-neutral).

Third, the approach initially drew some inspiration from the example of a particular SoP, the UK housing system as addressed by Michael Ball (1988 and 1990). His work from the mid-1980s took its point of departure from two aspects of the contemporary literature. On the one hand, there was a major preoccupation with the role of landed property in the housing system (drawing upon rent theory). On the other hand, the issue of forms of tenure was also extremely prominent. Ball persuasively argued that these issues needed to be located in relation not only to one another but also to the chain of activity running from access to landed property through the processes underpinning provision of, and access to, housing by consumers. Such an approach to the housing *system* suggested that other items of consumption should be similarly regarded as belonging to integral chains of activity that were specific to themselves. In this way, the conundrums associated with different disciplinary approaches to consumption could be resolved by attaching consumer theory to specific SoPs rather than overgeneralising horizontally across factors, such as gender for example (for which housing has no obvious and immediate bearing). By the same token, as already emphasised, each SoP takes on its own features in provision and culture to be discerned empirically.

Finally, the aim was to place emphasis upon *norms* of consumption. On the one hand, these involve not average but different levels or quality of consumption by socio-economic stratification. On the other hand, norms of consumption interact with the how as well as the what of provision, linking consumption (or living standards) to the SoP itself.

The approach is heavily inductive in application, leaving researchers to identify particular SoPs in practice. Given its inductive nature, the application of the SoP approach in practice is not simple, not least, for example, in identifying where one SoP begins and another ends (for the SoPs themselves and the object of inquiry). Indeed, there has been debate over whether the approach is legitimate at all given the interactions across different SoPs, whether within broader groups such as food systems as opposed to individualised sugar, meat and dairy systems. In a sense, this is to revisit the horizontal/vertical dualism in the study of consumption. This is itself acknowledged within the SoP approach by both seeking to identify integral forms of provisioning whilst also acknowledging that these interact with one another. SoPs also share common horizontal factors even if integrating them differently in extent and manner, at both national and international levels and across conditions such as equity and quality of provision, labour market conditions and macroeconomic impacts. Again, the example of gender is instructive but by no means unique as all manner of horizontal factors, such as socioeconomic status, affect and are affected (and effected by) SoPs in differentiated ways. Hence, as suggested, horizontal factors are different for different SoPs and so need to be examined within the framework of the SoP approach.

The SoP approach is also methodologically and theoretically open to a considerable degree although this does not mean that it is analytically neutral. Indeed, it definitely rejects many other approaches, not least where they are inconsistent with the SoP approach's more open stance (as against the universalising demand theory of mainstream economics for example). Finally, if to some extent easing rather than impeding application, the SoP approach allows for incorporation of other lesser comprehensive elaborations of production-consumption relations, in particular picking up and incorporating contributions that focus upon particular elements of the SoPs themselves. This might, though, involve transformation in the understanding of these elements in and of themselves and by virtue of locating them more broadly within the SoP approach (as with advertising for example and emphasis upon who advertises what and why and not just how as with semiotic treatments).

Significantly, the SoP approach was described over a decade ago by Leslie and Reimer (1999, p. 405) as "perhaps the most comprehensive elaboration of production-consumption relations", and has also been seen as one of the main approaches to the study of consumption, and cited as such in Jackson et al. (2004, p. 8). It has also been adopted in an OECD (2002, p. 8) study:[6]

> To analyse the key forces shaping consumption patterns, the report uses *the system of provision framework*. The systems of provision approach analyses consumption as an active process, with actors seeking certain lifestyles, and constructing their identity by selective consumption and practices. The 'systems of provision' is defined as the chain that unites particular systems of production with particular systems of consumption, focusing on the dynamics of the different actors (producers, distributors, retailers as well as consumers). In this light, it becomes clear that by the way governments design and transform energy, water and waste systems can either enable or obstruct household behaviour towards sustainable consumption.
>
> The *systems of provision* framework for understanding consumption patterns stresses the importance of exploring the mechanisms that shape everyday practices related to commodities and services and the extent to which they can be seen to support or impede sustainable consumption behaviour. In this light, household consumption is not the sum of

6 See Chapter 1 for the spread in use and application of the SoP approach.

> individual behavioural patterns, each consciously motivated and evaluated by the actor. Instead, household consumption is a whole set of behavioural practices that are common to other households ... They are social practices carried out by applying sets of rules and shared norms. They are also connected to production and distribution systems (technological and infrastructure network) that enable certain lifestyles that connect consumers to one another.

Such is an apt description of the SoP approach.

3 The Importance of Material Culture

More recently, especially in Fine (2002a) in an updating of Fine and Leopold (1993) to take account of subsequent developments in the field of consumer studies, the SoP approach has been influenced by, and responded to, the concept of material culture.[7] With reference to the study of consumption, material culture has emerged in response to the rise of neoliberalism and a corresponding waning of postmodernism in which discursive practices have become increasingly perceived to be a consequence of material circumstances (as well as giving rise to a proliferation and sequence of post-postmodernisms of various hues). As a consequence, the SoP approach has no longer sought to present itself in terms of departure from the two subjectivist extremes of rational choice and postmodernism but has focused on how to address the relationship between the material and culture in terms of the practices and meanings associated with consumption and the relationships between the two. It is not just the factors involved in the delivery of a service or the inputs into a good that constitute the SoP. Also relevant is the culture and meaning with which a good or commodity is associated, for both consumers and providers alike. Goods and services have cultural significance associated with modes of provision, as has been readily recognised in terms of the meanings of water contingent upon public or private delivery systems (which are themselves each subject to considerable variation).

Each SoP needs to be addressed by reference to the material and cultural specificities that take account of the whole chain of activity, bringing together production, distribution, access, and the nature and influence of the conditions under which these occur. The material properties of a good or service fundamentally affect consumption patterns (for example water has different

7 For more on the material culture of financialisation, see Fine (2013b).

material attributes than housing) and goods and services are imbued (often subtly) with cultural significance. For example, owner-occupied housing has different cultural meanings than privately rented tenures, and the narrowly defined physical characteristics attached to provision, and consumption, are necessarily culturally endowed in the widest sense. Such cultural content is also subject to wider considerations (such as gender, class and nationality) that range far beyond the immediate provision of the good itself.

A key example of the way in which our relationship with goods, services and commodities is culturally and socially dependent is demonstrated in the paradox of the recent parallel expansion of both unhealthy diets and healthy eating campaigns. This demonstrates that there is considerable complexity in the way in which information is translated into 'knowledge' and culture, and these in turn into behaviour. The provision of a good or a service, or of 'information' about it, does not necessarily mean these will be used as intended or anticipated. The SoP approach recognises that the cultural perceptions and identities of the users will be significant in the consumption and production processes, and these are heavily influenced if not rigidly determined by the material practices attached to the corresponding SoP.

The cultural content of a good is related not only to the material system of provision but also to wider cultural influences (again, reference can be made to gender, class and nationality, etc). Each SoP is attached to its own integral cultural system, and this cultural system derives content from each and every material aspect of the SoP. But consumers are reflexive and not passive recipients of culture. Nonetheless, the factors that shape cultural systems have been grouped by Fine (2013a) under ten headings (known as the 10Cs) and these interact with each other in complex and diverse ways as follows:

1. Constructed – the cultural systems attached to consumption are constructed in that they are influenced by the material practices of the SoP. Commodities have associated meanings for consumers, which may be variably responsive to what they know and experience of the chain of provision, and its distinctive material properties. These may also be subject to change and to manipulation (e.g. drinking a particular brand of bottled water may project a certain image as well as quenching one's thirst; buying a house in some locations may be a financial investment as well as a place to live).
2. Construed – objects of consumption are endowed with qualities construed by consumers. These can float free to a greater or lesser degree from the material properties of the objects themselves. The process of construal is influenced by a multiplicity of factors, and

these are derived from context. Sources of experience and knowledge are reacted to, or against, and imbued with meaning rather than simply received passively by the consumer.

3. Commodified – to greater or lesser degrees, cultures may be influenced by commodification even if the good is not. In the UK, even supposedly non-commodified services such as the health service may be understood in commodified terms with, for example, pressure for greater cost efficiency, or putatively non-commercialised aspects of a good used as a selling point (e.g. as good as home-made). The process of commodification serves to frame ways of thinking and interpreting what is consumed, including closing of certain cultures (as is explicitly recognised in notions of consumer society or consumerism as driving our consumption).
4. Conforming – regardless of what choices the consumer makes, meanings to them are influenced by the circumstances of provision, whether social as opposed to private housing is seen as a right or as a dependency for example. Commodity provision also, for example, tends to frame consumption in terms of market versus the state.
5. Contextual – cultures of consumption differ in time and place and what is consumed is not only located in specific circumstances (high or low price, good or bad quality) but these are associated with particular and variable meanings to the consumer (for example, an item of clothing may have different significance depending on the situation). One person's necessity may be another's luxury and, even for given consumption item, the distinctions may change over time, location and across income levels.
6. Contradictory – different agents and forces compete to give content to the cultural systems and these may provide a stimulus in opposite directions (e.g. compulsions to spend and to save; to eat and to diet).
7. Chaotic – material cultures draw together (or not) a multiplicity of practices and influences across a multiplicity of dimensions which are reflected on by households going about their daily life and so will be riddled with inconsistencies. This does not mean that there is no rationale but that these may differ and lead to tensions and unpredictable outcomes.
8. Closed – there is unequal participation in a SoP and unequal and differentiated roles in constructing cultures (for example: in the financial sector, while everyone may be involved, the process of intervention is both by, and for, an increasingly powerful financial elite with a corresponding loss of democratic accountability and

rise in inequality; and trade-marking standards, branding, regulations all shape cultures but only a select few are involved in their making).

9. Contested – different cultures of consumption may come into conflict for example with the Occupy movement or with global protests against privatisation of water. Contestation may also occur in terms of the conditions attached to the material practices along the SoP chain.
10. Collective – contestation is usually collective. While individuals may carry out acts of dissent, collective action is likely to be a more successful, unavoidable and enduring form of contestation.

The relevance and usefulness of the different Cs will vary depending on the type of good, the SoP and the reasons for which it is being investigated. For each SoP, consumption is, by virtue of material provision and material culture of consumption, differentiated in its own way in terms of socio-economic and socio-cultural characteristics. Patterns of consumption will be affected by gender, age, income level, location, occupation and (un)employment, race and ethnicity and so on, but in different ways and with different outcomes according to the specific SoP itself. As a result, the norms of consumption specific to each SoP need to be identified with a subsequent corresponding explanation for how these are reproduced or not.

4 Specifying SoPs in Practice

In principle, each SoP needs to be addressed by reference to the material and cultural specificities that take full account of the whole chain of activity, bringing together production, distribution (and access), and the nature and influence of the conditions under which these occur. Even at the level of empirical narrative, this leaves open some degree of ambiguity and choice. In part, this is because of the already indicated need to identify the scope of individual SoPs themselves. Thus, for example, private and public housing may not be integral with one another, as may be the case with private rented and owner-occupation, even though each will share some of their elements in common. Similarly, bottled and piped water will almost certainly be perceived as belonging to separate, if overlapping, SoPs. In addition, even if the SoP itself, and its elements, has been empirically identified, possibly uncontroversially, it is still open to be understood in very different ways both within and across disciplines, conceptualisations, methods and theories. Once again, the approach remains open in this respect (other than to approaches that are not open and especially if deterministic as with, for example, appeal to the optimising behaviour of individuals characteristic of mainstream economics). As a result, we draw freely upon standard ways of conceptualising and theorising across the social sciences by appeal to the following general, overlapping categories:

(i) *Structures* – broadly, this includes the historically-evolved and socially-specific institutional forms of provisioning, not least patterns of ownership, control and delivery. There may be structural divisions between public and private supply as well as demand, structures in access by price and quality, and so on.

(ii) *Processes* – each SoP is shaped by the interaction of the activities of labour and consumers, of service providers, of the state but also by wider processes such as commodification, decentralisation, globalisation, commercialisation and so on. It may be that a public sector structure of provision is subject to the process of privatisation so it is important to specify the dynamic of each SoP, how its structures and processes interact and may be in tension across and with one another.

(iii) *Agents/agencies* – SoPs are determined by the participants in the processes of production through to consumption. Incorporated are those who produce and those who consume but also wider bodies such as trade unions, consumer groups, regulators and those who affect delivery of finance, investment, technology and so on. Agencies reflect and interact with both structures and processes, again either reproducing or transforming in tension or conformity with one another.

(iv) *Relations* – structures, processes and agents/agencies are necessarily far from neutral, contingent upon who exercises power, and how, and with what purpose (and meaning to participants). So, the relations upon which (PS)SOPS are founded are differentiated by the roles of capital (or state as employer) and labour in production and other commercial (or non-commercial) operations through to the relational norms by social characteristics that are attached to levels and meanings of consumption. Significantly, the relations attached to, and underpinning, SoPs are crucial in understanding what and how conflicts arise and how they are or are not resolved.

Clearly, this is not the place to put forward a general framework for undertaking social theory although, at least implicitly, this is to some extent unavoidable. What we have sought to do, however, is to pincer the specification of SoPs between two ways of framing them. One is to follow the action, as it were, seeking to specify the chain of provision from production through to consumption at a more immediate empirical level. This approach also allows for a synthesis of the literature by locating what are often partial analyses (dealing with one or more aspects of the SoP alone) within the framing of the SoP as a whole. The other framing is to follow the chain of determinants across structures, processes, agencies and relations. Each of these aspects of analysis requires close attention both to the integral nature of the SoP and to its historical, social and material specificities (water is not housing). In addition, whilst we place emphasis on the integral nature of SoPs, we are also mindful that a focus can be placed on one particular element for closer analysis, either because it is of immediate concern and/or because it is particularly decisive in the functioning of the SoP itself, whether in promoting or obstructing delivery for example. And a particular focus is the purpose here, with respect to financialisation, with the presumption that the presence of finance will be differentiated across both national SoPs of the same type (the national water or housing systems) and the same SoPs across nations. And, whilst this is something to be explained by virtue of the SoPs taken as a whole, by the same token, the impact of financialisation will be differentiated, irrespective of the weight and form of its presence, dependent upon how it interacts within and on particular SoPs as a whole.

When it comes to practical application, the SoP framing does not offer a blueprint because by its nature, each SoP is different and specific. A SoP is, potentially, huge in analytical demands, if all aspects of material culture and production are connected to consumption. In practice, the way a SoP is identified depends on the research question at hand, and it is usually necessary to shine a spotlight on the elements of the SoP that are of particular relevance. For example, Ball's structures of provision approach originally served to argue that researchers interested in the incidence and impact of state subsidies on housing outcomes, especially distribution, needed to take account of considerations beyond tenure balance because the way that housing was provided determined the characteristics of different tenures. This is not the same as saying that *every* element in the chain of provision plus every relevant contextual or 'horizontal' factor needs to be thoroughly investigated before questions of subsidy and distribution can be addressed. The research framework needs to be narrowed down for practical application. In her investigation of housing and financialisation, Robertson (2014) identifies the relevant elements of the housing SoP. Some important wider elements of the SoP (such as housing associations, DIY, repair and maintenance, architecture) are not covered in her study because of the need to focus the analysis on the research question. Similarly looking at financialisation of water in England and Wales, Bayliss

(2014) focuses on interlinkages and distributional outcomes from modes of financing. Important components of the water SoP, such as river basin management, hydrology and climate change, are not addressed because they have lesser immediate relevance to the specific research interest.

5 PSSoPs and the Role of the State

Having outlined the broad principles of the SoP approach, we now turn to consider the specific application of the SoP approach to the role of finance in public services. To do so requires, first, consideration of what could or should be provided by way of public services, which leads to a deeper interrogation of underlying notions of the role of the state. Second, through this prism, this section looks at finance and financialisation, and how it is engaged in public provision in and of itself and as a more or less important determinant of the SoP or PSSoP. Does, for example, finance merely serve the funding of public service provision or have a profound effect on the provisioning processes themselves. This is addressed in more detail at the end of this section.

The SoP approach was originally devised as an alternative to theories of consumption that were entirely focused on private demand and supply although it was noted how traditional approaches tended to overlook public sector provision for individual or collective consumption. Effectively government provision tended to be seen as distinct from (private) consumption by being alternatively designated as social policy and/or as belonging to the welfare state. But such goods and services can also be understood as being attached to their own SoPs. A theory of social policy must accommodate a variety of structural determinants, how they interact across agencies, processes, relations and structures (and institutional forms) to give rise to a diversity of shifting outcomes. The conceptual gaps in consumption theory apply equally, if not more so, to provision within the public sector. Applying the SoP approach to modes of public provision gave rise to what Fine (2002a) has termed the public sector SoP or PSSoP approach.

The role of the states is both complex and diverse. While an extensive review of the literature on the role of the state is not possible here, some general themes can be highlighted. From a neoliberal perspective, states are at most required to respond to market failures that are generally deemed to be exceptional (and subject to cure worse than disease!). States do this (to varying degrees) by enforcing property rights, providing public goods and defining rents and raising taxation for social distribution, all of which is embedded in specific institutional structures. A successful state is deemed to be one that supports the market in delivering strong economic growth. Generally, however, states are considered to be constrained by diverse and opaque objectives as well as the utility-maximising interests of the individuals that attach themselves to its institutions broadly conceived. Accordingly, interventionist policies were subject to considerable criticism from the 1970s, particularly in the context of international development and the constraints imposed by tariff protection and financial controls. This gave rise to the notion of 'state failure' and calls for the role of the state to be limited to supporting market operations (Chang, 1999). The Washington Consensus (WC) emanating from the Bretton Woods institutions put forward a ten-point plan based around these themes (Williamson, 1990). Subsequent modifications, in the form of the post-Washington Consensus (PWC), brought adjustments to take account of market failures and externalities but the underlying principles were unchanged (for example, the World Bank 1997 World Development Report "The State in a Changing World").

Others, in contrast, see the state as essentially a means of defending the dominance of the capitalist class, and this may take different forms (capitalist, democratic, autocratic, etc). Jessop (2007) provides an overview of some of this literature, from Marx to Weber through to Miliband and Poulantzas. According to the Gramscian notion of cultural hegemony, the ruling class acts with the consent of the subordinated groups due to the cultural ethos that pervades society. In current conditions, and for the focus here on public provision, this raises issues of how the ruling class rules in the context of financialisation, with what substance and effects and how it reproduces legitimacy in doing so, especially in the wake of the Global Financial Crisis.

In terms of the appropriate functions of a state, the neoliberal perspective is of a minimalist state which facilitates the operation of a free market. State activities are limited to enforcing law and order and addressing the most serious market imperfections. The ideology of a free market suggests a neutral approach to policy in terms of interests but even to deliver the free market requires substantial state intervention. And such policy is far from neutral in relation to interests, as is most evident in labour legislation for example. In any case, in practice, neoliberalism relies heavily on extensive intervention. The state needs to set the rules for property rights, for labour laws, for regulation. But the state has a deeper significance. For welfare provision (and economic and social infrastructure more generally) is essential to social reproduction. Of course, this was acknowledged and targeted in the post-war boom and commitment to Keynesian/welfarism. Whilst the ideological thrust of neoliberalism is to withdraw such intervention, and to rely upon private capital and provision, the extent to which this has materialised in practice is extremely mixed and is caught on the dilemma of how to respond to the dysfunctions and inequities of neoliberalism itself, as is evidenced after the global crisis in the massive intervention in favour of a financial system putatively committed to free markets or at least deregulation. Such dilemmas extend beyond finance to public provision.

Alternative theories to neoliberalism inevitably suggest that states must play a major role in economic development. This was central to early theories of development economics. Chang (1999) cites Gerchenkron, Rosenstein-Rodan and others to show how states were considered crucial to industrialisation and economic transformation, and weakly interventionist states were contributors to underdevelopment. The Developmental State Paradigm (DSP) emerged in the 1980s as a major challenge to Washington Consensus (WC) orthodoxy drawing upon the success of the East Asian Newly Industrialising Countries (NICs) which had achieved success with extensive state intervention, especially in industrial policy, and explicit rejection of the policies of the WC.

The DSP has since been weakened by the crisis of the NICs themselves from 1997/8 as well as for other reasons (Fine et al. eds, 2013 for extensive discussion). Furthermore, there were limitations to the theory. It was narrowly focused on industrialisation and late industrialiser catch-up, and based on a state-market dichotomy. Other aspects of development were neglected. Class interests were confined to those of capitalists alone (in dealings with what was presumed to be the relatively autonomous state, or industrial ministry within it), and global developments were treated as external to the national structure and so were only considered in terms of how governments accessed trade, finance or technology, etc, and not in terms of the way in which the systemic functioning of the world economy is built on the integration of nation states. With the expansion of the range of explanatory factors used to explain the presence or not of developmental states, ranging across social, cultural, political and institutional factors, the DSP became so diluted as to lose meaning, especially when any single, specific example of developmental success attributed to government intervention (as opposed to wide-ranging developmental transformation) attracted the moniker of developmental state.

Studies of the state have also found it difficult to account for the great diversity observed. The Varieties of Capitalism (VoC) literature emerged in the 1990s to explain differences in types of capitalism and the role of institutions and national political economies and the extent to which they shape economic performance and social well-being (Hall and Soskice, eds, 2001). The approach is also constrained by its foundations in what might be termed methodological nationalism and, as with the WRA critically addressed above, marred by dependence upon ideal types that cannot accommodate the diversity within and between national economies, and see Jessop (2011) for a detailed critique that points to concessions of the WRA to neoliberalism.

What the DSP, VoC and WRA approaches all share in common are their deep roots in the conditions of the Keynesian/welfarism post-war boom irrespective of how well they capture that period. The ethos is to explain comparative economic performance in which the world economy, and most individual economies, are expanding as never before. This has a profound influence on how issues are framed, not least of course, in nostalgically seeking to reproduce the best facets, and performers, of that golden era. As a result, apart from the methodological nationalism already highlighted, there is a failure to address the global and systemic conditions and failures of the neoliberal era, as if these can simply be overcome by adopting policies other than those associated with neoliberalism (such as best practice Keynesian/welfarism). But that earlier era has been left behind together with its higher global levels of economic performance as particularly demonstrated by the global crisis. More specifically, these approaches have failed to acknowledge sufficiently what we have taken to be a defining feature of the neoliberal era, together with its influence on the role of the state and what policies might be possible and desirable. This is financialisation to which we now turn explicitly.

6 Financialisation[8]

Theories of the state have failed to address the extensive growth in financialisation witnessed in recent years. Relations between finance and the state have led to profound changes in the role of the state with implications for the delivery of public services. Financialisation is a broad term and different definitions have been proposed.[9] According to Epstein (2002, p. 1), "'Financialisation' refers to the increasing importance of financial markets, financial motives, financial institutions, and financial elites in the operation of the economy and its governing institutions, both at the national and international levels." For Palley (2007), similarly, financialisation is a process whereby financial markets, financial institutions, and financial elites gain greater influence over economic policy and economic outcomes. Others perceive financialisation in terms of a shift of emphasis and power from the 'real' to the 'financial' economy (Stockhammer, 2010; and Rossman and Greenfield, 2006) and where profits

8 See also Fine (2013b and 2013–14).

9 The following paragraphs draw on earlier work on this subject covered in Bayliss (2013).

accrue through financial channels rather than trade and commodity production (Krippner, 2005).

Financialisation can be observed in the escalation of activity on financial markets compared with real economic activity. For example, the financial sector's share of corporate profits has doubled since the 1980s; the stock of global financial assets has increased ninefold in real terms from 1980 to 2007 (Palma, 2009), three times faster than global GDP. Financialisation has led to an increase in the number of non-financial firms that are owned by the financial sector. These shareholdings have become assets that are traded, with ownership changing hands according to financial market indicators without a basis in real production, productivity, or jobs. This has the effect of financialising non-financial activities from health care to provision for old age. Privatisation, in the context of financialisation, has transformed the supply of welfare services into private assets, from the sale of social housing in the UK to the privatisation of water. The result is that provision is subject to the vagaries of stockholder and asset value, which has encouraged speculation, sell-offs, and subcontracting at the expense of direct production.

Financialisation is associated with increased inequality. Rentier incomes (interest, dividends, and capital gains) and financial sector bonuses have increased while wage shares have fallen. The fall in the labour share of income reflects a shift in the balance of power between capital and labour (Stockhammer, 2010; and Rodriguez and Jayadev, 2010). Managers, judged by the stock price, increasingly prioritise shareholder value, and the maximisation of return on equity overrides other objectives. Stock options have been used to align the interests of managers with those of shareholders (Rossman and Greenfield, 2006). As Epstein (2002, p. 6) puts it, financialisation has "magnified their rentier motivations". Non-financial companies have an incentive to trade in financial products rather than to produce goods and services. Overall, the effect is to withdraw capital from production and divert it towards financial markets (Krippner, 2005) with a negative effect on (real) investment.

The state has played a key role in supporting the flourishing of finance and has allowed the emergence of the financial rentier class with policies that are in their interests such as prioritising low inflation, the promotion of anti-union legislation, and financial deregulation (Jayadev and Epstein, 2007). Financial agencies are also proactive in trying to shape policy in favourable directions, as is most obviously demonstrated by the aggressive promotion of owner-occupation and mortgages by the US subprime mortgage lenders. Revolving doors between private finance and government positions have supported the position of finance in government. Finance has become so complicated that governments rely on the 'big four' accounting firms to help them design policy, further cementing the position of the financial sector at the heart of the state.

The recent economic crisis has further supported the rentiers according to Palma (2009) with minimal demands on big business in return for the state supporting this financial elite. Despite the role of the financial sector in causing the crisis, financial firms have recovered remarkably unscathed (apart from a few significant casualties). The emphasis has been on protecting shareholder value while losses are socialised. Public attention has focused on government spending as if it this is the cause of the crisis. Following this logic, social spending has been depicted as "unaffordable and burdensome" (Ortiz and Cummins, 2013, p. 11). Austerity measures have been the result.

Austerity policies have had devastating effects in some countries as, for example, cuts in health expenditure have crippled service provision. While government spending contracted in many affected countries, there were increases in household expenditure and health care services covered by private insurance. Public contraction has led to an increase in private financing of health services (Morgan and Astolfi, 2013). This has been the case in other sectors where the government's fiscal position has been constrained (after bailing out the financial sector) leading to a perceived need for more private investment in economic and social infrastructure. However, privatisation does not bring finance in and of itself. Any funds provided by the private sector need to be repaid (with a profit margin) out of payments by end users and/or taxpayers. But privatisation is attractive as a means of financing infrastructure when there are severe constraints on government spending, and this has been magnified since the financial crisis. Thus, the financial crisis has led to calls for greater involvement of private finance in areas of public consumption despite its catalytic role in the recession. Those that caused the problems are now being assigned the task of fixing them,[10] suggesting that alliances between states and finance capital are stronger than ever. This theme is picked up in more detail below.

---

10 This applies in other privatisation cases. For example, in the UK, several regional health providers are in financial difficulties, in large part due to payments to private providers for infrastructure services under concession arrangements with them. The response has been to increase franchising of services to the private sector to help these providers in managing their finances (NAO, 2012b).

7 From PSSoPs ...

As mentioned above, theories of the state and social policy have been oriented around two broad framings, either a regimes approach (WRA and VoC) or the new welfare economics (market imperfections). Aside from other weaknesses, both of these framings are limited in the way they unduly homogenise over contextually-specific policies and practices that are differentiated by programme and country. This is so whether by appeal to ill-fitting ideal types of welfare regimes or more or less efficient incorporation of marginalised if optimising individuals into a situation of one type of market imperfection or another. Moreover, both implicitly eschew earlier political economy approaches to social policy and the welfare state that locate them in terms of the contradictory tensions between economic and social reproduction.

In contrast to other theories, for the PSSoP approach, there is not necessarily any grand theory of the state or ideal-type states. The aim of SoP is to highlight diversity rather than to squeeze different structures into regime-shaped boxes. SoP studies are oriented towards specific chains of provision. The state is disaggregated into its different elements which are understood in their specific context in terms of the relations between agents. The SoP approach takes a systemic view. The origins and outcomes of policies are considered to be context-specific and part of a linked process. States consist of many layers from the administrative to the political and includes the formal legal framework and informal social norms. The role of the state will vary across countries and across sectors although some cross-cutting themes are present, if unevenly so, not least financialisation. Outcomes from state activities reflect social and political priorities as well as the bargaining strengths of different groups. While there are global structures and processes, the specific impact will be contextual.

The state can be involved in varieties of ways along the chain of provision, reflecting both material and cultural, including political, factors. These have been expressed traditionally in terms of factors such as aspirations for universal coverage (as with health, education and housing) or as a response to market imperfections whether as externalities or economies of scale and scope. For many PSSoPs with the objective of universal access or provision, there are significant issues of production *and* distribution, with corresponding issues of spatial differentiation in provision whether for water or housing, for example, with corresponding interactions with other elements of social construction of space in light of standards of public and private provision of social and economic amenities.

While broad trends are observable, there is considerable diversity across PSSoPs. Housing is different from education, for example, so that different principles and issues in delivery will arise. The essence of the approach is that each element of the SoP is attached to an integral and distinctive system – the health system, the education system and so on. Recognising diversity allows greater understanding of the issues which are historically-specific and depend on comparative location. As mentioned above, mainstream economics tends to take a market-oriented stance and interprets decisions as to the respective roles of the public and private sectors in terms of market and state failures. So, for example, externalities may require state regulation. However, the nature of such 'failures' is sector-specific and requires a deconstruction of the nature and attributes of a good or service within its context.

As with SoPs, consumption from PSSoPs is also differentiated by socio-economic and socio-cultural characteristics that cannot be determined in advance in terms of which of these characteristics are liable to be salient. They can range over gender, age, income level, location, occupation and (un)employment, race and ethnicity and so on. As a result, the norms of consumption specific to each (PS)SoP need to be identified, with a subsequent corresponding explanation for how these are reproduced or transformed, and the differentiated meaning to which consumption norms are attached. Thus, there is not only differentiation in access to, and quality of, housing by forms of tenure but also the meaning of housing to occupants is different, and potentially changing, across and within these forms of tenure. On the other hand, in case of water, it is the greater degree of homogeneity in access and quality (if not always use) of public supplies that provides the basis for privatised forms of bottled water as a form of consumption distinctive from that of the tap.

The PSSoP approach provides an appropriate mix of the general and the specific. It can focus on specific details such as the link between housing and finance (inevitably this is incorporated), but necessarily sets these in context of the SoP as a whole. At the other end of the scale the SoP approach is inductive and avoids abstract universal principles or posturing (as for example would be characteristic of a focus on market imperfections) as the aim is to recognise the difference between systems for different goods and services – the way water is provided, and the nature of provision, is very different from housing or health, for example, in what it means, as well as in how and to whom it is provided and the interactions between these, see next Section. In terms of policy, the SoP approach allows for much clearer specification of objectives and the paths by which these should be achieved. A systemic analysis of the chain of provision signals where provision is impeded or dysfunctional, and why and how it might be remedied.

8 … to a Material Culture of Public Services

The 10Cs introduced above were devised in relation to (private) consumption studies but can be applied equally to public consumption. Each aspect of service delivery has its own culture (of consumption). Rather than assuming that individuals are rational utility-maximisers operating in a vacuum, the SoP approach suggests that consumption is shaped by the nature of the provisioning of the good in question and the consumer. As a result, when it comes to devising a framework for analysing public provision of goods and services the possible permutations and combinations for outcomes are extensive. An off-the-shelf blueprint approach is impossible. Hence this chapter looks inductively at the stages and the processes by which one might devise a comprehensive analytical framework for addressing public provision rather than a universally applicable structure.

The SoP approach requires an assessment of the material culture and the way in which it impacts on the chain of production and consumption. In contrast to orthodox economics, the SoP approach does not take a set of preferences as given but seeks to determine the ways in which cultures of consumption emerge and change over time. Once it is recognised that there is great diversity in the way that services are provided and consumed, ideal-type construction has limited use.

Taking, for example, the case of housing in the UK, Robertson (2014) shows how preferences for owner-occupation, as compared with other forms of housing tenure, have changed over time. She attributes this to a range of factors including the decline in quality and availability of other tenure types and to changes in use values, as housing has become a financial asset as well as a form of shelter. In addition, successive governments have shaped cultures of consumption in the portrayal of homeownership as the tenure of choice for hardworking citizens. This contrasts to a mainstream economics in which there would be indifference between different types of housing tenure, subject to (imputed) rental cost, itself subject to 'market imperfections' in housing markets themselves or those related to housing markets (most obviously finance, but also transport, labour markets, schooling and so on, i.e. more or less everything of major importance to consumers!).

For water, there are material attributes that affect the way in which it is produced and consumed. It is heavy to transport and, therefore, tends to be used close to source. It is transported by pipes and pumps, and duplication is costly, with limited substitutability (aside from bottled water, no good for washing) so delivery is inherently monopolistic. It is essential for life and so there is a strong social element in sector policy. While in developed countries water is largely homogenous, cultural associations around water vary across societies and across different types of consumers within households to agricultural producers, and will depend on the level of scarcity. Water, then, has a unique material culture that is specific in time and location (Bayliss, 2014).

Components of welfare have their own material culture stemming from different elements of the 10Cs listed above, and these will be different across sectors. The material culture of education will be different from that of, say, physical infrastructures such as transport. Even within sectors, material culture will vary, for example, across different elements of health care (e.g. heart surgery as opposed to vaccinations), or for nursery as opposed to university education.

The introduction of private finance into the delivery of traditionally publicly provided services brings about fundamental changes in the PSSoPs. Finance – and financiers – needs to be located in the chain of provision. The extent and impact of private finance derives in part from the inherent characteristics of the service in question. Some elements of private provision of health and education have long co-existed alongside state provision in most countries although the relative weight attached to each varies across locations and over time. Thus, housing has been extensively provided by the private sector and even more so in the wake of reductions in social housing in the UK and elsewhere. In contrast, while the private provision of policing has emerged to some degree in the use of private security firms for personal or business protection, on the whole, policing remains in the public domain. So, some sectors have seen more privatisation than others. Some countries have privatised more than others. Privatisation itself can be considered to have its own material culture.

9 Material Culture of Privatisation

The diversity in the extent of privatisation across sectors, locations and over time indicates that the reasons for privatising (or not) derive not from empirical observation or theoretical analysis but rather are based on other factors such as the thresholds of political acceptability of the reaches of private capital as well as the appetite for particular investments on the part of the private sector. Privatisation is rooted in politics and often continues even when there is clear evidence of adverse impacts. In this way, privatisation can be considered to have its own material culture. This is explored below with reference to the 10Cs outlined above. These are not in any particular order and the relative significance of each C will vary across sectors and research questions.

First, it has been made clear in the above discussion that the material culture of privatisation is *Contextual* varying substantially across locations and over time. Some countries such as the UK, have privatised more than others. Privatisation in the so-called transition economies played out in a different way from privatisation in developing countries. Parker and Saal (2003) compile an extensive collection of case studies and conclude that results are mixed. The extent of what is deemed privatisable changes over time. For example, in the UK, the postal service was sold off in 2013, a step which was considered unacceptable a few years earlier. And there would also appear to be creeping privatisation of the health service through enforced or induced subcontracting.

Second, support for privatisation is *Constructed* in part through preparation of public entities for privatisation (through commercialisation) but also through external pressures and considerations. Going back to the Thatcher government in the UK in the early 1980s, privatisation was a political initiative with economic theory added later, see, for example, Kay and Thompson's (1986) *Economic Journal* paper entitled *Privatisation: a Policy in Search of a Rationale*. The original privatisation programme in the UK was in large part driven by a move to improve the government balance sheet with a shift to off-balance sheet financing. Political objectives were to weaken trade unions and to promote popular capitalism with wider shareownership and the right to buy council housing. The economic rationale came later.

More recently, the need for private finance is constructed in the terms and practice of policy. For example, deficiencies in infrastructure around the world are described as reflecting a 'financing gap', a term applied across public services from infrastructure to health provision which condenses all the complexities of service delivery down to the need for finance. And in the context of tight government budgets, itself a matter of policy and priorities and not of necessity, the obvious implication is that there is a need for private in the (constructed absence of public) finance. This can be so even though reliance upon private finance and participation can be more expensive than providing finance through the public sector directly, see next.

The way in which the culture of privatisation is constructed is also demonstrated in evaluation processes. According to the UK's National Audit Office (NAO, 2013a), the methodology used to evaluate private concessions ex ante is biased in favour of the private sector. Use is made of a "public sector comparator" which does not use the relatively cheap cost of government borrowing but instead uses a considerably higher "social time preference rate". This inflates the comparative public sector cost. Furthermore, public sector procurement costs are assumed to be front-loaded compared with the annual unitary costs of a private project. Again, this biases evaluation in favour of private outcomes.

The Treasury does not consider comparison with the cost of government borrowing (as is the approach used in the USA) to be appropriate because this is related to wider issues of fiscal policy. When the NAO reworked the VfM, Value for Money, calculations for six PFIs, private finance initiative, projects they found that in five of them, once these assumptions were changed, private costs were found to be higher than those of government procurement. According to Shaoul (2008, p. 9), "it is therefore difficult to avoid the conclusion that the government designed a system of appraisal that would provide a public justification for its policy of using private capital in public services".

Austerity measures are also used to justify cutting public finance, thereby increasing the space for private finance. As Uppenberg et al. (2011, p. 7) put it, "perhaps the decisive factor for a growing private role in financing and operating infrastructure has been the fiscal constraints facing governments, even though the actual economic case for this is weak."

Third, polemical debates continue to plague the cases for both public and private provision according to how privatisation is *Construed*. For privatisation to continue, it is essential to perpetuate a discourse that denigrates the state and promotes private capital. There are cultural associations attached to privatisation and private services (although the empirical foundations for these are weak). The private sector is associated with efficiency and dynamism while the state is often considered to be lumbering and bureaucratic. Private education is more attractive when state schools are seen to have lower attainment levels. Private health care is boosted by media stories of inefficiency and incompetence in the UK's National Health Service. Private health care and education have different cultural associations from those provided by the state, and these distinctions will vary across locations and over time. They can become self-perpetuating as the more that is (cherry-)picked up by the private sector, the more the state is left with the harder to serve (and social housing, for example, can be seen as inferior to owner-occupation if deprived of quality and repair and maintenance). The public sector in some circles has become synonymous with inefficiency and overspending.

Fourth, privatisation is *Closed* in that most consumers have little understanding of, and participation in decision-making in, the complexities behind the delivery of public services. Decisions on financing are left to experts both in the government and in international agencies such as the IMF, World Bank, EU and ECB. Decisions are restricted to an elite. Advisers are from a closed club (with revolving doors across corporate bosses, politicians, government consultants and civil servants). In southern European countries, privatisation is imposed by the troika (of European Commission and Central Bank and the

IMF) and in developing countries it is heavily promoted by the World Bank leading to a democratic deficit.

Fifth, public services are increasingly *Commodified*. This does not necessarily mean that services are provided for profit but their provision is evaluated in monetary form. According to Fine (2013b), monetary calculation can enter into our consciousness even if it does not enter our practices. However, commodification offers advantages as a precursor to privatisation. Once a monetary value is calculated for public services, the way is clearer for engagement of the private sector.

In the UK, public services have been transformed in the post-war era from national or local council provision towards a network of contracts with private providers. Along the way this has shaped state provision so that day-to-day operations are fused with financial criteria. This process of subcontracting "turns what remains of the state sector into an archipelago of financialised operating units" (Bowman et al. 2012, p. 10). Some aspects of health services are now subcontracted, and public and private providers are required to compete for contracts. This can benefit private providers over public counterparts due to their expertise and experience in competitive tendering, and they can select the easiest and most lucrative services, with the denigrated state remaining responsible for provider of last resort to those least commercially viable to serve.

Sixth, the privatisation of basic services can be regarded as *Contradictory* because the process introduces values and systems that run counter to public provision. Private financial capital is associated with certain attributes. The search for profits leads to fragmentation of services (as a result of cherry-picking), speculative short-termism and loss of transparency in the name of commercial confidentiality. These are not compatible with public services and infrastructure, with essential services often provided on a monopolistic basis from which households have no option but to consume (consider water and energy). Regulation is required to mediate these diverse interests that pervade once privatisation is introduced.

Seventh, *Contestation* comes from several angles. Privatisation is contested across the world as, for example, global groups protest against water privatisation, and organised workers struggle against both privatisation itself and its effects, thereby also indicating the *Collective* content of the material culture of privatisation. Different interests reflect different attitudes to, and understandings of privatisation. At the local level, protests take place against, for example, hospital closures and nationally against programmes of cuts (most noticeably in Greece, Portugal and Spain). Yet opposition has failed to make much of a mark on policy. Organisations see workers and managers contesting wage settlements and globally the right to shape national policy is contested against, for example, the Troika in Europe and the World Bank globally.

Ninth, the way in which privatisation has emerged has been haphazard (*Chaotic*). In the UK where privatisation gained considerable momentum under the Thatcher administration in the 1980s, there was never a master programme. Rather the approach was ad hoc and piecemeal (Parker 2004).

Finally, privatisation debates are increasingly *Conforming* with neoliberal criteria of performance, and accepted or rejected on these terms. Empirical validation is based on whether or not private firms are more efficient than public providers (see for, example, Gassner et al. 2009). Public providers are assessed on the extent to which they are like private entities with evaluation in terms of limited efficiency criteria.

10 Agents, Relations, Structures and Processes

The SoP approach consists of two strands. First there is the material culture of the good or service or policy in question, outlined above although, second, the material culture is contingent upon the chain of provision from production to consumption. The material aspects of the SoP approach are explored in more detail here. This section moves towards practical application of the SoP approach, highlighting some general themes and issues which would need to be adapted for a detailed specific SoP analysis, drawing on examples from the UK.

According to the SoP approach, outcomes are derived from the vertical chain linking consumption to production. At each stage of the process there exist agents which have specific interests and bargaining strengths. Agents' practices will be shaped by the institutional and legal framework as well as by social norms and power relations. The organising framework for a SoP study usually starts with a research question related to a specific good or commodity. The approach was originally devised in relation to consumption (for example of food and clothing). Recently completed studies have examined the role of finance in the UK provision of water and housing, with corresponding attention to material cultures (Bayliss, 2013; and Robertson, 2014, respectively).

Relations between agents are embedded in context- and service-specific structures and processes. The SoP approach offers a particular advantage over traditional perspectives on social policy in the theoretical recognition of such diversity. Chains of provision will differ for various services and for participants in the process. This systemic approach aims to show the interconnected processes by which SoPs are shaped, rooted in a specific context but not limited by national boundaries. International processes such as globalisation, neoliberalism and financialisation have had a profound impact on SoPs, but on some more than others, the impact depending in part on the nature of the SoP.

Relations between agents are rooted in contextual systems and processes. Cross-cutting trends meet with historically-evolved structures to create systems that are unique in location and in time. Social structures and relations are both shaped by, and shape, the behaviour of individuals. According to Fine and Milonakis (2009, p. 155):

> This does not mean that individual behaviour is totally determined by these properties of collectivities, only that individual action is necessarily *filtered through* and *conditioned* by these structural and social factors and institutions. In such a framework the individual is no longer the asocial, ahistorical, rational individual of standard economic theory but a social individual situated within a proper social and historical context.

Structures shape the behaviour of individuals regardless of whether they have the memory, habits or ideas that are associated with them. Fine and Milonakis (2009, p. 156) cite Giddens's 1979 notion of structuration: "structural properties of social systems are both the medium and the outcome of the practices that constitute those systems."

Global processes in privatisation, financialisation and globalisation have had a significant, but variable, impact on the extent and impact of private finance in basic service delivery. Other social norms such as gendered capitalist relations have an impact on the SoP. For Wöhl (2014) for example, the state represents social relations and, therefore, is an expression of gender relations which have been shaped by masculine hegemony. The result has been that women have suffered far more than men as a result of the financial crisis (MacLeavy, 2011). Meanwhile others, including van Staveren (2012), question whether there would even have been a crisis if women rather than men had been in charge of the financial sector.

The vertical approach is not to deny that there are complex cross-cutting themes (e.g. labour markets, gender, etc) but the impact of these varies across SoPs. As mentioned above, the SoP approach is heavily inductive, and each case requires the researcher to identify the relevant details. What is significant in one SoP may not be in another. The approach does not provide a set of blueprints/templates. Furthermore, the details of the chain of provision may not be obvious, and drawing the boundaries requires judgement. Public services in particular are interconnected with multiple and overlapping SoPs. Pensions, for example, interact with the broader system of economic and social provisioning including health, housing and social security, and then pensions are also linked into financial markets. Arguments to constrain the financial sector can also be seen as limiting the incomes of pensioners. Similarly primary health care is only one element of public health which relies on nutrition, sanitation, water, shelter, etc.

SoP studies are derived from the complexities of real-world dynamics. The notion of systems is already commonplace (for example, the health system, education system and the transport system). To operationalise the SoP framework requires careful disaggregation of systems from production through to consumption, to expose the details of relations between agents. Typically this then includes producers and consumers. The other agents included in the analysis will depend on the research question at hand. To address the impact of finance on public services, agents will include the state and financiers. Within these groupings lie further sets of agents. For example, 'producers' will include workers as well as managers and owners of enterprises, which may be state or private shareholders. And there are different types of private enterprise, for example, in the health sector ranging from a private hospital to a pharmaceutical company. Private finance will include debt and equity financing raised from shareholders and/or lenders. The state includes the frontline staff (if a service is not privatised), central and local government staff, possibly a regulatory authority, as well as the elected political party at the central and local levels that may be driven by political ambitions.

A focus on agency relations is not unique to SoPs. Other theoretical constructs are also derived, if more subtly, from the interactions between interest groups. According to orthodox theory, privatisation is said to improve the efficiency of an enterprise as the switch of ownership from the bureaucratic state to the profit-maximising private sector is supposed to sharpen and streamline the monitoring function. The essence of the theory is that private owners will make the operation run more efficiently because they stand to benefit financially. Unlike the SoP approach, orthodox privatisation theory makes standard neoliberal assumptions of atomistic utility-maximisers operating in circumstances devoid of context and so has questionable relevance in the real world. However, it is important to note that the introduction of the private sector brings a shift in agency relations.

The issues and implications for the SoP depend on the agents involved and the terms under which they are engaged in the delivery systems. This section advances a methodological framework for assessing the impact of private finance on the provision of public services, organised around three main agents: citizens, the private sector and the state (although each of these incorporates internal groupings of agents). This is proposed as a loose organising framework and not to suggest that these agents are in ring-fenced categories. There will be overlapping issues. For example, politics and elite power may run across public and private sectors. In addition, national boundaries are also fluid, not just with flows of private capital but also with supra-state agencies, such as the EU, the IMF, the ECB and the World Bank, taking a decisive role in policy making in some countries.

Clearly, to some degree, consumption is shaped by demand. However, the SoP approach rejects the notion that production moves in response to the whims of consumers and considers that provisioning is itself a major determinant of demand. It may be that producers actively push consumers to raise demand levels. Advertising, for example, attempts to imbue commodities with specific associations to increase their desirability and thereby to shape demand.

For the SoP approach, consumption is considered to be shaped by production. What is consumed is determined to some extent by what is available, and the way in which it is delivered. For example, households receiving piped water consume far more than those that obtain water from a standpipe. Housing production in the UK has failed to respond to increases in demand. Consumption then does not conform to demand. Many live in rented accommodation, or with their extended families, but would prefer to buy if they were not constrained in their ability to do this because of lack of supply (Robertson, 2014). Consumption and production are thus integrally related. This is explored in considerable detail and with further examples in Fine and Leopold (1993) and Fine (2002a).

Consumption and the role of consumers will vary according to the good or service in question and socio-economic and socio-cultural status (for example, gender, age, income-level, etc). Consumers will have more bargaining power in competitive, non-essential sectors. Basic services do not usually fit into this category. The state plays a significant role in the delivery of certain goods and services because they have particular qualities, for example, their consumption is socially desirable, they are monopolistic and/or their provision is required to meet certain basic human rights.

Introducing the private sector into the delivery of basic services can change production-consumption relationships as citizens become customer-consumers, although the impact depends on the good in question and the way in which the private sector is engaged. Subcontracting of hospital cleaning has a different impact from the private provision of primary health care services.

However, despite such diversity, the introduction of private finance focuses the attention on revenue (and costs). Where finance is repaid from user fees, the relations between provider and consumer become a commercial rather than a social one. Pricing can become a contested area. The price paid by customers needs to cover costs but what costs, and at what price? The state may intervene to regulate prices particularly where supply is monopolistic. However, in England and Wales, considerable reliance is placed on private firms to address social policy where consumers face affordability constraints. In the delivery of water, it is left to the private provider to decide on a social tariff for low-income households subject to the proviso that other consumers must approve any cross-subsidy (placing, as it were, social policy on the basis of contestation between groups of consumers) (Bayliss, 2014).

Orthodox privatisation theory considers that enterprises will become more efficient in the hands of the private sector because the profit motive will provide incentives for more effective monitoring and innovation. For the SoP approach, the impact of privatisation varies greatly, and can only be assessed in the context of the specific good, and the nature of engagement with, and the type of, private provider. The type of service and the nature of private involvement will also affect the details of the SoP. There is a spectrum of private sector involvement ranging from subcontracting to divestiture. Furthermore, the location of a private contract has great implications for the outcome. In the UK, investors are attracted to public sector contracts because they are considered to be relatively low risk (NAO, 2012a for PFI concessions, and Bayliss, 2014 for private water contracts). In contrast, efforts to introduce private finance into the water sector in developing countries are widely considered to have failed. After two decades of privatisation of provision, the amount of private finance raised was virtually zero (Marin, 2009). Accordingly, context has a major impact. Furthermore, privatisation has been shaped by wider processes such as financialisation and globalisation.

Private sector involvement in the provision of public services takes many forms including direct provision, lease/concessions, supply of products (as for example with the pharmaceutical industry), and the provision of finance. The private sector can incorporate large conglomerates and small local providers. As a result, it is not possible to make general predictions about what the 'private sector' will do as outcomes depend on the circumstances, the contractual framework, the sector, the country and an extensive range of other variables. This is why empirical assessments of the impact of privatisation lead to diverse conclusions, and assessment of outcomes can be used to support arguments for and against.[11]

---

11 See Bayliss (2011) for more on the 'cup half full or half empty' interpretations of water privatisation.

As mentioned earlier, SoPs have been shaped considerably, although to varying degrees, by financialisation. This has led to changes in the role of private enterprise in the delivery of basic services. Where privatisation may at one time have led to a takeover by an infrastructure company, now private financial capital is increasingly involved in basic services and is seeking new markets. In England and Wales, four of the ten water and sanitation companies, that were listed on the London Stock Exchange in 1989, are now owned by global consortia of private financial firms. In Senegal and Cote d'Ivoire, the long-term private water concessions have been sold by infrastructure firms to a private equity company, Finagestion. A similar process can be observed in the development of other infrastructure concessions in the UK. Long-term contracts under the PFI scheme often involve private equity investors at the start which then made considerable returns on the sale of equity to secondary investors in an established project (NAO, 2012a).

Privatisation in this context goes beyond the simple transfer of ownership to increase efficiency but is about a fundamental reshaping of the mechanisms of service delivery. Infrastructure has become an asset class and in ways that are a far cry from the notion and anticipation of shareholder democracy that was used to underpin the initial denationalisation programmes in the UK. Shareholders are often financial institutions such as investment or pension funds, themselves operating on behalf of private investors. The ultimate beneficiaries of dividend payments are, therefore, several steps removed from the company itself. Privatisation serves to place the delivery of basic services in the hands of, or at least under the influence of, the financial world, forming a component of investment portfolios of global capital. The SoP approach highlights relations between agents to show that payments either from taxpayers or from end users trickle up into the revenue of the firm and create investor returns in a systemic fashion that may be extremely 'distant' from the processes of service delivery themselves.

Globalisation has also shaped privatisation outcomes. Whereas at one stage local services may have been located within a municipal structure along with other local services, privatisation leads to a local decoupling and an alignment within a global portfolio of investments. Where a local municipality may have collective responsibility for service provision, privatisation has locked these into global chains.[12] Private finance is often an international collective.

12 For example, infrastructure in the UK is owned by companies with a string of global assets including airports and hotels as well as electricity providers. The biggest largest private provider of private hospital services in London is a company called Hospital Corporation of America, HCA.

Investment funds around the world buy and sell stakes in financial companies and these invest in assets delivering basic services. The effect has been to realign service delivery on global lines. Taking the example of water in England, these companies now form part of multi-country investment portfolios. Whereas local provision of water would have been grouped with the delivery of other local services (as is still the case in many countries), privatisation has led to regional water companies becoming parts of global conglomerates, for example, headquartered in Hong Kong or Malaysia, or pyramided in ownership structures that ultimately reside in tax havens.

Aside from privatisation, the private firm is already the site of considerable contestation. Workers, managers and shareholders typically compete for shares of revenues. The profits that accrue to the owners increase if workers are paid less and/or work harder. Workers' bargaining positions affect their share of income. Meanwhile, managers mediate between owners and workers. They are answerable to shareholders, and measures are taken to align their incentives with those of the owners, for example, with some elements of remuneration taking the form of a bonus, payable on achievement of specified targets as well as a proportion of shares allocated to managers (and sometimes employees). For the SoP approach, then, the role of the private sector needs to be unpicked to identify the specifics of the interaction with the other agents in the process of delivery.

Bringing private enterprise into the delivery of basic services creates further contestation when firms are operating in an area that is associated with social welfare and where social rather than commercial objectives are expected to prevail to a greater or lesser extent. Introducing private finance raises particular forms of conflict in the SoP. Private firms are under pressure to maintain the share price which puts the emphasis on maximising shareholder revenue. This puts upwards pressure on prices and downward pressure on costs. In some circles this can be considered to be an improvement in efficiency but, first, lowering wage costs can be exploitative and lead to a more vulnerable workforce (zero hours contracts); second, there is no guarantee that such gains will be shared with society and not just accrue to the private owner; third, private equity is also associated with short-termism and asset stripping which is arguably not compatible with the social interests associated with public provision. Finally, in accordance with the financialisation thesis of Palley (2013), privatisation has led to high levels of gearing and debt finance (Bayliss, 2014; and NAO, 2012a). This has the effect of creating high interest payments which are tax deductible (unlike dividends) but high gearing can create a more vulnerable financing structure, which is arguably not in the social interest.

11 Regulation and the State

For the SoP approach, the state is not a monolithic entity, and it is a site of contestation. Different state agencies co-exist, often with competing priorities, for example, one that focuses on environmental impacts may have an agenda that conflicts with one that is devoted to economic issues. Reference has already been made to the wider issues regarding the role of the state. When it comes to the SoP approach, the state's role is extensive in setting the parameters for different activities and the details would need to be specified. However, the details of a SoP analysis will depend on the sector in question. This section focuses on one specific role of the state activity in the context of private finance – that of a regulator.

Much has been written about how best to regulate privatised enterprises, for example, the relative merits of 'rate-of-return' as opposed to 'price-cap' regulation. These were originally devised with a view to mimicking the impact of competition in monopolistic sectors. For price-cap regulation, firms are allowed to make what profits they can, subject to a price set by the regulator, thereby providing an incentive for firms to increase efficiency as they would if they were a price-taker in a competitive market structure.

But this regulatory structure provides incentives for firms to do other things such as to overstate costs in the price-setting process, to withhold information from the regulator, to engage in transfer pricing, to skimp on quality, to reduce wages and increase workloads. Firms also have an incentive to misreport data on performance targets where these affect the allowable returns. Efforts to strengthen regulation by increasing the extent and complexity of reporting requirements has not led to greater effectiveness (Bayliss, 2014 on the water sector; and Haldane and Madouros, 2012 on the financial sector). Bowman et al. (2012 p. 5), citing Engelen et al. (2011), describe market "bricolage" in the financial sector where regulation does not impose constraints so much as create an input for further, more elaborate forms of creative profit-making. An alternative interpretation of regulation is that, rather than setting parameters for firms in the form of regulations, the state is setting obstacles that need to be overcome.

Regulation is less scientific and bounded than orthodox theory suggests, in part because of the blurring of agency relations between the state and the private sector. The perception of a state/market dichotomy is not valid in practice. One way in which boundaries are crossed is with the use of private consultants who work both for the government and for the private sector. For concession contracts in the UK, government evaluations of PFI are carried out by financial consultants with a vested interest as advisers, private sector partners in PFI deals or major subcontractors (Shaoul, 2008). This is also the case in the design of tax policy where the government relies on the 'big four' accounting firms who then advise clients on how to avoid paying tax (HoC, 2013, p. 4).

But the state increasingly needs to use consultants because they do not have the capacity for regulation, in large part because of the growing complexity of financial transactions. The state lacks the ability to regulate the private sector effectively. In the UK, the National Audit Office found that this was the case for PFI concession contracts (NAO, 2011). There is also growing evidence of this for the financial sector. Indeed, Bowman et al. (2012, p. 14) suggest the faith that the elites and the masses continue to hold in finance, despite mounting evidence of its failings, stems partly from the "scientisation of central banking which turned financial regulation into an arcane matter understood only by a small number of elite figures in the financial markets or in central banks and regulators". Increasing financial complexity, driven by greater involvement of finance in non-financial companies, makes the task of regulation more difficult.

Regulatory strength is also weakened by consolidation in the private sector as this effectively shrinks the pool of potential participants. In finance the 'big four' accounting firms dominate financial advice both for private firms and the government (Froud et al. 2011, p. 12). In the UK, regulation is constrained by a shrinking number of service providers in the wake of industry consolidation. It has also led to four firms dominating subcontracting in the country (G4S, Serco, Capital and Atos). This gives a sense of too big to fail and limits the extent and application of sanctions in the event of transgressions (NAO, 2013b).

Regulation may be compromised by conflicting state agendas. While, on paper, the regulator is tasked with reining in the excesses of private exploitation so that the privatised sectors work in the interests of society, the privatising government does not want to see privatisation fail. For that reason, states need the private sector to make profits and the terms of regulation not to be too onerous. In the UK, privatisations are often under-priced so investors see an immediate gain from the share price increase. State capture also emerges from political alliances. The financial sector has close ties with the government in the UK, for example with political donations (Froud et al. 2011, p. 13). Revolving doors between government and the private sector promote the private sector agenda.

12 Conclusion: Multiple and Contested SoPs

This chapter outlines an innovative approach to conceptualising the impact of finance on public provision. Until now, assessments have largely been in terms of the way that privatisation has or has not led to improvements in productive efficiency. Critiques have raised concerns regarding the conventional methodologies and approaches, but no significant appropriate alternative has been offered.

The literature on the impact of finance on public provision is notable for its ideological content. For some it is a great success while for others an abject failure. It has become increasingly clear from the empirical debates that that there are no guaranteed outcomes when it comes to privatisation. The only valid conclusion from a review of the literature is that the private and the public both contain the best and the worst of performers. The SoP approach is more nuanced. There are winners and losers and interpretations will vary according to the underlying assumptions and perspectives of the researchers.

There is, then, only small mileage to be gained from thinking in terms of the state/market dichotomy and far greater insights can be obtained from a systemic perspective. By shifting the approach to a vertical analysis, the emphasis is on the processes by which outcomes are reached. While the SoP approach starts from the premise that each case is different, the thematic approach does not preclude cross-sector and cross-country analyses. Cross-cutting themes play out in different ways across cases, and these differences give greater insight into the workings of national socio-economic relations. In some ways it is easier to understand one case in terms of how and why it differs from others. For this reason, the Fessud research programme is sponsoring a cross-country SoP study of finance and financialisation in the delivery of housing and water in five case-study locations.[13]

The inductive approach of SoPs has potential drawbacks in being, necessarily, contingent upon case study application. However, the level of abstraction and underlying assumptions of supposedly scientific econometric analyses also exhibit major failings, (see Bayliss, 2011 on water privatisation). For the SoP approach, considerable responsibility rests with the researcher. Perceptions of the SoP boundaries, the material culture and the vertical production-consumption chain are subject to framed judgements. However, this is a feature of much economic research, although elsewhere this is largely implicit.

13 UK, Turkey, South Africa, Poland and Portugal. The country studies and synthesis reports will be completed by June 2015.

Theoretical and empirical approaches have been limited by attempting to mould heterogeneity into systematic patterns with ideal types and syntheses of regimes. The real world is messy, complex and unpredictable with multiple and conflicting systems and processes, operating simultaneously with their own material cultures, historically and contextually determined ethos, and path dependence. For the (PS)SoP approach, this diversity is welcomed as the starting point of analysis. As such, it is anticipated that this will offer a useful framework for understanding and shaping policy outcomes.

CHAPTER 5

Housing and Water in Light of Financialisation and 'Financialisation'

Postscript as Personal Preamble

There is a logical progression from the previous chapters to this. It draws upon neoliberalism, Chapter 2, financialisation and systems of provision (SoPs), Chapter 3, and the role of the public sector (as the private sector becomes more involved) in social provisioning, Chapter 4. In doing so, and in drawing upon comparative case studies of housing and water across five countries, this Chapter is both more developed and more empirically informed than the earlier ones, quite apart from making use of other research across the Fessud project and more generally.

More specifically, there is a much more wide-ranging discussion of financialisation in practice and in theory (with some unavoidable repetition of some points), a similarly deeper discussion of the unpicking of commodification into commodification as such (C), commodity form (CF) and commodity calculation (CC), or CCFCC if all taken together. There is also some brief discussion of economic and social reproduction and their implications for gender. All of these issues, and more, have been taken up in later work, see Appendices to Chapter 1, but an important conclusion is the need both for general theory but for it to be able to be sensitive to variegation across time, place and sector in understanding what is provided, to whom, and why.

1 Introduction[1]

This chapter brings together findings based on a collection of cases that examined the systems of provision (SoPs) for water and housing in five selected locations – UK, Poland, Portugal, South Africa and Istanbul.[2] The case studies provide detailed analyses of the role of finance in the SoPs which demonstrate how financialisation works in practice in these two non-financial sectors. In

1 Appearing initially as Fine et al. (2016b).

2 Some knowledge of the SoP approach is presumed in what follows. See earlier chapters or, most recently, Bayliss and Fine (2021a).

 | DOI:10.1163/9789004706293_006

this chapter, we attempt to tease out the implications of these accounts for our understanding of financialisation, both as real economic phenomenon (financialisation) and as area of scholarship ('financialisation' although the inverted commas will be dropped as the meaning becomes clear).

Beginning with the latter, we argue that much existing literature on financialisation lacks a coherent theoretical foundation. While theory is not absent from the large and expanding literature on financialisation, it is often imputed from elsewhere, implicitly and without reflection. We have elsewhere advocated the SoP approach, which investigates financialisation by looking at the role and impact of finance on the concrete chain of activities that underpin production and consumption (Bayliss et al. 2013). The case studies demonstrate the merits of the approach – by analysing financialisation through SoPs, the case studies are able to grasp the commodity- and location-specific forms taken by processes of financialisation. In this chapter, though, we turn to a more abstract level of analysis, in order, on the one hand, to draw on the case study results to deepen our understanding of financialisation in general and, on the other, to give those case studies a deeper theoretical foundation.

The case studies show that financialisation has been associated with the increasing presence of the 'market' or 'market forces' in the provision of housing and water. In short, as finance is underpinned by money and commodity relations, so financialisation is underpinned by commodification. A deeper theorisation of financialisation must, therefore, begin with a relatively abstract understanding of the relationships between money, commodities, and finance, requiring a theory of money, the extension of that theory to finance, and the specification of the processes attaching finance to the non-financial.

A closer look, however, reveals the nature of the 'markets' for housing and water to be highly differentiated, with respect to both each other and across the different case studies. Further, that differentiation has significant implications for how those sectors relate to financialisation, and for how we understand the latter. We suggest that the differentiated market forms identified in the case studies can be grasped by distinguishing between commodification as such (production for private profit), the commodity form (periodic payments for a good or service, in the absence of the profit motive) and commodity calculation (application of a monetary logic, though without money changing hands). Each of these categories is then shown to vary in terms of how far they facilitate financialisation. We suggest that the application of these categories to housing and water can be used to illustrate and explain variegated outcomes across countries and sectors, and discuss their multiple and complex relations to financialisation.

Our approach to money and commodification serves as the basis for a more general discussion of financialisation, which traces the emergence of new opportunities for financial 'profit'. In particular, we argue that the proliferation of assets and asset trading has led to dramatic restructuring of social and economic life. Consequently, many distinguishing features and effects of financialisation – including the encroachment of finance into more areas of social and economic life and the expansion of fictitious capital at the expense of the real economy – can be understood in these terms.

We begin in the next section by discussing theoretical characteristics of the existing literature on financialisation, drawing attention to a lack of coherence and self-reflection. In the following section, we argue that an abstract understanding of financialisation, given the latter's systemic properties, needs to be rooted in a universal theory of money, and outline our categories for the different forms of monetised interactions. In sections four and five, we look at the role of money in generating new forms of profit-making though the financial sector, and the consequential expansion of that sector at the expense of the real economy, with application to housing and water, respectively. Section six then allows us to revisit the notion of financialisation in light of the case studies. Section seven explains how this leads to financialisation's encroachment on social and economic reproduction, and section eight discusses the implications of this for gender. Section nine concludes.

2 A New Term Is Borne and Born

Over the course of the financial crisis (or crises) and subsequent global recession, the term 'financialisation' has experienced a considerable growth in usage, one that seems set to continue for the foreseeable future. This is to be contrasted with its negligible presence previously. Although deployed for slightly longer within political economy (Arrighi 1994, most notably), Goldstein (2009) views the idea as having a significant presence only over the last decade.[3] Within the discipline of economics, its origins and continuing trajectory remain confined to the heavily marginalised fields of heterodox economics. Otherwise, if not quite a scholarly "buzzword",[4] it has found some purchase across the social sciences more generally, and is possibly in danger of attaining the status of

3 But see Magdoff and Sweezy (1987).

4 See Cornwall and Eade (eds) (2010).

a "fuzzword".[5] Specifically, it has been deployed with different meanings and with different methods and theories. In this respect, it carries a similar burden as more longstanding concepts such as globalisation, neoliberalism, and social capital, and has, significantly, overlapped with at least the first two of these.[6]

Three fundamental features, then, mark this rise of financialisation across the social sciences. One is the frequent observation of neglect of finance in the past.[7] Typical, for example, is Pike and Pollard (2010, p. 29), for whom there are, "long-standing concerns about the relatively marginal location of finance in economic geography".[8] Similarly, Moran and Payne (2014, p. 335) observe the limited attention to (the power of) finance in political science due to its primary concern with the state:

---

5 For Michell and Toporowski (2014, p. 80), seeking deeper explanations for the increased role of finance and its relationship to capitalist enterprises, "Without identifying and explaining those key relationships, 'financialization' cannot provide any insight beyond the evidence adduced for its existence. The challenge for users of that term is to provide analysis that reveals more than just what is already known. Lacking a clear account of the market processes of banking and finance (credit, credit innovation, and hedging), and banking and financial policy, financialization joins 'neoliberalism' and 'globalization' as a predicament that disempowers us. It disempowers us by distracting us from a necessary intellectual enquiry with an unformed and shadowy conclusion." Unsurprisingly, they conclude, "For this reason, the understanding of finance requires the abandonment of financialization as a project of intellectual inquiry", p. 80.

6 If not the third, as social capital has studiously avoided what are possibly its most obvious application, national and international elites in general, and those attached to finance in particular. See Fine (2010b) and Vitali et al. (2011). See also Sawyer (2014, p. 13) who observes in quoting Epstein (2005, p. 3), "In short, this changing landscape has been characterized by the rise of *neoliberalism, globalization* and *financialization*".

7 See Michell and Toporowski (2014) who view 'financialisation' as a neologism, reflecting overreaction to the greater presence of finance but its neglect in the past. See also Christophers (2015a).

8 Significantly, in light of our next two points, they continue, "We emphasize the integral role of finance in connecting the entangled geographies of the economic to the social, the cultural, and the political. In the wake of various 'turns' in the discipline, we develop this integrationist approach to finance in ways that retain political economies of states, markets, and social power in our interpretations of geographically uneven development. In this article, we discuss the plural nature of emergent work on financialization and develop three analytical themes to shape our discussion of financialization. Next, we elaborate our analytical approach by warning against functional, political, and spatial disconnections traced in the literature on the geographies of money. We then explore how financialization is broadening and deepening the array of agents, relations, and sites that require consideration in economic geography and is generating tensions between territorial and relational spatialities of geographic differentiation."

> In sum, with economics asserting a monopoly in the study of economic life and international political economy largely content with overarching analyses of global trends, political science was able, on the whole successfully, to assert and claim its own monopoly, so to speak, of the study of the state, and to do it, as we have seen, in its own distinctive way.

Notwithstanding diversity of foci within the field (see, for example, Kemeny and Lowe, 1998), the same is true of housing studies, where an exponential increase in literature on mortgage markets is a relatively new phenomenon. Similarly with water, and infrastructure more generally, finance attracted little attention until the last decade when deficiencies in provision began to be increasingly depicted in terms of a 'financing gap'.

A second feature of the literature, possibly in an understandable reaction against an unavoidable sense of neglect in the wake of recent events, has been the wide variety of approaches taken to financialisation, from pointing to the neoliberal subject variously as worker, consumer, entrepreneur and investor (as in Langley, 2007), and similarly within the 'state of the art' of van der Zwan (2014), who sees financialisation as straddling approaches to the nature of contemporary capitalism, shareholder value and everyday life. This breadth is reproduced in relation to housing, which has been implicated in both macroeconomic restructuring and the reconstitution of individual subjectivities (Crouch, 2009a; and Van Gent, 2010). In water, financialisation has often been related to enclosing the commons and financial involvement in natural resources (see for example, Friends of the Earth, 2013). The political economy of the financial sector in the provision of water has only recently been the subject of academic scholarship (Bayliss, 2013; and Allen and Pryke, 2013).

Third, closely related but distinct, is the equally wide variety of subject matter covered by financialisation, dealing in everything from the nature of the relationship between financialisation and neoliberalism in characterising contemporary capitalism to the eponymous influence of financialisation on everyday life, let alone as a generic term for finance itself (Sawyer, 2014). Housing and water appear in this context as two examples among many areas whose subjection to financialisation has been the subject of investigation.

No doubt, much of this is a consequence of the, now acknowledged, increasing pervasiveness and diversity of finance in general, however it is understood, with an equally compelling fluidity and innovation attached to financialisation (as with other 'grand' concepts). In short, financialisation has been configured in response to the unprecedented expansion of finance, variously understood, across both financial markets, the monetary system, commodification and its ethos and far beyond, with major impacts upon economic and social functioning more generally, usually with deleterious effects the more it is present.[9] Significantly, then, as proposed by Lee et al. (2009, p. 727–8), in locating it geographically, "financialisation is hardly a new phenomenon in circuits of capital. What is perhaps relatively new is the extent to which finance has found its way into most, if not all, of the nooks and crannies of social life. To illustrate, it is easily possible to identify at least *17 notions* of financialisation", emphasis added.

Each of housing and water offers up its own array of phenomena attached to financialisation. Following Robertson (2016), most conspicuous for housing is a vast expansion of mortgage lending, which has ensnared households in financial markets. Concomitant has been, on the one hand, the growth of secondary mortgage markets trading assets underpinned by mortgage repayments and, on the other, attempts to reconstitute individuals as neoliberal saver-investors (with partial success). More generally, housing provision has been increasingly governed by a commitment to market forms, which is not to say that states have not intervened, only that their interventions are constrained by a presumption against state provision and in favour of at times elusive market forms. This commitment is reflected, for example, in land markets. While states continue to intervene heavily in these markets via planning regulations, their interventions are increasingly dictated by allocating land to its highest value – in monetary terms – use. This shift has coincided with a growth in the importance of real estate investment in the broader economy, itself a facet of the ascendance of speculative over real investment.

Water, as a natural resource, seems to be far removed from the financial sector. Certainly the scope and nature of financialisation is more opaque than in housing. In most countries, water is provided by the state, and financial interventions are limited to bond issues with some hedging of interest rate and currency fluctuations. State water providers have increasingly been required to restructure themselves as independent water companies and to adopt private sector style financial management but privatisation has not been widespread as reflected in Fessud case studies. Where water has been privatised, this is usually in the form of long-term concession contracts. The exception is England and Wales (E&W) where privatisation has taken the form of divestiture. Here, the financial sector has taken root, and many of the features of financialisation are evident. The different forms of providing water found across the case

9 Here the original quotes at length from Ashman and Fine (2013, pp. 156/7) but this has already been deployed in two earlier chapters and so is replaced by a summary text.

studies have implications for the way in which financialisation has emerged in varying forms in the sector.

Each of the many features of financialisation can be demonstrated empirically and theoretically from a variety of points of view. This is even so, despite some temporary and mild setbacks from the global crisis, of those of a neoliberal bent who can offer explanations in terms of responses to random shocks in otherwise perfectly working markets (for the Chicago school of economic thought), or as a result of the uncertainties that inevitably accompany innovation and change (or too much state interference in this, for neo-Austrians). What is more at stake is how theory and empirical evidence is ordered within and across the various factors involved, something that is our purpose to take up later in some detail in the context of case studies around housing and water.

Yet one, possibly unsurprising, feature of the financialisation literature is the extent to which it is not explicitly theoretically innovative in addressing its object of study. One reason for this is that the literature has been sandwiched, if not squeezed, between the unavoidable weight of newly emerging and discovered empirical developments (however well identified, understood and incorporated) and the application and promotion of prior methodological, conceptual and theoretical stances. This does, however, allow the theory of financialisation to range from post-Keynesianism to performativity and beyond. So, it is not so much that theories, or framings, of finance are absent as that they remain at most and at best implicit and, generally, unquestioned despite their presumed suitability for new or newly-recognised empirical developments.

It is striking, for example, that financialisation does not appear within mainstream economics at all. This is to be expected given how it has treated money and finance in the most recent past, with the former primarily seen as belonging to macroeconomics and subject to state control over its supply, and the latter confined to microeconomics and the more or less efficient mobilisation and allocation of (financial) resources. In practice, this has involved an absence of systemic and dynamic determinants in their historical and social context that are essential factors in specifying financialisation. In other words, necessarily hypothetically, if mainstream economics had been genuinely drawn into seeking to conceptualise financialisation, it might reasonably be expected to have found its theoretical foundations in both microeconomics and macroeconomics to be seriously unfit for purpose (as, of course, might also be argued for its application to the pre-financialisation period).[10] Whether

10 The breakdown of the previously complacent New Consensus Macroeconomics without replacement in sight other than to appeal to greater realism, to more and more severe

in its efficient market hypothesis form, or what might be termed its inefficient market hypothesis form, mainstream approaches to finance have been seriously deficient in understanding its systemic effects. This is not accidental but a direct consequence of its undue reliance upon what has been termed its technical apparatus and technical architecture.[11]

At the other extreme, most of the other social sciences are familiar and comfortable with dealing with the systemic and the dynamic so that it is far less irksome for them, including political economy, to engage with financialisation. As a result, as seen, analyses of financialisation have blossomed across the social sciences (outside of mainstream economics) displaying a variety of conceptualisation, methods and applications with a corresponding collective lack of coherences and self-examinations.

Not surprisingly, then, Erturk et al. (eds) (2008) are able to identify a number of different approaches to financialisation, including their own synthesis that focuses upon the contemporary period as one of what they call "coupon pool" capitalism.[12] Their synthesis is explicitly made up out of a triangulation of four framings, each deriving from different intellectual traditions and different time periods in terms of origins and influence. These are, in their somewhat obscure terms, 1930s liberal collectivism, 1980s agency theory, the political economy of quantities (that is more longstanding across heterodox and Marxist schools of economics), and cultural political economy which, in its application to finance, primarily belongs to the new millennium. They are surely correct both to suggest that these framings are mutually incompatible *and* that each has something to offer. More questionable, though, is the assertion that these insights cannot be incorporated into a single frame, if taking each as critical point of departure, something that they seem to dismiss on the grounds of the fluid nature of finance itself, and the equally fluid and variable nature of its causes and consequences – financialisation is perceived as a

---

market imperfections, and to behavioural economics, is indicative of the inadequacy of the mainstream both before and after the crisis. See Fine (2016c).

11 Or TA[2], see Fine (2017b) most recently for example, with emphasis upon orthodoxy's undue reliance upon use of production and utility functions, and preoccupation with optimisation, efficiency and equilibrium, respectively, for apparatus and architecture. See also Fine (2024a–c).

12 For them, this involves the conjunctural specificity of mass (40%) participation of households in financial dealings of various sorts, the proliferation of financial intermediation, and the increasing distance between financial and productive assets, leading it to be "certainly helpful to distinguish between intermediary elite groups and financialized masses", pp. 26–7.

veritable "bricolage" as their favoured descriptive term to accommodate varieties of determinants and their interactions.[13]

What would appear to be at issue is whether financialisation can be grounded in a multi-purpose, if more abstract, theory that could serve to engender coherence, underpinnings and/or clarity in the forward march of financialisation within scholarship. Inevitably, this will appear to prove impossible if relying upon general methodological stances (around the systemic and dynamic – financialisation as culture or as agency for example), at one extreme, and the immediately empirical, at the other. For the latter, paying a water bill or taking out a mortgage has a greater or lesser attachment to financialisation without necessarily being, as it were, financialisation itself. To tease out the relations involved, it is imperative then to locate financialisation in relation to both the monetary system as a whole, of which it is but a part, and the non-monetary relations with which financialisation either directly or indirectly interacts.

Theories of money and finance, as illustrated most obviously by the financialisation literature itself, necessarily range over a huge landscape from accounts of the forms and meanings of money, through the macroeconomics of the money supply, to the more general interaction between putatively separate but intertwined monetary and real economies in generating employment, investment, inflation, crises and much else besides. And this is even before the global nature of money has been considered at one extreme, and everyday life (of the household) at the other. These are all crucial to a greater or lesser extent for how money and its effects are experienced and understood and so also for the material culture of financialisation. And, in particular, simple cultures involving money, in purchasing for consumption, deploying a credit card, and avoiding or negotiating indebtedness, have deep, and possibly elusive and distant, connections to a financial, and productive, system that heavily influences in practice how financialisation engenders meanings for those who are often unaware of how and how deeply they are embroiled within it. A complete survey of theories of finance and theories of money is beyond the scope of this chapter.[14] Instead our focus (in the next section) is limited to money as it relates to commodities and commodification.

---

13 See also Johal et al. (2014) for use of bricolage in the context of the building and exercise of the power of finance.

14 Our own approach draws upon Marxist political economy and its complex theory of forms of capital in exchange. For a simple exposition, see Fine and Saad-Filho (2016b) but also Fine (1985/6 and 1988) and especially Fine (2013–14). For other views from within political economy, see the contributions to the symposium in the same issue as the latter. See also Fine (2022).

3 From Money through Commodification and Beyond (CCFCC ...)[15]

In short, and ideally, analysing financialisation involves three components: a theory of money, its extension to finance, and specification of the processes attaching finance to the non-financial, with a corresponding account of the causes and consequences of the related outcomes. In this light, some elementary points are worthy of observation. For, whilst elementary, they provide the basis for addressing the complexity and diversity of the forms taken by, and impacts of, financialisation and how they are conceived. First is that money never exists in isolation but involves a close association with commodities. Equally, the domain of money is delimited, at least in part, by the domain of commodities although their common domain is far from fixed across time, place and character – all money-commodity relations are not the same, even if they share common elements by virtue of being depositories of exchangeable value despite the diversity of commodities themselves. The shifting domain of money is acknowledged in the notion of commodification (or, indeed, decommodification and re-commodification) whereby what was previously outside the domain (for example, water) is incorporated within it (or excluded or reincorporated, respectively). As is already apparent, then, insofar as finance takes monetary/commodity relations as its starting point, so financialisation is readily associated with commodification.[16] This is most obvious, for example, in the commercialisation and privatisation of state provision which opens up opportunities for the intervention of finance and financialisation in varieties of ways.

In its universally recognised roles as means of payment and unit of account, money is embroiled in a sphere or, more exactly, spheres of application that incorporate a wide range of economic and social activities. Most obviously, of course, is within the world of markets where commodities are bought and sold through the medium of money. This involves all sorts of credit relations to which financialisation can attach itself, as well as currency trading and state finances. But, in addition, in part if not primarily because of these roles,

15 Commodity, Commodity Form and Commodity Calculation.

16 Thus, as Botta et al. (2015, p. 2) implicitly observe, financialisation involves the "*commodification* of financial relationships", p. 2, but this necessarily requires previous commodification of non-financial relationships. Hence, as suggested by Callaghan (2015, pp. 333/4), citing (Apeldoorn and Horn, 2007, p. 215), "financialization depends on marketization, defined as the creation of regulatory preconditions for markets to arise and develop, thereby extending the market mechanism to new areas of social life". On the latter, see below.

monetisation is embroiled in interactions beyond market exchange as with the payment of bribes, taxes, interfamilial transfers and so on.

Commodification is widely used to denote the process of moving goods or services into monetised spheres of existence but there are different elements to this process, and each has significance for the nature and impact of financialisation. Here we can distinguish between commodification of production as such (reduced on a narrow definition to the production of commodities for the purpose of profitability) and the adoption of the commodity form (without commodification) where 'payments' of a more or less casual and periodic nature are made for whatever reason. More or less nominal user charges for a state-owned health service certainly involve the commodity form but not commodities as such. And arrangements of this type vary by degree of penetration of the commodity form, their influence (is payment token or not) and, equally important, their dynamics. While the commodity form may not be for profitable purposes this might, for example, be transitional to further commercialisation and privatisation (and even intended as such) or be a means of financially sustaining state provision against or simply in absence of privatisation, with the state potentially subsidising provision over partially covered costs. So commodity form, CF, can occur without commodification, C, but there cannot in general be C without CF (but see below on the peculiar commodity form taken by commodified water).

Further, the realm of monetisation/commodification extends beyond the activities attached to commodities and commodity forms themselves to their application in calculation or even qualitative reasoning in which neither commodities nor money are themselves necessarily present, i.e. for which money does not actually exchange hands, even as a matter of settling of accounts.[17] Money enters our consciousness even where it does not enter our practices. This tends to move to quantification – how much is something worth in monetary terms – but it can remain at the abstract level of whether we can evaluate something in such terms in principle irrespective of whether it is done in practice. Equally, whether it be virtue or otherwise, we may eschew such evaluations in placing certain 'commodities' beyond the cash nexus as it were.[18]

---

17 As Dodd (1994) observes of Simmel (1978), the latter's argument around money is not that money homogenises everything. Rather, the idea that money can do so is extremely powerful and very much enters our understanding of capitalist society. See below and also Gronow (1997) and discussion in Fine (2002a).

18 See Fine (2013c, p. 16), "For Margaret Radin (1996), in her book, *Contested Commodities*, the argument is put forward that the treatment in the field of economics and law, inspired by economics imperialism, has the effect of producing attitudes to sexual assault as if it were reducible to a violation of property with correspondingly damaging effects on incidence.

In short, the extent and scope of commodification, and commodity forms and calculation, have long since become sufficiently widespread and ingrained, that we are enabled to deploy them in the abstract, both individually and collectively, irrespective of whether money and 'commodity' are actually exchanged (or other activity occurs for monetary reward). Such is the nature of cost-benefit analysis in theory and practice, as well as decisions in our daily lives as we choose to save money or not by self-provisioning rather than purchasing – I saved (how much, an unknowable amount) by walking rather than catching a bus or going by car. CC can take place without CF or C. Whilst, CF can be a token payment or can be based on a more detailed CC, C generally requires both CC and CF (although these can take on peculiar characteristics in case of water, for example, as unit prices do not always prevail).

Significantly, the troika of commodification, commodity form and commodity calculation (CCFCC) has given rise to a debate over the nature of money itself which is worth rehearsing for it concerns how money and, hence, its derivative, financialisation, is to be understood systemically and, accordingly, enters into our daily lives. For Zelizer (1994, 1996, 1998 and 2000),[19] drawing upon different examples of the uses of money and the motivations for them, there can be no general, or universal, theory of money since it (even one currency note as opposed to another) carries different meanings contingent upon its origins (how it is obtained) and its destinations (how it is spent).[20] As a

A rather different but classic example of collective ethics is the *Gift Relationship* of Richard Titmuss (1970), and the free donation of blood in the UK that is more effective in soliciting supply than if it were paid for. I am an example myself. I would not have given blood if I were paid for it just as I will not submit to journals that charge for submission nor referee for those that pay for review since I consider these to be a collective intellectual responsibility. Of course, there are those who hold different views, especially those academics who receive huge fees for promoting the liberalisation of financial markets, secure in the certainty that if someone is willing to pay so much for this knowledge, that is what it must be worth with the added comfort that Gresham's law of the bad driving out the good money from circulation does not apply to knowledge any more than it does to efficient markets. The ethics of such plutonomy within the economics profession has been cruelly exposed, especially within the United States (Epstein and Carrick-Hagenbarth, 2010 and 2012; Fullbrook, 2012; Ferguson, 2010; and Mirowski, 2010). It is complemented by an ethics of agnotology, the more or less deliberate spread of ignorance about matters economic (Mirowski 2010; and Mirowski and Nik-Khah, 2013)."

19 Note that the origins of Zelizer's approach lie in the transition from the valued to the invaluable child, although valuing (quality of) life and limb has inevitably become standard in cost-benefit analysis and compensation claims.

20 For a, possibly unwitting, update of Zelizer from within a performativity perspective, see Langley (2008, p. 6) for whom it is denied that finance is spaceless and timeless, with its being de-territorialised and dematerialised particularly in relation to globalisation. Instead, a corrective is provided by, "Distinct cultural rituals, rulés and symbols;

result, each acquisition and/or use of money is potentially differentiated from others according to the motives, actions, indeed the cultures, of those who engage with it, whether it be the differences between how men and women engage in monetary relations, for example, or the rationalities associated with gambling or luxury display as opposed to saving for a rainy day.

By contrast, Fine and Lapavitsas (2000), Fine (2002a) and Lapavitsas (2003), whilst recognising the presence of such multiple monies as they are termed, suggest that this needs to be rooted in a universal theory of money (and equivalents). Indeed, it precisely because money is (almost literally) a blank sheet of paper (apart from numerical denominations) that it is able to perform its diverse roles as multiple monies and incorporate mixes of practices and motivations (across CCFCC). As French et al. (2011, p. 809) observe, however accurately, referencing Zelizer for support:

> Even accounts of financialization that have sought to think about money more as a mutable network still implicitly cleave to an understanding of money as necessarily disembedding and alienating, an agent that acts on social relations, rather than being constituted by social relations.

Admittedly, for example, banks and other financial agents have provided an increase in mortgage lending due to a growing culture of homeownership. The growth of this culture has in turn affected the practices, even the creation, of financial agents (subprime traders) but the culture itself could not have emerged without the lending practices. An expression of a preference for homeownership as the tenure of choice is only possible because of the availability of mortgage finance. Accordingly, social relations both shape and are shaped by interactions with finance. But that those engaging in monetary relations both act upon (make finance available for whatever, for example) and are constituted by (take savings from whomsoever) social relations (and, indeed, constitute them, the worlds of financial elites or payday loans for example) is as much an argument for, as against, a universal theory of money.[21]

For, although money takes on a range of forms and provides a range of functions, reflecting the diverse social relations in which it is embedded, the

---

relationships of trust, friendship, and cooperation; the acceptance of models, formulas, and calculations; and trading floors of computer screens, interlinked by high-technology communication channels".

21 Thus, the rigid separation between form and content (and so the making of social relations) is a false one, as was acknowledged long ago in Marx's theory of commodity fetishism.

multiple roles played by money are structured in part by common systemic factors, which, through interaction with financial agents, have efficacy in shaping monetary relations. To give an example, taking out a mortgage does not make the culture of owner-occupation what it is, nor is owner-occupation, as an integral part of the housing system, possible in the absence of mortgages. And, by the same token, paying a water bill does not lead to the culture of derivative trading by providers but remains essential to it. However, that these are both entirely distinct applications of money and finance, with determinants that are not self-contained, does not mean they are disconnected from one another and do not have common systemic influences, appropriately addressed through an underlying, universal theory of multiple monies, as it were.

In other words, it is the homogenising nature of money that allows it to be so diverse in application in both practice and thought (and calculation and, as it were, knowing the price of everything and the value of nothing).[22] By the same token, however, such a universal approach to the nature of money carries the implication that it is otherwise silent, even ignorant, around the origins and nature of the CCFCCs to which it is attached in practice and/or thought. Just give me the money (or assess monetary value) in exchange (possibly in thought alone) for whatever is at hand, it might be said. With the commodity, for example, the duality between use value and exchange value is one that is not simply comprised of useful properties and their evaluation exclusively at the point of sale. For use value, the physically and socially determined nature of the commodity will depend upon how it has been produced, distributed and sold as well as how it is subsequently used for further economic activity and/or consumption. Further, in case of CF and CC, these too have social origins with continuing effects although they are not necessarily (exclusively or primarily) rooted in the imperatives of the market mechanism (bribery is not [re]produced as a commodity nor is the payment of taxes and pocket money, although 'market forces' may exert an influence).

It might seem that the distinction between a theory of many monies and one of universal money with contingent and diverse outcomes is merely academic. However, it is at least symbolic of much deeper issues that go to the

22 Note also that the universal nature of money leads to the illusion that barter is simply commodity exchange without money and, vice versa, that commodity exchange is a more sophisticated, extensive and efficient form of barter. It is more appropriate to see barter and commodity exchange as simply different from each other (Lapavitsas, 2003) rather than either as an evolutionary sequence or as a less or a more advanced version of the other.

heart of methodological differences. The multiple monies approach is mindful both of avoiding undue (economic) determinism, whether derived from homo economicus or some form of structuralism, and of allowing for individual cultures and subjectivities. By contrast, the universal approach tends to be committed to systemic analysis and to emphasise how such individual subjectivities are constrained by both the nature of money and the social structures to which it is attached. A resolution of these differences is important not so much for the theory of money as such (and its various uses in day-to-day expenditure as is the preferred territory of the multiple monies approach) as for how such a theory underpins the more general and developed theory of finance in which money (as capital) is embroiled in unavoidable systemic effects, not least through financialisation as will be addressed in what follows. The virtue of the universal approach is that it attends to both systemic and specific roles of money as well as the pathways through which financialisation has both direct and indirect effects. And, for the indirect effects, 'finance' as such can be directly involved but not financialisation itself (the taking out of a mortgage or the paying of a water bill, for example) or it can even be detached from exchange relations as in the exercise of power or influence. This is, however, contingent on how financialisation is defined (as it is always involved if its definition is taken wide enough to incorporate the presence of money and/or monied interests and ethos).

In this light, observe that, although the nature of the commodity remains controversial within Marxist value theory (where it probably attracts the closest and most detailed attention in contrast to a more general tendency to depend upon a simple market/non-market dualism), it is imperative to draw the logical distinctions between commodities, commodity form and commodity calculation. Each also has different implications for financialisation. In reverse order, commodity calculation can at most facilitate financialisation as it does not itself involve monetary flows as such. Commodity form can be the basis for financialisation insofar as regular flows of money, not necessarily involving commodity production, are securitised, thereby creating an asset that can be traded.[23] Only with commodities, and their integration into the circuits of production and exchange, is the potential for financialisation fully released, allowing for whatever both CF and CC have to offer, as well as the range of financial processes underpinning production and sale.

23 See Leyshon and Thrift (2007) for emphasis upon securitisation as the new driving force of capitalism, and Pike and Pollard (2010) for securitisation of brands and even the weather. And for corresponding financialisation of the university, see Engelen et al. (2014) and Morrish and Sauntson (2013).

It also follows that these distinctions bear upon the processes as well as the presence of financialisation by which is meant at least the increasing weight of finance in economic and social life. For, the process of commodification itself (and so shifts from CC to CF and from CF to C) strengthens the potential for financialisation. In a slightly more refined way, this says little more than that expanding the realm of the market underpins the potential realm of financialisation. But it follows that financialisation is attached to a wide range of economic and social processes that are subject both to varying degrees of, and potential for, financialisation as they are themselves reproduced and/or transformed (for example, through commercialisation or privatisation).

So financialisation feeds on money (in ways as yet to be more fully specified), and money feeds on commodities and vice-versa, allowing for the more generalised presence of commodity forms and calculations. Such are the consequences of a universal theory of money, which allows for differentiation across the different processes to which it is attached, with a corresponding obligation to investigate the substance of the economic and social relations, structures, processes and agencies to which it is attached.[24] Wherever activities fall across the CCFCC divides, their monetary forms of expression are this and no more, innocent of why and how they belong where they do until exposed as such. This does not mean that money is a passive reflection of the activities to which it is attached, something that is forcibly realised in crises, but nor does it have a uniform let alone an independent existence from the highly varied worlds of CCFCC.

That financialisation is associated with the encroachment of monetary relations is evidenced in the case studies, which document a marked increase in the presence and influence of market forces in the provision of housing and water across the countries considered. Yet the case studies also show that simply to equate financialisation with commodification would be misleading. The provision of housing and water is highly variegated across the countries considered, and this variegation is underpinned by a range of market forms. We

24 Note that for Beckert (2011, p. 759), this leads to the idea that prices derive from social relations so that, "the outcome of struggles between market actors taking place within market fields is the sociological vantage point from which to analyse price formation" with the consequence that more or less everything is price-forming including networks, just norms, power (of cartels), trust, status, institutions, legitimacy, meaning, preferences, expectations, and so on. Indeed, Bourdieu is quoted to the effect that, "It is not prices that determine everything, but everything that determines prices". Ironically, there is nothing in this to bother the mainstream neoclassical economist. In contrast here, the position is that these elements attached to systems of provision are formative of the material culture underpinning use, as opposed to, exchange values.

suggest that the CCFCC triad can help to explicate this variegation by unpicking the diversity of arrangements concealed under the spread of a more amorphous notion of market forces.

4 Comparative Housing

The most striking feature of housing provision in the era of financialisation has been the rise of owner-occupation as the favoured tenure form (that is, the favoured set of arrangements for accessing housing).[25] Owner-occupation involves households purchasing and inhabiting their own dwelling, in contrast with the most common alternative tenures, private and social rental, whereby households rent their dwelling from a private or social landlord, respectively, with the latter usually involving some sort of rental subsidy. One of the merits of the SoP approach is that it looks beyond the allocation arrangements that are typically the focus of neoclassical economics, opening up the black boxes of production and consumption in order to investigate the entire chain of provision. In this context, the degree of commodification of owner-occupation becomes a question, not simply of whether houses are bought and sold in a market, but also of the nature of the rules governing land use and the character of housing producers. While owner-occupation can be fully commodified – if land is accessed through the market and the homes concerned are built and sold for profit – it is notable that it is not necessarily so. At the other extreme to production and sale for profit, it is possible for owner-occupied homes to be built and allocated without the profit motive playing a role at all – if, for example, the state were to requisition land, build housing and transfer ownership to inhabitants administratively.

In practice, owner-occupation in the case study countries has exhibited varying degrees and types of commodification along the chain of provision. Before discussing them in more detail, it should be noted that all of the case study countries had a significant commodified owner-occupation sector that preceded the period looked at in the case studies, with the exception of Poland, where housing was decommodified under socialism. We therefore follow the case studies in focusing on areas of transition in the housing sector.

Beginning with consumption, in Portugal owner-occupation expanded at the expense of the private rented sector and informal shanty towns in response

25 The following discussion is based on case study reports (Robertson, 2014 and 2016; Santos et al. 2015; Isaacs, 2016; Lis, 2015b; and Çelik et al. 2015; as well as the sectoral synthesis report, Robertson, 2016).

to increased availability of mortgages. Housing provision therefore underwent a shift from one form of commodified relations (rental) to another (purchase), with the aid of mortgage subsidies and state investment in infrastructure. In the UK and Poland, commodification of housing was given a big push by the privatisation of social housing from the 1980s and 1990s, respectively. However, the character of this shift is complex. On the one hand, prior to privatisation, social housing was characterised by the commodity form, in that occupants paid monthly rents to state providers, albeit at subsidised rates. On the other hand, the sale of this housing did not in itself transform that housing into commodities because the profit motive played no role. The privatised housing had been built by the state and was sold at a heavy discount to sitting tenants and, hence, is better understood as an alternative commodity form. The push given to commodification of housing by privatisation came from the way in which ownership of state-built housing facilitated entry into private housing markets. In the UK, this has been fully realised as there have been high rates of sale of privatised housing, allowing agents to enter secondary housing markets. In Poland this process has been impeded by the poor quality of the privatised housing stock.

The South African government has sought to spread homeownership to the poor black population by subsidising investment in basic housing units, which are allocated through an application process among those meeting income requirements. Access to housing for this section of the population relies on the commodity form only in so far as a small payment is involved in the bureaucratic process through which basic housing units are allocated. As in the UK and Poland, it was hoped that giving poorer households ownership rights over subsidised properties would facilitate entry of those households – and the subsidised properties – into the secondary housing market. However, the generally poor quality of the subsidised housing has prevented this from happening. The Turkish case study, which focuses on Istanbul, describes the way in with the Mass Housing Administration (TOKI) has collaborated with private developers to displace squatting communities and free up land for the development of middle- and upper-income housing. This process has seen one set of commodified relations (within squatting communities) replaced by another (middle- and upper-class flats). The lower-income residents displaced in the process have been rehoused in state-provided housing, for which they pay the state under arrangements captured by the commodity form.

Turning to production, irrespective of the range of acquisition arrangements, commodified relations dominated housing production in all case studies, with housebuilding carried out by capitalist agents for profit. This is the case even for production that is state-led, as for low-income housing in Turkey and South Africa. Here, investment comes from the state but private firms are contracted to carry out construction. The same is true of the small amount of state-subsidised housing that exists in the UK, Portugal and Poland. The only exceptions are those parts of the housing stock that were built by producers directly employed by the state and then privatised, in the UK and Poland, and self-build, which accounts for a significant part of supply in both Poland and Portugal. While self-build is decommodified, in the sense that households build for their own use rather than for profit, it is nonetheless embedded in a series of commodified relationships affecting land acquisition, materials and, in many cases, the employment of a contract builder to manage delivery.

Land is a central component of housing production, and arrangements governing access and use shape housing systems in important ways. Though not strictly a commodity, because not produced, land can be commodified (in form, CF) in the sense that access is determined through private property rights exchanged on a market. A trend reported across the case studies was that land use is increasingly governed by the logic of the market or 'best (monetary) value' use. However, within this trend, commodification across the case studies once again took varying forms. In Portugal, land is largely commodified, subject to land use regulations administered by the state. The case study documents, in addition, the incorporation of slum-cleared areas into formal land markets. In the UK, land is similarly largely commodified, and planning authorities' decisions over land use have become increasingly determined by monetary value, leading to the squeezing of social housing in desirable areas and growing investment in real estate assets. An unwillingness to intervene in land markets has also shaped the housing SoP in South Africa. In particular, it has confined subsidised low-income housing to areas remote from employment centres and lacking infrastructure. A similar relegation of the poor to low value land was evident in Turkey, though there we have seen a more active process of removal, with lower income communities compulsory relocated, often offering violent resistance . Land was rapidly commodified following Poland's transition from socialism, under which land was allocated administratively. Poland's 'shock therapy' put in place lax land use regulations, giving rise to chaotic patterns of development.

It is clear from this discussion that the promotion of owner-occupation in the era of financialisation cannot be reduced to commodification per se. Housing provision occurs through a series of arrangements embodying varying forms and degrees of commodification. This is compounded by the observation that owner-occupation is not the only way of commodifying housing provision. Private rental is also a commodified form of housing provision, especially if both the production and the rental of housing are carried out for the purpose of profit-making. What distinguishes owner-occupation – and makes it the quintessential form of financialised housing provision – is that the cost of housing relative to incomes entails that house purchase is dependent on credit for most households. Owner-occupation thus serves to incorporate households into financial markets, expanding the scope for financial profit, through both interest on mortgage payments and trading rights to those payments on secondary mortgage markets.

Indirectly, owner-occupation has also been associated with the spread of commodity calculation by reconstituting individuals as neoliberal agents. The idea here is that, by providing individuals with an asset that can be borrowed against and used to accumulate wealth through capital gains and climbing the housing ladder, owner-occupation serves to inculcate rational economic behaviour in individuals, expanding the scope of commodity calculation into more areas of daily life (Payne, 2012). In the extreme, owner-occupation has been seen as the lynchpin of an 'asset-based welfare system', in which widespread homeownership "serves as a tool or lever for governments to institute welfare reform" thus allowing "governments to pursue restructuring programmes that downsize other welfare services, notably social care and pensions, or allocate them to a local level" (Van Gent, 2010, p. 376).

To sum up, the financialisation of housing has fed off the extension of the scope of monetary relations within housing provision, with the particular form of debt-based form of monetary relations associated with owner-occupation being most prominent. Yet beneath this general trend lies a wide variety of forms of commodification and methods through which they have been extended, giving rise to variegated forms of financialisation across the housing systems considered.

Before we move on to water, this discussion of owner-occupation and the ways in which it provides a vehicle for financialisation requires some caveats. First, while the promotion of owner-occupation and incorporation of households into mortgage markets has been a clear goal of governments, it has not always been achieved and, when it has, has often proved dysfunctional. As mentioned, despite hopes that state subsidies would provide a launching pad for poor black households to climb up the housing ladder, South Africa's low-income housing market remains segregated from the secondary housing market, and low-income households are largely excluded from mortgage markets. Even in the UK and Portugal, countries in which owner-occupation is widespread and mortgage markets mature, a recent revival of the private rented sector suggests that the owner-occupation tenure form is reaching its limits.

Second, the tying of owner-occupation to the encroachment of commodity calculation on individual rationality is arguably more a facet of scholarship and policy than it is reality. The idea appears in academic literature more often as an analysis of the rationale governing policy than of the extent to which that policy agenda has been successful (see, for example, Payne, 2012; Van Gent, 2010; Crouch, 2009b; Finlayson, 2009; and Watson, 2009). Where the latter question has been asked it has been met with scepticism. For example, Toussaint and Elsinga (2009) distinguish between 'old' and 'new' asset-based welfare systems. In the former, associated with Southern Europe, housing plays a role in supporting welfare provision as a result of its being embedded in familial support structures. Only in the latter – associated with Anglo-American countries – is housing asset-based welfare linked to financialisation and commodity calculation. Even here, we should be wary of assuming that individuals are passively reformed in response to shifting forms of provision, as the imperative to treat housing as an asset runs into other meanings and uses that people attach to housing, most notably as a place of comfort, security and shelter (Robertson, 2014). What these caveats tell us is that variegation is not only a product of the different means through which commodification has been extended in different social and economic contexts, but also out of the dysfunctions, contradictions, and resistances to which commodification gives rise.

5 Comparative Water

The provision of water has also undergone something of a transformation since the 1980s in each of the case studies. As with housing, these show varying forms and degrees of commodification. For most of the last century water was provided as a strategic resource to support what Bakker (2005) terms a "state hydraulic" paradigm of water management characterised by centrally planned investments to provide for economic growth and social development. The high capital costs and long infrastructure lifetimes meant that public financing was crucial for the development of water supply across the world. Water was provided by the state with a focus on supply-side interventions following the cholera and typhoid epidemics of the cities in the nineteenth century. These aspects of water – the high cost and long-term nature of investment, combined with the public health elements of provision – meant that the system of water provision did not appear to lend itself easily to commodification.

Changes in the sector came in the 1980s with the rise of neoliberalism (Fine et al. 2016a) and increasing attention to state failure and environmental concerns. Water consumption had begun to tail off in many countries. In E&W, the system of centralised water planning failed to anticipate a dramatic decline in industrial water demand as the country's economic structure shifted from manufacturing to services. Ten regional water authorities were created in E&W in the 1970s. Their operations were financially ring-fenced from the local authority, and they were obliged to operate on a cost recovery basis. From the early 1980s they were able to borrow from private capital. The same pattern can be observed to varying degrees across all of the case studies, although this transformation came a decade or so later, with corporatisation of water companies becoming core sector policy. Cost recovery pricing was introduced across all locations, although in E&W the majority of households were still charged on the basis of the rateable value of their property rather than their water consumption. In most other countries water consumption is now metered although this is now an option in E&W and can even be imposed in case of a declaration of water shortage (on relatively easy criteria).

England and Wales were among the first in the world to introduce water privatisation. This took the form of listing the water companies on the London Stock Exchange (LSE) in 1989. The perception at this stage was that private financing could be substituted for public borrowing in a benign swap that had the advantage of appearing to reduce public borrowing. Elsewhere privatisation was introduced in different ways. In South Africa, water remains the responsibility of the municipality but private investors have been sought to undertake management contracts (e.g. in Johannesburg) or long-term concession contracts with municipalities. These were introduced in the late 1990s and just two remain. In Portugal also municipalities could enter into private concession contracts from 1993. These are skewed to the more wealthy areas with just 29 private concessions for retail water out of 380 managing entities. However, these cover 13% of the population. In Poland the sector was restructured in the early 1990s with water providers established at arm's length from the municipality with diverse ownership structures. Water was privatised in Gdansk in 1993. This then brought the production of water into the realm of commodity production but still a strong role for the state remained, often as provider and, even with privatised water, the state continues to govern pricing and production standards. The process of commodification of water has generally stopped short of water trading (except in a few locations, Grafton et al. 2010).[26]

There are ways in which the case of E&W differs from the other case studies and these have shaped the processes of commodification and financialisation. First, in this case the transition is permanent. Listing the water companies on the LSE sent a clear signal of commitment to commodification

26 This is the buying and selling of water access entitlements and allocations.

in perpetuity. For firms and financiers, this provides a more secure framework for long-term financing decisions than fixed term contracts. Second, water companies are regulated by the central economic regulator, Ofwat, which sets policy and answers to the central government. This is in contrast to the other concessions which are answerable to local municipalities. In Portugal there is a sector regulator, ERSAR, but only in 2014 did ERSAR take over water pricing from the municipalities. Third, this is a national programme where all water and sewerage companies were privatised (albeit at considerable discount to ensure interest from investors) and not just water but also energy, telecoms and the rail network were all privatised around the same time. In this country, then, privatisation was part of a national shift towards commodification of infrastructure. In contrast, privatisation accounts for only a small element of provision in the other case study countries. The result is that the transition is deeper and more far-reaching and attached to a bigger political project than privatisation in the other countries.

The case of E&W has also seen some changes over time as privatisation has matured. From the mid-1990s, firms were targets for takeovers with their large cash balances, low levels of debts and high and secure revenues. Initially the entrants were European and American infrastructure companies. Subsequently, out of ten water and sewerage companies that were listed on the LSE in 1989, three remain listed, two have been delisted and are owned by Asian conglomerates, one is a not-for-profit company and four are owned by financial sector companies. In the other case studies, Portugal has had the most privatisation. Here too there has been some consolidation as the global and domestic environment has changed. The initial investors were local Portuguese and Spanish construction companies. More recently, the last couple of years have seen the entry of Asian investors in the sector with Japanese conglomerate, Marubeni, taking over AGS in 2014, and Beijing Enterprises Water Group buying a group of water companies from Veolia in 2013.[27] In South Africa, many initial attempts at privatisation were short-lived and only two long-term contracts remain. Both of these have been consolidated and since 2012 have been owned by the Singapore-based company, Sembcorp (which is also the owner of an English water-only company in Bournemouth).

---

27 Indaqua is owned by Portuguese shareholders Mota Engil, Soares da Costa and Hidrante; Aquapor, formerly part of the state-owned utility AdP, was sold in 2007 to a consortium of Portuguese investors, DST and ABB. A third significant investor in the sector, AGS, was owned by Somague, a Spanish subsidiary of Sacyr Valleheremoso but in 2014 was sold to Marubeni.

The process of privatisation connects water consumers with circuits of global financial capital, of which they are largely unaware. The two largest investors in water privatisation contracts over the past ten years, Veolia Environnement and Suez, have been operating in each of the case study countries at various times since the early 1990s. These companies are linked to financial markets far removed from water consumption, via financial intermediaries, for example, with water-targeted investment funds which are traded on the New York Stock Exchange. Owners of shares in some of these financial products, such as Exchange Traded Funds (ETFs), include investment funds operating on behalf of high net worth individuals. In this way, stakes in water infrastructure have become an asset class and households are connected with the world's richest individuals via finance (see Bayliss, 2013 for more on this). In addition, some of these water-related financial products also include stakes in some of the LSE-listed English water companies, Severn Trent, Pennon and United Utilities. So, a water consumer in the south-west of England paying their water bill contributes to the same pool of funds as the bill payment from a customer of Veolia in South Africa or Portugal (at least, until recently as Veolia sold its stakes in each of these in 2012 and 2013, respectively) which trickles up to the high net worths at the top of the financial feed chain. Eventually returns from ETFs are paid out, via asset fund managers, to the world's richest individuals as well as to pension funds (although only the identity of five largest stakeholders are disclosed, so the ultimate beneficiaries from these company dividends are unknown).

Since the emergence of Asian investors on the scene, there has been further consolidation with finance in other parts of the world. For example, Sembcorp from Singapore which now owns the two South African water companies as well as Bournemouth Water, in England, is owned by the Government of Singapore (with 49.5%) and the balance of shares is listed on the Singapore Stock Exchange. As with E&W, financialisation processes have connected water consumers in English and South African towns to investors on the Singapore exchange.

Commodification via privatisation therefore unwittingly connects some households to the world's financial capitals through their consumption of water. However, the range is limited in the case study countries as privatisation was not widespread and was usually only implemented in the more affluent and profitable locations. There is a growing divide, with water consumers in the same country paying into global financial chains while others pay to the local municipality. Some are more directly part of financialisation processes than others.

6 From Financialisation …

Having outlined the analytical categories captured by CCFCC and discussed them in relation to housing and water, it remains to tie these categories to financialisation and contemporary capitalism more generally. We do this by considering another commonly observed function of money – that of store of value (however economic 'value' might be understood and determined). This function of money attains greater significance in the era of financialisation due to the proliferation of asset trading. Indeed, the role of money as store of value has underpinned the new forms and scales of profit-making that have emerged through the financial system over the last few decades. As we show in this section, the nature of these new forms and scales, and how they have played out in relation to both economic and social reproduction, can in turn be understood in part by drawing the distinction between capital extended in circulation for consumption and that extended for production.

As store of value, money, or the idea of monetary value, is represented symbolically as an asset. This symbolic representation can circulate independently of the purported value that it represents, as is the case with trade credit or a generalised system of IOUs. What these share in common is both a redistribution of payment and receipt of monetary values over time together with a redistribution of the values concerned (with later payment usually commanding greater value depending on interest effectively charged and in the absence of default). To give a housing-related example, claims to mortgage repayments, secured on the values of the houses to which those mortgages are attached, are traded as assets on financial markets in the form of residential mortgage-backed securities (RMBSs). In addition, the value of these RMBSs may fluctuate in response to supply and demand for such securities on financial markets, even if the value of the asset underpinning the security – directly, mortgages, indirectly, house prices – does not change. Certainly, in principle, the different values involved, and the relationship between them, can diverge as is sharply revealed in bubbles and crashes.

Accordingly, paper claims on (expanded) value were termed fictitious (capital) by Marx, not because the value on which they depend does not exist (other than by way of exception, especially fraud), but precisely because the paper claims involved can take on a value distinct from whatever value-generating process (or not) that is supposedly underpinning them (just as paper money is more or less worthless relative to the value it represents, only that represented value is intended to expand for fictitious *capital*). In other words, the fictitious nature of the paper does not make it *capital* as such. For this, the paper claim is contingent upon value that has yet to be produced and realised, or is in process. For Marx, and equally for Minsky if on a different basis drawing on the accounting and borrowing practices of firms, the distinction between monetary relations based on credit as such and those contingent upon continuing expansion (production and realisation of surplus value for Marx, and hedge, speculative and Ponzi borrowing for Minsky) is crucial.[28] In particular, for Marx, underpinning this distinction is a separation between different types of capital operating within exchange, namely, that facilitating consumption and that facilitating production. For the former, most readily associated with buying and selling commodities, especially on credit, as a function of commodity circulation, such capitals tend to earn a normal rate of profit similar to industrial capital. For the latter, capital in exchange, providing for the expansion of production by mobilising financial resources for that purpose, is not necessarily subject to the same form of competition and attracts interest, and a deduction from surplus generated, before it is distributed to other capitals.

Consider, for example, a bank that borrows (takes deposits) and lends without the need to use any capital of its own. Whatever return it makes by differences between rates of interest for borrowing and lending (and to cover expenses) will yield an infinite rate of profit. This could, of course, be reduced by competitive presence or entry of others into the sector but if there is, indeed, some minimum scale of capital required to enter and compete (let alone state regulation), then incumbents are not likely to make such capital available to potential rivals at their own expense. This is not to say that banks (or financial institutions more generally) can charge whatever they like for (some of) their services, only that the competitive process for them is different than for other capitals (since it does not tend to provide the financial means to compete with itself, only for competition in other sectors).

In addition, it cannot be predetermined, even if intentions are solid, whether financial services individually designed to promote a return by expanding provision do achieve this return in practice especially for the economy as a whole. An enterprise may fail and, vice-versa, a simple credit or transfer to fund consumption (pensions, for example, spent on food) may promote profitable provision (for food enterprises) for what would otherwise be an unsuccessful loan for the capitalist providing for that consumption. In short, the extent to which expansion of financial services coincides with expansion of material provision, whether as output or profitability, is of necessity highly variable as is sharply revealed in case of sectoral or economy-wide bubbles and collapses.

28 For Marx, this is the basis of interest-bearing capital for which see Fine (2013–14), Fine and Saad-Filho (2016b) and Fine (1985/6 and 1988) for exposition and for what follows.

This last point is illustrated by both housing and water. For housing, the distinction between monetary relations based on credit and those dependent on continuing expansion corresponds to that between mortgage lending for house purchase and lending to housing developers. Across the case studies, financialisation is associated with expanded mortgage lending, notwithstanding variation in the size and coverage of mortgage markets in the countries considered. There has thus been a reorganisation of housing provision that has served to expand finance's claim on incomes. In some cases – predominantly the USA and Britain, and to a lesser extent elsewhere – secondary mortgage markets have emerged on which these claims have been traded. Increased mortgage lending has served to expand financial sector profits, which, as mentioned above, arise from fluctuations in the value of RMBSs away from the value of the income stream underpinning the asset, as well as from the value of that income stream itself. Expanded mortgage lending has also tended to drive up house prices, but whether or not this is translated into expanded material provision is dependent on patterns of development finance as well as the way in which the housebuilding industry operates.

In general, the expansion of finance for production has been more limited than that of house purchase finance. Among the case study countries, only Portugal saw a significant increase in lending for house building. There, the construction and real estate sectors increased their share in total business lending from 10% in 1992 to 40% in 2008, and this created a housebuilding boom corresponding to the house price boom. Both Turkey and South Africa also experienced a boom in building, but this relied on the state providing land and investment finance, respectively. In the UK, by contrast, constraints on supply have been two-fold. First, mortgage lending expanded at a much faster rate than lending for development, meaning that finance inflated demand more than supply. Second, the structure of the housebuilding industry in Britain – most notably, the dominance of speculative housebuilders and a restrictive planning system – has channelled a large portion of the development finance that is available into land, hindering production volumes and inflating speculative land and house price bubbles prone to collapse when finance is withdrawn.

In water, financialisation has deepened in E&W with the arrival of a new type of investor in the water sector in the 2000s. Initial takeovers by American and European investors were sold out to Asian and private equity owners of water companies. The case study research indicates that the type of owner had an impact on the nature and extent of financialisation practices in the provision of water. Notably, the four water companies owned by private equity firms in E&W have introduced predatory financial practices to increase shareholder earnings. Mostly these companies are owned by special purpose vehicles (SPVs) put together by a group of financial investors, and their headquarters are registered offshore. The rise of the SPV is increasingly significant for infrastructure finance and has been widespread in public-private partnerships (PPPs). The project structure is attractive because there is no recourse to the assets of the investors, and finance is raised on the strength of the project or investment itself. The project assets are isolated from the rest of the other assets of the SPV shareholders. PPPs that are financed in this way tend to be highly leveraged. Investors in these water SPVs are asset managers, investment banks, pension funds and similar financial entities, and they receive the residual from the project or the operations of the water utility.

The water companies owned by SPVs have the most complex and least transparent of ownership structures. These four companies, Thames, Anglian, Yorkshire and Southern Water, all have a similar corporate group structure. The regulated water company is situated in a chain of companies, some of which are based in tax havens. Funds are transferred up and down the ownership chain in a dense sequence of dividends and interest payments on inter-group loans. Several holding companies with similar names in the chain of ownership do nothing apart from receive interest and/or dividends and then pay these out to other group companies with the SPV as the ultimate owner. Each of these has a group company in the Cayman Islands. This is to enable the buyer of the water company to add the debt incurred to buy the water company to the water company itself ('acquisition debt'), something not allowed by UK company law. This use of debt to buy the company, where the debt is raised on the strength of the company being bought, is a kind of leveraged buyout, popular with private equity firms and described by Investopedia as "an especially ruthless predatory tactic".

While such financial practices were not documented in the other case studies, in Portugal the purchase of the utility, CGEP, when it was acquired by Beijing Enterprises Water Group (BEWG) Ltd[29] from Veolia in 2013,[30] was in part financed by loans from the new shareholders to the water utility. The shareholder loan will be paid interest annually by CGEP to its parent holding company. So, the utility pays interest to the owners of the company on funds used to buy the company. Interest, where it is paid on loans from shareholders,

29 "BEWG successfully acquired Portugal assets of Veolia Water", Press Release, Beijing Enterprises Water Group Ltd, Hong Kong, 25 March, 2013.

30 Incorporated in Bermuda as an exempted company with limited liability, and the shares are listed on the Hong Kong Stock Exchange.

is another form of shareholder distribution along with dividends. And the interest is tax deductible.[31]

In E&W, the SPV-owned water companies have also carried out a complex corporate restructuring known as 'Whole Business Securitisation' (WBS) which has enabled them to raise the debts of the water company that are secured against the expected revenue from future bill payments which are securitised. The process of WBS is only possible in restricted circumstances where firms have a stable and predictable revenue stream, so a privatised water utility is ideal. One of the conditions of the water company licence, set by the regulator, is that the water company has to have a credit rating which is 'investment grade'. Increasing debt levels puts this rating at risk. The WBS process, however, enables a higher level of debt within the limits of the credit rating.

The WBS process was originally devised to enable a not-for-profit company to take over Welsh Water using high levels of debt. This financing structure was subsequently replicated by the private, equity-owned companies. Welsh Water now has one of the lowest levels of gearing and highest credit ratings in the sector while the private equity owned firms have the highest gearing levels and lowest credit ratings. This shows that it is not the financial structures or mechanisms as such that necessarily create financial extraction but the commodity production for profit.

Across the sector, levels of gearing have increased substantially since privatisation. To some extent, this has fed a significant increase in investment but firms have also used these debts to finance shareholder distributions. In common with wider experiences of financialisation, the sector has seen a large increase in 'rentier' payments. The yearly charge for net interest payable for the nine England Water and Sewerage Companies (WaSCs) increased from £288m to over £2,000m in the twenty years from 1993 to 2012 (in 2012 prices).[32] Where the interest paid is to shareholders on loans to the company, sometimes at 18% rate of interest, there are even greater benefits for the owners of water companies.

The financialisation of the sector is evident in the significant structural transformation that has taken place since privatisation with the shift in resource allocation away from wage labour towards 'rentier' provisioning (interest and dividends). Also in keeping with wider patterns has been a significant increase in remuneration of directors as reward for meeting shareholder interests, a feature permeating the whole sector. The Chief Executive of the

31 "BEWG successfully acquired Portugal assets of Veolia Water", Press Release, Beijing Enterprises Water Group Ltd, Hong Kong, 25 March, 2013.

32 Own calculations based on data from company reports.

regulator Ofwat, Jonson Cox was awarded £10m when he left his former position as CEO of Anglian Water in recognition of the substantial increase in the share price that had occurred under his leadership.

This reflects the wider pattern of financialisation where the enrichment of shareholders and company managers has been at the expense of workers' wages and benefits (Van der Zwan, 2014). In water companies, workers have faced downward pressure on wages and conditions both from dividend-focused shareholders as well as regulator pressure to improve 'productivity'. In E&W there was some evidence of companies reporting they would need to lay off staff to meet the conditions set in the regulatory price review.

Such financialised outcomes are overseen by the state. The sector is regulated according to a structure of price controls established at the time of privatisation in 1989, but the current nature and practices of the company owners have changed dramatically since then. Within this regulatory framework, company debt and dividends are considered to be 'market outcomes' and are not subject to any control (as long as the company retains a credit rating which is investment grade). In response to suggestions that Ofwat should specify a gap on gearing levels or set specific liquidity ratios, the regulator sees disadvantages in bringing such measures into the companies' licences mainly because Ofwat is no better able to assess what would be appropriate than the markets themselves or the credit ratings agencies, "We are unlikely to be in a better position than the credit rating agencies or the markets themselves to determine appropriate constraints on financial ratios and capital structure" (Ofwat, 2011, p. 4, cited in Bayliss, 2014).

7 ... through Economic to Social Reproduction

Across the previous two sections, then, we have sought to take further the theoretical, or framing, perspectives previously developed in which the notion of 'financialisation' as the eponymous presence of finance is unpicked into various categories around CCFCC, the presence of fictitious capital or not and the way in which these impinge upon the SoPs for water and housing across our case studies. It should be added that, as items of final consumption, both housing and water (which is also a commercial input) have peculiar characteristics as use values. For water, whilst in principle it could be charged for by the unit like many other commodities, especially with metering, in practice the pricing to which it is attached tends to be subject to more complicated forms of charging reflecting infrastructural or other costs and criteria in more or less arbitrary ways. For example, in E&W households cannot be disconnected for non-payment. This shapes credit relations in the sector as households are advised that water is not a priority debt, compared to electricity for example or even credit card 'abuse'. In South Africa some water is provided for free for some households. Paradoxically, this means to some degree that water is produced as a commodity but, in some instances, the commodity form to which it is attached is suspended. After all, getting water for free in these circumstances is not the same in anyway whatsoever as the free provision of water. It is simply the exception of the rule for water not being free in some ways as if the water had been stolen, signifying not the absence of commodity or other relations but breaches with them. And, more generally, just because water is regulated, this does not mean that it is not produced as a commodity but merely, and paradoxically, not in an 'ideal' or 'pure' commodity form.

In other words, even our disaggregation into CCFCC as the basis for addressing the scope for financialisation cannot tell the full story of provision, not least because these are fluid categories in practice both in and of themselves and in relation to one another. What can be discerned, however, is how financialisation is associated with the pressures to ease and draw upon transitions from CC to CF and from CF to CC in systems of provision, although such processes are influenced both by the material forms taken by what is provided and contestation over provision (as with free or subsidised water, regulation, etc). And, of course, similar considerations apply to the specificities of housing provision given its diverse forms of supply, tenure and financing. Most striking is that the financialisation of housing has advanced on the back of private homeownership, to which commodified housing production and access has been secondary, as evidenced by the state's role in building the privatised housing stock in the UK and Poland and in allocating low income housing in South Africa. This reflects the opportunities for mortgage lending and secondary mortgage trading created by private homeownership – forms of financialisation that can develop with relative independence from commodified housing production.

Such observations lead to three important implications concerning financialisation. The first is that the prodigious expansion and proliferation of financial markets over the past three decades is indicative of a secular, if irregular, trend of expansion of fictitious capital alongside and, arguably, at the net expense of the real economy. How else are we to describe, let alone explain, the disproportionate growth and spread of both financial markets and rewards (and corresponding inequalities)? Slow growth relative to the post-war boom as well as the crisis and recession that have followed it have, after all, occurred despite this prodigious expansion of finance *and* otherwise extraordinarily favourable conditions for both growth and productivity increase.[33]

Second, and as already noted in relation to housing, a standard mechanism for such effects is for finance to be drawn into the sale and resale of assets that have claims to incomes. This can lead to speculative bubbles and to pressures to sustain the processes involved through short-term profit-making and/or -taking. Such may be realised through cost-cutting at the expense of wages, working conditions, long-term investment and so on. The important point here is the greater pressure for short-term profit-making at the expense of longer-term and broader considerations, not least since wage-cutting, etc, are hardly unique to the era of financialisation and otherwise absented from the rationale of capitalist production and reproduction. The presumption is that financialisation induces poorer economic and social performance at many levels, if not for everyone all of the time. From this, it follows that the consequences of financialisation are differentiated by the sources of income upon which it depends and how it depends upon them, i.e. how these incomes are generated, and this cannot be derived from the presence of financialisation as such.

We can see this by contrasting the consequences of financialisation in housing and water. In the former, the financialisation of income streams arising from mortgage repayments has fed mortgage markets and speculative house price bubbles. This has in turn fuelled inequality by expanding the housing wealth of some while driving up housing costs of others. In other instances, financialisation can be associated with longer-term investments not least when these can themselves be bundled into more liquid forms of commercial assets for resale and/or access to enhanced levels of credit. For water, companies are able to issue bonds on the basis of identifiable cash flows from the operating revenues of a segment of a business. Loans are taken out on the basis of these future revenue streams. These are used to finance large-scale, long-term investments, contrary to some degree to the notion that financialisation involves short-termism at the expense of long-term investment. But the promise of secure revenues does allow water companies to raise short-term finance, and there is also evidence that debts have been raised to finance shareholder distributions, thereby expanding financial profits at the expense of real investment. The proximate effect is a transfer from the water consumers of the future to the shareholders of today.

33 Ashman and Fine (2013, p. 157) refer to favourable "'fundamentals' for capitalism in terms of availability of new technologies, expansion and weakening of global and national labour forces, and the triumph of neoliberalism in political and policy arenas", with the role of China also underpinning expansion as a source and destination.

Of course, the financial mechanisms for delivering financial rewards have themselves become extremely diverse, encompassing huge salaries and bonuses within the financial sector, as well as returns on various kinds of asset ownership. These have generated greater levels of inequality, with implications for levels and composition of demand. In addition, and third, the expansion of finance has been both intensive (within existing or traditional spheres of operation) as well as extensive, that is by incorporating activities either where they were previously absent or where they were not previously subject to incorporation into financialised circuits (futures markets for commodities, for example, following those of currencies are notable examples). Housing is illustrative of both, as we have seen intensive expansion in the form of the growth of secondary mortgage markets attached to already existing mortgage markets, and extensive expansion through the incorporation into mortgage markets of sections of the population previously excluded, most notably through subprime and reverse redlining in the USA. Within the literature, this expanding and increasing reach has been marked by reference to the increasing presence of financialisation in both economic and social reproduction.

For economic reproduction, an early insight in the context of financialisation was provided by reference to the rise of shareholder value, the increasing engagement of (industrial) corporations in targeting short-term financial as opposed to long-term productivity gains, and the increasing reliance of corporations upon profits drawn from financial dealing as opposed to producing things. In general, emphasis on corporate financialisation preceded more general accounts (i.e. of credit, the household and everyday life) by a short if distinct lag.[34] Significantly, though, the literature tends to be very Anglo-American in focus, to some extent reflecting that the processes of financialisation are themselves more advanced in the USA and the UK, itself an index of the relative strengths of (global and domestic) financial interests and their political representation through the state, (Engelen et al. 2008). New public management has also been observed, with Skaerbaek and Melander (2004) pointing to new principles of accounting associated with financialisation and privatisation, and the corresponding emergence of new actors and interests.

For social, as opposed to narrowly-conceived economic, reproduction, financialisation has in part been seen to be a consequence of attempts to sustain (norms of) consumption through increased borrowing in face of

34 For this and a sample of continuing literature, see special issue of *Economy and Society*, vol 29, no 1, 2000, Kadtler and Sperling (2002), Perotti and Gelfer (2001), Krippner (2011), O'Sullivan (2007), Muellerleile (2009), Engelen and Grote (2009), Zademach (2009), Buhlmann et al. (2012).

stagnating real wages (or unemployment), cuts in welfare provision, privatisation of social services (pensions, housing, health and education) and the interaction between these and the processes of financialisation. In the lead in this respect has been Lapavitsas' notion of exploitation (of us all) through financialisation.[35] Whatever its merits otherwise, this is, however, a misleading account in a number of respects. On the one hand, it unduly focuses upon the 'impoverished', as it were, for the incidence and even the drive behind financialisation (of the household), whereas whether in use of credit and access to financial(ised) assets, the process has arguably been led by, and has greater incidence with, those on higher incomes (and not driven by low income, unemployment, limited access to privatised welfare, etc).[36] Mortgage lending, for example, is correlated with income (Santos et al. 2016) and extending mortgage lending to less well-off households has proved an on-going problem (Robertson, 2016). On the other hand, as already suggested, not least by reference to CCFCC, the financialisation of social reproduction is highly contingent upon how finance is integrated with provisioning with implications for health, housing and education, let alone credit card (ab)use, liable to be extremely varied across different households and (national) locations.[37] So the US subprime market was predatory and can plausibly be regarded as colloquially exploitative due to its punitive and often outright deceptive repayment structures. But access to a mortgage in the UK is more associated with access to large capital gains and the accumulation of housing wealth than it is with default, negative equity, or unmanageable repayments.

Further, social reproduction involves much more than immediate household access to provisioning. Prominent in the literature has been the reproduction of the spatial environment. This is reflected through a wide range of studies across different applications and at different levels of empirical detail, such as Gruffydd Jones (2012) on Third World slums, Baud and Durand (2012) for global retailing, Christophers (2010, p. 105) for the financialisation of land as "the trend towards treatment of property as a pure financial asset" rather than for its use,[38] Sassen (2010) for subprime as primitive accumulation,

35 Although, for Lapavitsas, financialisation also ranges over new roles for banks and non-financial enterprises as well as households. For a critique, see Fine (2010a). See also Soederberg (2013) for an account of the "debtfare state and the credit card industry".

36 See Beaverstock et al. (2013) for the rise of the super rich and their access to financial products. See also Lysandrou (2011 and 2011/12) and Goda and Lysandrou (2014).

37 With an increasing financialisation of micro-credit (Bateman, 2010; Weber, 2014; and Mader, 2014).

38 See also Robertson (2016) and, for the heavy presence of financialisation in the 'land grab literature', see Isakson and Ryan (2014), Dixon (2014), Fairbairn et al. (2014), Fairbairn

Torrance (2009) for urban infrastructure, Robertson (2012) for ecosystem services, and Amin (2010) for agriculture, the Third World and primitive accumulation. Financialisation has also been closely linked to the inadequacies of responses to climate change (Fieldman, 2014; Layfield, 2013; Sullivan, 2013; and Lohmann, 2011).

Housing and water are, of course, heavily implicated in the reproduction of the built environment. Ivanova (2011, p. 398), like many, follows David Harvey, in arguing that, "The state can temporarily alleviate the tendency to overaccumulation in the primary circuit of capital by facilitating the switch of resources from industry and manufacturing into construction and real estate through a variety of public policies, such as the provision of long-term financing and the willingness to guarantee large-scale projects".[39] In brief, Harvey's "capital switching" thesis distinguishes between primary (commodities), secondary (fixed capital and the built environment) and tertiary (science and technology and social goods) circuits of capital, and argues that over-accumulation in the first will lead to the channelling of investment into the second, and so on. That the state is an active agent in this process is borne out by recent efforts to increase private finance in infrastructure. For example, the European Investment Plan for Europe includes the European Fund for Strategic Investments which aims to overcome the current 'investment gap' in the European Union by mobilising private finance for strategic investments in infrastructure, http://ec.europa.eu/priorities/jobs-growth-investment/plan/efsi/index_en.htm. In developing countries the World Bank's Global Infrastructure Facility has emerged to match private finance to infrastructure investments.

However, the housing case studies belie the idea of *temporary* 'switching' in response to over-accumulation in the primary circuit, by paying witness to long-term economic restructuring characterised by the foregrounding of real estate as a site of 'value creation' and appropriation (the relative balance between the two being a moot and contentious point) and the reshaping of the built environment in response to this restructuring. The reasons for this

(2014) and McMichael (2012), itself indicative of how financialisation is a hot issue for hot issues!

39 And the list could go on, in respect of the spatial and otherwise (although integral to one another even if finance and financialisation are in some sense disembodied whilst also needing to come down to earth). See Locke (2014) for differences between German and US financialisation, with differential impacts upon income distribution and education, Kaika and Ruggeiro (2016) for the transformation of a Milanese industrial district, Theurillat et al. (2010) for differential impact of pension funds on property development, and Weber (2010) for Chicago's securitisation of tax revenue to fund urban development. See later for financialisation of agriculture more generally.

restructuring are complex, but Haila (1988) usefully dissects them, starting with the relocation of industrial production to urban peripheries and emerging economies and consequent restructuring of urban environments around the service sector. This, in turn, is associated with the transformation of urban areas into consumption spaces, to which are attached symbolic meanings. In the context of a growing number of footloose firms and expanded international capital flows, these processes have served to increase the ground rents up for grabs in urban centres.

Another idea of Harvey's is useful in helping to understand these processes. This is that, in the course of capitalist development, land comes to behave like a financial asset which is underpinned by rent: "interest-bearing capital circulates through land markets perpetually in search of enhanced future ground rents" (Harvey, 1982, p. 368). It is not just mortgages, then, that are being financialised, but also ground rents themselves, as evidenced by the emergence of a number of specialised institutions for investing in real estate directly. But the relevance of Harvey's thesis goes beyond the creation of new financial assets underpinned by rent. Haila (1988, p. 91) also points to "the spread of a calculating attitude" with respect to land – CC, if we may – among non-financial agents. For Haila, these include non-financial firms, which "have begun to require maximum profitability also from their real property which has until now served as a framework for activity", p. 92, and the state, which "[i]n their role as landowners ... have recently begun to pursue a new kind of rationality", p. 92. The case studies suggest a third such property owner, as households are also being encouraged to employ a calculating attitude towards their housing by using it as a basis from which to accumulate and extract value. While we have stressed that financialisation's effect on individual subjectivities is complex and contradictory, a shift towards households treating their housing like a financial asset is evident across the case studies.

Harvey's notion of land coming to be treated more like a financial asset more powerfully captures the structural transformations associated with financialisation than does capital switching. Nonetheless, the point stands that the channelling of finance to real estate has had dramatic consequences for both the built environment and broader economic functioning, and that states have played a substantial role in this. A good illustration of the latter aspect is given by the active role of the state in displacing lower income communities from high value land. This was observed in central urban areas in the UK and Turkey and, in the form of slum clearances, in Portugal and South Africa and, in all cases, can be understood as serving to enhance rents and aid their capture.

8 ... to Gender

But reference to social reproduction inevitably raises the issue of gender relations and how these have interacted with financialisation. To a large extent, as with many other fields of study, the gender implications of a new concept and new material developments have been subject to neglect. This does not, however, appear to be primarily the consequence of gender blindness or oppression as such. Rather, it is the sheer complexity of what is involved that discourages grand theorising and generalisation.

Consider, for example, the careful empirical study of the US labour market by Arestis et al. (2013, p. 171/2):

> the empirical analysis of this study supports the notion that a growing wage premium exists for individuals working in managerial and financial occupations over the period 1983– 2009, and that this growing wage premium is not equally distributed among all gender and race groups present in the US labor market. For each ethnic group, men have taken an increasing share of the wage premium. More generally, white and Hispanic men have enjoyed a disproportionate share of this wage premium at the expense of black men, white women, and Hispanic women.
>
> Putting it boldly, the theoretical and empirical analyses suggest that financialization has been neither race nor gender neutral. It has in fact exacerbated gender and ethnic stratification in the US labor market. From this perspective, the gender and race stratification effects of the Great Recession are at least in part the long-run outcome of structural processes generated by the financialization process.

It will surely come as no surprise that they conclude that financialisation has been associated with, primarily, white male rewards in the wake of growing inequality. But how far does this generalise beyond the USA, to other outcomes deriving from financialisation and to non-economic reproduction?

Such issues are addressed by Adkins and Dever (2014) who, given women's role in social reproduction, acknowledge the multiple sources of impact upon gender relations through financialisation, not least implicitly differentiated by CCFCC as laid out here and, for them, in conditions of (the crisis of) postfordism. It is far from clear that the notion of postfordism helps in capturing this complexity, not least as it has long since gone out of fashion and, unlike the original conception of Fordism (and regulation) by Aglietta, postfordism has been relatively aloof from the role of finance. This does raise the issue of whether financialisation is distinctive in its implications for gender and, if so, in what ways. This is equally brought out by Allon (2014, p. 17) in drawing contrast with a stylised account of an earlier era for which, "The Fordist/Keynesian welfare state was underpinned by a series of gender, sexual and racial norms, including a gendered division of labour premised on the free gift of women's unpaid domestic work". By contrast post-fordist financialisation is perceived to break down these norms if not the household itself, p. 20:

> This entanglement of financial markets with spaces and activities not previously associated with processes of calculation, measurement and economic value suggests a considerable challenge to received understandings of the relationships between gender and economy, production and reproduction, and life and labour. But perhaps the greatest challenge is to the traditional identity of the home. Long represented as a realm of freedom beyond the market and state, and therefore a site beyond economic calculation, the home's identity has frequently been defined in opposition to the economy ... Rather than existing as a refuge from accumulation, the home has actually been well and truly reconfigured as a new frontier of accumulation.

This idea is prominent in the literature on housing asset-based welfare systems. It views growing homeownership and access to mortgage products as underpinning a shift towards individualised welfare provision in which asset ownership in general, and homeownership in particular, are central. Arguably, however, this is an idea that has more purchase in scholarship, or 'financialisation', and political rhetoric than it does in reality (Robertson, 2014).

Such an approach parallels the notion that the household has itself become a financial enterprise, a notion popularised by Bryan and Rafferty (2014). It is certainly worth questioning whether other developments, even in the earlier period, such as welfare provision and women's greater labour market participation, might not be at least as powerful in transforming the nature of the household, gender relations and social reproduction (and whether gendered norms within the household both persist and/or are transformed in conjunction with financialisation). In short, possibly uncontroversially, the relationships between gender and financialisation and economic and social reproduction need to be disentangled through close attention to the different aspects and processes involved. To the extent that financialisation is associated with increasing debts, a feature of both housing and water in several of the case studies, this is more prevalent in single parent households and these are predominantly headed by women.

More generally, there is, then, drawing upon the discussion so far, a recognisable tension in commitment to a universal theory of money, suitably developed to incorporate CCFCC, and, whether through financialisation or otherwise, acknowledgement that monetary and financial relations are extremely diverse or, as a preferred terminology, 'variegated'.[40] Choice of this term reflects a wish to avoid reliance upon ideal types, as for example with the terminologically close but distinct notion of Varieties of Capitalism.[41] The need is to be able both to identify general underlying determinants – whether as structures, processes, agents and/or relations – and to attach them to diverse outcomes. Accordingly, financialisation is uneven in its nature, incidence and impact,[42] and unsurprisingly, much the same will be true, if not more so, of its associated provisions and cultures, and associated gender relations.

9 Concluding Remarks

This chapter has sought to engage with both the array of trends and phenomena that constitute financialisation, and how they have been reckoned with through scholarship on 'financialisation', in light of case studies on financialisation of housing and water. The core of our theoretical analysis is that as finance is underpinned by money, which is itself constituted by commodified relations, so financialisation is underpinned by transformations of provisioning across the categories abbreviated as CCFCC. These transformations have opened up new income streams to financial capital, which has in turn transformed these income streams into financial assets to be traded. This gives rise to many of the phenomena associated with financialisation – most notably, the intensive and extensive expansion of finance into economic and social

40 See Jessop (2014) for example. Early use of the notion of variegated capitalism is to be found in Peck and Theodore (2007), and see also Brenner et al. (2010) for variegated neoliberalism.

41 For a critique of which, with application to South Africa, especially in the context of financialisation, see Ashman and Fine (2013).

42 The uneven and diverse nature of financialisation is more observed, the more analysis is extended beyond its Anglo-Saxon origins. See, for example, Lapavitsas and Powell (2013), Becker et al. (2010), Becker (2014), Erturk (2010), Garcia-Arias (2015), Levy-Orlik (2014), Datz (2014) in context of pensions, Zhang (2014) for East Asia in context of political influences, Carroll and Jarvis (2014) for Asia, Rethel and Sinclair (2014) for financialisation as an avenue for the developmental to become an entrepreneurial state in Asia, and Bonizzi (2014) for an overview in the context of development.

reproduction, and the expansion of the financial at the expense of the real economy. But the examples drawn from housing and water caution against excessive generalisation in drawing conclusions from our analyses. The nature of CCFCC, its relationship to finance, and the extent to which it has facilitated financialisation all exhibit wide variation across both housing and water and the different case studies. The implications for social and economic reproduction and for real investment similarly vary. All of this emphasises the need to couple the theoretical precepts drawn from our discussion of money and CCFCC with attention to the variegated forms taken, and influences exerted, by financialisation in practice.

Elsewhere, in addition, it has been argued that financialisation lies at the heart of neoliberalism and explains its longevity, Fine et al. (2016a). But, of course, the material culture of neoliberalism extends far beyond that of mere money. Or does it? In his classic novel of the Great Depression, *The Grapes of Wrath*, Steinbeck observes, "this *tractor* does two things – it *turns the land* and *turns* us off the *land*", and his novel charts the material cultures of those dispossessed, not only their heroic attempts to survive and prosper but also the material support they receive on occasion as well as the violence and stigma attached to their plight. But the author also makes clear that behind the tractor and the land lies the banker whose bottom line must be met irrespective of the economic and social costs.

To some extent, *The Grapes of Wrath* might be taken as a metaphor for the imperatives of financialisation. But like all metaphors, it has its strengths and weaknesses. As we have sought to indicate, financialisation proceeds both directly and indirectly through many channels attached to CCFCC and through the making and application of fictitious capital in economic and social reproduction. But such abstract considerations akin to a set of impersonal forces are realised concretely in the diverse outcomes attached to housing and water which, by necessity, cannot be taken as the equivalent of the tractor and the land in Great Depression America. What has been mercilessly exposed through our own and others' study of 'financialisation' is that it is much easier to point to the grave dysfunctions of financialisation in practice, and to propose remedies for them, than it is to build the political support for policy alternatives.

CHAPTER 6

The Endemic and Systemic Malaise of Mainstream Economics

Postscript as Personal Preamble

I have written too many times over the past five decades on what is the nature of mainstream economics that this piece came easy but also hard – for the latter, how to say something different, managed if marginally by focusing more than I normally do on macro in light of financialisation and the Global Financial Crisis (GFC), in deference to Fessud imperatives.[1] The topic lends itself to separate but related issues such as what is wrong with the discipline, how did it get to be the way that it is, how is the discipline evolving (or is it a case of plus ça change, toujours la même chose), what of methodology, the history of economic thought, interdisciplinarity and policy perspectives.

These and more are often but briefly touched upon here, and some working knowledge of recent developments in the mainstream is presumed to a large degree. Apart from the references already made in the first footnote (and the citations to be found within them), critical presentations of micro and macro are to be found in Fine (2016d) and Fine and Dimakou (2016).

Otherwise, I would point to an interesting development in my thinking within the text that follows – a glitch that probably arises out of a first drafting and a hasty revision for delivery of sheafs of working papers for inclusion prior to the close of the Fessud project. The starting point is that there are two phases of economics imperialism, with the second phase incorporating whatever variables the discipline cares to include alongside a market imperfection approach to the economy itself as the foundation for doing so. By the end of the paper, I am characterizing this as a separate, third phase of economics imperialism. And this has now stuck. Logically, it makes sense to distinguish the perfect and imperfect market foundations of economics imperialism, as well as these from the third phase of add on variables willy nilly. The rationale for not doing so is

1 For an obligatory contribution to the last Work Package, number 12, on Synthesis and Conclusions, for which this chapter contributes its main message in the spirit derived from the title of Fine (2013c), "Economics – Unfit for Purpose". For latest contributions, in light of economics imperialism, see first three volumes in this series (Fine, 2024a–c) and forthcoming volumes intended on the mainstream and its alter ego, heterodoxy.

 | DOI:10.1163/9789004706293_007

that, whilst all three phases are riddled with the logical flaws associated with Bringing Back In (BBI) what has been left out in establishing the core technical apparatus and architecture of the discipline (production and utility functions and general equilibrium in brief), those flaws attain new levels of intensity with the third phase of economics imperialism – as core principles are both deployed and suspended at the same time.

1 Introduction[2]

The poverty of mainstream, orthodox, neoclassical economics, I will use the terms interchangeably, in the wake of the crisis has become something of a cliché. As argued elsewhere, in the entirely different context of ethics, economics has become shown to be "unfit for purpose" (Fine, 2013c) and has even been accepted as such by its own practitioners. A striking if far from uncommon illustration of this is revealed by the work of Oliver Blanchard, erstwhile Chief Economist at the IMF. In the abstract of Blanchard (2008), a working paper with presumably relatively limited delay to publication, he suggests, emphasis added:[3]

> For a long while after the explosion of macroeconomics in the 1970s, the field looked like a battlefield. Over time however, largely because facts do not go away, a largely shared vision both of fluctuations and of methodology has emerged. Not everything is fine. Like all revolutions, this one has come with the destruction of some knowledge, and suffers from extremism and herding. None of this deadly however [sic]. *The state of macro is good.*

Just a short time later, Blanchard had entirely changed his tune, having in the interim joined the IMF (Blanchard et al. 2010). Effectively five 'confessions' of sins in outlook were made of the mea culpa variety, in explaining how the state

2 This chapter (originally Fine, 2016c) draws upon and adds to a number of earlier contributions, where the themes addressed are more fully developed and referenced. See Fine and Milonakis (2009 and 2011), Milonakis and Fine (2009), Fine (2015 and 2017b) and Fine and Dimakou (2016). For the inertia of the mainstream as "Zombieconomics", see Fine (2009a and 2010c).

3 The paper was eventually first published online as a Review in Advance on May 12, 2009, Blanchard (2009), and in print in September, 2009. The abstract was only amended to correct as, "None of this *is* deadly however", emphasis added. I have not checked for other changes in the substantive content of the text itself.

of macro was no longer good, that: low inflation should be a primary target of policy; this could be achieved through the single instrument of the interest rate; fiscal policy was of limited significance; financial regulation was not a macroeconomic matter; and, with the Great Moderation, continued stability was more or less guaranteed.

No doubt this commendable turnaround was prompted by the Global Financial Crisis (GFC), something that had been presumed to have been rendered extinct, as if a Black Swan event. However, turnaround as such is insufficient. It remains to be shown why macroeconomics should not only have become so complacent but to have done so on the basis of a set of propositions that can only be considered to be narrow and ill-conceived even in the absence of the prod to reconsider them in light of the GFC. In other words, it is not simply a matter of confessing to being foolish, not as an individual but as a profession, but also to understand how such foolishness could come about and what can be done to remedy it and make sure it does not happen again.

This is the purpose of this chapter. But it also covers wider terrain. For, first, whilst in particular, the poverty of macroeconomics has been exposed by the GFC, this can itself be misleading in revealing the discipline's weaknesses, and the reasons for them, through an undue focus on how finance as such has been handled as it understandably drew focused attention. Indeed, it will be argued that such deficiencies as are revealed and exposed by Blanchard in this way are merely the tip of the iceberg in terms of what are considerably larger and deeper inadequacies in mainstream economics and, of course, not just macroeconomics. Second, this will also shed light on why the response of the mainstream to the crisis has in practice been extremely limited, with little prospect for major change in either teaching or research.[4] Third, this is in part the consequence and reflection of the marginalisation of alternatives to the mainstream, of pluralist or heterodox economics, that is both systematic and continuing.

This chapter is organised as follows. It charts how mainstream got to be how it is across three sections, beginning with the passage from the marginalist to the formalist revolution in Section 2. This is then followed in Section 3 by an account of the evolution of mainstream economics after the second world war that ultimately witnessed the subordination of macroeconomics to an extremely reduced microeconomics at the time of the GFC (even if not as extreme as the New Classical Economics that preceded and influenced it).

4 For a sample of contributions on economics in the wake of the crisis, see Spaventa (2009), Krugman (2009), Buiter (2009), Besley (2011) and Blanchard et al. (eds) (2012).

Section 4, through reference to economics imperialism, accounts for how the mainstream has incorporated material from outside of its traditional analysis and has widened its scope of application. This has not, however, given rise to a genuine interdisciplinarity and has served more to veil rather than to address the reduced substance of the mainstream, whilst further consolidating its command over the discipline at the expense of alternative approaches. In this light, the final section suggests the prospects for the transformation of mainstream economics as a discipline are extremely bleak (although heterodox economics and political economy are prospering outside it), unless major external pressures are exerted upon it to change.

2 From Marginalist to Formalist Revolution

It is uncontroversial that over the past forty years, macroeconomics has become increasingly wedded to microeconomics. It warrants charting how this has come about over a longer period, going back at least to the marginalist revolution of the 1870s. The latter set in train a focus upon the optimising behaviour of individuals, whether in supply (basing itself on cost or production functions) or demand (utility functions in practice although amenable to more general formulation in terms of fixed, well-behaved preference orderings).

In this light, the passage from the marginalist revolution to what has been termed the 'formalist revolution' of the 1950s was marked by a particular technical problem – given utility and production functions and optimising individuals, what are the maximal restrictions that can be placed on the functional forms taken by supply and demand curves (whether for theoretical or empirical purposes in estimation). Ultimately, this issue was resolved through the Slutsky-Hicks-Samuelson conditions. However, for my purposes, this is of lesser significance than the process by which the results were obtained and on which they depend. I have described this as an 'implosion', as the casting of the problem was systematically reduced in ways that allowed it to be solved, throwing out whatever qualifications might be necessary and, it might be argued, losing sight of the original motivation of seeking to explain the determinants of supply and demand even if posed at the level of the individual agent.

Essentially, this implosion involved two processes. The first was in setting the problem for which it became essential to assume that utility is given and fixed, that its maximisation is the sole motive, and that goods are essentially defined by their physical properties and have no social content as such or in forming and fulfilling the subjectivities of consumers.[5] Similarly, for production, technology itself is given and conceived of as merely a (narrowly conceived technical) relationship between inputs and outputs. Such starting points necessarily preclude many of the issues that not only determine supply and demand but also what constitute their very nature. On the other hand, and second, even taking this implosion as starting point, merely allowing for optimisation to be achieved required further technical assumptions to be made, such as diminishing returns.

In short, the goal of establishing supply and demand curves, and of basing them on utility and production functions, became part and parcel of a method in which modelling assumed a high priority. At the time, and in retrospect, this has been described and justified as representing the deductive method and, falsely, seen as resembling the methods of the natural sciences. But a critical point of departure from the latter is the lack of basing assumptions on empirical observation, or some form of realism. Admittedly, individuals do (as well as do not) pursue self-interest but it is apparent that the reliance upon utility and production functions and individual optimisation (to be termed the mainstream's technical apparatus) is more or less arbitrary other than in pushing forward a solution to the problem posed on its own terms as opposed to those of the functioning individual let alone economy.

In some respects, then, the development of microeconomics in these terms might be thought of as not only an original sin, reflected in the implosive disregard for other factors and methods, but the transformation of that sin into virtue as far as the mainstream is concerned. This is also characteristic of the other great issue arising out of the passage from the marginalist to the formalist revolution, the development of general equilibrium theory. This, setting what will be termed the mainstream's technical architecture,[6] unquestioningly aggregated over individuals subject to the technical apparatus, to discover a given set of prices at which supply and demand would be equal to one another across all markets simultaneously. Again, without going into details, general equilibrium theory was propelled by the problem it was seeking to solve, discarding any obstacles in the way of seeking out the existence, uniqueness, stability and (Pareto) efficiency of such an equilibrium, consolidating the ethos of sin/virtue around the methods and assumptions involved. Indeed, it is no exaggeration to suggest that de jure, general equilibrium theory is conducive to rejecting its own relevance for understanding the economy given the thicket

5 Note this implies an entirely different individual subjectivity for mainstream economics (it is fixed) than for the postmodernist inventive consumer.

6 The terms derive from Al-Jazaeri (2008).

of assumptions and presumptions underpinning its construction. But de facto, these reservations are not only set aside in assuming, often implicitly, that general equilibrium does or could prevail, but also that the approach and assumptions attached to it are sacrosanct – not, it should be added, in the sense that they are always all made but that they are open to be adopted or not at the discretion of the discipline according to purpose and convenience, a point taken up later in the context of 'suspension'.

3 From Formalist Revolution to GFC

This is, however, to anticipate (the consequences of) the burgeoning influence of microeconomics. Crucially, though, over the period of the establishment of the technical apparatus (TA1) and technical architecture (TA2), or TA^2 taken together, especially in the 1930s, its presence and influence within the discipline was subordinate to other approaches. Most obviously, in retrospect, is the rise of (Keynesian) macroeconomics as its complement, slightly later but no less rapid and influential, together with what would now be thought of as heterodox economics, especially old institutional economics and the more general traditions of inductive economics, each of which dovetailed with study the of the history of economic thought as well as economic history and contemporary social and economic developments. This rendered monopolisation, corporate behaviour and organisation, labour relations, business cycles, distribution of income, and so on, subject to close attention.

In this respect, coming out of the second world war, there were three broad fields within the discipline – macroeconomics, microeconomics and a mixed bag of applied fields which was soon to incorporate development. Each flourished over the post-war boom. Whilst macroeconomics was captured by the so-called Keynesian neoclassical synthesis, IS/LM, it became heavily influenced by the formalist ethos attached to microeconomics, not least in being reduced to modelling quite apart from expunging the more radical elements of Keynesianism attached to the nature of the financial system (reduced to the liquidity trap by the synthesis as a special case of failure of Walrasian adjustment) and the role of uncertainty (reduced to risk). Nonetheless, the IS/LM framework in principle and in practice retained a distance from microeconomics, with some sort of commitment to systemic analysis, primarily through close attention to the determinants of macroeconomic aggregates and how they interact (consumption, investment, demand for money functions, etc). Applied fields tended to forge their own independent paths according to their subject matter but, of crucial significance, they did so in parallel with the core division between microeconomics and macroeconomics (one notable exception being the more or less vacuous field of welfare economics, deriving from Graaff (1957), and its telling contrast with the applied field of public economics as was).

The evolving relations between the applied fields have, however, increasingly involved the subordination of macroeconomics to microeconomics, surreptitiously to some degree during the post-war boom but deliberately and precipitously in its wake.[7] This convergence of microeconomics upon macroeconomics inevitably involved a corresponding convergence not only upon general equilibrium but also upon select elements of its associated TA^2. Here, though, it is important to disentangle two different aspects of general equilibrium. One is the reliance upon optimising individualism, and hence methodological individualism of a special type. In general, and in its full application, this had to wait upon the New Classical Economics, after which it continued to hold sway, even in new Keynesianism's breach with this extreme form of monetarism and reduction to microeconomics (see below).

The other aspect of general equilibrium is reliance upon Walras' Law – each (intended) supply must be matched by an (intended) demand and so the aggregate of all supplies and *demands* must sum to zero.[8] This is important in underpinning Patinkin's rejection of the classical dichotomy, itself an immediate consequence of the search to find compatibility between microeconomics and macroeconomics. What Patinkin showed is, first, that the classical dichotomy could not hold alongside Walras' Law and, effectively, lack of money illusion across whatever agencies (not necessarily individuals) determine supply and demand. For, with separate real and monetary economies, a hypothetical doubling of prices to explore the consequences for supply and demand would yield no change. Presuming, for convenience, that all goods markets are in equilibrium, they would remain so. But, with a fixed supply of money, and a positive (presumably proportionate) increase in demand for

7 As explicitly reflected by Lucas (1987, pp. 107–8), Nobel Prize winner and leading proponent of the New Classical Economics, our emphasis, in the oft-quoted, "The most interesting recent developments in macroeconomic theory seem to me describable as the reincorporation of aggregative problems such as inflation and the business cycle within the general framework of 'microeconomic' theory. If these developments succeed, the term 'macroeconomic' will simply disappear from use and the modifier 'micro' will become superfluous."

8 To be distinguished from what might be termed Say's Law that the same applies to goods markets alone, which is refuted by Walras' Law insofar as an excess supply of all goods (a glut) can complement an excess demand for money, as is emphasised by Keynes in his rejection of a stylised classical economics as flawed by adherence to Say's Law with the notable exception of Malthus.

money to undertake whatever real transactions are intended, there would be excess demand for money, violating Walras' Law.

Patinkin draws the conclusion that the classical dichotomy must be rejected and, by the same token, money matters to the real economy. Equally, in brief, the homogeneity postulate is also rejected unless taken to hold over prices *and* money – that, in equilibrium, all prices increase in proportion to the quantity of money. This all leads to the real balance effect appearing in the real economy but with neutrality of money being restored in the long run. An increase in money does not change the (long-run) equilibrium in real terms, it only changes the price level and the (unspecified) path to that unchanged equilibrium.

There is a point of running over these well-known results, generally if not universally incorporated into macroeconomics, and necessarily so where this aspect of general equilibrium is respected. It is that it is indicative across a number of dimensions of steps taken in macroeconomics that laid the foundation for the impoverished state of macroeconomics even if not directly responsible for it.

First is the dependence of macroeconomics upon an unchanged, unique, presumably efficient (or someone might do something about it), long-run equilibrium around which macroeconomics came to focus on terms of paths of adjustment. Second, then, and more broadly is to draw a firewall between short and long runs, conflating the different ways of understanding these as if they were all the same: namely, in equilibrium or not; the passage of time; and the relative speed of adjustment of variables (itself subject to theoretical and empirical dispute, not least between Keynesians and monetarists over quantity and price adjustment). Only through this conflation was it possible both to allow for short-run adjustment without long-run effects (for a recession, for example, surely reduces the levels of investment upon which the equilibrium rests). Third is the facile treatment of money as both fixed, or fixable, in supply, but also subject to equilibrium with demand as opposed to being part and parcel of a financial system that is more or less effective in mobilising and allocating resources for investment.[9] Last, Patinkin's contribution is indicative of what could be done, and how, to join micro and macro consistently together within the mainstream but, if only implicitly and subsequently overlooked, other aspects of the dualism between micro and macro, major preoccupations of applied economics and interwar institutional economics, were simply

9 It is noteworthy that the mainstream is essentially incapable of explaining why money emerges let alone why it would continue to be needed once equilibrium is attained.

disregarded because they could not be addressed. This includes monopolisation, labour relations, technical change, and business cycles as part and parcel of the growth process (for example, there is no way that Schumpeter's creative destruction could fit across the macro/micro divide).

Indicative of these developments is the rise of mainstream growth theory, not least through the Solow growth model of 1956. It represents the separation of growth theory from macroeconomics. And it continues to remain unclear whether growth theory belongs to macroeconomics or microeconomics in part because it is the technical apparatus of microeconomics, specifically use of the ubiquitous production function, which has underpinned what is essentially a macroeconomic issue, the long-term performance of the economy. And, of course, the theoretical and empirical traumas associated with such growth theory in the wake of the Cambridge Capital Controversies are simply set aside in the continuing commitment to the associated technical apparatus despite its lack of consistency and coherence even on its own terms.

In short, the relations across microeconomics, macroeconomics and other more applied fields were certainly not fixed nor without flaws but they did constitute a compromise around responsibility for subject matter even if with fluid boundaries. This compromise was rudely shattered by the demise of the post-war boom, the credibility of Keynesianism and the monetarist counter-revolution, spearheaded by Friedman and taken to extremes by New Classical Economics (NCE). Whilst Friedman's vertical Phillips Curve both placed (adaptive) expectations at the heart of macroeconomics and analytically reduced them to risk at the expense of uncertainty, the NCE denied even the minimal role that Friedman allowed the state, to affect unemployment albeit at the expense of an ever accelerating/decelerating price level.

The state ineffectiveness result (as well as the Lucas critique) involves the culmination of the convergences previously identified, not least the presumption that there are some (dogmatically privileged) irreducible fundamentals such as resources, preferences and technologies from which all else derives,[10] and their location within an extreme set of assumptions, and hence, consequences, not least representative individuals, perfectly working markets, rational expectations and state ineffectiveness. Notable for the latter, in particular, is that it follows less from the nature of the theory itself (although this is essential) than from the way in which the state is itself conceptualised. In a world in which there is a given long-run equilibrium, representative individuals with

10 For this as unquestioned common ground, in context of debate between NCE and NCM, see Chari et al. (2009).

given utility and production functions, where there is no health, education, welfare or industrial policy, no conflict over the distribution of income, and so on, the state is reduced to at most an individual with some special powers to shift supply and demand. It is hardly surprising given the powers of individuals in conditions of perfectly working markets that such a reduced state should be powerless in face of Ricardian equivalence-type results. The state is only enabled to do what individuals can and do neutralise.

Effectively, the NCE reduced macroeconomics to the consequences of monetary shocks. It was soon complemented by real business cycle, RBC, theory in which fluctuations in the economy are perceived to be the consequence of shocks in the rate of productivity increase, relieving the analysis of the need to consider monetary factors altogether. NCE and RBC theory were complemented by the efficient market hypothesis, EMH, for financial markets, to form a troika around which not only should state intervention be minimised but in which the free operation of financial markets could also provide for the best of all possible worlds.[11]

The troika, as critical point of departure, provided the basis for the new Keynesianism or New Consensus Macroeconomics, NCM, leading to Blanchard's assessment that the state of macro is good. But the NCM accepts as much, if not more, of the NCE than it rejects. It retains rational expectations, representative individuals and micro-foundations. Where it departs is in merely allowing for some markets to be inefficient in the limited sense of not clearing instantaneously. The result is that government policy can be effective in a limited way through interest rate manipulation, reflating or deflating the economy by decreasing or increasing the interest rate. This does, however, build inflationary inertia into the system, and higher interest rates will be needed to reduce inflation, inflationary expectations and expectations (or credibility) of government policy. Whilst it has been argued that this unduly neglects the role of fiscal policy, this is not a matter of choice but of the logic of the model since any fiscal expansion will be neutralised by countervailing private reduction in expenditure (Ricardian equivalence still holds in the 'long run') as a consequence of the model being tied to a given long-run equilibrium and rational expectations.

---

11 Significantly, the EMH is primarily about capacity, or not, to make abnormal returns within financial markets on the basis of available information; despite its name, it says nothing about the efficiency of the financial system in itself and for the economic system, and cannot do so without making assumptions about the existence of a unique, stable, Pareto-efficient equilibrium that is to be realised by the putatively efficient financial markets. See Guerrien and Gun (2011).

This more or less completes our review of how did it get there as far as macroeconomics on the cusp of the crisis is concerned. It has been subject to a division between macroeconomics and microeconomics (with a correspondingly separate terrain for an increasingly marginalised applied economics as it became reduced to microeconomics), a reduction of microeconomics to TA^2, the separation of short and long runs, a subordination and eventual reduction of macroeconomics to microeconomics, the driving of such macroeconomics to extremes of rational expectations, perfectly working markets and representative individuals, thereby reducing both the conceptualisation and the effectiveness of the state, and at most the mildest of reactions against these extremes to give rise to the NCM.

Crucially, the current world of mainstream economics is a far cry from that which prevailed in the post-war boom even though there are many elements of continuity. This is so much so that even those who played some considerable role in this evolution seem aghast at what has been (or they have in part) created. For Solow:[12]

> Suppose someone sits down where you are sitting right now and announces to me that he is Napoleon Bonaparte. The last thing I want to do with him is to get involved in a technical discussion on cavalry tactics at the Battle of Austerlitz. If I do that, I'm getting tacitly drawn into the game that he is Napoleon Bonaparte.

Even Milton Friedman lost patience with the developments in economics that he had done so much to spawn, bemoaning the discipline had become an arcane branch of mathematics.[13]

Usually omitted from the oft-quoted Solow is how he continues from above:

> Now, Bob Lucas and Tom Sargent like nothing better than to get drawn into technical discussions, because then you have tacitly gone along with their fundamental assumptions; your attention is attracted away from the

12 Cited in Klamer (1984, p. 146).

13 This is exemplified by the fate of Harry Markowitz, who received a Nobel Prize in economics in 1990 for his work on finance, but who completed his first work in the form of his (successful) University of Chicago doctoral dissertation in 1955. As reported by Harrison (1997, p. 176), citing Bernstein (1992), Friedman's comment on Markowitz's work was as follows, "Harry, I don't see anything wrong with the math here, but I have a problem. This isn't a dissertation in economics, and we can't give you a Ph.D. in economics for a dissertation that's not economics. It's not math, it's not economics, it's not even business administration."

> basic weakness of the whole story. Since I find that fundamental framework ludicrous, I respond by treating it as ludicrous – that is, by laughing at it – so as not to fall into the trap of taking it seriously and passing on to matters of technique.

This is significant in drawing a distinction between what is and what is not ludicrous with the presumption that Solow himself is well placed far within the correct side of the border. This reflects his dependence upon a wider set of less extreme principles applied on a much narrower scope of analysis. He is, for example, extremely hostile to new growth theory in minor part because of its false representation of old growth theory as predicting convergence which it did not.[14] For, in major part, Solow does not consider that the old growth theory was intended to explain productivity change within, let alone between, countries as it depended upon country-specific non-economic variables that had been excluded from the analysis (which, after all, only drew upon weighted combinations of inputs to measure technical change as a residual from warranted output increases). Yet, Solow's reduction of growth within a country to the microeconomic, technical apparatus of a single production function might itself be considered ludicrous (and invalid, as demonstrated by the Cambridge Critique).

4 Economics Imperialism

Such a digression on the relationship between old and new growth theory raises the more general issue of the scope as well as of the content of economic analysis. For, so far, the focus has been upon the way in which macroeconomics has been reduced by the processes involved. Most obviously, and recognised as such, in the wake of the GFC, the reduction of the analysis of money to supply and demand, mediated as a market by the rate of interest and wedded to a greater or lesser extent to the EMH, represents the most impoverished treatment of the financial system by confining it, however well conceptualised as such, to the nether regions of microeconomics whilst the financial system in practice was busy preparing itself for the most spectacular of macroeconomic displays.

In this respect, it is crucial to recognise that the problem with economics is not that it has in some absolute sense excluded consideration of relevant

14 See Solow (2006) for example as well as contributions in critique of Lucas' growth theory.

factors and issues from its scope of analysis. Far from it even if this is the case for its macroeconomic analysis as covered in the passage to the NCM. Indeed, as a discipline, economics is now more far-ranging than ever before in the scope of analysis and variables that it incorporates. Accordingly, it is essential to understand how this is the case and yet that macroeconomics can have been as it is.

The answer is to be found in the evolution of economics imperialism by which is meant the increasing application of (an evolving) mainstream economics, primarily microeconomics, to other social sciences. This essentially has its origins with the formalist revolution of the 1950s. For, having established the microeconomic principles attached to TA^2, it was at least implicitly recognised that they were subject to a tension that can be termed the historical logic of economics imperialism. Initially, the microeconomic problem was posed as addressing the implications of the optimising individual in a market context, to explain supply and demand in response to prices leaving aside other motivations for individual behaviour and social determinants. However, and this is the logic, once the problem was solved and the methods established with credibility as a core part of the discipline, it became apparent that the technical apparatus of utility and production functions is of universal application without confinement to the market and to supply and demand. This pushed for wider applicability of the technical apparatus, with success contingent upon disciplinary acceptability.

In what is termed the first phase of, or old, economics imperialism, especially associated with Gary Becker, the principles are applied outside the market but as if a market is present. Prior to the demise of Keynesianism, this gave rise but was confined to three notable successes – cliometrics (the new economic history), public choice theory (politics as horse trading subject to costs and benefits) and human capital theory (education and skills as if reduced to an investment good). However, with the monetarist counter-revolution and the subordination of macroeconomics to microeconomics, economics imperialism enjoyed greater leeway, not least engaging fields within economic itself, most notably macroeconomics but also, for example, the *new* development economics (although this was based on the *old* economics imperialism).

However, paradoxically, the greatest impetus to the second phase of, or new, economics imperialism derived from a reaction against the analytical thrust of the first in its reliance upon perfectly working markets. In part, this was motivated by the wish to restore Keynesianism through rejecting the instantaneous market clearing attached to the NCE. In doing so, reliance was placed on explaining inefficient, sticky or absent markets through microeconomic principles by setting aside perfect for asymmetric information on one or other side of the acts of exchange, with Akerlof's market for lemons the paradigmatic exemplar.[15] In this way, the non-market became amenable to analysis in the much more palatable form (to economists and non-economists alike) as the response to market imperfections as opposed to the reflection of market perfections.[16] The result was to induce a whole new range of fields extending economic analysis to the non-economic, or revitalising those fields that had previously been subject to the old economics imperialism. By the same token, most of the disparate fields, dubbed applied economics earlier, came under the sway of microeconomics, with mathematical models and econometrics displacing inductive methods and content.

Six aspects of the second phase of economics imperialism are worth highlighting over and above its scale and scope of subject matter and disciplinary coverage. First is that the marriage of TA^2 with concepts from the traditions, methods and theories of the other social sciences is inevitably, despite being primarily on the terms of economics, conducive to inconsistency if not incoherence. Generally, for example, enriched content in the motivation underpinning individual behaviour raises questions over where each form of behaviour begins and ends, and the use of social categories, such as gender, race or class begs the question of how these are compatible with methodological individualism. In other words, economics has now become subject to what can be termed 'suspension', prioritising its TA^2 more or less unquestioningly but being prepared more or less arbitrarily to set it aside as the determinant of behaviour in deference to other explanatory factors. Significantly, both the confidence in TA^2 and the timing of the inclination to complement it with other factors is highlighted by the commentary of Herbert Simon (1999, p. 113) who suggests of the 1930s that he offered economics two gifts, "organizational identification" and "bounded rationality". He bemoans the fact that, "The gifts were not received with enthusiasm. Most economists did not see their relevance to anything they were doing, and they mostly ignored them and went on counting the angels on the heads of neoclassical pins". Similarly, despite being developed by mainstream economists soon after the second world war, game theory was only heavily integrated into mainstream economics once

15 For the new economics imperialism as Kuhnian paradigm, see Fine (2004b) and, in the context of the newer development economics, Fine (2002b).

16 Note also an alternative route for the new economics imperialism by allowing for market imperfections in the presence of increasing returns to scale (and/or externalities). This is especially associated with Paul Krugman (and new trade theory and new economic geography) and new growth theory. For critical expositions, see Fine (2010e) and Fine (2000, 2003 and 2006b), respectively.

its potential (suspended) inconsistencies with individualism could be overlooked – the need, in light of conjectural variation, to take a view of other players' world views and vice-versa so that preferences and actions are inevitably interdependent and certainly not conducive to single equilibrium. In short, game theory and behavioural economics have attained a particularly strong presence within the mainstream as they allow for an almost unlimited scope and are conducive to policy analysis that is far more rounded than that relying upon TA^2 alone.[17]

Second, such ill-considered promiscuity in the promotion and suspension of its own economic principles has itself developed to such an extent that it can be considered a third or newest phase of economics imperialism, one in which the basic principles have been more or less discarded altogether leaving behind a shell of mathematical modelling and econometric estimation. This has, for example, led the leading exponent of critical realism in economics, Tony Lawson (2013), to argue that essentially there is no such thing as neoclassical economics (in part by reference to how Veblen defined it which is hardly relevant to the present day) and to characterise (the deficiencies of) the mainstream in terms of its being reduced simply to reliance upon deterministic mathematical models in search of empirical regularities (and a correspondingly fallacious, because deterministic, social ontology). This is, however, to overlook that the principles of the mainstream, organised around TA^2, have been far from absolutely suspended and continue to lie at the centre of and inform the vast majority of teaching and, if less so given the novelty of suspensions, research within the discipline. In the event, though, the character of the third phase of economics imperialism is well captured by the terminology of freakonomics and the economics of almost everything.

Third, this latest phase of economics imperialism gives rise to an extraordinary extension of scope but in ways which are fragmented and incoherent. There is simply a proliferation of fields and analyses with little or no unifying frame of analysis, connecting them to one another, other than (suspended) commitment to TA^2 as well as contingent ideological predilections in favour of the market (as has been the case for free trade, for example), or otherwise (as for the newly-discovered favour for minimum wages). With a starting point in TA^2, and the determinants of supply and demand upon the market, economics

17 For a critique of 'nudge', now prominent in policy circles, in this vein, see Fine et al. (2015). And for a parallel path to that taken by bounded rationality in seeking to engage a more realistic approach to consumption, now more readily acknowledged and accommodated, consider the work of George Katona and his contribution to behavioural economics. See Hosseini (2011).

has reached out to the world beyond these in a big bang of filling out the rest of the universe. Such anarchy is reflected, for example, in the simultaneous development of the new institutional economics and the application of social capital within economics, each of which has separate intellectual origins, but each of which performs the same function of accounting for the non-economic's impact upon the economy. Yet, these two literatures sit side-by-side with little or no interaction between them, as in the work of Nobel Prize winner, Elinor Ostrom (Fine, 2010d). And, in addition, the social capital and rent-seeking literatures incorporate exactly the same analytical frameworks whilst drawing entirely opposite conclusions concerning the impact of the non-economic upon the economic (Fine, 2010b). Much the same lack of unifying framing of the discipline is characteristic of more insular economic analysis itself, in contrast for example to the Keynesian/monetarism world visions (or, indeed, those of classical political economy). After all, we are primarily left with the vision that some markets work well and some do not, which means that the same applies to macroeconomies.

Fourth, this is all indicative of what has been termed bringing back in, BBI. As outlined, the TA^2 was established by an implosion, the systematic exclusion of any factor, method, realism or even narrow technical assumption that stood in its way. Economics imperialism's big bang has ultimately seen that implosion reversed, with TA^2 exploding within the discipline and across other disciplines. Although there tend to be no go areas, most notably those social sciences in the wake of postmodernism engaging in the meaning of economic and social activity, ethnography and so on (and especially, in this light, the world of consumption within the other social sciences which is not reducible to fixed utilities/identities and includes symbolic content of goods), BBI is quintessentially the inconsistent/incoherent form taken by the suspended character of economics imperialism. This is precisely and perversely because TA^2 could only be established by precluding the content which is now brought back in to be explained or to be used as explanatory variable (thereby subsequently allowing for what essentially undermines the starting point).

Fifth, and more generally, this is indicative of both the strengths and the weaknesses of the mainstream. The intellectual, institutionalised strengths lie in the unquestioned commitment to TA^2 even though it is subject to a suspension that might have led it to be challenged in earlier times (through bounded rationality and/or game theory, for example, that are now allowable). The weaknesses are twofold. On the one hand, it is accepted that the discipline's core principles are incapable of explaining the economy let alone broader issues and, so, it is necessary to range beyond those principles to include an unspecified and unspecifiable set of non-economic variables and analyses.[18] On the other hand, the corresponding explosion across the other social sciences to explain the economy let alone the non-economic (as economics imperialism) exposes the discipline to alternative methodologies, methods, theories and conceptualisations with which it is entirely incompatible and both outdated and extreme, as is evidenced for example in its reliance upon methodological individualism, empiricism, deductivism and so on.

Sixth, at least intellectually, this explains the absolute intolerance of the mainstream not only to alternative approaches but also to fields such as the history of economic thought and the methodology of economics. So intellectually fragile is the mainstream to alternatives that it can only prosper by marginalising and failing to engage with them other than on its own narrow terms, if bolstered by suspension and BBI. Indeed, this is rationalised by stigmatising heterodox economics for lacking the supposed scientific rigour associated with the mainstream's theoretical and empirical methods, even though these border on the inconsistent and incoherent and are from the borders of the scientific methods in the natural sciences that are putatively emulated.[19]

5 Prospects

The purpose of this wide-ranging overview of the discipline in a broader context is to explain why the mainstream has proven incapable not so much to explain the GFC, and to offer policy to move beyond it, but to be unable to respond to this lack of capacity itself. It is not because of its lack of scope of analysis, given the pervasive reach of economics imperialism, nor even, as most would suppose, the deadweight path dependence of what was previously thought to be the good state of macro. Rather, the problem lies both in how the discipline broaches broader material and in how this precludes moving forward to alternative analyses other than in a marginal way. It is a consequence of suspended TA^2 as the content and form taken by the latest phase of economics imperialism. It is only able to offer fragmented and inadequate analyses

18 This is most apparent in new growth theory and Barro-type regresssions, see Fine (2000, 2003 and 2006b).

19 Note, in particular, that deductive rigour (i.e. mathematical modelling) is always sacrificed at the altar of analytical content – if the maths does not give what we want, too bad, as with Cambridge Capital Theory, the conditions for the existence, uniqueness, stability and efficiency of general equilibrium, the theory of the second best, etc.

whilst offering the illusion of being capable of including more or less anything at will.

This syndrome is ideally illustrated by reference to where the mainstream will not go, to heterodox political economy.[20] More specifically, especially in the wake of the GFC, the notion of financialisation has over little more than a decade mushroomed across the social sciences, incorporating an extremely wide range of disciplines, methodologies, methods, theories, conceptualisations and subject matter, often from what is acknowledged to be undue neglect of finance in the past. Particularly striking is the failure of mainstream economics to have participated in this academic venture in any way whatsoever. Nor is it difficult to discern why, in contrast to other buzzword and fuzzword concepts such as globalisation and social capital, in which it has been able to participate from its own perspectives. The obstacles to embracing financialisation are that it is systemic, involving structures, relations, processes and agencies, conflict and power. Both individually, and especially collectively, these are anathema even to the most open and suspended forms of economics imperialism – financialisation as behavioural economics, I don't think so!

But, equally important, as signalled earlier, even if sharply revealed by the GFC as the most explicit form taken by its inadequacies, the nature of mainstream economics that renders it incapable of addressing financialisation hangs heavily over the treatment of other issues that it either neglects or impoverishes, whether it be technical change, distribution, monopolisation, the role of health and education in economic performance, and so on. As argued, it is not at all that these are not covered but that they are only so on the basis of a piecemeal, fragmented and suspended TA^2 which, paradoxically, continues to provide considerable innovative momentum to the discipline and the marginalisation of alternatives whether the latter be within heterodox political economy or through genuine interdisciplinarity with the other social sciences.

This is truly a bleak picture and draws a sharp contrast with the previous major crises of the 1930s and the 1970s, when Keynesianism and the monetarist counter-revolution marked major changes in the discipline. By contrast, it seems today relatively undisturbed, changing rapidly if only to remain the same given the shifting forms taken by the latest phase of economics imperialism. Indeed, in earlier work, Fourcade (2010) has suggested that the scope

20 This is not absolute as, of course, economics imperialism, especially in its latest phase, also colonises heterodoxy with, for example, segmented labour markets as a leading example of the application of asymmetric information economics, a topic that was previously shunned by the mainstream (Fine, 1998).

for heterodox economics and its influence upon policymaking is highly contingent upon country context. Somewhat later, however, she has felt obliged to tease out what constitutes the supposed superiority of economists and how they sustain it (Fourcade et al. 2015). This has, however, strengthened and broadened over time, with one of her exceptional cases, France, seemingly falling in line with the mainstream.[21] The one exception, that more than proves the rule, seems to be Greece where the Syriza Government is flush with professors of heterodox economics. Possibly, this signals that the only secure way to bring about an alternative economics alongside, let alone in place of, the mainstream is through an equally radical change in policies, itself contingent on strengthening the political forces in favour of them.[22]

---

21 See http://assoeconomiepolitique.org/petition-pluralism-now/ See also Heise and Thieme (2015) for the earlier history of the decline of German heterodox political economy if, to some extent, falling into blaming the victim. See Lee (2012) for a more general defence of heterodoxy against critics of its being responsible for its own fate.

22 Although the Syriza venture ultimately proved a disastrous disappointment whether by virtue of its economics or otherwise.

CHAPTER 7

Reports of My Death Are Greatly Exaggerated: The Persistence of Neoliberalism in Britain

Personal Preamble

This preamble can be brief and, unlike for most of the other chapters, is not designated as a postscript. This is because the chapter is newly drafted if having been through many earlier versions. Essentially, this is a chapter we would now write if Fessud were still up and running. It covers in a more up to date form much of the theory and case study material that comes earlier albeit at the inevitable expense of some repetition. It is, however, the theme and context that is different – not least how the state interventionism attached to, and accelerated by, the COVID-19 pandemic is emblematic of neoliberalism, and its dependence upon financialisation, as opposed to its demise.

1 Introduction[1]

The extent of the economic intervention by the British Government during the COVID-19 pandemic, its heavy fiscal costs (estimated around £310–410bn, HOC 2023), and the policy turn of 'Bidenomics' in the USA led many to declare neoliberalism dead and to herald the return of the state. In rapid sequence, commentators have postulated a new era of interventionism (Mascaro, 2023; MacFarlane, 2021; O'Kane, 2023; Rainey, 2021; and Tooze, 2021). UK television's leading pundit, Robert Peston (2020) claimed that, "COVID-19 turned Boris Johnson into more Castro than Castro … an economy … more socialist … than at any point in British history".

Political economy has long exposed such false dichotomies between state and market, highlighting the tensions between neoliberalism in theory, ideology, and practice, and the continuing dependence of neoliberalism on the state, generally concluding that "the so-called 'roll-back of the state' is … an ideological misnomer for the process of its neoliberal restructuring" (Šumonja, 2021, p. 220; see also Davies, 2014; Fine and Saad-Filho, 2016a; Paul and

1 Based on a longer and revised version of Bayliss et al. (2024).

 | DOI:10.1163/9789004706293_008

Cumbers, 2021; and Peck and Theodore, 2019).[2] When looking beyond the *fact* of extensive state intervention under neoliberalism to its (shifting) *nature*, the literature often becomes eclectic. For example, Šumonja (2021, p. 217) claims the state is "the organising force of neoliberal assault on all political obstacles to the profitability of capital accumulation" and lists a disconcertingly diverse account of what overcoming such obstacles involves, including "crushing … trade unions, cuts in social provision, privatisation of public industries and services, deregulation of financial markets, monetary policies predicated on price stability and so on". Peck and Theodore (2019, p. 249) argue that the neoliberal state leads "a generalized assault on social-welfarist or left-arm functions, coupled with an expansion of right-arm roles and capacities in areas like policing and surveillance". For Duncan (2021, p. 3), the state's main role is to reconstitute people as neoliberal subjects through the "state disciplinary technique of responsibilization".

These diffuse understandings of the role of the state in neoliberalism reflect the variety of functions of states across countries and over time. Understandably, many accounts of neoliberalism tend to focus upon particular general aspects of capitalism, possibly if unwittingly because they are on occasion more extreme, if not uniquely so, over the current period – the list is endless ranging over austerity, authoritarianism, individualistic responsibility, laissez-faire (ideology), assaults upon the working class and its organisations, populism, distributional conflict (wage repression) and inegalitarianism, and so on. Correspondingly, lack of a coherent account of the role of the neoliberal state has reinforced the aforementioned tendency to declare the end of neoliberalism after any expansion of state spending or newly interventionist stance (see also Stiglitz, 2008). There is a parallel tendency to emphasise the political role of the state creating the background conditions for accumulation under neoliberalism, at the expense of detailed examination of how states (re)produce neoliberal forms of accumulation (Fine and Saad-Filho, 2016a; Mudge, 2008; Saad-Filho, 2017; and Stedman Jones, 2012). Regulation Theory, (Jessop, 1993 and 1995 for example), is a partial exception, attempting to theorise

2 A burgeoning literature on state capitalism (Silverwood and Berry, 2022) grapples with a perceived shift towards "more muscular forms of statism" (Alami and Dixon, 2021, p. 4). This chapter represents a challenge to the 'state capitalism' thesis insofar as it implies that state intervention in capital accumulation represents something new or distinct compared with earlier phases of neoliberalism. Instead, we argue, the state's role in accumulation should be viewed in terms of ongoing transformations (of both forms of accumulation and of the state itself) with the state playing an essential and ongoing role in quintessentially neoliberal reforms such as privatisation and marketisation.

systematically the nature and role of the neoliberal state in accumulation. But it is ultimately unable to accommodate variation over time and place other than through ill-fitting of neoliberalism into its one-size-fits-all regime.

We identify two aspects of the role of the British state in accumulation under neoliberalism, which not only persist but also *account for* neoliberalism's shapeshifting nature. The first concerns the creation of, and support for, opportunities for financial accumulation by extending corresponding monetary relations to new areas of social provision. In this way, the state has played a constitutive role in wider processes of financialisation which, we argue, distinguish neoliberalism from previous stages of capitalism owing to the scale and range with which financialisation has been distinctively engaged in economic and social reproduction in the neoliberal period. The instabilities directly attached to, and deriving from, financialisation have meant the intensification of volatile and variegated vulnerabilities around each and every element of economic and social reproduction under neoliberalism.[3] The second aspect of the state's role, therefore, involves the management of the fallout arising from the first aspect and, more generally, ever-deepening dysfunctions the longer neoliberalism persists.

In this light, our aim is two-fold. First, we seek to identify precisely the *economic* functions of the state under neoliberalism from the angle of commodification and financialisation, in contrast with accounts which view the state's role primarily in terms of the political requirements for whatever form is taken by accumulation. Second, by foregrounding the form(s) taken by capital accumulation, our discussion sheds light on the transformations of neoliberalism in the UK in particular.

Our account derives from a detailed examination of the role(s) of Britain's neoliberal state in accumulation in three critically important areas of social provision where, ostensibly, the state was "rolled back" decades ago, housing, water and health. We show the state has driven restructuring of these sectors fronted by different forms of privatisation and, crucially and deliberately, embedding the extraction of financial profits by global capital into the provision of (domestic) public goods and services. Consequently, essential human needs have been turned into financialised revenue streams secured by public institutions and public revenues. As indicated, the restructuring required to open up these sectors to financial accumulation has made their operations dysfunctional in variegated – but specifically neoliberal – ways. They have also

3 This approach is related with the growing literature on derisking, which approaches similar issues from a different angle (Amarnath et al. 2023; Gabor, 2023; and McArthur, 2024).

created a permanent role for the state in managing the consequences, including low investment, volatility, periodic crises, and at least nominal provision for the market-excluded. In short, we offer an original interpretation of how accumulation under neoliberalism has been financialised in particular sectors, and how this has been underpinned by the state; these processes have relied upon extensive restructuring of economic and social reproduction driven by public policy, and involved significant shifts in the character and operations of the state itself.

The next section elaborates two key functions of the neoliberal state in theoretical terms. Three subsequent sections cover the cases of housing, water and health. The final section reflects on implications for debates on the transcendence of neoliberalism.

2 Towards a Theory of Neoliberalism's Active State

A notable early attempt to theorise systematically the nature and role of the neoliberal state, including its relationship to accumulation, was offered by Regulation Theory. Regulationists sought to identify the "ensembles of complementary economic and extraeconomic mechanisms and practices which enable capital accumulation to occur in a relatively stable manner over long periods" (Jessop, 1995, p. 1613), particularly in relation to the alleged transition from Fordism to postfordism. For example, Jessop (2003) characterises this shift in terms of a movement from a Keynesian welfare state to a Schumpeterian workfare regime, with the latter corresponding to a neoliberal accumulation strategy comprising six elements: liberalisation, deregulation, privatisation, commodification, internationalisation and reduced direct taxation. While undoubtedly touching on important features of neoliberalism, this characterisation, by Jessop's own admission, relies on ideal-type theorising which involves "the one-sided accentuation of empirically observable features" (Jessop, 2002, p. 254). Such theorising can inevitably only partially capture phenomena and our case studies confirm this for Jessop's six elements. As a result, and "notwithstanding the caveats that were scrupulously issued" (Peck, 2022, p. 176), Regulation Theory has ultimately proved incapable of grasping or explaining neoliberalism's variegation, instability and adaptations – "Neoliberalism, in other words, refuses to fit into any of the prefabricated boxes associated with régulation theory", (Peck, 2022, p. 182).

We see neoliberalism not as a mode of regulation but as a distinct stage of capitalism that is underpinned by, while not reducible to, financialisation. In brief, we distinguish stages of capitalism by the different ways in which the production of surplus value is integrated into economic and social reproduction. The monopoly capital stage, associated with the production of relative as opposed to absolute surplus value, involved not only reductions in the value of labour power but also measures to limit the crudest exploitation of the working class (with limitations on the length of the working day most prominently remarked by Marx). Subsequently, the variously designated Keynesian/welfare stage incorporated extensive state intervention in directly promoting capital accumulation (not least through public enterprise) but also through expenditure on economic and social provisioning, not least in health, education, social security, etc. The neoliberal stage has witnessed the intensified and extensive presence of financialisation in the governance of economic and social reproduction without, as already emphasised, this being at the expense of continuing state intervention as such (neoliberal ideology of reliance upon the market to the contrary).

Of course, finance has always been important to capitalism, and the idea that it has become more prominent in contemporary capitalism, and neoliberalism, is most obvious in references to its financialisation. There is a vast literature on financialisation (see, for example, Fine 2010a, 2013–14 and 2022; Mader et al. eds, 2020; Sawyer, 2022; and van der Zwan, 2014). Unlike a general trend across the literature in which financialisation is amorphously seen as the ever greater presence of monetary practices and motives, we define financialisation tightly as the intensive and extensive accumulation of what Marx called interest-bearing capital (IBC), that is, the growth of activities geared to making 'profit' out of investments in money and paper assets, including certificates of ownership of 'real' property and purely financial instruments ('fictitious capital'), rather than using wage-labour to produce goods or services for sale. It is the unprecedented involvement of financialisation, thus understood, in diverse aspects of economic and social reproduction, that sets neoliberalism apart from previous periods. Inevitably, the effects of financialisation reach far beyond the immediate presence of IBC in the circulation of capital in economic reproduction, not least in light of 'commodification', the nature and incidences of which we carefully unpick below not least as they are felt through social reproduction.

Under neoliberalism, the scale of this intensive and extensive accumulation of interest-bearing capital, and its effects, renders it a leading force in economic restructuring and social reproduction. In contrast with the industrialists, who both dominated and represented pre-World War I 'liberal' capitalism and the alliances between the state and large business that ruled in post-World War II Keynesianism, under neoliberalism the global financial sector, and financial interests and practices, increasingly encroach over all nodes of economic and social reproduction. This leads to the restructuring of economic and social provision through the expansion of monetary relations, giving rise to diverse financialised patterns of accumulation, with equally diverse impacts on provisioning. It is this relationship between financialisation and the structures and institutions of social and economic reproduction that establish the material basis of neoliberalism as a system of accumulation (see, for example, Albo, 2008; and Saad-Filho and Johnston, eds. 2005).

Below we identify two integral roles played by Britain's neoliberal state in this system of accumulation. First is the opening up new areas of social reproduction to financial accumulation through various forms of commodification and sustaining the conditions for financial accumulation. Far from being one-off acts, privatisation, for example, has invariably required an ongoing role for the state in replicating what is ideologically perceived to be (a necessarily imperfect) market-like competition through (more or less state) regulation, at least implicitly underwriting future profits (to finance and for financialisation). Second, the counterpart to such commodification is that it falls on the state to intervene where the market fails or is absented, although these interventions themselves take on distinctly neoliberal forms whilst also contradicting them – most transparently in extremis in the support to finance in the wake of the Global Financial Crisis, and to labour markets in the pandemic.

The value of our approach is in integrating concrete variations across time and place into a core definition of neoliberalism as a stage of capitalism in which economic and social reproduction is increasingly restructured through financialisation. Thus, neoliberalism's variegated and contextually specific evolution across time, place and issue can be coherently understood as driven by tensions derived from, or expressed through, processes of financialisation and reactions to these tensions, whether in the form of class struggle or attempts to stabilise the system.

3 Financialisation through Commodification

Financialisation is necessarily grounded on the expansion of monetary relations underpinned by the state, albeit in differentiated ways depending on activity and context, and it captures the distinctive nature of contemporary capitalism, that is, neoliberalism. The expansion of these monetary relations can be broken down into three categories (Fine and Bayliss, 2022; and Hermann, 2021). First, *commodification* (C) involves commercial activity for profit, typically the production of commodities for sale. Second, *commodity form* (CF) concerns the movement of money without the production or circulation of commodities for profit. Examples include most state revenues and expenditures, and a range of services charging arbitrary prices including, for example, fees paid by UK university students. C and CF can facilitate financialisation, for example, if they underpin streams of revenue that can be securitised and traded as assets, permitting the capture of rewards by finance.[4]

Third, and weakest in the range of monetary relations, is *commodity calculation* (CC). This is the use of monetary, pseudo-monetary or purely abstract 'market-like' criteria in decision-making, even when relations are not marketised and products do not take the commodity form, for example, in cost-benefit analysis or the valuation of education in terms of human capital.[5] CC is a ubiquitous feature of material cultures in financialised economies, where money is driven into our consciousness even when it does not (yet) directly enter our practices (Engelen et al. 2014; Graeber, 2014; and Morrish and Sauntson, 2013).

These categories, abbreviated as CCFCC, underpin our analysis of the restructuring of social provision under neoliberalism. They provide a spectrum along which neoliberal policies and 'reforms' (marketisation, privatisation, regulation, austerity and so on) can shift the provision of goods and services from the state to financialised accumulation while, also, promoting behaviours, practices and cultures that reinforce neoliberal social relations. But this does not happen in a linear or unidirectional fashion. Although the provision of key basic goods has become more marketised under neoliberalism, this has not been the outcome of a straightforward 'rollback' of the state, or the advance of a simple process of commercialisation. Instead, marketisation has been the outcome of state intervention across all areas of social reproduction, taking place in specific, continuing, variegated, shifting, and financialised forms.

Neoliberalised forms of provision tend to intensify inequalities and to expose certain groups to variegated vulnerabilities concentrated on the hard to employ, house, educate, provide for in old age, raise out of poverty, provide for health services, etc. Despite neoliberalism's anti-state rhetoric, when the market is absented or fails, pressures inevitably emerge for the state to offer remedies. Common across the case studies presented below is that the state

---

4 Both IBC and securitisation can be traced back several centuries (Buchanan, 2014). However, neoliberalism is uniquely based upon the *extensive* and *intensive* reach of such securitisation into economic and social reproduction (Fine, 2022).

5 Brown (2015, p. 10) identifies CC in extreme form. "All conduct is economic conduct: all spheres of existence are framed and measured by economic terms and metric, even when those spheres are not directly monetized ... we are only and everywhere *homo oeconomicus*". The classic reference for CC is Simmel (1978); (see also Brown, 2015; Davies, 2014; Jessop, 2015; and Haiven, 2014).

has been expected to resolve anomalies in provision, whether due to 'undue' benefits (to be cut) or 'undue' harshness (to be alleviated), with shifting perceptions of what is 'fair' or 'tolerable' given ideology, economic constraints and political contestations. While the state's involvement must be ongoing across all areas of provision, even if in complex and *ad hoc* forms, it is noticeable that extreme forms of absolute and relative deprivation have emerged under neoliberalism, and they have tended to become normalised.[6]

The residualisation of the hard-to-reach through market-based provision is one example of neoliberal dysfunctions that the state is expected to address. Others include insufficient investment, industrial fragmentation, and operational and profitability crises. The case studies show that these circumstances can be so frequent that state intervention cannot be limited to economic strategy; instead, it must also encompass day-to-day operations. The piecemeal and *ad hoc* nature of the involvement of the British state in social provision has been compounded by growing centralisation of decision-making, which has often limited the ability of frontline providers to deliver, especially local authorities, not least through the syndrome of responsibility to provide without resources to do so.[7]

As areas of social reproduction have traversed, unevenly, along CCFCC, social policymaking itself has increasingly become subjected at least to CC, with the state playing a significant role in this transformation and, thereby, transforming itself. In each sector, 'competition' and 'efficiency' have become the discursive mantra of policy reform, eclipsing equity, environmental sustainability, the public good and other goals, and fostering a material culture driving the neoliberalisation of everyday life (Montgomerie, 2020). In particular, under neoliberalism social policy tends to be framed around financial(ised) constraints on public policy, for example by quantifying the unquantifiable in pseudo-monetary terms (e.g. who is deserving of social security), evaluating the invaluable (what is a minimum standard of life), and prioritising the essential (we cannot afford it all). This is closely associated with the proliferation of public sector management techniques seeking to mimic 'the market',

6 See Palma (2009) for the capacity of the top 10% of the income distribution to grow at the expense of the bottom 40%.

7 Dagdeviren and Karwowski (2021) review the financialisation of Local Councils under 'austerity', and Bayliss (2022) and Bayliss and Gideon (2020) focus on the financialisation of health and social care. Haines-Doran (2022) shows that rail privatisation has involved more detailed government intervention than under nationalisation, for example, across timetabling and pricing. Fearn (2024) shows that the crisis-ridden UK energy system focuses on the protection of private companies rather than users, while Ward (2020) examines the process of financially 'liquefying' the Port of Liverpool.

for example, through audit cultures, cost-benefit analysis and performance management.

The three sectors in our case studies have undergone neoliberal reforms to different degrees, with the state playing a central role implementing those reforms and managing the sectors themselves and the ensuing social conflicts and crises. We show that state interventions have not declined under neoliberalism, but their nature has changed as provision, and the state itself, have undergone profound shifts. Our case studies demonstrate that these changes in provision, and in the state itself, can be understood in terms of the extension of monetary relations through CCFCC and the attempts to deal with the fall out arising from the ensuing financialisation.

4 Housing

The financialisation of Britain's housing system was driven by the expansion of both mortgage lending and homeownership, with the state playing a pivotal role in both. Far from passively 'freeing up' housing finance through the removal of market constraints, the state encouraged the aggressive expansion of housing credit and securitisation through regulatory changes and subsidies (Oren and Blythe, 2019; and Wainwright, 2009). As a result, the ratio of mortgage debt to income increased from under 25% to over 100% between 1980 and the start of the Global Financial Crisis (GFC), in 2008 (Bank of England, 2021; Grafe and Mieg 2019; and Kohl, 2021 shows that the explosion of mortgage finance has not led to a proportional expansion of housing supply across seventeen advanced economies).

The expansion of the demand for mortgages and the availability of (collateralisable) housing assets was achieved through the winding down of state provision and the subsidised transfer of state-owned social housing to tenants (Robertson, 2017a and b). In England, 1.8 million council-built and owned properties were purchased under 'Right to Buy' between 1980 and 2014, while the number of dwellings owned by local authorities declined from 5.1 to 1.7 million (DCLG Select Committee, 2015). Since this privatisation process involved the transfer of ownership of existing housing, it implied a shift from one commodity form (social rent) to another (purchase, generally with a mortgage, with potential rents to follow in secondary markets). This meant erstwhile social housing went from being shielded from the logic of profitability to being governed by it, eventually becoming a site for value extraction by (securitised mortgage) finance, private rentals and speculative capital gains. This process complemented the imposition of restrictions on council housebuilding, and growing reliance on for-profit housebuilders, which acquire land and build for sale, dramatically increasing the commodification or, more exactly, the CF (other than for new build) of the British housing system.

Additional housing finance available on easier terms fed long-term increases in house prices (i.e., capitalised rents or capital gains); house prices in Britain increased on average by 7% per year for thirty years after 1980 (ONS, 2016). These price increases encouraged investment-driven demand for homeownership inducing, and induced by, targeted inflows of international capital. They allowed house prices, especially in London, to be drawn from the global pool of (surplus) value, rather than being limited by local factors. The symbiotic relationship between mortgage finance and house prices supported the intensive accumulation of IBC through the repackaging of claims to future mortgage payments into Residential Mortgage-Backed Securities (RMBSs) traded on international markets (Robertson, 2017a).[8] In other words, securitisation converted rents into fictitious capital, as it turned homes into liquid financial assets.

The sale of large tracts of state-owned land to the private sector and the transformation of land into financial assets were also crucial, as they created pressures for land use to be determined by exchange value rather than use value – a shift from non-commodity to commodity form. The state played a key role in these processes, by privatising public lands (reversing historic trends of acquisition), and by regulating property rights, the construction of new housing, and the financing to pay for them (Bradley, 2021; and Christophers, 2017 and 2019).

The extension of monetary relations in housing through shifts along CCFCC paved the way for the financialisation of housing production. The business model of speculative housebuilders revolves around rent capture, as they seek to maximise the uplift between the price paid for land and the price for which it is sold, with housebuilding itself becoming an intermediate step. In Britain, where developable land is limited, housebuilders have strong incentives to sit on land in rising markets, and to limit house sales to lift prices (Ball, 2003; and Edwards, 2015). Both strategies restrict supply and raise the rents and (builders') capital gains that, in turn, feed securitisation and financial extraction. These gains lure additional finance into housing, driving bubbles that must eventually burst.

The financialisation of housebuilding intensified after the GFC. Archer and Cole (2014 and 2021) show that, since 2008, financial investors have extracted

8 For the case of Spain, see Moore (2020).

more capital from the industry than they have put in. For example, between 2010 and 2017 the output of new homes grew by 70%, while housebuilder revenues grew by 178% and pre-tax profits by 703%; in turn, dividends increased both in absolute terms and as a proportion of profits. The post-GFC wave of housing financialisation in Britain also saw the financialisation of rental housing. The forerunner was purpose-built student accommodation, with student housing Real Estate Investment Trusts (REITs) now a "mature and globally recognised" asset (Savills, 2015), listed on the London Stock Exchange (Sanderson and Özogul, 2022). In the wider rental market, Britain has experienced a growing Build to Rent sector, where institutional investors such as REITs and pension funds convert or build property for rent. This sector's pipeline grew by 478% between 2013 and 2018 (Savills, 2018), and its market share is expected to reach 13% by 2026 (Savills, 2022; and Aveline-Dubach, 2022 examines the financialisation of nursing homes through REITs).

None of this could have occurred without state intervention to make markets and create new asset classes. Beswick et al. (2016) and Nethercote (2019) show how British governments encouraged the growth of the Build to Rent asset class including: new instruments to securitise rental properties; public subsidies (such as the £1.1bn Build to Rent Fund, in 2013); regulations removing the need for planning permission from office to residential conversions; government guarantees for capital market financing; legislation allowing REITs; and exemptions of finance from capital gains tax. The extent to which governments have sought to drive financial investment in the rental sector is also evident in the review of "barriers to institutional investment in private rented homes" (DCLG, 2012).

The state is also encouraging financialisation, and hence erosion, of social housing, primarily through the removal of protections that shielded it from the (commercial) logic of accumulation. Cuts to Housing Association (HA) grants have forced providers to become almost entirely self-financing and, therefore, increasingly responsive to demand rather than need. A rule change in 2010 made it legal to profit from social housing, and the introduction of fixed-term tenancies and the redefinition of affordable rents as 80% of market rent increased the scope for profits (Beswick et al. 2016). In response, capital market funding for HAs increased from under £1bn in 2010–11 to more than £4.1bn in 2014–15 (THFC, 2016, p. 32). The integration of HAs into financial markets is shifting their operation and values, with economic taking precedence over social values (Wainwright and Manville, 2017). The number of For Profit Registered Providers (FPRP) of affordable housing is also growing rapidly (Savills, 2021), driven by perceived opportunities to close rent gaps (Christophers, 2022).

The British state has, then, played a vital role facilitating the penetration of finance into housing provision and sustaining financial accumulation within it. This inevitably requires managing the dysfunctional consequences of financialised provision, most strikingly through the measures introduced to contain the collapse of housing markets and the wider financial system after the GFC. This role has continued, through regular interventions to support house prices and mortgage lending. For example, the ironically named "Help to Buy" scheme sought to kickstart the housing market after the GFC by providing first-time buyers with loans, but it has been criticised for inflating prices and thereby making it harder to buy, while increasing the profit margins and share prices for housebuilders (Archer and Cole, 2014 and 2021; and Hammond, 2022).

The financialisation of housing has necessarily given rise to countertendencies centred on those whose housing needs cannot be met on the market, though how and to what extent is contextually driven. The privatisation of large swathes of social housing, combined with declining affordability in an owner-occupied sector awash with credit, has pushed many households into costly private rentals. Even though owner-occupation has been a dominant vehicle for financialisation, homeownership itself has contracted as rising prices created an 'affordability gap' (Byrne, 2020), despite the extraordinarily low interest rates between the GFC and the inflationary spike following the COVID-19 pandemic. Homeownership peaked in 2003 at 71% of households, and declined to 65% by 2019–20 (HoC, 2021a). The counterpart of the state's retreat from direct provision is a ballooning housing benefit bill, rising from £11bn in 1999–2000 to £20bn in 2009–10 (HoC, 2021b).[9] Essentially, state investment in a publicly-owned asset has been replaced by benefits paid to tenants priced out of owner-occupation. These benefits immediately flow to their landlords, subsidising private ownership and fuelling further house-price increases and speculative purchases of properties often on a large scale by inward global finance.

Under austerity, the British government legislated to limit the housing benefit bill. This included reducing and, later, freezing rates; requiring social landlords to reduce rents by 1% each year between 2016 and 2020; reducing entitlements for young people; introducing an under-occupation deduction (the 'bedroom tax'); and capping household benefits. These measures slowed the growth of housing benefit expenditure (notwithstanding rising claims during the pandemic), but they had knock-on effects on homelessness – for every

9 This has been commonplace across much of western Europe, National Housing Federation (2017).

£1 saved by Central Government on the housing benefit bill, local authority spending on temporary accommodation increased by 53p (Fetzer et al. 2020). Recent interest rate rises have generated demands for mortgage support to those experiencing large increases in repayments. Thus far, the Government has resisted such pressure beyond encouraging lenders to show forbearance to those struggling, signalling its priority of reducing inflation (Bell, 2023).

The contradictory role of the state, driving the incorporation of housing into financial circuits, *and* having to manage the fallout, is reflected in tensions between branches of government. Responsibility for housing the growing numbers excluded from Britain's commodified and financialised housing system falls to local authorities, but their capacities and funding have been drastically reduced. Prior to the GFC, this tension was mediated by third-sector bodies, that either took over social housing and management responsibilities from local governments, or outsourced them to the private sector (Pawson, 2007). Beswick (2021, p. 17) shows that post-GFC austerity "has driven local governments towards financialisation"; for example, several councils in London have engaged in "financialised municipal entrepreneurialism". This involves partnering with finance to boost housing supply by building for sale and using the revenue to help fund council services or, more boldly, creating a market for inter-council lending and borrowing (Dagdeviren and Karwowski, 2021).

In summary, the neoliberal state has driven the financialisation of housing in Britain. On the one hand, local governments have gradually shifted from providers of decommodified housing, to overseers of third-sector and private organisations, to financialised entrepreneurs and even bankers. On the other hand, the shift at the level of central government is not just that housing benefit must provide for the market-excluded, but that access to housing benefit has become increasingly determined by CC, with questions of who is entitled to what being formulated in terms of cost rather than need. The same goes for planning and land use, where policy is increasingly determined by calculations that privilege financialised rent extraction over use value (Christophers, 2017 and 2022).

5 Water

Water in England and Wales was privatised in 1989, when the ten regional water and sewerage companies were floated on the London Stock Exchange (LSE). These flotations were heavily subsidised; for example, the government cancelled the debts of the regional utilities at a cost of £4.9bn, and injected £1.5bn in cash, at 1989 prices (the 'green dowry'). Considering these costs, the fiscal gains from privatisation were nil (Ofwat/DEFRA, 2006). In contrast, share prices increased rapidly. At first, the shareholders were a dispersed set including many customers, and the government retained a golden share of 15% of voting rights, presumably to prevent any individual or company gaining control. When the government shares were sold in 1994, concentration of ownership followed almost immediately. Given their large cash balances, low debt and secure revenue streams, the water companies became immediate targets for corporate buyouts.

While the initial investors tended to be American, European and Asian infrastructure firms, financial investors began to take over from 2003. Currently, water in England is provided by fifteen water and sewerage and smaller, water-only, companies. Only three were still listed on the LSE in March 2023 (Severn Trent, United Utilities, and South West Water, which is owned by Pennon Group PLC). Another three were delisted and are owned by Asian conglomerates (Northumbrian Water, Wessex Water and SES Water). The remaining nine are owned by financial, largely private equity (PE), investors via special purpose vehicle (SPV) companies, and ownership stakes are regularly traded. One smaller water company, Bristol Water, was sold to Pennon Group in late 2021 (Bayliss et al. 2022).

The rise of PE investors in water reflects their increased role in the British economy (Appelbaum and Batt, 2014). Their entry into the water sector, as elsewhere, went largely unnoticed. The names of the water providers are unchanged and, for the users, there is no apparent difference in supply; however, the new owners have been associated with a radical restructuring of corporate finances.

In line with financialisation practices, PE investors have boosted shareholder returns via financial means unrelated to productivity – primarily by raising corporate debt. Under the terms of their licence, company debt is limited by the need to maintain investment-grade credit rating, so some PE investors set up complex securitisation structures via offshore jurisdictions to allow them to increase gearing (the ratio of net debt to regulatory capital) in ways that did not weaken their credit rating. Industry debt was low after privatisation, but it began to increase in the 2000s. By 2004, net debt reached £20.8bn, equivalent to a gearing of 60% (Ofwat/DEFRA, 2006); in 2020, Thames Water had a gearing of 86%, and Anglian Water of 82% (Moody's, 2021). Southern Water and Yorkshire Water also had very high gearing, but the measure fails to capture their indebtedness because it excludes pension obligations (Plimmer, 2021b). Total net debt exceeded £60bn in March 2022, while the average gearing reached 68%, if down from 73% in 2021 (Ofwat, 2022). At the same time as increasing debt, partly to fund their own acquisitions, the water companies have paid dividends of £72bn since privatisation, alongside generous pay and bonuses to their directors (Horton, 2022). Rising interest rates placed additional strain on highly-indebted companies. In June 2023, Thames Water, England's largest water company, was reported to be in dire financial difficulties due to the costs of servicing its £14bn debt (Plimmer et al. 2023).

The water system has, therefore, been restructured by the state to generate a stream of returns to (mostly financial) capital, funded by consumer revenues, while investors have taken advantage of the security of the revenue stream provided by the essential nature of water to put together an extractive financial architecture to their own benefit. This restructuring has involved an ongoing, though shifting, role for the state in regulating privatised water to balance the competing pressures of sustaining financial extraction and meeting (shifting perceptions of) social need and environmental protection.

Three regulatory agencies govern water provision in England – the Drinking Water Inspectorate, the Environment Agency, and the Water Services Regulation Authority (Ofwat) that focuses on the economics of supply. Other state agencies also have a say in service operation, especially the Competition and Markets Authority (CMA). Sectoral policy has been framed by the perception of the water system as an 'imperfect market', which is reflected in Ofwat's mandate to protect consumers by promoting competition where possible (Ofwat, n.d.) The regulatory structure is putatively designed to mimic aspects of a competitive market.

Water utilities are governed by price controls, where the regulator sets maximum tariffs for a fixed period (usually five years), based on the RPI-X formula, with the retail price index (RPI) measuring inflation, adjusted by a factor, X, derived from expected costs and performance targets. These price controls have been presented as the outcome of an independent process balancing the interests of investors and consumers, limiting companies' ability to charge monopoly prices, compelling them to raise productivity, and offering incentives for firms to pursue social and environmental goals (NIC, 2019). However, regulation is unavoidably embedded in complex and contested social relations framed by neoliberalism. In particular, until recently, regulation avoided addressing financial engineering by PE investors, instead prioritising regulatory stability and investor confidence. The narrative of the sector as an imperfect market steered the regulator away from intervening in company practices securing shareholder returns, including the accumulation of debt and high dividend payments, which were presented as market outcomes (Bayliss et al. 2022).

More recently Ofwat has started curbing financialisation. Only since 2015, have companies been required to demonstrate financial resilience. This regulatory response is too little too late, taking effect long after securitisation had begun, by which time some PE investors had already sold up. Moreover, the CMA upheld an appeal by four companies against PR19, on the grounds that tighter rules would limit their investments. In response, Ofwat (2020, p. 3) stated to the CMA, "we can have no confidence that ... higher returns will translate into investment services for the benefit of consumers and the environment". The tensions between the CMA and Ofwat illustrate the contestation surrounding the financialisation of infrastructure in Britain; different state agencies chase distinct goals (e.g. regulating shareholders versus attracting investment) precisely because the state plays a dual role of facilitating financialisation and managing its fallout.

Water regulation has become increasingly complex over time. PR19 generated thousands of pages in company, regulator and consultancy reports and, for the first time, one price review overlapped with its successor, as the 2024 Review started before PR19 was completed. Costs have grown significantly, as firms and the regulator must draw on legal and consultancy services to support their negotiations. Water companies say they spent three years and £140m on preparing for PR19, aside from the costs of regulating water quality and environmental impacts (Plimmer, 2021a). This shows that, far from privatisation being a retreat of the state, the public sector must play a continuing and intricate set of roles in water provision. In doing this, the state has set up a regulatory framework that is now widely acknowledged to be biased towards profit-extracting investors rather than consumers (HoC, 2015; and Ofwat, 2017, p. 2). Even the UK National Infrastructure Commission notes a systemic bias towards investors in the regulatory architecture (NIC, 2019). The long-term failings of regulation are coming to light, as companies have been criticised for low investment, water leakage rates averaging 20% and record levels of pollution, as well as financial fragility. The regulator has been incredibly slow to intervene. In July 2023, it was announced that Ofwat would have new powers to stop the payment of dividends if they would risk the company's financial resilience, but only from April 2025 (Ofwat, 2023). Thus, the state's ability (and will) to curb extraction is both limited and curtailed by cumbersome practices, in contrast to the agility of private finance.

Household level effects manifest differently for water than for housing (where growing numbers are denied access to the preferred tenure of owner-occupation, and rents are unaffordable). English households cannot be disconnected from the network for non-payment; however, one-quarter of households have reported difficulties paying their bills (Bayliss et al. 2020). Nevertheless, consumers must fund the financialisation of water; around £1.8bn was paid each year between 2007 and 2016 on dividends, plus £1.4bn in annual financing costs (Bayliss and Hall, 2017). Also, unlike housing, where the state intervenes directly to support the hard-to-house, water companies are required to set a lower social tariff. However, these (differing for each company) must be cost-neutral, meaning that revenues must be balanced, for example, by lower debt recovery costs. In addition, since the social tariff is funded by other residential bill-payers (non-household customers are excluded), subsidies must be acceptable to other customers. This is assessed through consultation with households over their views on 'suitable beneficiaries' and appropriate social tariffs which, by construction, promotes judgements about deserving versus undeserving poor (Bayliss, 2017).

In summary, social policy in water is structured by a notion of fairness in which everyone must pay for what they consume, and affordability is addressed via (indirect) handouts from better-off to poorer households, which is closer to charity than to progressive redistribution (Bayliss et al. 2020). This system smooths some edges of the financialisation of water, but the fundamental inequity remains, whereby households must pay into a system that transfers millions to directors and billions to shareholders. Beyond company-level social tariffs, affordability issues must be picked up by the wider benefit system, but utility providers can apply for householders' universal credit payments to be deducted by up to 5% to pay for gas, electricity and water, plus 10–20% for rent (UK Government, n.d.).

Complex regulatory interventions to address social and environmental failings do not sit comfortably with the narrative of mimicking a market. One example is that a reduction in water consumption is desirable for environmental reasons; however, such a fall in revenue is unacceptable for firms remunerated according to units consumed. A solution was found by setting consumption reduction as a performance target so, if demand falls, firms are rewarded by being able to increase unit prices. In other words, if a household lowers water consumption, their bill may not decline. In this way, the state intervenes to derisk private investment at the immediate expense of end users. Regulation has also failed to protect the environment. In 2023, the UK experienced devastating outpourings of raw sewage into rivers and seas. In large part, this was due to regulatory neglect; storm overflows were not monitored until recently, companies have underinvested, funding for the Environment Agency has been slashed, and the number of prosecutions against companies has fallen (Colbert, 2022) – and, now that bills need to increase to finance new investment, there is no guarantee that the additional revenue will not leak into financialised extraction through payments of loan interest and dividends to offshore shareholders.

In short, water privatisation in Britain has progressed through financialisation, sponsored by the state. Meanwhile, global corporations have manipulated revenue streams from water bills to extract profits for themselves.

6 Health

The NHS is under unprecedented strain. While funding has increased in real terms each year since it was established in 1948, in line with economic growth and an increasing population, the rate of increase was at its lowest from 2010 until the start of the Covid-19 pandemic (Warner and Zaranko, 2021). Access to health services has been in decline as a result, accelerating since the pandemic. Key waiting time targets for treatments are consistently being missed. NHS providers are in deficit and under intense pressure to do more with less resources. A detailed study of the UK alongside eighteen other comparable countries finds the NHS lags behind on some important resources, such as having fewer CT and MRI scanners and hospital beds. The UK also has fewer levels of clinical staff per head than most of its peers. These deficiencies are having an impact on health outcomes and, in particular, the UK performs noticeably worse on important indicators including life expectancy (Anandaciva, 2023). Those that have the means are opting out, using private health services (Thomas et al. 2022).

NHS England has undergone extensive reforms since 1999, generally aiming to increase the scope of market forces in the system and the role of the private sector in state-funded services (Bayliss, 2022). Yet, the expected levels of privatisation itself have not materialised and have been exaggerated in popular discourse, at least in the form of privately provided (but publicly funded) health services, with the share of public health spending going directly to the independent sector remaining around 7% (Department of Health and Social Care, accounts, various years) Nevertheless, the private sector is well-established in segments of the publicly-financed NHS, and social care has been almost completely privately provided since the 1990s. Furthermore, the rise in out-of-pocket spending on health is contributing to a growing market for the private sector outside the public system.[10]

From the 1990s, NHS England was structured around an institutional split between 'buyers' and 'sellers' of services meant to mimic the market, though

10 Goodair and Reeves (2022) show that an annual increase of one percentage point of outsourcing to the private-for-profit sector corresponded with an annual increase in treatable mortality of 0·38%, or 0·29% deaths in the following year.

provisioning has mostly remained in the public sector. Since 2012, 'purchasing' has been the responsibility of more than two hundred Clinical Commissioning Groups (CCGs).[11] They 'commission' services from providers, including GPs and NHS trusts, encompassing hospitals, mental health, ambulance and community services, as well as private companies. This is indicative of CC (if not CF, or even C, depending on the sector, service and circumstances), with finances being distributed according to targets and performance, and provision following an imitation of commercial logic, but (mostly) without production directly for profit (Bushell, 2020; and Hunter and Murray, 2019).

Within and alongside this expanding pseudo-market for health services within the public sector, a fully-commodified private sector sells services to the NHS. This includes the (discontinued) Private Finance Initiative (PFI), through which large investments, such as hospitals, were financed and built by the private sector, to be reimbursed by the state over decades. These turned out to be hugely costly for the government, raising £13bn of capital investment at a cost of £80bn; in 2019, a year after PFI was stopped, £55bn was still outstanding, with payments extending until 2052 (Thomas, 2019). In 2003, under a Labour Government, commodification extended into outsourcing diagnostic tests and low-risk surgeries to (private) Independent Sector Treatment Centres (ISTCs), rationalised by the goal of reducing waiting times and expanding NHS capacity. The ISTCs also provided much-trumpeted 'choice', with patients allowed to decide which hospital to attend for some procedures, including for-profit providers. The scope of for-profit companies was extended further under the 2012 HSCA, which required CCGs to allocate funds through competitive tendering, with both private and NHS providers able to bid, unless a rationale was otherwise provided.[12]

Since the NHS does not disclose information on contracts, the extent of publicly-funded private provision must be gleaned from freedom of information requests and independent surveys. It appears that the private sector provides a significant and growing share of NHS-funded routine elective procedures (e.g. hip and knee replacements), and is heavily represented in community and mental health services. For example, a Care Quality Commission (CQC, 2018) study of mental health rehabilitation inpatient services found that 53% were provided by the private sector, rising to 78% for beds categorised as "locked rehabilitation" or "complex care".

11 These were renamed Integrated Care Boards (ICBs) in 2022, in a nominal measure to address health and care together across delivering agencies.

12 With NHS providers wary of legal action should they self-provide.

Some aspects of mental health provision have become overtly financialised, with services being provided by companies owned by PE investors extracting returns through financial engineering. For example, The Priory is the largest provider of NHS-funded private mental health services, with over 90% of revenue from public sources, and reportedly operating 10% of NHS-funded mental health care beds (Plimmer, 2021c). The company has been bought and sold back and forth by PE and US health corporations since it was established in 1980, and it has been loaded with debt, often due to leveraged buyouts. In 2021, around 12% of company income (£110m) was directed towards servicing debt owed to a holding company within the same group, based in the Cayman Islands. Thus, NHS funds are being directed towards murky corporate structures benefitting offshore shareholders, profiting both from securitised NHS contract revenues, and from legalised tax avoidance.

Another dimension to financial engineering is 'sale and leaseback', where ownership is separated from provision, and health care assets are bought from, and then leased back to, the service provider. For example, some properties owned by The Priory were sold to and leased back from a US real estate fund in 2021. Similarly, some GP practices have been taken over by property investors, with Assura PLC owning 6% of GP premises in the UK (Bayliss, 2022). These arrangements release capital to the current owners, while tying them into long-term rental agreements with annual rent increases; in turn, real estate investors are attracted by the secure revenues ultimately provided by the NHS. Sale and leaseback expand the chain of financial interests extracting profits from public resources, either succeeding with no additional contribution to health care, or creating vulnerabilities where costs are imposed through spiralling rental charges. This arrangement contributed directly to the collapse of the care home chain, Southern Cross, in 2011 (Bayliss and Gideon, 2020).

Since the NHS was established in 1948, some elements of primary care have always remained in private hands, operating in close co-ordination with the public health system. Dental and GP services, for example, have always been provided by individual practices. However, recent years have seen a major shift in the nature of such private ownership. Following a change in legislation in 2004, some GP partnerships began to buy out others and build chains of practices. In 2021, the US health care company, Centene, purchased some of these, operating seventy practices in England, around 1% of the total (We Own It, 2021). While not privatisation as such, since these practices were already privately owned, this shift changes the nature of provision, with small partnerships passing into the hands of (often) major corporations, with the nature and scope of services increasingly reflecting the imperatives of securing revenues for a financialised business model (including service charges, casualised staff, restrictions on visits to cut costs, and long waits for appointments).

Another dimension to the commodification of health provision is that the NHS can itself, increasingly, provide private services. The 2012 HSCA lifted the cap that NHS providers could earn from private patients from 2% to 49% of income. While not yet triggering a sharp increase in private income shares, the legislation has created new relationships between the state and private service providers. For example, the Christie NHS Foundation Trust and HCA International Ltd have set up a private cancer treatment centre in Manchester, called Christie Private Care LLP, which generates profits accruing to the NHS. While seemingly harmless, this mode of operation turns the public health sector into a player in the private health care market, complicating the statutory duty to prioritise patient care according to need rather than disposable income.

The state has maintained a more obvious role in health care provision than in housing or water since, for the most part, health has not undergone a straightforward or wholesale privatisation but, rather, a sequence of reforms to extend the scope of CCFCC and enable, if not promote, financialisation. This drove significant shifts in the role and functions of the state, for example, at least prior to the 2022 Health and Care Bill (HCB), forcing NHS bodies to compete for services that they can themselves and do traditionally deliver.

The British state has addressed the need to support the hard-to-provide-health-for as well as the political imperative to facilitate financial extraction from health services in three significant ways. First, as with housing, it falls to the state to manage crises, most clearly the COVID-19 pandemic. England entered COVID-19 with a relatively weak health system; for example, it had higher bed-occupancy rates, and fewer beds, doctors, nurses, and capital assets per capita than most high-income countries. Unsurprisingly, England experienced relatively high rates of excess deaths. In the aftermath of the pandemic, health care waiting lists, already long before COVID-19, subsequently passed seven million, the highest levels since records began,[13] while staff strikes spread in unprecedented ways and the number of unfilled vacancies reached 100,000, as the government proved unable to address any of the key challenges facing the health service. Proposed spending increases will take years to turn into capacity improvements, especially in terms of staffing, implying waiting lists are likely to rise further. Simultaneously, since the 1970s, out-of-pocket

13 See HoC (2022) and https://www.itv.com/thismorning/articles/nhs-waiting-lists-hit-new-record-high-of-7-7-million.

spending on health as a percentage of GDP has risen faster in England than any other G7 nation, leading to a noticeable uptick in private sector revenues (Thomas et al. 2022).

Second, although, like water, health provision is a universal entitlement, the state plays an ongoing role in determining access to specific treatments and shaping the wider determinants of health. The expansion of private provision and austerity have eroded service provision through the encroachment of payments for services and parallel provision of private care in NHS facilities while, as was shown previously, waiting lists became unprecedentedly long. These shortcomings reveal a wider shift in NHS ethos, with health and social care being undervalued while the social determinants of health drive widening inequalities, most clearly around life expectancy (Marmot et al. 2020).

While the wholesale privatisation of the NHS has not taken place, the private sector has positioned itself to extract government revenue, attaching itself to lucrative revenue streams. For example, the NHS is suffering from critical staffing shortages (Morgan, 2022). Private equity investors are behind a growing number of staffing agencies that supply temporary staff at high cost to NHS hospitals to address staff shortages (for example, the largest nursing staff agency, Thornberry, is owned by Onex, a Canadian private equity firm). As mentioned, property companies are buying up GP practices through transactions known as 'sale and leaseback' where practice premises are bought and then rented back to the doctors. Part of the attraction to investors is that the GP rents are reimbursed by NHS bodies (see for example The PHP Group). As such the private sector is sequestering government funds in ways that do not feature in policy overtly but are facilitated by a state that is permissive of such practices.

Finally, again like water, the state imposes continual reforms, involving ad hoc and multidirectional movements along the CCFCC spectrum as the dysfunctions of previous reforms become intolerable. Thus, the NHS has moved into a huge restructuring after COVID-19. The Health and Care Bill (HCB) 2022 ostensibly heralded a redirection from competitive structures within the NHS to a more collaborative and integrated structure, where providers work together and with other actors such as local authorities, to create a more preventative and holistic health system. The shift in approach in the HCB can be seen as a response to the catastrophe early in the pandemic, when patients were forcibly transferred from hospitals into ill-prepared care homes, to free up hospital beds. However, close examination of the reforms show that HCB will present at most a marginal shift in, rather than a significant departure from, the neoliberalisation of provision.

This is because, first, there is now a strong private health care lobby reliant on NHS funding, and the government sees an expanded role for NHS-funded privately-provided health care to address waiting lists for elective treatments. But, in practice, as already observed, the impact of the private sector is limited, particularly prevalent in simple day surgery procedures (notably cataract surgery). Orthopaedic services (joint replacements) are also being outsourced but these take longer and independent sector activity is not easy to scale up (Coughlan et al. 2023). This policy became apparent during the pandemic, when private providers benefitted from a deluge of government contracts, some of them later challenged because of allegations of corruption (Iacobucci, 2021; and NAO, 2022), while much of the additional capacity was either unnecessary or could not be utilised for lack of staff (Ryan et al. 2021). More generally, while the HCB does not directly promote greater private sector involvement, it also does not commit to the NHS as the preferred service provider. The reforms also focus on areas where the private presence is already greatest, especially the intersection between the NHS and local authorities with responsibility for social care. This is part of a shift from meeting minimum legally-required standards as cheaply as possible (or delaying provision as long as possible), to one of paring those standards and hoping to get away with it – obvious in case of waiting times for treatment and emergency services, and increasingly endemic in major shortages of provision for social care.

Second, while the HCB avowedly promotes an integrated public health system, important aspects of the earlier framework remain, such as 'patient choice'. Contrary to the narrative of cooperation, the policy of patient choice turns patients into consumers, while retaining elements of competition among providers even though its welfare benefits are, at best, ephemeral.

Finally, substantive improvements in health care provision are impossible without sustained increases in spending; however, notwithstanding the COVID-19 surge, rising levels of public spending do not sit comfortably with the prevailing political regime. In March 2022, the (then) Health Secretary, Sajid Javid, gave an indication of the political direction, stating the government's commitment to a small "but strong" state. Javid promoted the image of an overblown public sector, by claiming that health spending in England was bigger than the GDP of Greece, paving the way for lower expectations alongside an invocation for families (read women) to plug the gaps left by a retreating public sector (Javid, 2022).

In short, rather than marking a turning point in neoliberal health provision, the HCB is an attempt to patch up the most egregious dysfunctions of the previous reforms, consolidate uneven delivery across populations and services, and continue to ignore the social determinants of (ill-)health, while further supporting the shift of health provision in England along the CCFCC spectrum. As with the other case studies, this is an example of state restructuring in response to the competing demands of social pressures and financial extraction.

7 Conclusion

Despite considerable variegation, two key state roles emerge from our case studies across the current stage of neoliberalism as experienced in Britain: creating and sustaining opportunities for financialised accumulation by extending CCFCC in (social) provisioning; and managing perceptions of 'market failure' and insufficient provision to the 'deserving' through shifts in both directions along the CCFCC spectrum. Norms of provision, in terms of who gets what and how this is perceived, have also been transformed. Our case studies also highlight changes in the nature of the state under neoliberalism, with enabling and regulatory functions increasingly displacing direct provision within an increasingly financialised framework. This all follows from the transformations that have taken place under neoliberalism in terms of how interests are represented and how policy is correspondingly formed and implemented.

More specifically, our case studies show that COVID-19 did not bring about either a 'retreat' from neoliberalism nor the 'return of the state' – it never went away. Instead, the pandemic has led to marginal (if costly and often dysfunctional) adjustments in modes of regulation, financing, and accumulation. In effect, the British state's pandemic response represented neoliberal crisis management *par excellence in extremis*, since it involved the state addressing dysfunctions, while sustaining the monetary and other relations upon which neoliberal accumulation depends.

The significance of our analysis is three-fold. First, it enriches understandings of the role of the British state in supporting capital accumulation, highlighting, in particular, its increasingly financialised nature and its constitutive role in even archetypal neoliberal reforms. Second, this study stresses the economic functions of the state under neoliberalism, offering an alternative to perspectives that focus on the role of the state in maintaining the political conditions for neoliberal accumulation. In doing so, this chapter puts on a stronger footing that the state has *not* retreated under neoliberalism, both before and after the pandemic. Third, by demonstrating that intervention to address crises and anomalies in provision is an ongoing function of the British state within neoliberalism, this chapter provides a framework for understanding the pandemic response as not only compatible with neoliberalism but an inherent component of it. In summary, the pandemic response was not only consistent with how previous systemic crises like the GFC were handled, but it also aligns with continual restructuring in reaction to economic and political pressures as seen through our case studies.

It can be concluded that the pandemic interventions were fully aligned with neoliberal approaches to public policy. Key functions, such as the provision of protective equipment and the test-and-trace system, were assigned to the private sector, while the NHS contracted services from private hospitals at huge cost to expand its own depleted capacity to protect the 'nation'. The decentralisation of responsibilities not backed up by essential resources created tensions throughout the pandemic, most notably in the way that care homes, themselves extensively privatised but excluded from those (favoured) centralised networks, were placed in extraordinarily vulnerable positions. Vaccination led by the NHS was the most successful element of the government's pandemic strategy, but it was also an anomaly, and it was largely discontinued along with most data collection as soon as this could be done in practice.

What is often missing from accounts that infer the return of the state or the end of neoliberalism from the pandemic response and its aftermath, or from other examples of state intervention, is attention to their wider effects, and whose interests are served by them. They reveal that government interventions have been uniformly aimed at preserving the current social and economic configuration. In short, the interventions by the Johnson government during and after the pandemic, followed by the (catastrophic but fortunately short) administration led by Liz Truss, and the politically paralysed government led by Rishi Sunak, were entirely consistent with what one would expect from a neoliberal state. They offer another testimony to neoliberalism's ability to weather crises through adaptation and retrospective justification.

What, then, would it take to create a rupture, and turn a crisis *in* neoliberalism to one *of* neoliberalism (Saad-Filho, 2011)? The differentiated incidence and severity of the pandemic has revealed the importance of health, housing, and other public goods and services, and their mutually reinforcing effects, and the prevalence of low wages and poor working conditions in terms of outcomes, with ethnic minorities and the less healthy (and those in social care) most at risk. Related changes in employment and social life, the declining presence of trade unions and other mass organisations, and the atrophy of collective forms of dissent, have reinforced the construction of neoliberal subjectivities and financialised social intercourse to an extent that would have been unimaginable a few decades ago. At the same time, the GFC and the austerity in its aftermath were associated with the fracturing of the ideological hegemony of neoliberalism, potentially opening new spaces for contestation, over time, across the commodification/CCFCC of public goods, services and, especially, of the environment. Experiences of success deserve attention and potential replication; for example, the remunicipalisation of water and definancialisation of provision in Valladolid (Garcia-Arias et al. 2022), and proposals for the definancialisation of nursing care (Aveline-Dubach, 2022) and housing (Wijburg, 2020). The constraints on beginning the transitions from neoliberalism, then, are neither technical nor even financial, they are political.

References

Aalbers, M. (2015) "The Potential for Financialization", *Dialogues in Human Geography*, vol 5, no 2, pp. 214–19.

Aalbers, M. and B. Christophers (2014) "Centring Housing in Political Economy", *Housing, Theory and Society*, vol 31, no 4, pp. 373–94.

Adkins, L. and M. Dever (2014) "Housework, Wages and Money", *Australian Feminist Studies*, vol 29, no 79, pp. 50–66.

Al-Jazaeri, H. (2008) "Interrogating Technical Change through the History of Economic Thought in the Context of Latecomers' Industrial Development: The Case of the South Korean Microelectronics, Auto and Steel Industries", University of London, unpublished Phd Thesis.

Alami, I. and A. Dixon (2021) "Uneven and Combined State Capitalism", *Environment and Planning A*, vol 55, no 1, pp. 72–99.

Albo, G. (2008) "Neoliberalism and the Discontented", in Panitch and Leys (eds) (2008), pp. 354–62.

Albritton R., B. Jessop and R. Westra (eds) (2007) *Political Economy and Global Capitalism: The 21st Century, Present and Future*, London: Anthem Press.

Alexander, N. (2014) "The Emerging Multi-Polar World Order: Its Unprecedented Consensus on a New Model for Financing Infrastructure Investment and Development", Heinrich Böll Foundation North America, http://us.boell.org/sites/default/files/alexander_multi-polar_world_order_1.pdf.

Allen, J. and M. Pryke (2013) "Financialising Household Water: Thames Water, MEIF, and 'Ring-Fenced' Politics", *Cambridge Journal of Regions, Economy and Society*, vol 6, no 3, pp. 419–39.

Allon, F. (2014) "The Feminisation of Finance", *Australian Feminist Studies*, vol 29, no 79, pp. 12–30.

Alt, J. and K. Shepsle (eds) (1990) *Perspectives on Positive Political Economy*, Cambridge: Cambridge University Press.

Amarnath, S., M. Brusseler, D. Gabor, C. Lala and J. Mason (2023) "Varieties of Derisking", https://www.phenomenalworld.org/interviews/derisking/.

Amin, S. (2010) "Exiting the Crisis of Capitalism or Capitalism in Crisis?", *Globalizations*, vol 7, no 1–2, pp. 261–73.

Anandaciva, S. (2023) "How Does the NHS Compare to the Health Care Systems of Other Countries?", Report for The King's Fund, https://www.kingsfund.org.uk/sites/default/files/2023-06/How_NHS_compare_2023.pdf.

Apeldoorn, B. and L. Horn (2007) "The Marketization of European Corporate Control: A Critical Political Economy Perspective", *New Political Economy*, vol 12, no 2, pp. 211–35.

Appelbaum, E. and R. Batt (2014) *Private Equity at Work: When Wall Street Manages* Main Street, New York: Russell Sage.

Archer, T. and I. Cole (2014) "Still Not Plannable? Housing Supply and the Changing Structure of the Housebuilding Industry in the UK in 'Austere' Times", *People, Place and Policy*, vol 8, no 2, pp. 97–112.

Archer, T. and I. Cole (2021) "The Financialisation of Housing Production: Exploring Capital Flows and Value Extraction Among Major Housebuilders in the UK", *Journal of Housing and the Built Environment*, vol 36, no 4, pp. 1367–87.

Arestis, P. and M. Sawyer (eds) (2004) *The Rise of the Market*, Camberley: Edward Elgar.

Arestis, P. and M. Sawyer (eds) (2008) *Critical Essays on the Privatisation Experience*, London: Palgrave Macmillan.

Arestis, P., C. Aurélie and G. Fontana (2013) "Financialization, the Great Recession, and the Stratification of the US Labor Market", *Feminist Economics*, vol 19, no 3, pp. 152–80.

Arrighi, G. (1994) *The Long Twentieth Century*, London: Verso.

Ashman, S. and B. Fine (2013) "Neo-liberalism, Varieties of Capitalism, and the Shifting Contours of South Africa's Financial System", *Transformation*, no 81/2, pp. 144–78.

Ashman, S., B. Fine and E. Karwowski (2021), "The Relevance of Financialization for African Economies: Lessons from South Africa", SOAS Department of Economics Working Paper, no 245, London: SOAS University of London, https://eprints.soas.ac.uk/36164/1/wpsamandewa.pdf.

Aveline-Dubach, N. (2022) "Financializing Nursing Homes? The Uneven Development of Health Care REITs in France, the United Kingdom and Japan", *Environment and Planning A: Economy and Space*, vol 54, no 5, pp. 984–1004.

Ayers, A. (ed.) (2008) *Gramsci, Political Economy and International Relations Theory: Modern Princes and Naked Emperors*, London: Palgrave.

Ayers, A. and A. Saad-Filho (2008) "Production, Class, and Power in the Neoliberal Transition: A Critique of Coxian Eclecticism", in Ayers (ed.) (2008), pp. 147–72.

Ayers, A. and A. Saad-Filho (2015) "Democracy against Neoliberalism: Paradoxes, Limitations, Transcendence", *Critical Sociology*, vol 41, no 4–5, pp. 597–618.

Bakker, K. (2005) "Neoliberalizing Nature? Market Environmentalism in Water Supply in England and Wales", *Annals of the Association of American Geographers*, vol 95, no 3, pp. 542–565.

Ball, M. (1988) *Rebuilding Construction: Economic Change and the British Construction Industry*, London: Routledge.

Ball, M. (1990) *Under One Roof – Retail Banking and the International Mortgage Finance Revolution*, Brighton: Harvester Wheatsheaf.

Ball, M. (2003) "Markets and the Structure of the Housebuilding Industry: An International Perspective", *Urban Studies* vol 40, no 5–6, pp. 897–916.

Bank of England (2021) *Financial Stability Report*, https://www.bankofengland.co.uk/-/media/boe/files/financial-stability-report/2021/december-2021.pdf.

Barber, W. (1995) "Chile con Chicago: A Review Essay", *Journal of Economic Literature*, vol 33, no 4, pp. 1941–49.

Barnes, T. (2004) "Culture: Economy" in Cloke and Johnston (eds) (2004), pp. 61–80.

Bateman, M. (2010) *Why Doesn't Microfinance Work?: The Destructive Rise of Local Neoliberalism*, London: Zed Press.

Baud, C. and C. Durand (2012) "Financialization, Globalization and the Making of Profits by Leading Retailers", *Socio-Economic Review*, vol 10, no 2, pp. 241–66.

Bayliss, K. (2011) "A Cup Half Full: The World Bank's Assessment of Water Privatisation", in Bayliss et al. (eds) (2011), pp. 73–98.

Bayliss, K. (2013) "The Financialization of Water", *Review of Radical Political Economics*, vol 20, no 10, pp. 1–16.

Bayliss, K. (2014) "The Financialisation of Water in England and Wales", FESSUD Working Paper Series no 52, https://fessud.org/wp-content/uploads/2015/03/Case-study-the-financialisation-of-Water-in-England-and-Wales-Bayliss-working-paper-REVISED_annexes-working-paper-52.pdf.

Bayliss, K. (2016a) "The System of Provision for Water in Selected Case Study Countries", FESSUD, Working Paper Series, no 194, https://fessud.org/wp-content/uploads/2015/03/FESSUD_WP194_The-System-of-Provision-for-Water-in-Selected-Case-Study-Countries.pdf.

Bayliss, K. (2016b) "Neoliberalised Water in South Africa", FESSUD, Working Paper Series, no 204, https://fessud.org/wp-content/uploads/2015/03/FESSUD_WP204_Neoliberalised-Water-in-South-Africa.pdf.

Bayliss, K. (2017) "Material Cultures of Water Financialisation in England and Wales", *New Political Economy*, vol 22, no 4, pp. 383–97, reproduced in Bayliss et al. (eds) (2018), pp. 29–43.

Bayliss, K. (2022) "Can England's National Health System Reforms Overcome the Neoliberal Legacy?", *International Journal of Health Services*, vol 52, no 4, pp. 480–91.

Bayliss, K. and B. Fine (2021a) *A Guide to the Systems of Provision Approach: Who Gets What, How and Why*, Basingstoke: Palgrave MacMillan.

Bayliss, K. and B. Fine (2021b) "Food, Diet and the Pandemic", *Theory and Struggle*, vol 122, no 1, pp. 46–57.

Bayliss, K. and B. Fine (eds) (2008) *Privatization and Alternative Public Sector Reform in Sub-Saharan Africa: Delivering on Electricity and Water*, London: Palgrave MacMillan.

Bayliss, K., B. Fine and M. Robertson (2013) "From Financialisation to Consumption: The Systems of Provision Approach Applied to Housing and Water", FESSUD, Working Paper Series, no 02, https://fessud.org/wp-content/uploads/2013/04/FESSUD-Working-Paper-021.pdf.

Bayliss, K., B. Fine and M. Robertson (eds) (2017) "Material Cultures of Financialisation", special issue of *New Political Economy*, vol 22, no 4, reproduced as Bayliss et al. (eds) (2018).

Bayliss, K., B. Fine and M. Robertson (eds) (2018) *Material Cultures of Financialisation*, London: Routledge, reproduced from Bayliss et al. (eds) (2017).

Bayliss, K., B. Fine, M. Robertson and A. Saad-Filho (2024) "Reports of My Death Are Greatly Exaggerated: The Persistence of Neoliberalism in Britain", *European Journal of Social Theory*, DOI: 10.1177/13684310241241800, forthcoming.

Bayliss, K., B. Fine and E. Van Waeyenberge (eds) (2011) *The Political Economy of Development: The World Bank, Neoliberalism and Development Research*, London: Pluto Press.

Bayliss, K. and J. Gideon (2020) "The Privatisation and Financialisation of Social Care in the UK", SOAS Working Paper Series, no 238.

Bayliss, K. and D. Hall (2017) "Bringing Water into Public Ownership: Costs and Benefits", Technical Report, Public Services International Research Unit (PSIRU), University of Greenwich, https://gala.gre.ac.uk/id/eprint/17277/.

Bayliss, K., G. Mattioli and J. Steinberger (2020) "Inequality, Poverty and the Privatization of Essential Services: A Systems of Provision Study of Water, Energy and Local Buses in the UK", *Competition and Change*, vol 25, no 3–4, pp. 478–500.

Bayliss, K., E. Van Waeyenberge and B. Bowles (2022) "Private Equity and the Regulation of Financialised Infrastructure: The Case of Macquarie in Britain's Water and Energy Networks", *New Political Economy*, vol 28, no 2, pp. 155–72.

Beaverstock, J., S. Hall and T. Wainwright (2013) "Servicing the Super-Rich: New Financial Elites and the Rise of the Private Wealth Management Retail Ecology", *Regional Studies*, vol 47, no 6, pp. 834–49.

Becker, J. (2014) "The Periphery in the Present International Crisis: Uneven Development, Uneven Impact and Different Responses", *Spectrum*, vol 5, no 1, pp. 21–41, http://spectrumjournal.net/wp-content/uploads/2014/05/Joachim-Becker.pdf.

Becker, J., J. Jäger, B. Leubolt and R. Weissenbacher (2010) "Peripheral Financialization and Vulnerability to Crisis: A Regulationist Perspective", *Competition and Change*, vol 14, no 3–4, pp. 225–47.

Beckert, J. (2011) "State of the Art: Where Do Prices Come from? Sociological Approaches to Price Formation", *Socio-Economic Review*, vol 9, no 4, pp. 757–86.

Bell, T. (2023) "What the Government Might Actually Do to Tackle the Mortgage Crunch", Resolution Foundation, https://www.resolutionfoundation.org/comment/what-the-government-might-actually-do-to-tackle-the-mortgage-crunch/.

Bellamy Foster, J. and R. McChesney (2012) "The Global Stagnation and China", *Monthly Review*, vol 63, no 9, pp. 1–28.

Bendix, R. (1977) *Nation-Building and Citizenship*, Berkeley: University of California Press.

Bernstein, P. (1992) *Capital Ideas: The Improbable Origins of Modern Wall Street*, New York: Free Press.

Besley, T (2011) "Rethinking Economics: Introduction and Overview", *Global Policy*, vol 2, no 2, pp. 163–4.

Beswick, J. (2021) *Public Rental Housing after the Global Financial Crisis: The Emergence of Financialised Municipal Entrepreneurialism in London*, PhD Thesis, University of Leeds, https://etheses.whiterose.ac.uk/29430/1/COMPLETED%20PhD%20-%20after%20corrections.pdf.

Beswick, J., G. Alexandri, M. Byrne, S. Vives-Miró, D. Fields, S. Hodkinson and M. Janoschka (2016) "Speculating on London's Housing Future", *City*, vol 20, no 2, pp. 321–41.

Binderkrantz, A., P. Christiansen and H. Pedersen (2015) "Interest Group Access to the Bureaucracy, Parliament, and the Media", *Governance*, vol 28, no 1, pp. 95–112.

Birch, K. and V. Mykhnenko (eds) (2010) *The Rise and Fall of Neoliberalism: The Collapse of an Economic Order?*, London: Zed Books.

Blanchard, O. (2008) "The State of Macro", NBER Working Paper, no 14259, http://www.nber.org/papers/w14259.pdf, published as Blanchard (2009).

Blanchard, O. (2009) "The State of Macro", *Annual Review of Economics*, vol 1, pp. 209–28.

Blanchard, O., G. Dell'Ariccia, and P. Mauro (2010) "Rethinking Macroeconomic Policy", IMF Staff Position Note, http://www.imf.org/external/pubs/ft/spn/2010/spn1003.pdf.

Blanchard, O., D. Romer, M. Spence and J. Stiglitz (eds) (2012) *In the Wake of the Crisis: Leading Economists Reassess Economic Policy*, Cambridge: MIT Press.

Bobek, A., M. Milus and M. Sokol (2023) "Making Sense of the Financialization of Households: State of the Art and Beyond", *Socio-Economic Review*, vol 21, no 4, pp. 2233–58.

Boffo, M, A. Brown and D. Spencer (2017) "From Happiness to Social Provisioning: Addressing Well-Being in Times of Crisis", *New Political Economy*, vol 22, no 4, pp. 450–462

Bonizzi, B. (2014) "Financialization in Developing and Emerging Countries: A Survey", *International Journal of Political Economy*, vol. 42, no. 4, pp. 83–107.

Botta, A., E. Caverzasi and D. Tori (2015) "Financial-Real Side Interactions in the Monetary Circuit: Loving or Dangerous Hugs?", Greenwich Papers in Political Economy, no 14069, University of Greenwich Political Economy Research Centre.

Bowman, A., I. Erturk, J. Froud, S. Johal, J. Law, A. Leaver, M. Moran and K. Williams (2012) "The Finance and Point-Value-Complex" CRESC Working Paper, no 118, Centre for Research in Socio-Cultural Change, Manchester University.

Bradley, Q. (2021) "The Financialisation of Housing Land Supply in England", *Urban Studies*, vol 58, no 2, pp. 389–404.

Brassett, J., L. Rethel and M. Watson (2010) "The Political Economy of the Subprime Crisis: The Economics, Politics and Ethics of Response", *New Political Economy*, vol 15, no 1, pp.1–7.

Brennan, D., D. Kristjanson-Gural, C. Mulder and E. Olsen (eds) (2019) *The Routledge Handbook of Marxian Economics*, London: Routledge.

Brenner, N., J. Peck and N. Theodore (2010) "Variegated Neoliberalization: Geographies, Modalities, Pathways", *Global Networks*, vol 10, no 2, pp. 182–222.

Bresnahan, R. (2003) "Chile since 1990: The Contradictions of Neoliberal Democratization", *Latin American Perspectives*, vol 30, no 5, pp. 3–15.

Brown, W. (2015) *Undoing the Demos: Neoliberalism's Stealth Revolution*, Cambridge: MIT Press.

Bryan, D. and M. Rafferty (2014) "Political Economy and Housing in the Twenty-First Century – From Mobile Homes to Liquid Housing", *Housing, Theory and Society*, vol 31, no 4, pp. 404–412.

Buchanan, B. (2014) "Back to the Future: 900 Years of Securitisation", *Journal of Risk Finance*, vol 15, no 4, pp. 316–33.

Budgen, S., S. Kouvelakis and S. Žižek (eds) (2007) *Lenin Reloaded: Toward a Politics of Truth*, Durham, NC: Duke University Press.

Buhlmann, F., T. David and A. Mach (2012) "The Swiss Business Elite (1980–2000): How the Changing Composition of the Elite Explains the Decline of the Swiss Company Network", *Economy and Society*, vol 41, no 2, pp. 199–226.

Buiter, W. (2009) "The Unfortunate Uselessness of Most 'State of the Art' Academic Monetary Economics", March 6, www.voxeu.org/index.php?q=node/3210.

Bushell, R. (2020) *Emergent Forms of Social Reproduction Financialisation: Social Investment and Adult Social Care*, PhD thesis, Coventry University.

Byrne, M. (2020) "Generation Rent and the Financialization of Housing: A Comparative Exploration of the Growth of the Private Rental Sector in Ireland, the UK and Spain", *Housing Studies*, vol 35, no 4, pp. 743–65.

Cahill, D. (2014) *The End of Laissez-Faire? On the Durability of Embedded Neoliberalism*, Cheltenham: Edward Elgar.

Callaghan, H. (2015) "Who Cares about Financialization?: Self-Reinforcing Feedback, Issue Salience, and Increasing Acquiescence to Market-Enabling Takeover Rules", *Socio-Economic Review*, vol 13, no 2, pp. 331–50.

Callon, M. (ed.) (1998) *Laws of the Markets*, Oxford: Wiley.

Carroll, T. and D. Jarvis (2014) "Introduction: Financialisation and Development in Asia under Late Capitalism", *Asian Studies Review*, vol 38, no 4, pp. 533–43.

Castree, N. (2006) "Commentary", *Environment and Planning A*, vol 38, no 1, pp. 1–6.

Çelik Ö., A. Topal and G. Yalman (2015) "Finance and System of Provision of Housing: The Case of Istanbul, Turkey", FESSUD Working Paper Series, no 152, https://fessud.org/wp-content/uploads/2015/03/Housing_Istanbul_WP152-FESSUD.pdf.

Chang, H.-J. (1999) "The Economic Theory of the Developmental State", in Woo-Cummings (ed.) (1999), pp. 182–99.

Chang, H.-J. (2011) *23 Things They Don't Tell You about Capitalism*, London: Penguin.

Chang, H.-J. (ed.) (2003) *Rethinking Development Economics*, London: Anthem Press.

Chang, K.-S., B. Fine and L. Weiss (eds) (2012) *Developmental Politics in Transition: The Neoliberal Era and Beyond*, Basingstoke: Palgrave Macmillan.

Chari, V., P. Kehoe, E. McGrattan (2009) "New Keynesian Models: Not Yet Useful for Policy Analysis", *American Economic Journal: Macroeconomics*, vol 1, no 1, pp. 242–66.

Christophers, B. (2010) "On Voodoo Economics: Theorising Relations of Property, Value and Contemporary Capitalism", *Transactions of the Institute of British Geographers*, vol 35, no 1, pp. 94–108.

Christophers, B. (2013) *Banking Across Boundaries: Placing Finance in Capitalism*, Chichester: Wiley-Blackwell.

Christophers, B. (2015a) "The Limits to Financialization", *Dialogues in Human Geography*, vol 5, no 2, pp. 183–200.

Christophers, B. (2015b) "From Financialization to Finance: For 'De-Financialization'", *Dialogues in Human Geography*, vol 5, no 2, pp. 229–32.

Christophers, B. (2017) "The State and Financialisation of Public Land in the UK", *Antipode*, vol 49, no 1, pp. 62–85.

Christophers, B. (2019) *The New Enclosure: The Appropriation of Public Land in Neoliberal Britain*, London: Verso.

Christophers, B. (2020) *Rentier Capitalism: Who Owns the Economy, and Who Pays for It?*, London: Verso.

Christophers, B. (2022) "Mind the Rent Gap: Blackstone, Housing Investment and the Reordering of Urban Rent Surfaces", *Urban Studies*, vol 59, no 4, pp. 698–716.

Christophers, B. and B. Fine (2020) "The Value of Financialization and the Financialization of Value", in Mader et al. (eds) (2020), pp. 19–30.

Christopherson, S., R. Martin and J. Pollard (2013) "Financialisation: Roots and Repercussions", *Cambridge Journal of Regions, Economy and Society*, vol 6, no 3, pp. 351–57.

Churchill, J. (2014) "Towards a Framework for Understanding the Recent Evolution of Pension Systems in the European Union", FESSUD Working Paper, no 12, https://fessud.org/wp-content/uploads/2013/04/Towards-a-framework-for-understanding-the-recent-evolution-of-pension-systems-in-the-European-Union-FESSUD-working-paper-12.pdf .

Cloke, P. and R. Johnston (eds) (2004) *Spaces of Geographical Thought Deconstructing Human Geography's Binaries*, London: Sage.

Coe, N., P. Lai and D. Wójcik (2014) "Integrating Finance into Global Production Networks", *Regional Studies*, vol 48, no 5, pp. 761–77.

Colbert, M. (2022) "Environment Agency Prosecutions 6% of the Level They Were a Decade Ago", *Byline Times*, November 9.

Cornwall, A. and D. Eade (eds) (2010) *Deconstructing Development Discourse: Buzzwords and Fuzzwords*, Oxfam and Rugby: Practical Action Publishing.

Coughlan, E., J. Keith, T. Gardner, S. Peytrignet, J. Hughes and C. Tallack (2023) "Waiting for NHS Hospital Care: The Role of the Independent Sector in Delivering Orthopaedic and Ophthalmic Care", The Health Foundation Long Read, https://www.health.org.uk/publications/long-reads/waiting-for-nhs-hospital-care-the-role-of-the-independent-sector.

CQC (2018) *Mental Health Rehabilitation Inpatient Services*, Care Quality Commission, https://www.cqc.org.uk/sites/default/files/20180301_mh_rehabilitation_briefing.pdf.

Crouch, C. (2009a) "Privatised Keynesianism: An Unacknowledged Policy Regime", *British Journal of Politics and International Relations*, vol 11, no 3, pp. 382–99.

Crouch, C. (2009b) "What Will Follow the Demise of Privatised Keynesianism?", *Political Quarterly*, vol 8, no S1, pp. S302–15.

Crouch, C. (2011) *The Strange Non-Death of Neo-liberalism*, Cambridge: Polity.

Dagdeviren, H. and E. Karwowski (2021) "Impasse or Mutation? Austerity and (De) financialisation of Local Governments in Britain", *Journal of Economic Geography*, vol 22, no 3, pp. 685–707.

Dale, G. (2012) "Double Movements and Pendular Forces: Polanyian Perspectives on the Neoliberal Age", *Current Sociology*, vol 60, no 1, pp. 3–27.

Dardot, P. and C. Laval (2013) *The New Way of the World: On Neoliberal Society*, London: Verso.

Datz, G. (2014) "Varieties of Power in Latin American Pension Finance: Pension Fund Capitalism, Developmentalism and Statism", *Government and Opposition*, vol 49, no 3, pp. 483–510.

Davies, W. (2014) *The Limits of Neoliberalism: Authority, Sovereignty and the Logic of Competition*, London: Sage.

Davis, J. (ed.) (1997) *New Economics and Its History, History of Political Economy*, vol 29, Supplement, Durham, NC: Duke University Press.

DCLG (2012) *Barriers to Institutional Investment in Private Rented Homes*, London: DCLG.

DCLG Select Committee (2015) *The Impact of the Existing Right to Buy and the Implications for the Proposed Extension of Right to Buy to Housing Associations*, https://www.parliament.uk/globalassets/documents/commons-committees/communities-and-local-government/Full-Report-for-Select-Committee-141015final.pdf.

Dixon, M. (2014) "The Land Grab, Finance Capital, and Food Regime Restructuring: The Case of Egypt", *Review of African Political Economy*, vol 41, no 140, pp. 232–48.

Dodd, N. (1994) *The Sociology of Money: Economics, Reason and Contemporary Society*, Cambridge: Polity Press.

Doherty, M. (2011) "It Must Have Been Love ... But It's Over Now: The Crisis and Collapse of Social Partnership in Ireland", *European Review of Labour and Research*, vol 71, no 3, pp. 371–85.

Duménil, G. and D. Lévy (2004) *Capital Resurgent: Roots of the Neoliberal Revolution*, Cambridge: Harvard University Press.

Duménil, G. and D. Lévy (2011) *The Crisis of Neoliberalism*, Cambridge: Harvard University Press.

Duncan, J. (2021) "The Death of Neoliberalism? UK Responses to the Pandemic", *International Journal of Human Rights*, vol 26, no 3, pp. 494–517.

Edwards, M. (2015) *Prospects for Land, Rent and Housing in UK Cities*, https://assets.publishing.service.gov.uk/government/uploads/system/uploads/attachment_data/file/440527/15-28-land-rent-housing-uk-cities.pdf.

Engelen, E., R. Fernandez and R. Hendrikse (2014) "How Finance Penetrates Its Other: A Cautionary Tale on the Financialization of a Dutch University", *Antipode*, vol 46, no 4, pp. 1072–91.

Engelen, E. and M. Grote (2009) "Stock Exchange Virtualisation and the Decline of Second-Tier Financial Centres – the Cases of Amsterdam and Frankfurt", *Journal of Economic Geography*, vol 9, no 5, pp. 679–96.

Engelen, E., M. Konings and R. Fernandez (2008) "The Rise of Activist Investors and Patterns of Political Responses: Lessons on Agency", *Socio-Economic Review*, vol 6, no 4, pp. 611–36.

Epstein, G. (2002) "Financialisation, Rentier Interests, and Central Bank Policy", paper for Financialisation of the World Economy, Political Economy Research Institute (PERI), University of Massachusetts, Amherst, December 7–8, 2001.

Epstein, G. (2005) "Introduction: Financialization and the World Economy", in Epstein (ed.) (2005), pp. 3–16.

Epstein, G. (ed.) (2005) *Financialization and the World Economy*, Cheltenham: Edward Elgar.

Epstein, G. and J. Carrick-Hagenbarth (2010) "Financial Economists, Financial Interests and Dark Corners of the Meltdown: It's Time to Set Ethical Standards for the Economics Profession", Political Economy Research Institute Working Paper, no 239, University of Massachusetts, Amherst.

Epstein, G. and J. Carrick-Hagenbarth (2012) "Dangerous Interconnectedness: Economists' Conflicts of Interest, Ideology and Financial Crisis", *Cambridge Journal of Economics*, vol 36, no 1, pp. 43–63.

Erturk, I. (2010) "Post-Crisis Alternative Views of Finance in Emerging Economies: An Introduction", *Competition and Change*, vol 14, no 3–4, pp. 221–24.

Erturk, I., J. Froud, S. Johal, A. Leaver and K. Williams (eds) (2008) *Financialization at Work: Key Texts and Commentary*, London: Routledge.

Fairbairn, M. (2014) "'Like Gold with Yield': Evolving Intersections between Farmland and Finance", *Journal of Peasant Studies*, vol 41, no 5, pp. 777–95.

Fairbairn, M. (2015) "Reinventing the Wheel? Or Adding New Air to Old Tires?", *Dialogues in Human Geography*, vol 5, no 2, pp. 210–13.

Fairbairn, M., J. Fox, S. Isakson, L. Ryan, M. Levien, N. Peluso, S. Razavi, I. Scoones and K. Sivaramakrishnan (2014) "Introduction: New Directions in Agrarian Political Economy", *Journal of Peasant Studies*, vol 41, no 5, pp. 653–66.

Fasenfest, D. (ed.) (2022) *Marx Matters*, Leiden: Brill.

Fearn, G. (2024) "The End of the Experiment? The Energy Crisis, Neoliberal Energy, and the Limits to a Socio-Ecological Fix", *Environment and Planning E: Nature and Space*, vol 7, no 1, pp. 212–33.

Ferguson, C. (2010) "Larry Summers and the Subversion of Economics", *The Chronicle Review*, October 3, available at http://chronicle.com/article/Larry-Summers the/124790/.

Ferguson, J. (2007) "Formalities of Poverty: Thinking about Social Assistance in Neoliberal South Africa", *African Studies Review*, vol 50, no 2, pp. 71–86.

Fetzer, T., S. Sen and P. Souza (2020) "Housing Insecurity, Homelessness and Populism: Evidence from the UK", *CEPR Discussion Paper, no DP14184*, https://papers.ssrn.com/sol3/papers.cfm?abstract_id=3504613.

Fieldman, G. (2014) "Financialisation and Ecological Modernisation", *Environmental Politics*, vol 23, no 2, pp. 224–42.

Fine, B. (1985/6) "Banking Capital and the Theory of Interest", *Science and Society*, vol XLIX, no 4, pp. 387–413.

Fine, B. (1988) "From Capital in Production to Capital in Exchange", *Science and Society*, vol. 52, no 3, pp. 326–37.

Fine, B. (1990) *The Coal Question: Political Economy and Industrial Change from the Nineteenth Century to the Present Day*, London: Routledge, 1990, reprinted as Routledge Revival, 2013.

Fine, B. (1998) *Labour Market Theory: A Constructive Reassessment*, London: Routledge.

Fine, B. (2000) "Endogenous Growth Theory: A Critical Assessment", *Cambridge Journal of Economics*, vol 24, no 2, pp. 245–65.

Fine, B. (2002a) *The World of Consumption: The Cultural and Material Revisited*, London: Routledge.

Fine, B. (2002b) "Economics Imperialism and the New Development Economics as Kuhnian Paradigm Shift", *World Development*, vol 30, no 12, pp. 2057–70.

Fine, B. (2003) "New Growth Theory", in Chang (ed.) (2003), pp. 201–17.

Fine, B. (2004a) "Examining the Idea of Globalisation and Development Critically: What Role for Political Economy?", *New Political Economy*, vol 9, no 2, pp. 213–31.

Fine, B. (2004b) "Economics Imperialism as Kuhnian Revolution", in Arestis and Sawyer (eds) (2004), pp. 107–44.

Fine, B. (2005) "Addressing the Consumer", in Trentmann (ed.) (2005), pp. 291–311.

Fine, B. (2006a) "Debating the 'New' Imperialism", *Historical Materialism*, vol 14, no 4, pp. 133–56.

Fine, B. (2006b) "New Growth Theory: More Problem than Solution", in Fine and Jomo (eds) (2006), pp. 68–86.

Fine, B. (2009a) "Development as Zombieconomics in the Age of Neo-Liberalism", *Third World Quarterly*, vol 30, no 5, pp. 885–904.

Fine, B. (2009b) "The Economics of Identity and the Identity of Economics?", *Cambridge Journal of Economics*, vol 33, no 2, pp. 175–91.

Fine, B. (2009c) "Political Economy for the Rainbow Nation: Dividing the Spectrum?", prepared for 'Making Sense of Borders: Identity, Citizenship and Power in South Africa', South African Sociological Association, Annual Conference, June/July, Johannesburg, available at http://eprints.soas.ac.uk/7972/1/sasa_benfine.pdf.

Fine, B. (2010a) "Locating Financialisation", *Historical Materialism*, vol 18, no 2, pp. 97–116.

Fine, B. (2010b) *Theories of Social Capital: Researchers Behaving Badly*, London: Pluto Press.

Fine, B. (2010c) "Zombieconomics: The Living Death of the Dismal Science", in Birch and Mykhnenko (eds) (2010), pp. 53–70.

Fine, B. (2010d) "Beyond the Tragedy of the Commons: A Discussion of *Governing the Commons: The Evolution of Institutions for Collective Action*", *Perspectives on Politics*, vol 8, no 2, pp. 583–86.

Fine, B. (2010e) "Flattening Economic Geography: Locating the World Development Report for 2009", *Journal of Economic Analysis*, vol 1, no 1, pp. 15–33.

Fine, B. (2012) "Financialisation and Social Policy", in Utting et al. (eds) (2012), pp. 103–22.

Fine, B. (2013–14) "Financialisation from a Marxist Perspective", *International Journal of Political Economy*, vol 42, no 4, pp. 47–66.

Fine, B. (2013a) "Consumption Matters", *Ephemera*, vol 13, no 2, pp. 217–48, http://www.ephemerajournal.org/contribution/consumption-matters.

Fine, B. (2013b) "Towards a Material Culture of Financialisation", FESSUD Working Paper Series, no 15, https://fessud.org/wp-content/uploads/2013/04/Towards-a-Material-Culture-of-Financialisation-FESSUD-Working-Paper-15.pdf, published as revised as Fine (2017a).

Fine, B. (2013c) "Economics – Unfit for Purpose: The Director's Cut", SOAS Department of Economics Working Paper Series, no 176, http://www.soas.ac.uk/economics/research/workingpapers/file81476.pdf, revised and shortened to appear as, "Economics: Unfit for Purpose", *Review of Social Economy*, vol LXXI, no 3, 2013, pp. 373–89.

Fine, B. (2014) "The Continuing Enigmas of Social Policy", prepared for the UNRISD project on Towards Universal Social Security in Emerging Economies, UNRISD Working Paper, no 2014–10, June, http://www.unrisd.org/80256B3C005BCCF9/%28httpAuxPages%29/30B153EE73F52ABFC1257D0200420A61/$file/Fine.pdf, shortened and revised in Ye (ed.) (2017), pp. 29–60.

Fine, B. (2015) "Neoclassical Economics: An Elephant is not a Chimera But Is a Chimera Real?", in Morgan (ed.) (2015), pp. 180–99.

Fine, B. (2016a) "The Systemic Failings in Framing Neo-Liberal Social Policy", in Subaset (ed.) (2016), pp. 159–77.

Fine, B. (2016b) "Across Developmental State and Social Compacting: The Peculiar Case of South Africa", ISER Working Paper no. 2016/1, Grahamstown: Institute of Social and Economic Research, Rhodes University. https://eprints.soas.ac.uk/34148/1/iserwp.pdf.

Fine, B. (2016c) "The Endemic and Systemic Malaise of Mainstream Economics", FESSUD, Working Paper Series, no 190, https://fessud.org/wp-content/uploads/2015/03/FESSUD_WP190_The-EndemicSystemic-Malaise-of-Mainstream-Economics.pdf, see Chapter 6.

Fine, B. (2016d) *Microeconomics: A Critical Companion*, London: Pluto.

Fine, B. (2017a) "The Material and Culture of Financialisation", *New Political Economy*, vol 22, no 4, pp. 371–82, reproduced in Bayliss et al. (eds) (2018), pp. 17–28.

Fine, B. (2017b) "From One-Dimensional Man to One-Dimensions Economy and Economics", *Radical Philosophy Review*, vol 20, no 1, pp. 49–74.

Fine, B. (2019) "Post-Apartheid South Africa: It's Neoliberalism, Stupid!", in Reynolds et al. (eds) (2019), pp. 75–95.

Fine, B. (2020a) "Framing Social Reproduction in the Age of Financialisation", in Santos and Teles (eds) (2020), pp. 257–72.

Fine, B. (2020b) "Situating PPPs", in Gideon and Unterhalter (eds) (2020), pp. 26–38.

Fine, B. (2022) "From Marxist Political Economy to Financialisation or Is It the Other Way about?", in Fasenfest (ed.) (2022), pp. 43–66.

Fine, B. (2024a) *Economics Imperialism and Interdisciplinarity: Before the Watershed; Critical Reconstructions of Political Economy*, Volume 1, Leiden: Brill, and Chicago: Haymarket.

Fine, B. (2024b) *Economics Imperialism and Interdisciplinarity: The Watershed and After; Critical Reconstructions of Political Economy*, Volume 2, Leiden: Brill, and Chicago: Haymarket.

Fine, B. (2024c) *Cliometrics as Economics Imperialism: Across the Watershed: Critical Reconstructions of Political Economy*, Volume 3, Leiden: Brill, and Chicago: Haymarket.

Fine, B. and K. Bayliss (2016) "Paper on Theoretical Framework for Assessing the Impact of Finance on Public Provision", FESSUD, Working Paper Series, no 196, https://fessud.org/wp-content/uploads/2015/03/FESSUD_WP192_Theoretical-Framework-for-Assessing-the-Impact-of-Finance-on-Public-Provision.pdf.

Fine, B. and K. Bayliss (2022) "From Addressing to Redressing Consumption: How the System of Provision Approach Helps", *Consumption and Society*, vol 1, no 1, pp. 197–206.

Fine, B., K. Bayliss and M. Robertson (2016b) "Housing and Water in Light of Financialisation and 'Financialisation'", FESSUD, Working Paper Series, no 156, https://fessud.org/wp-content/uploads/2015/03/Housing-and-Water-in-Light-of-Financialisation-and-"Financialisation"-working-paper-156.pdf, see Chapter 5.

Fine, B., K. Bayliss and M. Robertson (2016c) "From Financialisation to Systems of Provision", FESSUD, Working Paper Series, no 191, https://fessud.org/wp-content/uploads/2015/03/FESSUD_WP191_From-Financialisation-to-Systems-of-Provision.pdf, see Chapter 3.

Fine, B. and O. Dimakou (2016) *Macroeconomics: A Critical Companion*, London: Pluto.

Fine, B. and D. Hall (2012) "Terrains of Neoliberalism: Constraints and Opportunities for Alternative Models of Service Delivery", in McDonald and Ruiters (eds) (2012), pp. 45–70.

Fine, B. and L. Harris (1985) *The Peculiarities of the British Economy*, London: Lawrence and Wishart.

Fine, B., D. Johnston, A. Santos and E. Van Waeyenberge (2016b) "Nudging or Fudging: The World Development Report 2015", *Development and Change*, vol 47, no 4, pp. 640–63.

Fine, B. and K. Jomo (eds) (2006) *The New Development Economics: After the Washington Consensus*, Delhi: Tulika, and London: Zed Press.

Fine, B. and C. Lapavitsas (2000) "Markets and Money in Social Theory: What Role for Economics?", *Economic and Society*, vol 29, no 3, pp. 357–82.

Fine, B., C. Lapavitsas and J. Pincus (eds) (2001) *Development Policy in the Twenty-First Century: Beyond the Post-Washington Consensus*, London: Routledge.

Fine, B. and E. Leopold (1990) "Consumerism and the Industrial Revolution", *Social History*, vol 15, no 2, pp. 151–79.

Fine, B. and E. Leopold (1993) *The World of Consumption*, London: Routledge.

Fine, B. and D. Milonakis (2009) *From Economics Imperialism to Freakonomics: The Shifting Boundaries Between Economics and Other Social Sciences*, London: Routledge.

Fine, B. and D. Milonakis (2011) "'Useless but True': Economic Crisis and the Peculiarities of Economic Science", *Historical Materialism*, vol 19, no 2 pp. 3–31, the Isaac and Tamara Deutscher Memorial Lecture, London, November 12, 2010.

Fine, B., A. Petropoulos and H. Sato (2005) "Beyond Brenner's Investment Overhang Hypothesis: The Case of the Steel Industry", *New Political Economy*, vol 10, no 1, pp. 43–64.

Fine, B. and G. Pollen (2018) "The Developmental State Paradigm in the Age of Financialisation", in Hyland and Munck (eds) (2018) pp. 211–27.

Fine, B. and A. Saad-Filho (2014) "Politics of Neoliberal Development: Washington Consensus and post-Washington Consensus", in Weber (ed.) (2014), pp. 154–76.

Fine, B. and A. Saad-Filho (2016b) *Marx's 'Capital'*, London: Pluto, sixth edition.

Fine, B., A. Saad-Filho, K. Bayliss and M. Robertson (2016a) "Thirteen Things You Need to Know about Neoliberalism", FESSUD, Working Paper Series, no 155, https://fessud.org/wp-content/uploads/2015/03/13-Things-you-need-to-know-about-Neoliberalism-working-paper155.pdf, see Chapter 2.

Fine, B., J. Saraswati and D. Tavasci (eds) (2013) *Beyond the Developmental State: Industrial Policy into the 21st Century*, London: Pluto.

Finlayson, A. (2009) "Financialisation, Financial Literacy, and Asset-Based Welfare", *British Journal of Politics and International Relations,* vol 11, no 3, pp. 400–21.

Fiorentini, R. (2015) "Neoliberal Policies, Income Distribution Inequality and the Financial Crisis", *Forum for Social Economics*, vol 44, no 2, pp. 115–32.

Fourcade, M. (2010) *Economists and Societies: Discipline and Profession in the United States, Britain, and France, 1890s to 1990*, Ithaca: Princeton University Press.

Fourcade, M., E. Ollion and Y. Algan (2015) "The Superiority of Economists", *Journal of Economic Perspectives*, vol 29, no 1, pp. 89–114.

French, S., A. Leyshon and T. Wainwright (2011) "Financializing Space, Spacing Financialization", *Progress in Human Geography*, vol 35, no 6, pp. 798–819.

Friends of the Earth (2013) "Economic Drivers of Water Financialisation", Report by Friends of the Earth International, Amsterdam.

Froud, J., S. Johal and K. Williams (2002) "Financialisation and the Coupon Pool", *Capital and Class*, no 78, pp. 119–51.

Froud, J., S. Johal, A. Leaver, M. Moran and K. Williams (2011) "Groundhog Day: Elite Power, Democratic Disconnects and the Failure of Financial Reform in the UK" CRESC Working Paper, no 108, Centre for Research in Socio-Cultural Change, Manchester University.

Froud, J., A. Leaver and K. Williams (2007) "New Actors in a Financialised Economy and the Remaking of Capitalism", *New Political Economy*, vol 12, no 3, pp. 339–47.

Fullbrook, E. (2012) "The Political Economy of Bubbles", *Real-World Economics Review*, no. 59, pp. 138–154, available at http://www.paecon.net/PAEReview/issue59/Fullbrook59.pdf.

Gabor, D. (2023) "The (European) Derisking State", *SocArXiv Papers*, https://osf.io/preprints/socarxiv/hpbj2/.

Gabor, D. and S. Brooks (2017) "The Digital Revolution in Financial Inclusion: International Development in the Fintech Era", *New Political Economy*, vol 22, no 4, pp. 423–36, reproduced in Bayliss et al. (eds) (2018), pp. 69–82.

Garcia-Arias, J. (2015) "International Financialization and the Systemic Approach to International Financing for Development", *Global Policy*, vol 6, no 1, pp. 24–33.

Garcia-Arias, J., H. March, N. Alonso and M. Satorras (2022) "Public Water without (Public) Financial Mediation? Remunicipalizing Water in Valladolid, Spain", *Water International*, vol 47, no 5, pp. 733–50.

Gassner, K., A. Popov and N. Pushak (2009) "Does Private Sector Participation Improve Performance in Electricity and Water Distribution?", Trends and Policy Options no 6, World Bank and PPIAF, IBRD, Washington, DC.

Gideon, J. and E. Unterhalter (eds) (2020) *Critical Reflections on Public Private Partnerships*, London: Routledge.

Gingrich, J. (2015) "Varying Costs to Change? Institutional Change in the Public Sector", *Governance*, vol 28, no 1, pp. 41–60.

Goda, T. and P. Lysandrou (2014) "The Contribution of Wealth Concentration to the Subprime Crisis: A Quantitative Estimation", *Cambridge Journal of Economics*, vol 38, no 2, pp. 301–27.

Goldstein, J. (2009) "Introduction: The Political Economy of Financialization", *Review of Radical Political Economics*, vol 41, no 4, pp. 453–57.

Goodair, B. and A. Reeves (2022) "Outsourcing Health-Care Services to the Private Sector and Treatable Mortality Rates in England, 2013–20: An Observational Study of NHS Privatisation", *Lancet Public Health*, 7: e638–46.

Gowan, P. (1999) *The Global Gamble: America's Faustian Bid for World Dominance*, Verso: London.

Graaff, J. (1957) *Theoretical Welfare Economics*, Cambridge: Cambridge University Press.

Graeber, D, (2014) "Anthropology and the Rise of the Professional-Managerial Class", *Hau Journal of Ethnographic Theory*, vol 4, no 3, pp. 73–88.

Grafe, F. and H. Mieg (2019) "Connecting Financialization and Urbanization: The Changing Financial Ecology of Urban Infrastructure in the UK", *Regional Science*, vol 6, no 1, pp. 496–511.

Grafton, R., C. Landry, G. Libecap, S. McGlennon and R. O'Brien (2010) "An Integrated Assessment of Water Markets: Australia, Chile, China, South Africa and the USA", Working Paper, no 16203, National Bureau of Economic Research, Cambridge MA.

Graves-Brown, P. (2000) "Introduction", in Graves-Brown (ed.) (2000), pp. 1–9.

Graves-Brown, P. (ed.) (2000) *Matter, Materiality and Modern Culture*, London: Routledge.

Gronow, J. (1997) *The Sociology of Taste*, London: Routledge.

Gruffydd Jones, B. (2012) "Bankable Slums: The Global Politics of Slum Upgrading", *Third World Quarterly*, vol 33, no 5, pp. 769–89.

Guerrien, B. and O. Gun (2011) "Efficient Market Hypothesis: What Are We Talking about?", *Real-World Economics Review*, no 56, pp. 19–30, http://www.paecon.net/PAEReview/issue56/GuerrienGun56.pdf.

Gurney, C. (1999) "Pride and Prejudice: Discourses of Normalisation in Public and Private Accounts of Home Ownership", *Housing Studies*, vol 14, no 2, pp. 163–83.

Haila, A. (1988) "Land as a Financial Asset: The Theory of Rent as a Mirror of Economic Transformation", *Antipode*, vol 20, no 2, pp. 79–101.

Haines-Doran, T. (2022) *Derailed: How to Fix Britain's Broken Railways*, Manchester: Manchester University Press.

Haiven, M. (2014) *Cultures of Financialization: Fictitious Capital in Popular Culture and Everyday Life*, Basingstoke: Palgrave Macmillan.

Haldane, A. and V. Madouros (2012) "The Dog and the Frisbee" text of speech given at the Federal Reserve Bank of Kansas City's 36th Economic Policy Symposium, "The Changing Policy Landscape", Jackson Hole, Wyoming.

Hall, P. and D. Soskice (eds) (2001) *Varieties of Capitalism: The Institutional Foundations of Comparative Advantage*, Oxford: Oxford University Press.

Hammond, G. (2022) "Help to Buy Has Pushed up House Prices in England", *Financial Times*, January 10.

Hands, D. (2010) "Economics, Psychology and the History of Consumer Choice Theory", *Cambridge Journal of Economics*, vol 34, no 4, pp. 633–648.

Happer, C. (2013) "Financialisation, Media and Social Change", FESSUD Working Paper Series, no 10, https://fessud.org/wp-content/uploads/2013/04/Financialisation-Media-and-Social-Change-FESSUD-Working-Paper-10-.pdf, published as revised as Happer (2017).

Happer, C. (2017) "Financialisation, Media and Social Change", *New Political Economy*, vol 22, no 4, pp. 437–49, reproduced in Bayliss et al. (eds) (2018), pp. 83–95.

Harrison, P. (1997) "A History of an Intellectual Arbitrage: The Evolution of Financial Economics", in Davis (ed.) (1997), pp.172–87.

Hart, G. (2002) *Disabling Globalization: Places of Power in Post-Apartheid South Africa*, Durban: University of Natal Press.

Hart, G. (2008) "The Provocations of Neoliberalism: Contesting the Nation and Liberation after Apartheid", *Antipode*, vol 40, no 4, pp. 678–705.

Harvey, D. (1982) *The Limits to Capital*, Oxford: Basil Blackwell.

Harvey, D. (2005) *A Brief History of Neoliberalism*, Oxford: Oxford University Press.

Hein, E. (2022) "Varieties of Demand and Growth Regimes – Post-Keynesian Foundations", Institute for International Political Economy, Berlin School of Economics and Law, Working Paper, no 196/2022, https://www.ipe-berlin.org/fileadmin/institut-ipe/Dokumente/Working_Papers/ipe_working_paper_196_-_Hein2p.pdf.

Heise, A. and S. Thieme (2015) "What Happened to Heterodox Economics in Germany after the 1970s", Discussion Paper, no 49, Zentrum für Ökonomische und Soziologische Studien Universität Hamburg, http://www.wiso.uni-hamburg.de /fileadmin/sozialoekonomie/zoess/DP_49_Heise_Thieme.pdf.

Hermann, C. (2021) *The Critique of Commodification*, Oxford: Oxford University Press.

Hillier, B., R. Phillips and J. Peck (eds) (2022) *Regulation Theory, Space and Uneven Development: Conversations and Challenges*. Vancouver: 1984 Press.

HoC (2013) "Tax Avoidance: The Role of Large Accountancy Firms" Forty-fourth Report of Session 2012–13, Report ordered by the House of Commons, London.

HoC (2015) "Economic Regulation of the Water Sector", House of Commons Committee of Public Accounts Report, https://publications.parliament.uk/pa/cm201516/cmsel ect/cmpubacc/505/505.pdf.

HoC (2021a) "Extending Homeownership: Government Initiatives", House of Commons Library Briefing Paper, no 03668.

HoC (2021b) "The Rent Safety Net: Changes since 2010", House of Commons Library Briefing Paper, no 05638.

HoC (2022) "NHS Backlogs and Waiting Times in England", House of Commons Committee of Public Accounts Report, https://committees.parliament.uk/publicati ons/9266/documents/160332/default/.

HoC (2023) "Public Spending during the COVID-19 Pandemic", House of Commons Library, Briefing Paper, no 09309.

Hood, C. and R. Dixon (2015a) "What We Have to Show for 30 Years of New Public Management: Higher Costs, More Complaints", *Governance*, vol 28, no 3, pp. 265–67.

Hood, C. and R. Dixon (2015b) *A Government that Worked Better and Cost Less?*, Oxford: Oxford University Press.

Horton, H. (2022) "Calls to Cut Bonuses for UK Water Bosses until Reservoirs Built and Leaks Fixed", *Guardian*, August 15.

Hosseini, H. (2011) "George Katona: A Founding Father of Old Behavioral Economics", *Journal of Socio-Economics*, vol 40, no 6, pp. 977–84.

Hunter, B. and S. Murray (2019) "Deconstructing the Financialization of Healthcare", *Development and Change*, vol 50, no 5, pp. 1263–87.

Hyland, M. and R. Munck (eds) (2018) *Handbook on Development and Social Change*, Cheltenham: Edward Elgar.

Iacobucci, G. (2021) "COVID-19: One in Five Government Contracts Had Signs of Possible Corruption, Report Finds", *British Medical Journal*, April 23, http://dx.doi .org/10.1136/bmj.n1072.

Isaacs, G. (2016) "The Commodification, Commercialisation and Financialisation of Low-Cost Housing in South Africa", FESSUD Working Paper, no 200, https: //fessud.org/wp-content/uploads/2015/03/FESSUD_WP200_Commodificat ion-Commercialisation-Financialisation-Low-Cost-Housing-in-South-Africa.pdf.

Isakson, S. and L. Ryan (2014) "Food and Finance: The Financial Transformation of Agro-Food Supply Chains", *Journal of Peasant Studies*, vol 41, no 5, pp. 749–75.

Ivanova, M. (2011) "Housing and Hegemony: The US Experience", *Capital and Class*, vol 35, no 3, pp. 391–414.

Jackson, P., P. Russell and N. Ward (2004) "Commodity Chains and the Politics of Food", Cultures of Consumption and ESRC-AHRB Research Programme, Working Paper, no 18, http://www.consume.bbk.ac.uk/working_papers/jackson.doc.

Javid, S. (2022) "Health and Social Care Secretary Speech on Health Reform", delivered at Royal College of Physicians, https://www.gov.uk/government/speeches/health-and-social-care-secretary-speech-on-health-reform.

Jayadev, A. and G. Epstein (2007) "Correlates of Rentier Returns in OECD Countries" Political Economy Research Institute Working Paper Series, no 123, Amherst, MA.

Jessop, B. (1993) "Toward a Schumpeterian Welfare State? Preliminary Remarks on Post-Fordist Political Economy", *Studies in Political Economy*, vol 40, no 1, pp. 7–39.

Jessop, B. (1995) "Towards a Schumpeterian Workfare Regime in Britain?", *Environment and Planning A*, vol 27, no 10, pp. 1613–26.

Jessop, B. (2002) *The Future of the Capitalist State*, Cambridge: Polity Press.

Jessop, B. (2003) "From Thatcherism to New Labour: Neo-liberalism, Workfarism and Labour-Market Regulation", in Overbeek (ed.) (2003), pp. 137–53.

Jessop, B. (2007) "Dialogue of the Deaf: Reflections on the Poulantzas-Miliband Debate", in Wetherly et al. (eds) (2007), pp. 132–157.

Jessop, B. (2011) "Rethinking the Diversity of Capitalism: Varieties of Capitalism, Variegated Capitalism, and the World Market", in Wood and Lane (eds) (2011), pp. 209–37.

Jessop, B. (2014) "Variegated Capitalism, das Modell Deutschland, and the Eurozone Crisis", *Journal of Contemporary European Studi*es, vol 22, no 3, pp. 248–60.

Jessop, B. (2015) "Hard Cash, Easy Credit, Fictitious Capital: Critical Reflections on Money as a Fetishised Social Relation", *Finance and Society*, vol 1, no 1, pp. 20–37.

Jessop, B. and N. Sum (2001) "Pre-Disciplinary and Post-Disciplinary Perspectives", *New Political Economy*, vol 6, no 1, pp. 89–101.

Johal, S., M. Moran and K. Williams (2014) "Power, Politics and the City of London after the Great Financial Crisis", *Government and Opposition*, vol 49, no 3, pp. 400–25.

Jomo, K.S. (ed.) (2006) *Globalization under Hegemony: The Changing World Economy*, Oxford: Oxford University Press.

Kadtler, J. and H. Sperling (2002) "After Globalisation and Financialisation: Logics of Bargaining in the German Automotive Industry", *Competition Change*, vol 6, no 2, pp. 149–68.

Kaika, M. and L. Ruggeiro (2016) "Land Financialization as a 'Lived' Process: The Transformation of Milan's Bicocca by Pirelli", *European Urban and Regional Studies*, vol 23, no 1, pp. 3–22.

Karacimen, E. (2014) "Dynamics behind the Rise in Household Debt in Advanced Capitalist Countries: An Overview", FESSUD Working Paper Series, no 9, https://fessud.org/wp-content/uploads/2013/04/Dynamics-behind-the-Rise-in-Household-Debt-FESSUD-Working-Paper-09-1.pdf.

Kay, J. and D. Thompson (1986) "Privatisation: A Policy in Search of a Rationale", *Economic Journal*, vol 96, no 381, pp. 18–32.

Kear, M. (2013) "Governing Homo Subprimicus: Beyond Financial Citizenship, Exclusion, and Rights", *Antipode*, vol 45, no 4, pp. 926–46.

Kemeny, J. and S. Lowe (1998) "Schools of Comparative Housing Research: From Convergence to Divergence", *Housing Studies*, vol 13, no 2, pp. 161–76.

Kiely, R. (2005) *The Clash of Globalisations: Neo-Liberalism, the Third Way and Anti-Globalisation*, Leiden: Brill.

Klamer, A. (1984) *Conversations with Economists*, Totowa, NJ: Rowman and Allanheld.

Kliman, A. and S. Williams (2015) "Why 'Financialisation' Hasn't Depressed US Productive Investment", *Cambridge Journal of Economics*, vol 39, no 1, pp. 67–92.

Kohl, S. (2021) "Too Much Mortgage Debt? The Effect of Housing Financialization on Housing Supply and Residential Capital Formation", *Socio-Economic Review*, vol 19, no 2, pp. 413–40.

Kotz, D. (2015) *The Rise and Fall of Neoliberal Capitalism*, Cambridge: Harvard University Press.

Kotz, D., T. McDonough and M. Reich (2010) (eds) *Contemporary Capitalism and Its Crises: Social Structure of Accumulation Theory for the 21st Century*, Cambridge: Cambridge University Press.

Kozul-Wright, R. (2006) "Globalization Now and Again", in Jomo (ed.) (2006), pp. 100–32.

Krippner, G. (2005) "The Financialisation of the American Economy", *Socio-Economic Review*, vol 3, no 2, pp. 173–208.

Krippner, G. (2011) *Capitalizing on Crisis: The Political Origins of the Rise of Finance*, Cambridge: Harvard University Press.

Krugman, P. (2009) "How Did Economists Get It So Wrong?", September 2, www.nytimes.com/2009/09/06/magazine/06Economic-t.html?_r=1&emc=eta1.

Labica, G. (2007) "From Imperialism to Globalisation", in S Budgen et al. (eds) (2007), pp. 222–38.

Langley, P. (2007) "Uncertain Subjects of Anglo-American Financialization", *Cultural Critique*, vol 65, pp. 67–91.

Langley, P. (2008) *The Everyday Life of Global Finance: Saving and Borrowing in Anglo-America*, Oxford: Oxford University Press.

Lapavitsas, C. (2003) *Social Foundations of Markets, Money and Credit*, London: Routledge.

Lapavitsas, C. (2013) *Profiting without Producing: How Finance Exploits Us All*, London: Verso.

Lapavitsas, C. and J. Powell (2013) "Financialisation Varied: A Comparative Analysis of Advanced Economies", *Cambridge Journal of Regions, Economy and Society*, vol 6, no 3, pp. 359–79.

Lawrence, G. (2015) "Defending Financialization", *Dialogues in Human Geography*, vol 5, no 2, pp. 201–05.

Lawson, T. (2013) "What Is This 'School' Called Neoclassical Economics?", *Cambridge Journal of Economics*, vol 37, no 5, pp. 947–83, reproduced in Morgan (ed.) (2016), pp. 30–80.

Layfield, D. (2013) "Turning Carbon into Gold: The Financialisation of International Climate Policy", *Environmental Politics*, vol 22, no 6, pp. 901–17.

Lee, F. (2012) "Heterodox Economics and its Critics", *Review of Political Economy*, vol 24, no 2, pp. 337–51.

Lee, R., G. Clark, J. Pollard and A. Leyshon (2009) "The Remit of Financial Geography before and after the Crisis", *Journal of Economic Geography*, vol 9, no 5, pp. 723–47.

Lemke, T. (2001) "The Birth of Bio-Politics: Michel Foucault's Lecture at the Collège De France on Neo-Liberal Governmentality", *Economy and Society*, vol 30, no 2, pp. 190–207.

Leslie, D. and S. Reimer (1999) "Spatializing Commodity Chains", *Progress in Human Geography*, vol 23, no 3, pp. 401–20.

Levy-Orlik. N. (2014) "Financialization and Economic Growth in Developing Countries: The Case of the Mexican Economy", *International Journal of Political Economy*, vol 42, no 4, pp. 108–127.

Leyshon, A. and N. Thrift (2007) "The Capitalization of Almost Everything: The Future of Finance and Capitalism", *Theory, Culture & Society*, vol 24, no 7–8, pp. 97–115.

Lis, P. (2015a) "Financialisation of the System of Provision Applied to Housing in Poland", FESSUD Working Paper Series, no 100, https://fessud.org/wp-content/uploads/2015/01/2-LisP_FESSUD_WP8_housingPoland-working-paper-100.pdf.

Lis, P. (2015b) "Financialisation of the Water Sector in Poland", FESSUD Working Paper, no 101, https://fessud.org/wp-content/uploads/2015/03/FESSUD_WP8_Financialisation_of_the_water_sectorInPoland_working-paper101.pdf.

Locke, R. (2014) "Financialization, Income Distribution, and Social Justice: Recent German and American Experience", *Real-World Economics Review*, no 68, pp. 74–89.

Lohmann, L. (2011) "Financialization, Commodification and Carbon: The Contradictions of Neoliberal Climate Policy", in Panitch et al. (eds) (2011), pp. 85–107.

Lucas, R. (1987) *Models of Business Cycles*, Oxford: Basil Blackwell.

Lusardi, A. and J. Streeter (2023) *Journal of Financial Literacy and Wellbeing*, vol 1, no 2, pp. 169–198.

Lysandrou, P. (2011) "Global Inequality as One of the Root Causes of the Financial Crisis: A Suggested Explanation", *Economy and Society*, vol 40, no 3, pp. 323–44.

Lysandrou, P. (2011/12) "The Primacy of Hedge Funds in the Subprime Crisis", *Journal of Post Keynesian Economics*, vol 34, no 2, pp. 225–54.

MacFarlane, L. (2021) "Covid Has Forced a Neoliberal Retreat, but State Intervention Isn't Always Progressive", *Guardian*, April 29.

MacLeavy, J. (2011) "A 'New Politics' of Austerity, Workfare and Gender? The UK Coalition Government's Welfare Reform Proposals" *Cambridge Journal of Regions, Economy and Society*, vol 4, no 3, pp. 1–13.

Mader, P. (2014) "Financialisation through Microfinance: Civil Society and Market-Building in India", *Asian Studies Review*, vol 38, no 4, pp. 601–19.

Mader, P., D. Mertens and N. van der Zwan (eds) (2020) *The Routledge International Handbook of Financialization*, London: Routledge.

Madra, Y. and F. Adaman (2014) "Neoliberal Reason and Its Forms: De- Politicisation through Economisation", *Antipode*, vol 46, no 3, pp. 691–73.

Magdoff, H. and P. Sweezy (1987) *Stagnation and Financial Explosion*, New York: Monthly Review Press.

Marin, P. (2009) "Public-Private Partnerships for Urban Water Utilities: A Review of Experiences in Developing Countries", Public Private Infrastructure Advisory Facility, Trends and Policy Options, no 8, Washington, DC: IBRD.

Marmot, M., J. Allen, T. Boyce, P. Goldblatt and J. Morrison (2020) *Health Equity in England: The Marmot Review 10 Years on*. London: The Health Foundation.

Marron, D. (2013) "Governing Poverty in a Neoliberal Age: New Labour and the Case of Financial Exclusion", *New Political Economy*, vol 18, no 6, pp. 785–810.

Martin, R. (2011) *Under New Management: Universities, Administrative Labor, and the Professional Turn*, Philadelphia: Temple University Press.

Mascaro, L. (2023) "'Bidenomics' Delivered a Once-in-Generation Investment. It Shows the Pros and Cons of Policymaking", https://apnews.com/article/biden-ira-congress-ev-bidenomics-4d1e74d2cf21326e8833885972ad2891.

Mavroudeas, S. (1999) "Regulation Theory: The Road from Creative Marxism to Post-Modern Disintegration", *Science and Society*, vol 63, no 3, pp. 311–37.

Mavroudeas, S. (2006) "A History of Contemporary Political Economy and Postmodernism", *Review of Radical Political Economics*, vol 38, no 4, pp. 499–518.

Mazzucato, M. (2018) *The Value of Everything: Making and Taking in the Global Economy*, Harmondsworth: Penguin.

McArthur, J. (2024) "The UK Infrastructure Bank and the Financialization of Public Infrastructures amidst Nationalist Neoliberalism", *Competition and Change*, vol 28, no 1, pp. 46–66.

McDonald, D. and G. Ruiters (eds) (2012) *Alternatives to Privatisation: Exploring Non-Commercial Service Delivery Options in the Global South*, London: Routledge.

McMichael, P. (2012) "The Land Grab and Corporate Food Regime Restructuring", *Journal of Peasant Studies*, vol 39, no 3, pp. 681–701.

McNally, D. (2014) *Global Slump: The Economics and Politics of Crisis and Resistance*, Oakland: PM Press.

Medema, S. (2009) *The Hesitant Hand: Taming Self-Interest in the History of Economic Ideas*, Princeton: Princeton University Press.

Merton, R. (1957) *Social Theory and Social Structure*, New York: Free Press.

Michell, J. and J. Toporowski (2014) "Critical Observations on Financialization and the Financial Process", *International Journal of Political Economy*, vol 42, no 4, pp. 67–82.

Milonakis, D. and B. Fine (2009) *From Political Economy to Economics: Method, the Social and the Historical in the Evolution of Economic Theory*, London: Routledge.

Mirowski, P. (2009) "Postface: Defining Neoliberalism", in Mirowski and Plehwe (eds) (2009), pp. 417–56.

Mirowski, P. (2010) "The Great Mortification: Economists' Responses to the Crisis of 2007–(and Counting)", *The Hedgehog Review*, vol 12, no 3, pp. 28–41, available at http://www.iasc-culture.org/publications_article_2010_Summer_mirowski.php.

Mirowski, P. and E. Nik-Khah (2013) "Private Intellectuals and Public Perplexity: The Economics Profession and the Economic Crisis", *History of Political Economy*, vol 45, Supplement 1, pp. 279–311.

Mirowski, P. and Plehwe, D. (eds) (2009) *The Road from Mont Pèlerin: The Making of the Neoliberal Thought Collective*, Cambridge: Harvard University Press.

Montgomerie, J. (2009) "The Pursuit of (Past) Happiness? Middle-Class Indebtedness and American Financialisation", *New Political Economy*, vol 14, no 1, pp.1–24.

Montgomerie, J. (2020) "Indebtedness and Financialization in Everyday Life", in Mader et al. (eds) (2020), pp. 380–89.

Moody's (2021) "Thames Water Utilities Ltd. Moody's Credit Opinion", May 29, https://www.thameswater.co.uk/media-library/home/about-us/investors/debt-investors/thames-water-utilities/thames-water-utilities/Ratings-agencies-reports/moodys-april-2021.pdf .

Moore, G. (2020) *From Francoism to Financialisation: The Financialisation of Mortgages in Spain, a Case Study Analysis and a Framework for Future Studies*, unpublished PhD thesis, SOAS, University of London.

Moran, M. and A. Payne (2014) "Introduction: Neglecting, Rediscovering and Thinking Again about Power in Finance", vol 49, no 3, pp. 331–41.

Morgan, B. (2022) "NHS Staffing Shortages: Why Do Politicians Struggle to Give the NHS the Staff It Needs?" Report for The King's Fund, available at https://www.kingsfund.org.uk/sites/default/files/2022-11/NHS_staffing_shortages_final_web%20%282%29.pdf.

Morgan, D. and R. Astolfi (2013) "Health Spending Growth at Zero: Which Countries, Which Sectors Are Most Affected?", OECD Health Working Papers, no 60, OECD Publishing, http://dx.doi.org/10.1787/5k4dd1st95xv-en.

Morgan, J. (ed.) (2016) *What Is this 'School' Called Neoclassical Economics?: Debating the Issues*, London: Routledge.

Morrish, H. and L. Sauntson (2013) "Business-Facing Motors for Economic Development: An Appraisal Analysis of Visions and Values in the Marketised UK University", *Critical Discourse Studies*, vol 10, no 1, pp. 61–80.

Mudge, S. (2008) "What Is Neo-liberalism?", *Socio-Economic Review*, vol 6, no 4, pp. 703–31.

Muellerleile, C. (2009) "Financialization Takes off at Boeing", *Journal of Economic Geography*, vol 9, no 5, pp. 663–77.

Murphy, L. (2015) "Financialization (Un)Limited", *Dialogues in Human Geography*, vol 5, no 2, pp. 206–209.

NAO (2011) "Lessons from PFI and Other Projects", National Audit Office, London.

NAO (2012a) "Equity Investment in Privately Financed Projects", National Audit Office, London.

NAO (2012b) "The Franchising of Hinchingbrooke Health Care NHS Trust", National Audit Office, London.

NAO (2013a) "Review of the VFM Assessment Process for PFI", National Audit Office, London.

NAO (2013b) "The Role of Major Contractors in the Delivery of Public Services", National Audit Office, London.

NAO (2022) *Investigation into the Management of PPE Contracts*, National Audit Office, https://www.nao.org.uk/press-releases/investigation-into-the-management-of-ppe-contracts/.

National Housing Federation (2017) "Public Expenditure on Housing: The Shift from Capital Spend to Housing Allowances. A European Trend?", http://s3-eu-west-1.amazonaws.com/pub.housing.org.uk/public_spending_housing_europe_uk_briefing.pdf.

Nethercote, M. (2019) "Build-to-Rent and the Financialization of Rental Housing", *Housing Studies*, vol 35, no 5, pp. 839–74.

NIC (2019) *Strategic Investment and Public Confidence*, UK National Infrastructure Commission.

O'Kane, C. (2023) "Bidenomics: Why It's More Likely to Win the 2024 Election than Many People Think", https://theconversation.com/bidenomics-why-its-more-likely-to-win-the-2024-election-than-many-people-think-213281.

O'Sullivan, M. (2007) "Acting out Institutional Change: Understanding the Recent Transformation of the French Financial System", *Socio-Economic Review*, vol 5, no 3, pp. 389–436.

OECD (2002) "Household Energy and Water Consumption and Waste Generation; Trends, Environmental Impacts and Policy Responses", Sector Case Study Series, Working Party on National Environmental Policy, Organisation for Economic Co-operation and Development, Paris.

Ofwat (2011) "Financeability and Financing the Asset Base – a Discussion Paper," Report by Ofwat, Birmingham.

Ofwat (2017) *Future of Utilities – Water 2017*, Cathryn Ross speaking notes, November 21, London: Ofwat.

Ofwat (2020) *Reference of the PR19 Final Determinations: Overview – Response to CMA Provisional Findings*, London: Ofwat.

Ofwat (2022) "Monitoring Financial Resilience Report, 2021–2022" https://www.ofwat.gov.uk/wp-content/uploads/2022/12/MFR_2021-22.pdf.

Ofwat (2023) "Decision under Sections 13 and 12A of the Water Industry Act 1991 to Modify the Ring-Fencing Licence Conditions of the Largest Undertakers", https://www.ofwat.gov.uk/wp-content/uploads/2022/07/Decision_document_financial_resilience_proposals.pdf.

Ofwat (n.d.) *Our Duties*, https://www.ofwat.gov.uk/about-us/our-duties/.

Ofwat/DEFRA (2006) *The Development of the Water Industry in England and Wales*, Report by Ofwat and DEFRA.

ONS (2016) *Housing and Homeownership in the UK*, Office for National Statistics, https://www.ons.gov.uk/peoplepopulationandcommunity/housing/articles/ukperspectives2016housingandhomeownershipintheuk/2016-05-25.

Oren, T. and M. Blythe (2019) "From Big Bang to Big Crash: The Early Origins of the UK's Finance-Led Growth Model and the Persistence of Bad Policy Ideas", *New Political Economy*, vol 24, no 5, pp. 605–22.

Ortiz, I. and M. Cummins (2013) "The Age of Austerity: A Review of Public Expenditures and Adjustment Measures in 181 Countries", Paper for Initiative for Policy Dialogue (New York) and the South Centre (Geneva).

Ost, D. (2000) "'Illusory Corporatism' in Eastern Europe: Neoliberal Tripartism and Postcommunist Class Identities", *Politics and Society*, vol 28, no 4, pp. 503–30.

Ost, D. (2011) "Illusory Corporatism Ten Years Later", *Warsaw Forum of Economic Sociology*, vol 2, no 1, pp. 19–49.

Ouma, S. (2015) "Getting in between M and M′ or: How Farmland Further Debunks Financialization", *Dialogues in Human Geography*, vol 5, no 2, pp. 225–28.

Overbeek, H. (ed.) (2003) *The Political Economy of European Employment*, London: Routledge.

Palley, T. (2007) "Financialisation: What Is It and Why It Matters", The Levy Economics Institute, Working Paper, no 525.

Palley, T. (2013) *Financialization: The Economics of Finance Capital Domination*, London: Palgrave Macmillan.

Palma, G. (2009) "The Revenge of the Market on the Rentiers: Why Neo-Liberal Reports of the End of History Turned out to be Premature", *Cambridge Journal of Economics*, vol 33, no 4, pp. 829–69.

Panitch, L., G. Albo and V. Chibber (eds) (2011) *The Crisis and the Left, Socialist Register*, 2012, vol 48, London: Merlin Press.

Panitch, L. and S. Gindin (2012) *The Making of Global Capitalism: The Political Economy of American Empire*, London: Verso.

Panitch, L. and M. Konings (2008) (eds) *American Empire and the Political Economy of Global Finance*, London: Palgrave.

Panitch, L. and C. Leys (eds) (2005) *The Empire Reloaded, Socialist Register*, 2005, vol 41, London: Merlin Press.

Panitch, L. and C. Leys (eds) (2008) *Global Flashpoints: Reactions to Imperialism and Neoliberalism, Socialist Register*, 2008, vol 44, London: Merlin Press.

Parker, D. (2004) "The UK's Privatisation Experiment: The Passage of Time Permits a Sober Assessment", CESifo Working Paper, no 1126.

Parker, D. and D. Saal (eds) (2003) *International Handbook on Privatisation*, Cheltenham: Edward Elgar Publishing.

Paul, F. and A. Cumbers (2021) "The Return of the Local State? Failing Neoliberalism, Remunicipalisation, and the Role of the State in Advanced Capitalism", *Environment and Planning A*, vol 55, no 1, pp. 165–83.

Pawson, H. (2007) "Restructuring England's Social Housing Sector Since 1989: Undermining or Underpinning the Fundamentals of Public Housing?", *Housing Studies*, vol 21, no 5, pp. 767–83.

Payne, C. (2012) *The Consumer, Credit, and Neo-Liberalism: Governing the Modern Economy*, London: Routledge.

Peck, J. (2010) *Constructions of Neoliberal Reason*, Oxford: Oxford University Press.

Peck, J. (2022) "Confessions of a Recovering Regulation Theorist", in Hillier et al. (eds) (2022), pp. 169–90.

Peck, J. and N. Theodore (2007) "Variegated Capitalism", *Progress in Human Geography*, vol 31, no 6, pp. 731–72.

Peck, J. and N. Theodore (2019) "Still Neoliberalism?", *South Atlantic Quarterly*, vol 118, no 2, pp. 245–65.

Peet, R. (2000) "Culture, Imagery and Rationality in Regional Economic Development", *Environment and Planning A*, no 32, pp. 1215–34.

Perotti E. and S. Gelfer (2001) "Red Barons or Robber Barons? Governance and Investment in Russian Financial-Industrial Groups", *European Economic Review*, vol 45, no 9, pp. 1601–17.

Peston, R. (2020) "Twitter Status, October 22, 2020", https://twitter.com/peston/status/1319314159708889090.

Pike, A. and J. Pollard (2010) "Economic Geographies of Financialization", *Economic Geography*, vol 86, no 1, pp. 29–51.

Plimmer, G. (2021a) "UK Water Groups Pour £26m Down the Drain in Dispute with Regulator", *Financial Times*, April 10.

Plimmer, G. (2021b) "UK Water Monopolies in Poor Financial Health, Warns Watchdog", *Financial Times*, November 30.

Plimmer, G. (2021c) "Priory Property Deal Saddles Mental Health Chain with High Rents", *Financial Times*, February 6.

Plimmer, G., J. Pickard and M. O'Dyer (2023) "UK Government Looks at Nationalising Thames Water as Crisis Deepens", *Financial Times*, June 28.

Polanyi Levitt, K. (2001) *The Great Transformation: The Political and Economic Origins of Our Time*, Boston: Beacon Press.

Polanyi Levitt, K. (2013) *From the Great Transformation to the Great Financialization*, London: Zed Books.

Pollard, J. (2013) "Gendering Capital: Financial Crisis, Financialization and (an Agenda for) Economic Geography", *Progress in Human Geography*, vol 37, no 3, pp. 403–23.

Poovey, M. (2015) "On 'the Limits to Financialization'", *Dialogues in Human Geography*, vol 5, no 2, pp. 220–24.

Prügl, E. (2015) "Neoliberalising Feminism", *New Political Economy*, vol 20, no 4, pp. 614–31.

PWC (2013) "Cost of Capital for PR14: Methodological Considerations", Price Waterhouse Coopers Report for Ofwat.

Radin, M. (1996) *Contested Commodities*, Cambridge: Harvard University Press.

Rainey, M. (2021) "A Quick Guide to 'Bidenomics'", https://www.thefiscaltimes.com/2021/04/08/Quick-Guide-Bidenomics.

Regan, A. (2009) "The Impact of the Eurozone Crisis on Irish Social Partnership: A Political Economic Analysis", ILO International Training Centre, http://www.ilo.org/dyn/migpractice/docs/69/wcms_195004[1].pdf.

Rethel, L. and T. Sinclair (2014) "Innovation and the Entrepreneurial State in Asia: Mechanisms of Bond Market Development", *Asian Studies Review*, vol 38, no 4, pp. 564–81.

Reynolds, J., B. Fine and R. Van Niekerk (eds) (2019) *Race Class and the Post-Apartheid Democratic State*, Pietermaritzburg: University of KwaZulu-Natal Press.

Robertson, Mary (2014) "Case Study: Finance and Housing Provision in Britain", FESSUD Working Paper, no 51, https://fessud.org/wp-content/uploads/2013/04/Case-Study_-Finance-and-Housing-Provision-in-Britain-working-paper-51.pdf.

Robertson, Mary (2016) "The System of Provision for Housing in Selected Case Study Countries", FESSUD Working Paper, no 193, https://fessud.org/wp-content/uploads/2015/03/FESSUD_WP193_The-System-of-Provision-for-Housing-in-Selected-Case-Study-Countries.pdf.

Robertson, Mary (2017a) "The Great British Housing Crisis", *Capital and Class*, vol 41, no 2, pp. 195–215.

Robertson, Mary (2017b) "(De)constructing the Financialised Culture of Owner-Occupation in the UK, with the Aid of the 10Cs", *New Political Economy*, vol 22, no 4, 398–409, reproduced in Bayliss et al. (eds) (2018), pp. 398–409.

Robertson, Morgan (2012) "Measurement and Alienation: Making a World of Ecosystem Services", *Transactions of the Institute of British Geographers*, vol 37, no 3, pp. 386–401.

Rodriguez, F. and A. Jayadev (2010) "The Declining Labor Share of Income", Human Development Research Paper, no 2010/36, New York, UNDP.

Rosenberg, J. (2000) *The Follies of Globalisation Theory*, London: Verso.

Rosenberg, J. (2005) "Globalization Theory: A Post Mortem", *International Politics*, vol 42, pp. 2–74.

Rossman, P., and G. Greenfield (2006) "Financialisation: New Routes to Profit, New Challenges for Trade Unions", *Labour Education*, Quarterly Review of the ILO, Bureau for Workers Activities, no 142, www.iufdocuments.org/www/documents/Financialisation-e.pdf.

Rude, C. (2005) "The Role of Financial Discipline in Imperial Strategy", in Panitch and Leys (eds) (2005), pp. 82–107.

Ryan, S., D. Rowland, D. McCoy and C. Leys (2021) *For Whose Benefit? NHS England's Contract with the Private Hospital Sector in the First Year of the Pandemic*, Centre for Health and the Public Interest.

Rydin, Y. (1998) "The Enabling Local State and Urban Development: Resources, Rhetoric and Planning in East London", *Urban Studies*, vol 35, no 2, pp. 175–191.

Saad-Filho, A. (2007) "Monetary Policy in the Neoliberal Transition: A Political Economy Review of Keynesianism, Monetarism and Inflation Targeting", in Albritton et al. (eds) (2007), pp. 89–122.

Saad-Filho, A. (2008) "Marxian and Keynesian Critiques of Neoliberalism", in Panitch et al. (eds) (2008), pp. 337–45.

Saad-Filho, A. (2010) "Crisis in Neoliberalism or Crisis of Neoliberalism?", in Panitch et al. (eds) (2010), pp. 242–59.

Saad-Filho, A. (2017) "Neoliberalism", in Brennan et al. (eds) (2017), pp. 245–54.

Saad-Filho, A. (ed.) (2003) *Anti-Capitalism: A Marxist Introduction*, London: Pluto Press.

Saad-Filho, A. and D. Johnston (2005) "Introduction", in Saad-Filho and Johnston (eds) (2005), pp. 1–6.

Saad-Filho, A. and D. Johnston (eds) (2005) *Neoliberalism: A Critical Reader*, London: Pluto Press.

Saad-Filho, A. and G. Yalman (eds) (2010) *Transitions to Neoliberalism in Middle-Income Countries: Policy Dilemmas, Economic Crises, Mass Resistance*, London: Routledge.

Sanderson, D. and S. Özogul (2022) "Key Investors and their Strategies in the Expansion of European Student Housing Investment", *Journal of Property Research*, vol 39, no 2, pp. 170–96.

Santos, A. (2014) "Financial Literacy, Financialisation and Neo-liberalism", FESSUD Working Paper Series, no 11, https://fessud.org/wp-content/uploads/2015/03/FESSUD_WP172_Cross-national-comparative-analysis-household-well-being.pdf, published as revised as Santos (2017).

Santos, A. (2017) "Cultivating the Self-Reliant and Responsible Individual: The Material Culture of Financial Literacy", *New Political Economy*, vol 22, no 4, pp. 410–22, reproduced in Bayliss et al. (eds) (2018), pp. 56–68.

Santos, A., N. Serra and N. Teles (2015) "Finance and Housing Provision in Portugal", FESSUD Working Paper Series, no 79, https://fessud.org/wp-content/uploads/2015/01/FESSUD_Working-Paper-Series_Santos-Serra-Teles-2015-79.pdf.

Santos, A. and N. Teles (2014) "Recent Trends in Household Financial Behaviour", FESSUD Working Paper Series, no 171, https://fessud.org/wp-content/uploads/2015/03/FESSUD_WP171_Recent-Trends-Household-Financial-Behaviour.pdf.

Santos, A. and N. Teles (eds) (2020) *Financialisation in the European Periphery: Work and Social Reproduction in Portugal*, London: Routledge.

Santos, A., N. Teles, R. Matias, A. Brown and D. Spencer (2016) "Cross-National Comparative Analysis of Household Well-Being", FESSUD Working Paper Series, no 172, https://fessud.org/wp-content/uploads/2015/03/FESSUD_WP172_Cross-national-comparative-analysis-household-well-being.pdf.

Saritas, S. (2014), "Review of Pension Provision across the European Union Countries", FESSUD Working Paper Series, no 13, https://fessud.org/wp-content/uploads/2013/04/REVIEW-OF-THE-PENSION-PROVISION-ACROSS-THE-EUROPEAN-UNION-COUNTRIES_13.pdf.

Sassen, S. (2010) "A Savage Sorting of Winners and Losers: Contemporary Versions of Primitive Accumulation", *Globalizations*, vol 7, no 1–2, pp. 23–50.

Savills (2015) "Spotlight UK Student Housing", https://pdf.euro.savills.co.uk/residential---other/spotlight--uk-student-housing-2015.pdf.

Savills (2018) "Investing in Private Rent", https://pdf.euro.savills.co.uk/uk/residential---other/report---investing-in-private-rent.pdf.

Savills (2021) "Spotlight: Private Capital in Affordable Housing", https://www.savills.co.uk/research_articles/229130/316439-0.

Savills (2022) "UK Build-to-Rent Market Update – Q4 2021", https://www.savills.co.uk/research_articles/229130/323830-0.

Sawyer, M. (2014) "What Is Financialization?", *International Journal of Political Economy*, vol 42, no 4, pp. 5–18.

Sawyer, M. (2022) *Financialization: Economic and Social Impact*, Newcastle upon Tyne: Agenda Publishing.

Seabrooke, L. (2010) "What Do I Get? The Everyday Politics of Expectations and the Subprime Crisis", *New Political Economy*, vol 15, no 1, pp. 51–70.

Shaoul, J. (2008) "The Political Economy of the Private Finance Initiative", in Arestis and Sawyer (eds) (2008), pp. 1–38.

Silverwood, J. and C. Berry (2022) "The Distinctiveness of State Capitalism in Britain: Market-Making, Industrial Policy and Economic Space", *Environment and Planning A*, vol 55, no 1, pp. 122–42.

Simmel, G. (1978) *The Philosophy of Money*, London: Routledge and Kegan Paul, first published in 1900.

Simon, H. (1999) "The Potlatch between Economics and Political Science", in Alt et al. (eds) (1999), pp. 112–19.

Skaerbaek P. and P. Melander (2004) "The Politics of the Changing Forms of Accounting: A Field Study of Strategy Translation in a Danish Government-Owned Company under Privatisation", *Accounting, Auditing and Accountability Journal*, vol 17, no 1, pp. 17–40.

Smith, A. (2009) *An Inquiry into the Nature and Causes of the Wealth of Nations*, Available at: http://www.gutenberg.org/files/3300/3300-h/3300- h.htm.

Soederberg, S. (2013) "The US Debtfare State and the Credit Card Industry: Forging Spaces of Dispossession", *Antipode*, vol 45, no 2, pp. 493–512.

Solow, R. (2006) "Comments on Papers by Saint-Paul, Aghion, and Bhidé", *Capitalism and Society*, vol 1, no 1, Article 3, http://www.bepress.com/cas/vol1/iss1/art3/.

Spaventa, L. (2009) "Economists and Economics: What Does the Crisis Tell Us?", http: //www.cepr.org/pubs/PolicyInsights/PolicyInsight38.pdf.

Stanley, L. (2014) "'We're Reaping What We Sowed': Everyday Crisis Narratives and Acquiescence to the Age of Austerity", *New Political Economy*, vol 19, no 6, pp. 895–917.

Stedman Jones, D. (2012) *Masters of the Universe: Hayek, Friedman, and the Birth of Neoliberal Politics*, Princeton: Princeton University Press.

Stiglitz, J. (2008) "The End of Neoliberalism?", https://www.project-syndicate.org/commentary/the-end-of-neo-liberalism.

Stockhammer, E. (2010) "Financialisation and the Global Economy", Working Paper, no 240, Political Economy Research Institute, University of Massachusetts Amherst.

Subaset, T. (ed.) (2016) *The Great Financial Meltdown: Systemic, Conjunctural or Policy Created?*, Cheltenham: Edward Elgar.

Sullivan, S. (2013) "Banking Nature?: The Spectacular Financialisation of Environmental Conservation", *Antipode*, vol 45, no 1, pp. 198–217.

Summers, L. (2015) "Demand Side Secular Stagnation", *American Economic Review*, vol 105, no 5, pp. 60–65.

Šumonja, M. (2021) "Neoliberalism Is Not Dead – on Political Implications of Covid-19", *Capital and Class*, vol 45, no 2, pp. 215–27.

Teles, N. (2015) "Financialisation and Neoliberalism: The Case of Water Provision in Portugal", FESSUD Working Paper, no 102, https://fessud.org/wp-content/uploads/2015/03/Financialisation-and-neoliberalism-the-case-of-water-provision-in-Portugal-working-paper-102.pdf.

Theurillat, T., J. Corpataux and O. Crevoisier (2010) "Property Sector Financialization: The Case of Swiss Pension Funds (1992–2005)", *European Planning Studies*, vol 18, no 2, pp. 189–212.

THFC (2016) *Investing in Affordable Housing*, London: THFC.

Thomas, C. (2019) *The 'Make Do and Mend' Health Service: Solving the NHS's Capital Crisis*, London: Institute for Public Policy Research.

Thomas, C., V. Poku-Amanfo and P. Patel (2022) *The State of Health and Care*, London: Institute for Public Policy Research.

Titmuss, R. (1970) *The Gift Relationship: From Human Blood to Social. Policy*, London: Allen and Unwin.

Tooze, A. (2021) "Has Covid Ended the Neoliberal Era?", *Guardian*, September 2.

Torrance, M. (2009) "Reconceptualizing Urban Governance through a New Paradigm for Urban Infrastructure Networks", *Journal of Economic Geography*, vol 9, no 6, pp. 805–22..

Toussaint, J. and M. Elsinga (2009) "Exploring 'Housing Asset-Based Welfare'. Can the UK Be Held up as an Example for Europe?", *Housing Studies*, vol 24, no 5, pp. 669–92.

Trentmann, F. (ed.) (2005) *The Making of the Consumer: Knowledge, Power and Identity in the Modern World*, Oxford: Berg.

UK Government (n.d.) "Help Paying Bills Using Your Benefits: How Deductions Work", https://www.gov.uk/bills-benefits:~:text=If%20you%20get%20Universal%20Credit&text=Your%20Universal%20Credit%20will%20be,10%25%20and%2020%25%20for%20rent.

Uppenberg, K., H. Strauss and R. Wagenvoort (2011) "Financing Infrastructure: A Review of the 2010 EIB Conference in Economics and Finance", European Investment Bank, Luxembourg.

Utting P., S. Razavi and R. Buchholz (eds) (2012) *Global Crisis and Transformative Social Change*, London: Palgrave MacMillan.

van der Zwan, N. (2014) "Making Sense of Financialization", *Socio-Economic Review*, vol 12, no 1, pp. 99–129.

Van Gent, W. (2010) "Housing Policy as a Lever for Change? The Politics of Welfare, Assets and Tenure", *Housing Studies*, vol 25, no 5, pp. 735–53.

van Staveren, I. (2012) "The Lehman Sisters Hypothesis: An Exploration of Literature and Bankers", ISS Working Paper Series/General Series, vol 545, Erasmus University Rotterdam, http://hdl.handle.net/1765/32567.

Venugopal, R. (2015) "Neoliberalism as Concept", *Economy and Society*, vol 44, no 2, pp. 165–87.

Vitali, S., J. Glattfelder and S. Battiston (2011) "The Network of Global Corporate Control", http://arxiv.org/pdf/1107.5728v2.pdf.

Wacquant, L. (2009) *The Neoliberal Government of Social Insecurity*, Durham, N.C.: Duke University Press.

Wade, R. (2013) "How High Inequality Plus Neoliberal Governance Weakens Democracy", *Challenge*, vol 56, no 6, pp. 5–37.

Wainwright, T. (2009) "Laying the Foundations for a Crisis: Mapping the Historico-Geographical Construction of Residential Mortgage Backed Securitization in the UK", *International Journal of Urban and Regional Research*, vol 33, no 2, pp. 372–88.

Wainwright, T. and G. Manville (2017) "Financialization and the Third Sector: Innovation in Social Housing Bond Markets", *Environment and Planning A*, vol 49, no 4, pp. 819–38.

Ward, C. (2020) "Contradictions of Financial Capital Switching: Reading the Corporate Leverage Crisis through the Port of Liverpool's Whole Business Securitization", *International Journal of Urban and Regional Research*, vol 45, no 2, pp. 249–65.

Warner, M. and B. Zaranko (2021) "Pressures on the NHS: IFS Green Budget, Chapter 6", Institute for Fiscal Studies, https://ifs.org.uk/sites/default/files/output_url_files/6-Pressures-on-the-NHS-.pdf.

Watson, M. (2009) "Planning for a Future of Asset-Based Welfare? New Labour, Financialized Economic Agency, and the Housing Market", *Planning, Practice and Research*, vol 24, no 1, pp. 41–56.

We Own It (2021) "Here Are the GP Practices Taken over by US Health Insurance Giant Centene", https://weownit.org.uk/blog/here-are-gp-practices-taken-over-us-health-insurance-giant-centene.

Weber, H. (2014) "Global Politics of Microfinancing Poverty in Asia: The Case of Bangladesh Unpacked", *Asian Studies Review*, vol 38, no 4, pp. 544–563.

Weber, H. (ed.) (2014) *Politics of Neoliberalism: A Survey*, London: Routledge.

Weber, R. (2010) "Selling City Futures: The Financialization of Urban Redevelopment Policy", *Economic Geography*, vol 86, no 3, 251–74.

Webster, E., K. Joynt, and A. Metcalfe (2013), "Repositioning Peak-Level Social Dialogue in South Africa: NEDLAC into the Future" Johannesburg: NEDLAC.

Wetherly, P., C. Barrow and P. Burnham (eds) *Class, Power and the State in Capitalist Society: Essays on Ralph Miliband*, Basingstoke: Palgrave.

Wijburg, G. (2020) "The De-Financialization of Housing: Towards a Research Agenda", *Housing Studies*, vol 36, no 8, pp. 1276–93.

Williamson, J. (1990) "What Washington Means by Policy Reform", in Williamson (ed.) (1990), pp. 5–38.

Williamson, J. (ed.) (1990) *Latin American Adjustment: How Much Has Happened?*, Washington, DC: Institute for International Economics.

Witztum, A. (2013) "Behavioural Economics, Game Theory and Das Adam Smith Problem", http://www.eshet.net/conference/paper_view.php?id=1012&p=38, published in *Eastern Economic Journal*, vol 42, no 4, 2016, pp. 528–56.

Wöhl, S. (2014) "The State and Gender Relations in International Political Economy: A State-Theoretical Approach to Varieties of Capitalism in Crisis", *Capital and Class*, vol 38, no 1, pp. 87–99.

Woo-Cummings, M. (ed.) (1999) *The Developmental State*, New York: Cornell University Press.

Wood, G. and C. Lane (eds) (2011) *Capitalist Diversity and Diversity within Capitalism*, London: Routledge.

Ye, I. (ed.) (2017) *Towards Universal Health Care in Emerging Economies: Opportunities and Challenges*, London: Palgrave MacMillan.

Yilmaz, G. and Ö. Çelik (2016) "Finance and System of Provision of Water: The Case of Istanbul", FESSUD Working Paper Series, no 153, https://fessud.org/wp-content/uploads/2015/03/Water_METU_WP_FESSUD-153.pdf.

Zademach, H.-M. (2009) "Global Finance and the Development of Regional Clusters: Tracing Paths in Munich's Film and TV Industry", *Journal of Economic Geography*, vol 9, no 5, pp. 697–722.

Zelizer, V. (1994) *The Social Meaning of Money*, New York: Basic Books.

Zelizer, V. (1996) "Payments and Social Ties", *Sociological Forum*, vol 11, no 3, pp. 481–95.

Zelizer, V. (1998) "The Proliferation of Social Currencies", in Callon (ed.) (1998), pp. 58–68.

Zelizer, V. (2000) "Fine-Tuning the Zelizer View", *Economy and Society*, vol 29, no 3, pp. 383–89.

Zhang, X. (2014) "Coalitional Dynamics, Power Structure and Financial Markets in East Asia", *Government and Opposition*, vol 49, no 3, pp. 511–41.

Zysman, J. (1983) *Governments, Markets and Growth*, London: Cornell University Press.

Index